HEALTHY AGING

THROUGH THE SOCIAL DETERMINANTS OF HEALTH

For access to digital chapters,
visit the APHA Press bookstore (www.apha.org).

HEALTHY AGING
THROUGH THE SOCIAL DETERMINANTS OF HEALTH

EDITORS
Elaine T. Jurkowski PhD, MSW
M. Aaron Guest PhD, MPH, MSW

APHA PRESS
AN IMPRINT OF AMERICAN PUBLIC HEALTH ASSOCIATION

American Public Health Association
800 I Street, NW
Washington, DC 20001-3710
www.apha.org

Georges C. Benjamin, MD, Executive Director

Printed and bound in the United States of America
Book Production Editor: Blair Reynolds
Typesetting: The Charlesworth Group
Cover Design: Alan Giarcanella
Printing and Binding: Sheridan Books

Library of Congress Cataloging-in-Publication Data

Names: Jurkowski, Elaine Theresa, editor. | Guest, M. Aaron, editor.
Title: Healthy aging through the social determinants of health / [edited
   by] Elaine T. Jurkowski PhD, MSW, M. Aaron Guest PhD, MPH, MSW.
Description: Washington : American Public Health Association, 2021. |
   Includes bibliographical references and index. | Summary: "This book
   provides a public health perspective of aging, based on the five social
   determinants of health. These determinants form the framework for these
   chapters, as they outline a lifespan approach to healthy aging. This
   book is for practitioners and public health professionals who work with
   older adult populations"-- Provided by publisher.
Identifiers: LCCN 2020055963 (print) | LCCN 2020055964 (ebook) | ISBN
   9780875533155 (paperback) | ISBN 9780875533162 (ebook)
Subjects: LCSH: Older people--Social conditions. | Older people--Health and
   hygiene. | Older people--Care. | Aging--Social aspects.
Classification: LCC HQ1061 .S64813 2021 (print) | LCC HQ1061 (ebook) |
   DDC 305.26--dc23
LC record available at https://lccn.loc.gov/2020055963
LC ebook record available at https://lccn.loc.gov/2020055964

This book is dedicated to those unsung heroes within the public health arena who are working to make the lives of people growing older optimal.

This book is also dedicated to the APHA Aging and Public Health Section; and in memoriam of Steven P. Wallace, PhD, for his many contributions to and leadership in the field of public health and aging, including his tireless research and advocacy related to the Social Determinants of Health and Aging.

Contents

Online Supplement
Available at: https://bit.ly/3l3HBDG

Foreword

This is an important book at an important time. America's—indeed the world's—population is rapidly aging. The COVID-19 pandemic has taken a huge toll on the country, and especially older people. Our society is becoming ever more unequal, with a bigger gap between the haves and the have-nots. And, many of the latter are seniors struggling to get along.

The sad fact is that where one lives, "zip code risk," is a greater indication of health and life span than one's genetic code. This is part of the American story. No, life isn't fair. We don't all line up equally at the starting line.

Healthy Aging Through The Social Determinants of Health provides direction to make things better. It is a field guide for social change. I had a favorite book about social impact that I used to take with me, for example, to work on a family planning program in Egypt. This book is like that—a practical guide for action.

Elaine T. Jurkowski and M. Aaron Guest have organized their book along the five major social determinants of health: health and health care; neighborhood and the built environment; social and community; education; and the economics of aging.

These areas line up with what people say they want and need, and what they seek out for fulfillment. Health and financial security are usually at the top, and other common elements are the ability to contribute and to be connected to their communities. If you are studying public health, advocating for public policies, or engaged in community programs, this book has what you need.

I have spent a good deal of my career working on health promotion and disease prevention. When I was CEO of AARP, President of the Campaign for Tobacco-Free Kids, and engaged in international development with USAID, I could have really benefited from this book. Today, in teaching in the MBA program at Georgetown University, I will integrate it into my leadership and incorporate social responsibility courses.

I've always been partial to public health professionals. I often talk of nurse power, and today I'm involved in advanced illness and end-of-life care through the Coalition to Transform Advanced Care (C-TAC), where we interact with social workers, nurses, community activists, and chaplains. Public health workers are dedicated change agents, and I admire them for it.

The authors point out the importance of thinking across generations in addressing aging issues. At AARP, I emphasized this with the example of osteoporosis, a pediatric disease with geriatric consequences. And, there are lots of young people caring for parents and grandparents. In addition, many health care employees are young workers. Recently,

Georgetown University studied 18 to 39-year-olds during the COVID-19 pandemic. We learned that many of them were having a tough time, especially young women, and were not able to fund their retirement accounts. Clearly, we need intergenerational strategies.

If we're going to create a better future for older Americans, we have a big challenge ahead: a national political stalemate that soon will have to confront the costs of Social Security, Medicare, and Medicaid. The latter is already a political football. And of course, we are well aware of the unsustainable costs of our health care system. Public health practitioners will be critical players in all of this.

Now, who should read this book? As I said, it's a valuable field guide for those in the trenches. It also belongs in the classroom, where tomorrow's leaders are learning their trade. I also recommend it for Corporate America. If you want to do well by doing good (create bottom line success by incorporating social strategies into your core business) the future of aging is for you. Read this book.

Bill Novelli, MA
Professor and Founder of Business for Impact,
McDonough School of Business, Georgetown University
Former CEO of AARP

About This Book

AGING AND PUBLIC HEALTH SECTION OF THE AMERICAN PUBLIC HEALTH ASSOCIATION

Established in 1978, the Aging and Public Health Section* of the American Public Health Association (APHA) promotes individuals' health and well-being as they age by improving their health, functioning, quality of life, and financial security throughout the field of public health and beyond. Empowered by a Public Health Nursing Section Annual Meeting Session by Maggie Kuhn, the head of the Gray Panthers, a contingency of APHA members established a Task Force on Aging to bring attention to the importance and the multidisciplinary nature of aging and public health. Overcoming fear within the field of public health that aging lacked widespread interest, a fear ever present to this day, Section leaders such as Philip Weiler, Anne Zimmer, and Tom Hickey led the charge in developing a formal body within APHA for those working at the interface of aging and public health.

The Aging and Public Health Section aims to include all aging-related issues, and to recognize aging as a process that occurs across the life span. The Section has long prided itself on bringing financing and service delivery innovations to the public health arena, thereby improving older adults' health, functioning, quality of life, and financial security.

The Aging and Public Health Section is incredibly proud of its portfolio of awards, which is the largest of any APHA Section promoting scholarship and innovative aging practice. These awards recognize scholarship in older women, minorities, rural and environmental issues, global aging, and research done by students and new investigators, among others.

Through an endowment established by Archstone Foundation in 1997 and expanded in 2017, the Aging and Public Health Section has awarded the Archstone Award for Excellence in Program Innovation. This award recognizes innovative programs that demonstrate best practice models that effectively link academic theory with applied practice in public health and aging. In 2017, the Section celebrated 20 years of this partnership, with more than 58 award winners and honorable mentions. In addition, the Retirement Research Foundation has continuously funded masters and doctoral student awards since 1998.

The Aging and Public Health Section is committed to advancing policies that enhance older adults' lives and has been particularly active in contributing to policy positions on

---

*Established originally as the Gerontological Health Section.

issues such as Medicare prescription drugs and end-of-life issues. The Section also fulfills its mission through its vibrant Annual Meeting programming. The Section regularly hosts a variety of scientific sessions that showcase the interdisciplinary nature of aging research and practice. The annual mentoring session with experts in aging and public health provides a unique opportunity for new and emerging professionals to engage with scholars in the field. The Aging and Public Health Section's annual networking dinner provides opportunities for Section members to interact in an informal social setting. The Section's famed Auction at the Annual Meeting helps to provide financial support for awards.

The Aging and Public Health Section's future is bright due to the quality of the scholarship, practice, and advocacy of all of our members and their unflagging commitment to advancing issues of public health and aging. We welcome new members, including all those whose work or interests relate to aging in some way. As we celebrated our 40th anniversary in 2018, the Aging and Public Health Section rededicated itself toward work with APHA to promote individuals' health and well-being as they age.

Introduction

People are growing older and experiencing a much longer life span than that of prior generations. Many people over the age of 60 are healthier today and living in place within their home-based communities with noninstitutionalized care. In addition, only about 5% of the older adult population is living in institutional care. Despite this reality, the focus on older adults in much of the previous research has focused on institutional care. It is only within the last decade that we have begun to see publications related to healthy aging and community-based opportunities through the lens of public health. To date, there has been precious little attention to how we discuss and frame aging through a public health lens. To this end, the Aging and Public Health Section of the American Public Health Association has worked to provide a seminal piece of work, this book on healthy aging, to help practitioners and public health professionals better prepare for their work with the older adult populations.

ORIGINS

At the November 2018 Business Meeting of the Aging and Public Health Section, Elaine T. Jurkowski brought back up the idea of an Aging and Public Health supported text. The Section discussed the idea, along with the interest from APHA Press. At the conclusion of the Business Meeting it was decided that Elaine T. Jurkowski and M. Aaron Guest, along with Section leadership, would reconvene to further flesh out the idea. Dr. Jurkowski had worked as lead editor for a similar project with the Social Work and Public Health Section, resulting in a book entitled *Handbook for Public Health Social Work* (Springer Publishing Company).

Between January 2019 and May 2019, several phone meetings were scheduled with APHA Press and Section leadership. The initial framework of the text and target audience were defined with the assistance of APHA Press staff. Dr. Jurkowski and Dr. Guest took on leadership in the role of editors on behalf of the Section to move the project forward. From May 2019 to August 2019, a needs assessment survey was developed and distributed to Section membership regarding their interest, the perceived need for the proposed text, and potential chapter topics. Once the results were tabulated, a framework for the book evolved, including potential chapter headings and sections of the book, specific to the social determinants of health. In August 2019, a call for abstracts and authors was distributed, resulting in interest from academic and practice-based aging and public health professionals.

The editors sent out a call for chapter abstracts to the Section membership and received a plethora of proposals. From this pool, a series of abstracts were selected to form the text that you are about to embark upon.

THE SOCIAL DETERMINANTS OF HEALTHY AGING

The Social Determinants of Healthy Aging include the areas of health and health care, neighborhood and built environment, social support, education, economics, and policy, along with how these areas influence healthy aging. Using these themes, you will find, as you review this book, how each of these five areas play a role in the healthy aging process.

Section I of this book provides an overview of how the social determinant of health care and access to health care play a role in the course of healthy aging. Examples from both normal and nonnormative aging are discussed. Access to care and its role in healthy aging is also addressed within this section.

Section II on neighborhood and the built environment addresses the impact that neighborhood and different types of built environments have on the health and social outcomes of older adults. Neighborhoods and the types of livable communities available to one as they grow older will play a major role in one's health, well-being, and functioning. This section examines these issues through neighborhood factors, assistive technology, diversity, and housing options.

Section III addresses the critical role that social support plays within the process of healthy aging. Social support, caregiving, and the role of these supports are important factors within the healthy aging process. This section addresses these areas and provides the reader with some insight into the interface between social support and healthy aging, as well as the valuable contribution social support plays in one's well-being.

Section IV addresses education, access to education, and the impact of education on health outcomes and health literacy. This is accomplished through the lens of overall educational achievement, lifelong learning, retirement options, and workforce development.

Lastly, Section V deals with economic and policy issues that play a role in the healthy aging process. Factors such as pensions, economic resources, and policies that shape these outcomes are discussed in this section.

The editors have attempted to structure the chapters with a specific format in mind. Each chapter includes background, critical issues, the role of public health, and examples of best practices. Policies relevant to programs and services are briefly addressed within the chapters, and the book concludes with a host of resources, laid out by chapter.

This effort would not be possible without the support of the Aging and Public Health Section of the American Public Health Association, and many specific individuals. While many hands played a key role in this project, the editors would like to acknowledge Section past chairs Daniella Freedman, Mary Gallant, Carolynn Mendez-Luck, and

Annie Nguyen for endorsing and supporting this project. We are also grateful to Rich Lampert and Dan Doody from APHA Press for their work with us in the conceptualization, needs assessment, and contract process. Lastly, we are grateful for our support systems, Bill, our girls, and sideline editors, Momo, Miss Kitty, and Pemberton.

This volume has attempted to address a gap in the literature which examines how social determinants of health interface with the process of healthy aging and to make it accessible to those who interact with our older adult population. We hope that this text will be an effective tool for public health practitioners in the field and will help enhance the lives of people growing older.

I. HEALTH AND HEALTH CARE

This section provides an overview of how the social determinant of health care and access to health care play a role in the healthy aging process. Access to health care services for various health conditions is discussed within all chapters.

The section is led by an exploration of the biology of aging and weaves concepts related to Alzheimer's Disease and dementias throughout the chapter.

Polypharmacy is a serious issue and factor that plays a role in the functioning or lack of functioning among people growing older. The number of medications that individuals are prescribed is often staggering. A grasp of what these medications are and how they interact with each other is paramount to optimal functioning within older adults.

Hearing, vision, and oral health are three senses which impact one's functioning and quality of life. Chapter 3 addresses the incidence, prevalence of hearing loss, and relationship with healthy aging. Chapter 4 covers vision and oral health and affirms the relationship between oral health and overall health. This chapter expands on what the average practitioner understands about oral health care, especially within the realm of older adults, and addresses access to oral health care at local levels. Degenerative diseases which impact one's vision can play a central role in the ability to function in the least restrictive environment day to day.

This section concludes with Chapter 5 on mental health and healthy aging. It provides the reader with an overview of mental health issues and concerns that people growing older face. The notion of stigma as it relates to access to adequate mental health care will also be discussed, as well as common mental health concerns as people advance in age.

1

Aging and Dementia

Jordan Weiss, PhD and John Shean, MPH

BACKGROUND

Population aging is largely considered a success story, with more and more people living longer lives overall, but its implications for population health are pressing and widespread. This is especially true for age-related conditions, such as dementia, for which the primary risk factor is age.

Dementia is a syndrome characterized by deficits in cognitive abilities, such as memory and language, that interfere with an individual's ability to perform everyday activities, including feeding and clothing oneself. Although mild changes in cognition are considered a normal part of the aging process, a dementia-level of impairment is not caused by the aging process alone and is distinguished by its noted effect on an individual's ability to perform activities of daily living. The many symptoms that comprise dementia vary from person to person; what might be considered normal aging for one individual might not be considered normal for another. This is partially attributable to differences in individual level risk factors, such as the level of educational attainment one has achieved, but may also be driven by the type of dementia a person has.

Unlike some chronic conditions which may be clearly defined, dementia exists along a continuum (see Figure 1-1) that progressively worsens over time and with advancing age. This continuum includes the following[1]:

- Healthy cognitive functioning: most people have healthy cognitive functioning without any significant cognitive impairment throughout their lives.
- Mild cognitive impairment: a slight but measurable decline in cognitive abilities including thinking and memory.
- Early stage dementia: cognitive abilities have declined significantly enough to interfere with everyday life, but do not yet cause major disruption. People with early stage dementia may function independently, drive, work, and be part of social activities, but may forget familiar words or have difficulty recalling the location of everyday objects.

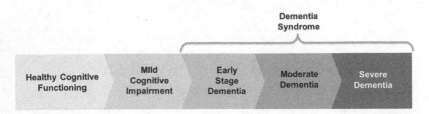

Source: Adapted with permission from the Alzheimer's Association and the Centers for Disease Control and Prevention.[1]
Note: Dementia occurs along a continuum. Most people will have healthy cognitive functioning throughout their lives, but for those who develop dementia, they will progress through mild cognitive impairment into dementia.

Figure 1-1. Dementia Continuum

- Moderate dementia: individuals have more difficulties with everyday tasks as a result of dementia. People with moderate dementia may be unable to pay bills or manage their medication as they previously had, may experience more trouble communicating, or may experience mood or behavior changes.
- Severe dementia: people in this final stage of dementia lose the ability to respond to their environment, lose the ability to communicate, and, eventually, lose control of movement. Individuals in the severe stage of dementia may become bed-bound and require around-the-clock care.

There are many types of dementia, most of which feature a gradual worsening of symptoms over time. In the United States and other Western nations, Alzheimer's disease (AD) is the chief cause of dementia. Though often used interchangeably, AD and dementia are not the same. AD is an irreversible, degenerative brain disorder characterized by progressive accumulation of the protein fragment beta-amyloid (i.e., plaques) outside neurons in the brain and twisted strands of the protein tau (i.e., tangles) inside neurons.[2,3] AD accounts for an estimated 60%–80% of dementia cases.

Another common subtype is vascular dementia, caused by diseased blood vessels which reduce the supply of blood, oxygen, and nutrients to the brain. Less common subtypes include Lewy body disease, frontotemporal lobar degeneration, and Parkinson's disease. Despite different etiologies, recent large autopsy studies have revealed that most cases of dementia feature pathologies of multiple subtypes; for example, AD and vascular dementia, which is referred to as mixed dementia.[4,5]

Pooled together, all-cause dementia is a leading cause of death, disability, and dependency in the United States. Its impact on population health is expected to rise in response to population aging. Dementia already places a substantial burden on patients, their families, and health care systems. The number of adults living with dementia is expected to more than double in the coming decades, from more than an estimated 5.8 million in 2020 to more than 13.8 million by 2050.[6]

In 2020, the annual expenditure for health care services, including long-term care and hospice, is expected to exceed $305 billion, making it America's most expensive medical condition.[7] Nearly one in five Medicare dollars will be spent on dementia in 2020. This is expected to increase to one in every three dollars by 2050 (unpublished tabulations based on data from the Medicare Current Beneficiary survey for 2011; prepared under contract by the Lewin Group for the Alzheimer's Association, June 2015), when the estimated costs of dementia are expected to exceed $1.1 trillion. These costs do not include the value of unpaid caregiving by family and friends which, in 2019, was estimated to reach nearly $244 billion.[7] In addition to the costs of unpaid labor, informal care providers face high risk of morbidity and mortality due to the increased strain of providing unpaid care with no relief or respite. Thus, in addition to focusing on dementia patients themselves, public health initiatives must also consider the health and well-being among the caregivers and family members of adults with dementia. In the absence of a cure, improving the health and well-being of persons with dementia and their families rests on surveillance, risk reduction, and early detection, which are key facets of public health.

PUBLIC HEALTH BURDEN OF DEMENTIA

The burden of dementia is far reaching, affecting those living with dementia, their caregivers and families, health care systems, and society more broadly. Patients and informal caregivers face reduced quality of life and increased mortality. Health care systems face increased public expenditures, whereas the careers of people with dementia and their families, quality of life, and economic systems impact the costs to society.

All-Cause Dementia Mortality

Vital statistics rank all-cause dementia as the third most common cause of death in the United States and AD alone ranks as the sixth leading cause of death.[8] Dementia remains the only cause of death in the top 10 without a viable prevention or cure. The actual mortality burden of all-cause dementia is likely higher, as recent studies indicate the large degree of underreporting of dementia on death certificates.[9]

Caregiver Burden

A majority of individuals living with dementia live in the community, typically with a family member who provides unpaid care (unpublished tabulations based on data from the Medicare Current Beneficiary Survey for 2011; prepared under contract by Avalere Health for the Alzheimer's Association, March 2016). In fact, nearly 50% of all caregivers in the United States who provide help to older adults do so for someone with dementia.[10] Caregivers, especially those for patients with dementia, tend to experience high levels of stress in addition to physical and emotional exhaustion due to the demands placed on them. In fact, studies have linked caregiving to increased rates of depression and premature mortality.[11] However, recent intervention studies have also indicated that behavioral interventions, such as increasing levels of physical activity, may help mitigate some of this burden.[12] Collectively, this body of work underscores the importance of the public health response to consider the health and well-being of caregivers.

Racial, Ethnic, and Gender Disparities

The social and economic burden of dementia is unequally distributed across racial/ethnic and gender groups in the United States. On average, women tend to be at greater risk for dementia compared with men[13] with studies indicating a divergence at around age 80.[14,15] The extant literature on drivers of this disparity are inconclusive but several hypotheses have been put forth.[16-21] For example, it is believed that women's life expectancy, which is on average longer than men's, could contribute to the disparity in the lifetime dementia risk.[21] Studies have also reported that genetic[17] or preclinical markers[19] could differentially alter the risk of dementia onset in men and women.

The absolute number of non-Hispanic White adults with dementia exceeds those of any other demographic subgroup in the United States, but this is driven by the larger share of non-Hispanic White adults in the population. The actual prevalence of dementia among non-Hispanic White adults is lower than their minority counterparts, with estimates indicating that the prevalence of dementia may be twice as high among non-Hispanic Black adults[22,23] and one and one-half times higher among Hispanic adults,[24] relative to age-matched non-Hispanic White adults. These disparities are believed to stem from differences in the onset risk of dementia rather than survival with dementia, which remains important but of a lesser magnitude in comparison.[25-28]

Risk Factors, Prevention, and Control

It is widely believed that dementia develops as a result of multiple risk factors across numerous domains (e.g., demographic, health, lifestyle, genetic) over the life course, with potential cohort effects depending on the characteristics of the population and cultural context.[29,30] This underscores the importance of taking a life span approach to investigate determinants of dementia as well as to motivate public health initiatives at different stages of the life course to implement prevention at all ages in the absence of a cure or disease-modifying strategy.

Among the leading priorities of public health are identifying, preventing, and controlling risk factors. A recent report which consolidated the state of knowledge on preventive and management strategies for dementia reviewed more than 500 scientific peer-reviewed articles, systematic reviews, and meta-analyses, and calculated that nearly one-third of dementia cases may be preventable through intervention on modifiable risk factors, including educational attainment, social engagement, physical activity, and management of medical comorbidities.[29]

It is well established that lower levels of educational attainment are associated with a higher risk of dementia, although the underlying mechanisms remain unclear.[31] The relationship between educational attainment and socioeconomic status has long been recognized and is suggested as a pathway through which lower educational attainment could increase the risk of dementia.[32,33] It has also been suggested that, together with other early-life experiences, educational attainment helps shape cognitive reserve which, it has been postulated, may account for individual differences in susceptibility to age-related brain changes or dementia-related pathology.[34] Moreover, educational attainment has been tied to engagement in health behaviors and medical comorbidities which could influence one's risk of dementia.

Numerous studies have identified mid-life risk factors for dementia that include obesity and smoking. Obesity, typically determined by measuring body mass index, is hypothesized to influence dementia risk through its association with cardiometabolic disease risk (e.g., vascular disease, diabetes).[35,36] Studies that examine associations between smoking and dementia, while accounting for the competing risk of mortality, report an increased risk of dementia among smokers.[37-40] As with obesity and other lifestyle factors, smoking is believed to influence cognitive health and dementia through its influence on cardiometabolic disease risk.[41] While some longitudinal studies that investigate associations between smoking and incident dementia report a protective effect,[42] this is likely an artefact of the statistical methods utilized in such studies. Smoking increases one's risk of early mortality; if one dies prior to dementia onset, it could appear that smoking protects against dementia even after adjusting for age. While obesity and smoking are associated with increased dementia risk, physical activity has been linked to reduced risk of dementia in several meta-analyses of randomized control trials.[43,44]

Together with these demographic and lifestyle risk factors, medical comorbidities have also been implicated in dementia onset. It is well established that the presence of one or more cardiometabolic diseases increases dementia risk.[45,46] This includes diabetes, stroke, and hypertension. Numerous studies have reported strong associations between a mid-life cardiovascular risk score and dementia risk in later-life[47] highlighting the importance and lasting implications of mid-life cardiometabolic health for determining dementia onset at older age.

THE ROLE OF PUBLIC HEALTH

Several facets of public health are and can be used to improve the health and well-being of families impacted by dementia. This includes surveillance, efforts to promote health and reduce risk profiles, and early identification.

Early Identification and Treatment

An early diagnosis of dementia or mild cognitive impairment allows patients and their families to make more informed decisions about their care pathway while planning for their future. Typically, it is through a diagnosis that individuals may access pharmacological and non-pharmacological treatments. Although there has yet to be a proven medication to inhibit dementia, early treatment may improve a patient's quality of life.[48] Importantly, with information regarding one's diagnosis, they can determine their eligibility to enroll in clinical trials and some evidence indicates that modifying certain health behaviors may even help delay the progression of dementia, extending the time a person lives with mild symptoms before developing more severe complications from dementia.

Health Promotion and Risk Reduction

Efforts to promote cognitive health can occur at any stage of the life course. A large body of work has implicated early-life experiences, educational attainment, mid-life health behaviors, occupational characteristics, and social engagement as important ways to protect against cognitive decline and dementia.[30] Targeting these modifiable risk factors may help reduce the overall burden of dementia while also improving health profiles overall. Public health initiatives in the medical and community settings can be used to drive this risk reduction.

Surveillance

Public health surveillance is a tool that can be used to estimate and track the health status and behaviors of populations and geospatial variation therein. Surveillance is useful, and in many ways critical, for measuring the extent of the dementia burden in terms of its prevalence, disparities, and associated risk profiles. This information can be used to identify opportunities to intervene and to aid decision-makers to more effectively manage efforts to reduce the burden of dementia in a timely manner.

In the United States, there are several systems that track health and behaviors, such as the Centers for Disease Control and Prevention's (CDC) Behavioral Risk Factor Surveillance System (BRFSS). In recent years, the BRFSS has introduced modules to assess cognitive decline and caregiving which have been implemented in 52 and 48 states/ territories, respectively.[49] Results from these surveys are being used to track trends and patterns, guide research, inform public policy, and to evaluate programs and policies among other tasks.

POLICY AND LEGISLATIVE EFFORTS

The National Plan to Address Alzheimer's Disease[50] guides the federal response to Alzheimer's and dementia, in particular its hallmark goal of developing an effective treatment for dementia by 2025 through aggressive research investment. Created from the bipartisan National Alzheimer's Project Act,[51] the National Plan has five overarching goals: develop an effective treatment, enhance care quality and efficiency, expand supports for people with dementia and their families, enhance public awareness of dementia, and improve data collection. Updated annually, an Advisory Council (jointly staffed by an equal share of representatives from the federal government and nongovernmental experts) assists with the development and evaluation of the National Plan. The Office of the Assistant Secretary of Planning and Evaluation within the US Department of Health and Human Services coordinates the National Plan overall.

Since the publication of the National Plan in 2012, research funding for AD and dementia at the National Institutes of Health has increased more than 400%.[52] While no cure has yet been established for Alzheimer's dementia, advances in biomarker research has helped expand understanding of etiology and increase early detection. Similarly, several enhancements to dementia care and support have been made in concert with the National Plan, including standardized workforce training curriculum,[53] development of nationwide recommendations for improved care and support services across care settings,[54] and Medicare reimbursement for comprehensive care planning services delivered to people with cognitive impairment.[55]

At the state level, nearly every state government has published a state-specific Alzheimer's plan to address dementia, cognitive health, and dementia caregiving for their residents. State Alzheimer's plans are tailored to the unique needs of the state's population and recent state plans have focused attention on public health interventions, particularly increasing public awareness about the importance of early detection and ensuring individuals have access to quality services and supports (unpublished analysis of state Alzheimer's disease plans; prepared under contract by Emory Centers for Training and Technical Assistance for the Alzheimer's Association, May 2020). An online repository of state dementia plans is available from the Alzheimer's Impact Movement.[56]

Additionally, other federal and state attention is directed toward unpaid caregivers through either specific plans or task forces. Dementia caregivers make up a sizable proportion of all unpaid caregivers nationally, as well as in many states.[57]

Government-Related Programs

The CDC houses the Alzheimer's Disease and Healthy Aging Program (AD+HAP), which is charged with implementing the Healthy Brain Initiative (HBI). The HBI is a public-private initiative that aims to make brain health an integral component of public health. To help guide the public health response, HBI partners have published a series of Road Maps; the most recent include *State and Local Public Health Partnerships to Address Dementia: The 2018-2023 Road Map*[1] and the *Road Map for Indian Country*.[58]

AD+HAP sponsors the Healthy People 2030 Dementia, including Alzheimer's Disease, topic area[59] and the Cognitive Decline and Caregiver optional modules of BRFSS. Additionally, AD+HAP partners with a variety of nationwide organizations to extend the reach of the HBI into every state and among diverse populations. Current and past partners include the American College of Preventive Medicine, the Association of State and Territorial Health Officials, the Balm in Gilead, Inc., the National Association of Chronic Disease Directors, the National Indian Health Board, and the Alzheimer's Association. In 2020, the AD+HAP distributed nearly $10 million, as appropriated through the Building Our Largest Dementia (BOLD) Infrastructure for Alzheimer's Act.[60] This money was used to support implementation of the HBI Road Maps through grants to state, local, and tribal public health programs and to establish nationwide Centers of Excellence to advance early detection, risk reduction, and dementia caregiving.

The Administration for Community Living maintains the National Alzheimer's and Dementia Resource Center which coordinates grants to states through the Alzheimer's Disease Supportive Services Program and the Alzheimer's Disease Initiative-Specialized Supportive Services Program. These two programs expand the availability of community-based services and supports for people living with dementia and their caregivers, including high-risk populations.

At the state level, individual Area Agencies on Aging provide many home- and community-based services that help people living with dementia remain in the community for as long as possible. Services include adult day services, meal assistance, respite care for caregivers, case management, and personal care services.

Several state governments have specific Alzheimer's and Dementia Programs. These programs include dedicated full-time state employees who oversee implementation of the state Alzheimer's plan, coordinate between state agencies and community organizations, evaluate existing dementia services and supports (including services access and gaps), and increase awareness of dementia overall. States with a dedicated Alzheimer's and Dementia Program include Georgia, Texas, Utah, Virginia, and Wisconsin.

PUBLIC HEALTH AND DEMENTIA: BEST PRACTICES

As with all other chronic conditions, strong public heath attention is needed to mitigate the future impacts of Alzheimer's and other dementias. This is even more important currently as treatments and cures for the underlying disease that cause Alzheimer's are not yet available. Public health can dually educate the public and health care providers about the best available evidence on strategies that reduce the risk of cognitive decline. There is sufficient evidence that certain modifiable risk factors, including quitting smoking, increasing physical activity, and managing cardiovascular health, reduces the risk of future cognitive impairment.[4,5,6]

Public health can take similarly successful public awareness campaigns on tobacco cessation, physical activity, and diabetes prevention and incorporate attention to cognitive health. Such campaigns should educate both the public and health care providers about ways to reduce their individual risk, when cognitive concerns warrant discussion with providers, and recognition of the early warning signs of dementia (see "Case Study" in this chapter for an example). Similarly, traditional tools and techniques of public health can ensure better early detection and diagnosis of dementia. These include educational campaigns, especially for health care providers about the early warning signs of dementia and available care planning services. Public health can use needs assessments to identify gaps in services, supports, and education, and better identify underserved populations.

With the number of people living with dementia estimated to reach nearly 14 million by 2050,[6] dedicated public health attention is needed now to mitigate those impacts and lessen the trajectory.

Special Considerations

Traditionally marginalized groups, including Black people, Latinx individuals, and Native American/Alaska Native adults have higher incidence and prevalence rates of dementia than their White peers.[7] These groups also have higher rates of other chronic conditions which offers workers in the field of public health an opportunity to integrate cognitive health education into existing outreach efforts.

Women also shoulder a disproportionate share of dementia as both individuals living with dementia and as caregivers.[22] Nearly two-thirds of Americans living with Alzheimer's are women, and nearly two-thirds of caregivers for people with dementia are women. Traditional gender roles, especially "women as care providers", may explain why more caregivers are women than men.

There has not been large-scale, focused research on dementia among the lesbian, gay, bisexual, and transgender communities. However, many associated risk factors with dementia are more common among these communities including smoking,[61] heart disease,[62] and depression.[63]

The number of Native American/Alaska Native individuals aged 65 years and older is projected to grow over five times between 2014-2060.[64] As the Native American/Alaska Native cohort ages, so too will the burden of cognitive impairment grow. The high prevalence of chronic conditions among Native American/Alaska Native communities, including diabetes,[65] heart disease,[66] and smoking,[67] offers a prime opportunity to improve cognitive health through culturally sensitive public health action.

Opportunities for Interdisciplinary Connections

Public health workers interface with all facets of the health care system and health care providers. As health education and communication experts, public health practitioners can leverage their trusted leadership with the health care community to train the current workforce, including physicians, nurses, and social workers, about dementia, the need for early detection, and ways to reduce population-level risk of cognitive decline. Supportive service staff, including home health aides, nursing assistants, and respite providers, likewise benefit from additional education. The future workforce cannot be overlooked, either. Students in schools of public health, nursing, social work, and medicine can benefit from specific training on older adult health and dementia. The readymade, introductory curriculum *A Public Health Approach to Alzheimer's and Other Dementias*[68] is available for faculty to incorporate into existing syllabi.

CASE STUDY

The Georgia Department of Public Health (GA DPH) operates a robust public awareness campaign on how the public can reduce their risk of cognitive decline and what they can do if they become worried about their own cognitive health. This campaign, called Think About It,[69] teaches the public about the warning signs of dementia, such as memory loss that disrupts everyday life or difficulty completing familiar tasks, as well as strategies people can take to protect their cognition, such as staying physically active and quitting smoking. The Think About It campaign encourages individuals to discuss cognitive health concerns with their health care provider. The campaign featured prominent transit ads on buses, trains, and billboards.

Think About It is a classic example of a largescale public service announcement. The Georgia Department of Public Health translated the latest science into digestible information for a lay audience to reach a large portion of the public. Additionally, the campaign drove individuals toward a single, accomplishable action.

The Georgia Department of Public Health has an early and thorough history of action on Alzheimer's and cognitive health, demonstrating how dedicated attention to this issue area can have wide-reaching results. The agency has steadily increased expertise within the department, expanded staffing, and increased their community partnerships to reach underserved populations.

Other public health agencies at the state and local level can take similar action to increase public awareness of healthy aging, especially how to reduce the risk of cognitive decline. Their unique networks reach underserved and vulnerable populations, and their experience working with these groups helps tailor the messaging to ensure cultural competence and accessibility. These culturally-appropriate messages should encourage healthy behaviors that can lower cognitive decline risk, and provide information on which cognitive warning signs warrant discussions with health care providers.

Subject matter expertise and buy-in from senior leadership is necessary to ensure success. As seen in the Think About It campaign, GA DPH utilized their deep history addressing Alzheimer's and used designated funding from the state legislature to scale up the project. Other public health agencies may have similar expertise in public awareness efforts for smoking cessation or hypertension prevention that can be readily adapted to cognitive health. These classic public health topics are ripe for integration of cognitive health messages since both smoking and heart health are risk factors for cognitive decline. For agencies ready to invest more heavily in addressing cognitive health, specific campaign design can better meet the needs of their most vulnerable populations.

CONCLUSION

Mitigating the burden of dementia will rely on successful interventions at the level of the individual and their families, the community, society, health care systems, and policy more broadly. The success of these efforts will be driven by the ability of local, state, and national actors to form partnerships and work in unison within the communities they serve, and across the nation to address the needs of our aging population. The traditional tools and techniques of public health, including surveillance, risk reduction, and early detection, can be adapted to improve the quality of life, health, and well-being of people living with dementia, their caregivers, and their families. Specifically, public health can

1. Recognize the role of aging across the life span and how healthy behaviors that protect physical health can also protect cognitive health,
2. Utilize existing infrastructure for chronic conditions to also address dementia, and
3. Employ broad-based changes to policies, systems, and environments to ensure access to services, a competent and dementia-capable workforce, and a public educated in cognitive aging, risk reduction, and early detection.

As our understanding of dementia continues to evolve, it is necessary to adopt culturally sensitive and relevant programming to meet the needs of an increasingly diverse population of older adults. Moreover, considering recent evidence suggesting that changes in the brain associated with AD may begin years or even decades before symptoms emerge,[70] these efforts should not be restricted to older age but instead should be viewed within the context of the life course. While researchers are working to identify underlying pathways and mechanisms that may shape trajectories of poor cognitive health, state and federal public health agencies are shifting more resources in response to the expected increases in the number of adults affected by dementia. However, in many circumstances, state and federal funding are insufficient to target and fund programs related to healthy aging.

As with prior and co-occurring matters related to public health, multilevel partnerships are necessary to expand the reach and impact of work addressing the burden of dementia. It is critical that state and federal agencies, including those that oversee Medicare and Medicaid, chronic disease, and workforce development, be involved in the response.

Nearly 10,000 adults in the United States celebrate their 65th birthday each day, a feat brought about by demographic and epidemiological transitions in the population. Indeed, population aging brings about dynamic challenges that society must face. The tools of public health helped promote our longevity; now, they must be used to continue our success story.

REFERENCES

1. Alzheimer's Association and Centers for Disease Control and Prevention. Healthy brain initiative, state and local public health partnerships to address dementia: The 2018–2023 Road Map. 2018. Available at: https://www.alz.org/media/Documents/healthy-brain-initiative-road-map-2018-2023.pdf. Accessed February 16, 2021.

2. Hardy JA, Higgins GA. Alzheimer's disease: the amyloid cascade hypothesis. *Science.* 1992;256(5054):184–185.

3. Selkoe DJ. Alzheimer's disease results from the cerebral accumulation and cytotoxicity of amyloid\beta-protein. *J Alzheimers Dis.* 2001;3(1):75–82.

4. Kapasi A, DeCarli C, Schneider JA. Impact of multiple pathologies on the threshold for clinically overt dementia. *Acta Neuropathol.* 2017;134(2):171–186.

5. Brenowitz WD, Hubbard RA, Keene CD, et al. Mixed neuropathologies and estimated rates of clinical progression in a large autopsy sample. *Alzheimers Dement.* 2017;13(6):654–662.

6. Hebert LE, Weuve J, Scherr PA, Evans DA. Alzheimer disease in the United States (2010–2050) estimated using the 2010 Census. *Neurology.* 2013;80(19):1778–1783.

7. Alzheimer's Association. 2020 Alzheimer's disease facts and figures. *Alzheimers Dement.* 2020;16(3):391–460.

8. Kramarow EA, Tejada-Vera B. Dementia mortality in the United States, 2000–2017. *Natl Vital Stat Rep.* 2019;68(2):1–28.

9. James BD, Leurgans SE, Hebert LE, Scherr PA, Yaffe K, Bennett DA. Contribution of Alzheimer disease to mortality in the United States. *Neurology*. 2014;82(12):1045–1050.

10. Spillman B, Wolff J, Freedman V, Kasper J. *Informal Caregiving for Older Americans: An Analysis of the 2011 National Health and Aging Trends Study*. Washington, DC: US Department of Health and Human Services, Office of the Assistance Secretary for Planning and Evaluation; 2014.

11. Fredman L, Lyons JG, Cauley JA, Hochberg M, Applebaum KM. The relationship between caregiving and mortality after accounting for time-varying caregiver status and addressing the healthy caregiver hypothesis. *J Gerontol A Bio Sci Med Sci*. 2015;70(9):1163–1168.

12. Puterman E, Weiss J, Lin J, et al. Aerobic exercise lengthens telomeres and reduces stress in family caregivers: A randomized controlled trial - Curt Richter Award Paper 2018. *Psychoneuroendocrinology*. 2018; 98:245–252.

13. Podcasy JL, Epperson CN. Considering sex and gender in Alzheimer disease and other dementias. *Dialogues Clin Neurosci*. 2016;18(4):437–446.

14. van der Flier WM, Scheltens P. Epidemiology and risk factors of dementia. *J Neurol Neurosurg Psychiatry*. 2005;76(suppl 5):v2–v7.

15. Licher S, Darweesh SK, Wolters FJ, et al. Lifetime risk of common neurological diseases in the elderly population. *J Neurol Neurosurg Psychiatry*. 2019;90(2):148–156.

16. Rocca WA, Grossardt BR, Shuster LT. Oophorectomy, estrogen, and dementia: a 2014 update. *Mol Cell Endocrinol*. 2014;389(1–2):7–12.

17. Altmann A, Tian L, Henderson VW, Greicius MD, Investigators AsDNI. Sex modifies the APOE-related risk of developing Alzheimer disease. *Ann Neurol*. 2014;75(4):563–573.

18. Lin KA, Choudhury KR, Rathakrishnan BG, et al. Marked gender differences in progression of mild cognitive impairment over 8 years. *Alzheimers Dement*. 2015;1(2):103–110.

19. Snyder HM, Asthana S, Bain L, et al. Sex biology contributions to vulnerability to Alzheimer's disease: A think tank convened by the Women's Alzheimer's Research Initiative. *Alzheimer Dement*. 2016;12(11):1186–1196.

20. Babulal GM, Quiroz YT, Albensi BC, et al. Perspectives on ethnic and racial disparities in Alzheimer's disease and related dementias: Update and areas of immediate need. *Alzheimers Dement*. 2019;15(2):292–312.

21. Mielke MM. Sex and gender differences in Alzheimer's disease dementia. *Psychiatr Times*. 2018;35(11):14–17.

22. Potter GG, Plassman BL, Burke JR, et al. Cognitive performance and informant reports in the diagnosis of cognitive impairment and dementia in African Americans and whites. *Alzheimer Dement*. 2009;5(6):445–453.

23. Gurland BJ, Wilder DE, Lantigua R, et al. Rates of dementia in three ethnoracial groups. *Int J Geriatr Psychiatry*. 1999;14(6):481–493.

24. Samper-Ternent R, Kuo YF, Ray LA, Ottenbacher KJ, Markides KS, Al Snih S. Prevalence of health conditions and predictors of mortality in oldest old Mexican Americans and non-Hispanic whites. *J Am Med Dir Assoc.* 2012;13(3):254–259.

25. Wu Y-T, Beiser AS, Breteler MMB, et al. The changing prevalence and incidence of dementia over time — current evidence. *Nat Rev Neurol.* 2017;13:327–339.

26. Barnes LL, Bennett DA. Alzheimer's disease in African Americans: risk factors and challenges for the future. *Health Aff.* 2014;33(4):580–586.

27. Chin AL, Negash S, Hamilton R. Diversity and disparity in dementia: the impact of ethnoracial differences in Alzheimer disease. *Alzheimer Dis Assoc Disord.* 2011;25(3):187–195.

28. Mehta KM, Yaffe K, Pérez-Stable EJ, et al. Race/ethnic differences in AD survival in US Alzheimer's Disease Centers. *Neurology.* 2008;70(14):1163–1170.

29. Livingston G, Sommerlad A, Orgeta V, et al. Dementia prevention, intervention, and care. *Lancet.* 2017;390(10113):2673–2734.

30. Ganguli M. The times they are a-changin': cohort effects in aging, cognition, and dementia. *Int Psychogeriatrics.* 2017;29(3):353–355.

31. Sharp ES, Gatz M. Relationship between education and dementia: an updated systematic review. *Alzheimer Dis Assoc Disord.* 2011;25(4):289–304.

32. Yaffe K, Falvey C, Harris TB, et al. Effect of socioeconomic disparities on incidence of dementia among biracial older adults: prospective study. *BMJ.* 2013;347:f7051.

33. Karp A, Kåreholt I, Qiu C, Bellander T, Winblad B, Fratiglioni L. Relation of education and occupation-based socioeconomic status to incident Alzheimer's disease. *Am J Epidemiol.* 2004;159(2):175–183.

34. Stern Y. Cognitive reserve. *Neuropsychologia.* 2009;47(10):2015–2028.

35. Anjum I, Fayyaz M, Wajid A, Sohail W, Ali A. Does obesity increase the risk of dementia: A literature review. *Cureus.* 2018;10(5):e2660–e2660.

36. Kivimäki M, Luukkonen R, Batty GD, et al. Body mass index and risk of dementia: Analysis of individual-level data from 1.3 million individuals. *Alzheimer Dement.* 2018;14(5):601–609.

37. Chang C-CH, Zhao Y, Lee C-W, Ganguli M. Smoking, death, and Alzheimer's disease: a case of competing risks. *Alzheimer Dis Assoc Disord.* 2012;26(4):300–306.

38. Gorina Y, Kramarow EA. Identifying chronic conditions in Medicare claims data: evaluating the Chronic Condition Data Warehouse algorithm. *Health Serv Res.* 2011;46(5):1610–1627.

39. Zhong G, Wang Y, Zhang Y, Guo JJ, Zhao Y. Smoking is associated with an increased risk of dementia: a meta-analysis of prospective cohort studies with investigation of potential effect modifiers [published correction appears in *PloS ONE.* 2015:10(4):e0126169]. *PloS ONE.* 2015;10(3):e0118333.

40. Anstey KJ, von Sanden C, Salim A, O'Kearney R. Smoking as a risk factor for dementia and cognitive decline: a meta-analysis of prospective studies. *Am J Epidemiol.* 2007;166(4): 367–378.

41. Samieri C, Perier M-C, Gaye B, et al. Association of cardiovascular health level in older age with cognitive decline and incident dementia. *JAMA.* 2018;320(7):657–664.

42. Graves A, Van Duijn C, Chandra V, et al. Alcohol and tobacco consumption as risk factors for Alzheimer's disease: a collaborative re-analysis of case-control studies. *Int J Epidemiol.* 1991;20(suppl 2):S48–S57.

43. Denkinger M, Nikolaus T, Denkinger C, Lukas A. Physical activity for the prevention of cognitive decline. *Z Gerontol Geriatr.* 2012;45(1):11–16.

44. Farina N, Rusted J, Tabet N. The effect of exercise interventions on cognitive outcome in Alzheimer's disease: a systematic review. *Int Psychogeriatr.* 2014;26(1):9–18.

45. Kivimäki M, Singh-Manoux A, Pentti J, et al. Physical inactivity, cardiometabolic disease, and risk of dementia: an individual-participant meta-analysis. *BMJ.* 2019;365:l1495.

46. Kontari P, Smith KJ. Risk of dementia associated with cardiometabolic abnormalities and depressive symptoms: a longitudinal cohort study using the English longitudinal study of ageing. *Int J Geriatr Psychiatry.* 2019;34(2):289–298.

47. Exalto LG, Quesenberry CP, Barnes D, Kivipelto M, Biessels GJ, Whitmer RA. Midlife risk score for the prediction of dementia four decades later. *Alzheimers Dement.* 2014;10(5): 562–570.

48. Prince M, Bryce R, Ferri C. World Alzheimer Report 2011: The benefits of early diagnosis and intervention. London, United Kingdom: Alzheimer's Disease International; 2011.

49. Alzheimer's Disease and Healthy Aging Data Portal. Centers for Disease Control and Prevention. Available at: https://www.cdc.gov/aging/agingdata/index.html. Accessed February 16, 2021.

50. Office of the Assistant Secretary for Planning and Evaluation. National Alzheimer's Project Act: National plans to address Alzheimer's disease. 2020. US Department of Health and Human Services. Available at: https://aspe.hhs.gov/national-plans-address-alzheimers-disease. Accessed February 16, 2021.

51. The National Alzheimer's Project Act, 42 USC §11225 (2011).

52. National Institutes of Health. NIH bypass budget proposal for fiscal year 2021: Together we succeed: Accelerating research on Alzheimer's disease and related dementias. 2019. Available at: https://www.nia.nih.gov/sites/default/files/2019-07/FY21-bypass-budget-report-508.pdf. Accessed February 16, 2021.

53. Health Resources and Services Administration. Train health care workers about dementia. 2020. Available at: https://bhw.hrsa.gov/grants/geriatrics/alzheimers-curriculum. Accessed February 16, 2021.

54. National Institute on Aging. Research Summit on Dementia Care, Building evidence for services and supports: Main summit recommendations. 2018. Available at: https://aspe.hhs.gov/system/files/pdf/259186/Recommendations.pdf. Accessed February 16, 2021.

55. Alzheimer's Association. Cognitive assessment and care planning services: Alzheimer's Association Expert Task Force recommendations and tools for implementation. 2018. Available at: https://www.alz.org/media/Documents/cog-impair-assess-care-plan-code.pdf. Accessed February 16, 2021.

56. Alzheimer's Impact Movement. State priorities (state dementia plans available from My State dropdown menu). 2019. Available at: https://alzimpact.org/priorities/state_priorities. Accessed February 16, 2021.

57. Edwards VJ, Bouldin ED, Taylor CA, Olivari BS, McGuire LC. Characteristics and health status of informal unpaid caregivers–44 states, District of Columbia, and Puerto Rico. *MMWR Morb Mortal Wkly Rep.* 2020;69(7):183–188.

58. Alzheimer's Association and Centers for Disease Control and Prevention. *Healthy Brain Initiative, Road Map for Indian Country.* Chicago, IL: Alzheimer's Association; 2019.

59. US Department of Health and Human Services. Dementias. Healthy People 2030. Available at: https://health.gov/healthypeople/objectives-and-data/browse-objectives/dementias. Accessed March 8, 2021.

60. Building Our Largest Dementia Infrastructure for Alzheimer's Act, 42 USC §280c, 280c–3, 280c–4, and 280c–5 (2018).

61. American Lung Association. *The LGBT Community: A Priority Population for Tobacco Control.* Chicago, IL: American Lung Association; 2018.

62. Caceres BA, Brody A, Luscombe RE, et al. A systematic review of cardiovascular disease in sexual minorities. *Am J Public Health.* 2017;107(4):e13–e21.

63. Haas AP, Eliason M, Mays VM, et al. Suicide and suicide risk in lesbian, gay, bisexual, and transgender populations: review and recommendations. *J Homosex.* 2011;58(1):10–51.

64. Matthews K, Xu W, Gaglioti A, Holt J, Croft J, Mack D, McGuire L. Racial and ethnic estimates of Alzheimer's disease and related dementias in the United States (2015–2060) in adults aged ≥65 years. *Alzheimers Dement.* 2019;15(1):17–24.

65. Centers for Disease Control and Prevention. Summary Health Statistics Tables: National Health Interview Survey, 2018, Table A-4a: Age-adjusted percentages (with standard errors) of selected diseases and conditions among adults aged 18 and over, by selected characteristics: United States. 2018. Available at: https://ftp.cdc.gov/pub/Health_Statistics/NCHS/NHIS/SHS/2018_SHS_Table_A-4.pdf. Accessed February 16, 2020.

66. Centers for Disease Control and Prevention. Summary Health Statistics Tables: National Health Interview Survey, 2018, Table A-1a: Age-adjusted percentages (with standard errors) of selected circulatory diseases among adults aged 18 and over, by selected characteristics: United States.

2018. Available at: https://ftp.cdc.gov/pub/Health_Statistics/NCHS/NHIS/SHS/2018_SHS_Table_A-1.pdf. Accessed February 16, 2021.

67. Center for Behavioral Health Statistics and Quality. *2016 National Survey on Drug Use and Health: Detailed Tables*. Rockville, MD: Substance Abuse and Mental Health Services Administration; 2017.

68. Alzheimer's Association and the Centers for Disease Control and Prevention. A public health approach to Alzheimer's and other dementias. 2020. Available at: https://www.alz.org/professionals/public-health/core-areas/educate-train-professionals/public-health-curriculum-on-alzheimer-s. Accessed February 16, 2021.

69. Georgia Department of Public Health. Alzheimer's/Dementia: Think About It. Available at: https://dph.georgia.gov/alzheimersdementia-think-about-it. Accessed March 21, 2021.

70. Sperling RA, Aisen PS, Beckett LA, et al. Toward defining the preclinical stages of Alzheimer's disease: Recommendations from the National Institute on Aging-Alzheimer's Association workgroups on diagnostic guidelines for Alzheimer's disease. *Alzheimers Dement*. 2011; 7(3):280–292.

Polypharmacy and Medication Safety in Older Adults

Rafia S. Rasu, MPharm, MBA, PhD, Jude des Bordes, MBChB, DrPH, CPH,
Rana Zalmai, PharmD, Aliza R. Karpes Matusevich, PhD, and
Nahid Rianon, MD, DrPH
Case Study 2: Nicole S. MacFarland, PhD, MSW and Darren Cosgrove, PhD, MSW

INTRODUCTION

Aging is associated with changes in physiological reserves and biological function. Altered physiologic functions also affect pharmacodynamics (PD) and pharmacokinetics (PK) of drugs, posing greater risk of adverse drug events (ADE) in older adults.[1] As chronic diseases become more common with age, multiple health conditions increase the need for numerous medications in an attempt to maintain optimal health and function. However, the interactions of multiple medications, known as polypharmacy, is of critical concern among aging populations. Polypharmacy often becomes an inseparable term from the medical life of an aging person. Excessive use of medications and cumulative medication exposure (whether in number or dosage) may negatively affect physical and cognitive functions, which often becomes a cause of more prescriptions for managing unintentional side effects.[2] Use of multiple medications leads to the risk of inappropriate medication use, medication non-adherence, and ADE with poor health outcomes. Medication safety has become an important aspect of health management and quality of life in the older age group.

POLYPHARMACY

Polypharmacy is defined as the simultaneous use of five or more medications for the prevention or treatment of one or multiple conditions.[3,4] While polypharmacy usually refers to concurrent, chronic, prescription medication use, it can include consecutive medications, short-term treatment (e.g. oral antibiotics for an infection), vitamins, supplements and over-the-counter (OTC) medications.[5] Polypharmacy is common in those with chronic conditions managed with several medications and thus becomes prevalent in older adults. Multimorbidity, the existence of two or more chronic conditions, is common. It occurs in 90% of adults aged 65–74, 96.5% in those aged 75–84, and 99% in those over 85 years of age,[6] with 9.7%, 16.7%, and 31.8% respectively having more than 10 chronic conditions.[7] (See Figure 2-1.)

Although generally viewed as undesirable, prescribing many drugs may be necessary to maintain optimal health; therefore, polypharmacy becomes an unavoidable medical necessity requiring appropriate management to cope with chronic disease management and to optimize therapeutic outcomes. The term "appropriate polypharmacy" has been used to describe a situation where a patient with complex or multiple conditions is prescribed many medications based on the best evidence and is in accordance with patient's clinical needs and maintenance of quality of life.[8–10] Thus, in striving to promote healthy aging, we aim to improve the situation through proper management of polypharmacy.

Prescriptions are meant to reduce morbidity and mortality, improve disease-specific end points such as blood pressure and glucose, improve quality of life, and prevent complications. However, more medications also increase the probability of medication errors and ADE.[11] This is exacerbated by health care systems and professionals who are trained to focus on individual conditions.[12] Polypharmacy potentially leads to ADE, falls, hospitalizations, reduced quality of life, and increased mortality.[12] Furthermore, multimorbidity and polypharmacy complicate the matter as a patient is already burdened with diseases and navigating complex health systems, including financial aspects.[13]

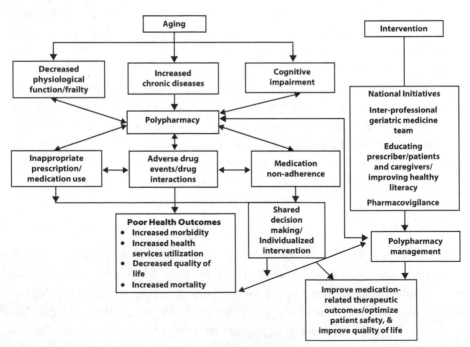

Note: "Polypharmacy is a growing and global issue, affecting primary and secondary care. It is predominantly driven by an ageing, multimorbid population coupled with the increasing use of evidence-based clinical guidelines."[5]

Figure 2-1. Polypharmacy and Multimorbidities

It has been estimated that 50% of people taking any medication are taking more than two medications, with 30% of older adults taking more than four medications daily and 5% taking more than eight medications.[14] Whether this complex situation is due to cultural influence or a true prevalence of multimorbidities among patients driving the prescribing trend of polypharmacy is a query that needs further investigation. On the other hand, direct consumer advertising for pharmaceutical products, which is not common in other parts of the world, may also have played a role behind the popularity of increase in medication utilization.

PREVALENCE OF POLYPHARMACY

The prevalence of polypharmacy is between 35%–40%, with 2.6%–8.6% of older adults taking at least 10 different medications.[15] Studies conducted in community-dwelling older adults found more than one third of older adults use five or more prescription medications and almost 40% use over-the-counter (OTC) medications. The percentages and the number of medications is even higher in older adults residing in skilled nursing facilities. The use of five or more medications in adults 65 and older has been on an upward trajectory increasing from 12.8% in 1988–1991 to 39.0% in 2009–2010.[16] Increasing rates of polypharmacy are attributed to high rates of multimorbidity augmented by over-zealous prescribing and inadequate monitoring. The more conditions, the greater the median annual health care expenditure.[7] People with two or more chronic conditions have more than double the total annual expenditures than those with none or one ($13,139 vs $5,849) and their out of pocket expenditures are almost double ($1,437 vs $839).[6] Some classes of medication are prescribed or used more often than others. These medications are commonly for metabolic syndrome, such as hypertension, hyperglycemia, hyperlipidemia, and central nervous system medications.

Consequences of inappropriate polypharmacy are numerous. They include impairment of physical function, (including contributing to development of geriatric syndromes of frailty and urinary incontinence) and cognitive function. These may reinforce each other and negatively impact physical and cognitive functions and may result in increased risk of frailty, hospitalizations, reduced quality of life, and increased mortality.[12] "Judicious prescribing, preserving the balance between the benefits and harms of medicines, may optimize functional abilities in frail adults or even prevent frailty."[17]

Declining cognitive function has been associated with polypharmacy, and it is not uncommon to see polypharmacy in groups with impaired cognition and/or dementia. A study of 2,306 participants with either Alzheimer's Disease, vascular dementia, or Lewy body dementia, using data from the National Alzheimer's Coordinating Center, demonstrated that more than three-quarters were taking five or more medications.[18] Of greater concern is the 28% with "hyperpolypharmacy."[18] Hyperpolypharmacy is a newer term usually defined as taking 10 or more medications which have been associated with functional and cognitive decline,[19,20] poor nutritional status,[20] and mortality risk.[21]

It has also been defined as the "inappropriate" use of multiple medications, "polyphar-macy of uncertain benefit",[22] or "hyperpharmacotherapy."[23]

CONSEQUENCES OF POLYPHARMACY

Adverse Drug Events

As mentioned earlier, taking multiple medications is not intrinsically harmful. However, the potential benefits of each additional medication must be balanced with the potential for medication errors and ADEs. An ADE is an umbrella term referring to any injury that occurs as a result of medical intervention related to a drug.[24] This includes harms incurred from off-label use (i.e., using a drug for an unapproved indication or in an unapproved age group, at an unapproved dose or using an unapproved route of administration), med-ication errors, or when reducing a dose or stopping a medication.[25] Low health literacy,[26] polypharmacy, and multimorbidity with increasing age, particularly among those 80 years and older, have been associated with ADE.[27,28] It is estimated that there are over 265,000 emergency department visits each year due to ADE for people aged 65 and older. Over one-third (37.5%) of these visits result in hospitalization and most of them are due to unintentional overdose (45.7 of ED visits and 65.7% of hospitalizations) or an adverse drug reaction (ADR) (30.2 of emergency department visits and 27.7% of hospitaliza-tions).[28] It is estimated that 66% of ADE are preventable.[29]

Adverse Drug Reactions

An ADR has a narrower definition than that of ADE, and ADR is the preferred term for side effects. An ADR is an unintended harmful or unpleasant consequence of the recom-mended doses of a pharmaceutical product and often requires treatment to resolve, as well as dosage changes or cessation of that medication.[30,31] These reactions can be dose-dependent and predictable based on the pharmacology of the medication. They may be associated with long-term drug exposure and thus have a time element. Adverse drug reac-tions can also be idiosyncratic and possibly attributed to person-specific pathological, bio-logical and genetic factors which will be discussed below.[30] Importantly, in the context of polypharmacy, ADRs are more common when more medications are taken. Comorbidities and age-related pharmacokinetic and pharmacodynamics changes further increase the risk of ADRs for older adults.[32] Adverse drug reactions are complicated by the fact that they are often accepted as symptoms of aging or a new condition and not recognized for what they are, resulting in adding new prescription to the list.[14,33] Lastly, allergies and allergic reac-tions, which are ADRs involving the immune system, account for approximately 20% of emergency department visits for this population and 5.6% of hospitalizations.[28]

Drug Interactions

Drug interactions are changes in a drug's action caused by recent or concurrent use of another drug or drugs (i.e., drug-drug interaction or DDI), ingestion of food or drink (i.e., drug-nutrient interaction), another underlying condition (i.e., drug-disease interaction) or due to individual genetic variations (i.e., drug-genome interaction). These changes can result in cancellation of a drug's therapeutic action, exacerbation of a drug's detrimental effect or creation of a new risk.

Age-related changes in PK and PD expose older adults to greater risk of ADR and drug interactions.[33] Pharmacokinetics refers to the movement of drugs within the body and is affected by absorption, distribution, metabolism and elimination.[34] Pharmacodynamics, on the other hand, studies how these processes affect the organs in which they take place.[34] For example, decrease in body water and increase in body fat can change distribution of lipophilic drugs, increasing its concentration in the central nervous system, which is worse in patients with Alzheimer's disease.[35] Chronic comorbidities increase older adults' susceptibility to ADRs by altering effects of PK and PD due to physiological changes in older adults' bodies.[33] Caring for older adults requires considerations of all chronic conditions, potential DDIs, drug-disease interactions, and drug PK in addition to patient preferences and therapy goals. Fortunately, various and recent assessment tools are available for helping clinicians with appropriate use of medication in older adults.

Drug-Drug Interactions

Drug-drug interaction (DDI) is when two or more medications interact with each other. Obviously, polypharmacy increases the likelihood of DDI. The interactions may cause increased effects of one drug, inhibit the effects of a drug, or cause an unexpected side effect. These interactions can occur with prescription medications as well as OTC medications, supplements, and herbal substances (e.g., a synergistic effect of sedatives and anti-histamines). There is a 50% risk with five to nine medications and up to 100% with 20 or more concurrent use of medications. Over 84% of patients experience at least one DDI,[5] which account for approximately 20% of ADRs.[14]

One in 10 community dwelling older adults experience a DDI when using OTC medication or supplement.[36,37] One OTC medication, primarily non-steroidal anti-inflammatory drugs, was involved in the most potential DDIs.[36,37] Common examples of DDI related to PK is interaction between an OTC proton pump inhibitor (e.g., omeprazole, frequently taken for gastro-esophageal reflux known as "heart burn") and a prescription of citalopram usually taken for depression; or a calcium supplement and prescription of levothyroxine, used for treating hypothyroidism.[35]

Drug-Nutrition Interactions

Interactions between food and medication may increase or decrease the pharmacologic effects of drugs. These are commonly caused by food-induced changes to the bioavailability of the medication or interaction with the active ingredient of the medication. A common interaction illustrating this is of warfarin and foods high in vitamin K. Other well-known drug-nutrient interactions include the antagonistic effect alcohol has on some antibiotics or its synergistic effect on benzodiazepines.[4]

Drug-Disease Interactions

The metabolism of drugs may be altered with certain diseases or conditions. Several cytochrome P450 enzymes, involved in the metabolism of drugs, can be inhibited by infections or inflammation. This can result in decreased metabolism of drugs and thereby reduced concentrations of prodrugs and increased concentrations of active drugs. Other diseases may directly alter concentrations of drugs in the body through declined functioning of the organs. Impaired renal or liver function can increase ADR by altering drug clearance or metabolism.

Drug-Genome Interactions

The new field of pharmacogenomics studies how genes affect an individual's reaction to drugs. Most drugs today are prescribed without the knowledge of how specific people will respond to them, if at all, and who will experience which adverse drug events. However, 15% of prescriptions in the United States are for the 30 most commonly prescribed drugs with known pharmacogenetics.[38] With the mapping of the human genome, researchers are starting to learn how pharmacokinetics and pharmacodynamics are affected by inherited differences in our genome and how this influences our response to drugs (i.e., drug-gene interactions).[33]

Medication Errors

Medication errors are mistakes made when prescribing, transcribing, dispensing, administering, taking, or monitoring a drug. Mistakes that can be made when taking a drug include incorrect storage procedures, keeping discontinued medications and hoarding, duplicating treatment, not having a set medication-taking routine, poor adherence, and confusing the generic and trade names of the medications.[27] These do not necessarily cause ADE,[25] but are correlated with polypharmacy, multimorbidity, and increasing age.[27] As DDI and ADE become more common in older adults with polypharmacy, the process of aging becomes more pronounced with worsening impairment of physical and cognitive function, both of which are required to maintain activities of daily living (e.g., bathing, dressing, feeding, ambulation) and instrumental activities of daily living (e.g., cooking, cleaning, driving, shopping, medication management). All body systems become more susceptible to ADE, which is worse in those patients with polypharmacy. Polypharmacy and cognitive function and polypharmacy and physical function are two such areas. People with dementia are at greater risk of ADE because of their age, multimorbidity, and higher likelihood of taking more neuroactive medications.[33] Polypharmacy has been associated with worse outcomes for people with dementia. At the same time, polypharmacy itself is a risk factor for cognitive decline with certain medications being linked to acute cognitive impartment, although less is known about long-term exposure as a modifiable risk factor.[39] Risk of delirium and cognitive impairment in relation to inappropriate medication use is discussed in cases described below. Polypharmacy is associated with sarcopenia, a geriatric syndrome characterized by loss of muscle strength and skeletal muscle mass, may negatively impact physical function, and increase fall risk.[40] Increased risk of fall, decreased mobility due to multiple chronic conditions (e.g., arthritis, osteoporosis, and related fractures), and complications from cardiovascular and metabolic diseases often have a snowball effect on physical functioning.

CHRONIC PAIN AND OPIOIDS USAGE: A PUBLIC HEALTH CONCERN

Chronic pain is more prevalent in older adults, occurring in 30% of older adults.[41] Pain in these patients may be managed with short-acting or long-acting opioids or a combination of both.[41] However, pain is difficult to manage in older adults due to other comorbidities, increased ADE, and medication interactions. Furthermore, older patients with pain may also develop insomnia and anxiety, which can exacerbate the pain, and the pain can exacerbate insomnia and anxiety, creating a vicious cycle for these patients.[42,43] Due to efficacy and safety concerns, the Centers for Disease Control and Prevention (CDC) guidelines recommend the use of opioid therapy for chronic pain only if the expected benefits for both pain and function are anticipated to outweigh the risk to patients.[44] The potential barriers to evidence-based practice seem to be ambiguity, disagreement, and sometimes, lack of understanding with clinical recommendations and risks of opioid prescribing.[45,46] Among patients prescribed opioids and central nervous system depressants, older adults are most at risk given these patients experience more adverse events due to comorbidities and other medication interactions.

MEDICATION NON-ADHERENCE

Polypharmacy and complexity of medication regimens increase the drug burden on the patient and may make it difficult to adhere to the medication regimen. Non-adherence is a risk for increased morbidity, hospitalization, and mortality[47] and could lead to further polypharmacy. Medication non-compliance leads to drug wastage and increased health care cost.

MANAGEMENT OF POLYPHARMACY

Several initiatives have been adopted to promote and strive for excellence in maximizing therapeutic outcomes through judicious prescribing, thus preserving the beneficial effects of medication, optimizing practical purpose, or even improving quality of life for older adults who are on several necessary medications. Management of polypharmacy is multifaceted and complex, as not all polypharmacy status is problematic or inappropriate for older adult patients. As multimorbidity situations vary by patients, individualized therapy approach and customized therapy management are required since a combination of medication may influence the PK and PD properties of medications in an already at-risk older adult. Thus, a holistic approach should be taken for management of polypharmacy. Applying an individual's treatment goals in a stepwise manner and considering shared decision-making preferences to ultimately improve quality of life can be adopted as necessary steps for managing polypharmacy. Simplifying regimens, improving formulations, engaging patient and caregiver, and developing an improved means of communication are some of the techniques used by interprofessional geriatric teams to enhance therapy adherence and compliance. Management of polypharmacy involve various management techniques described below.

Training Interprofessional Geriatric Teams Including Prescribers

Clinicians along with their interprofessional team (including pharmacists, nurses, physical and occupational therapists, nutritionist, speech therapist, social worker/case manager, and medication intake coordinator), who manage medical conditions in older adults need to be empowered through training and medication safety tools to recognize inappropriate medication use and individuals at risk of ADE. The Joint Commission, the largest standard-setting and accrediting body in health care in the United States, recently emphasized medication safety as one of the primary national patient safety goals.[48] Similarly, the Agency for Healthcare Research and Quality specifically funds research to reduce medication errors and improve medication management.[49] Continuing medical education (CME) on polypharmacy management could be a way to update physicians on medication safety for older adults (e.g., grand rounds, CME conferences organized by professional organizations). An inter-professional team for optimal management of geriatric patients is essential. Collaboration between pharmacists and physicians in both inpatient and outpatient settings has been shown to improve medication management and decreasing ADEs.

Health Literacy

Health literacy is necessary for patients to safely use their medications. Recognizing a universal health literacy toolkit is a key to optimize medication literacy. Clinicians are encouraged to apply teach-back health literacy communication methods in all levels of patient communications to provide more consistent and easy-to-understand information for patients. This is particularly applicable to patient counseling that involves educating patients on medication effects, side effects, and clinical use of specific medications and diseases.

Medication Reconciliation and Maintenance of Updated List of Medication

Going over a patient's list of medication is one of the most important part of a geriatric patient visit for both inpatient and outpatient settings. Matching medication with a diagnosis through the reconciliation process helps to avoid duplication of medication. At the same time, going over medication side effects and matching with the patient's presenting symptoms will help physicians to decide on strategies (see Figure 2-2).

Deprescribing

Deprescribing is the planned and programmed reduction in the number or dosage of medications by a health care professional. The goal of deprescribing is to reduce polypharmacy and improve outcomes while properly managing disease conditions. However, deprescribing is found to be difficult in older adults and requires consideration of multiple factors. Different approaches, such as pharmacist-led medication reviews, prescriber feedback, and multidisciplinary interventions have been trialed in response to polypharmacy with

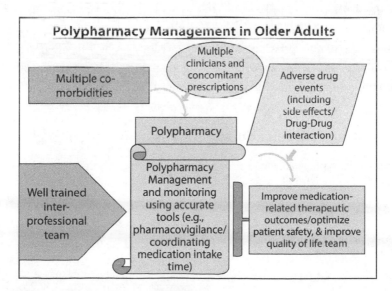

Figure 2-2. Polypharmacy Management in Older Adults

deprescribing. Deprescribing involves identifying, and ideally, stopping potentially inappropriate medications. A drug is considered unsuitable when the risk of possible ADE surpasses the clinical benefit expected, or when the risk-benefit ratio is unclear. Medication reviews for older adults reduces the risks of emergency room visits and hospitalization.

Instruments for Deprescribing

Multiple tools are available to aid in proper medication therapy in older adults, including the Beers Criteria, the STOPP tool, the IPET, and the McLeod Criteria.

The AGS Beers Criteria for Potentially Inappropriate Medication (PIM) in Older Adults is published by the American Geriatric Society and updated every 3 years.[50] The Screening Tool of Older Persons' Prescriptions (STOPP) is a European checklist-based explicit tool. The Improved Prescribing in the Elderly Tool (IPET), also known as the "Canadian Criteria" is a 14-point list of inappropriate drug-disease combinations. Finally, the McLeod criteria is a Canadian adaptation of the Beers Criteria.

Out of these tools and criteria, the Beers Criteria and the STOPP tool are used most frequently in practice. Drug classes that are relatively more amenable to deprescribing include antihistamines, vitamins, and supplements, while anti-psychotics have proved to be difficult despite their association with increased all-cause mortality.[51]

Older adults may have multi-morbidities and may be receiving many medications for management of chronic diseases. It is important to mention that avoiding polypharmacy should not deny a patient needed medications. Appropriate prescribing for such older people must take into consideration the goals of treatment, dose optimization, potential risks for ADE, risk-benefit ratio, and patient preferences.[52] On the other hand, medications that are determined to be ineffective or with a current unfavorable risk-benefit profile should be discontinued. The process of discontinuing or withdrawing a medication determined inappropriate, under the supervision of a health care professional and with the aim of improving outcomes and managing polypharmacy, is referred to as deprescribing when dealing with multimorbidities.[53]

Simplification of Medication Regimens

A patient with polypharmacy may be overwhelmed with not only the number of pills but also with the complexity of prescription regimen. Taking more than one medication at the same time (e.g., early in the morning on an empty stomach following complex instructions) can bring frustration on the patient's part and increases risk of non-compliance. Prescribing long-acting pills (e.g., once a month) with a required daily pill (e.g., thyroid medication) can help in such instances. Combined pills, often known as polypill, is also another way of simplifying regimen and decreasing the number of pills taken.

Policy Considerations: Prescription Drug Monitoring Program (PDMP)

The abuse of prescription drugs is a serious public health and public safety concern. Recently, the CDC and the office of National Drug Control Policy created a prescription drug monitoring program (PDMP) for each state. PDMP, an electronic database that tracks controlled substance prescriptions to prevent misuse, is a public health initiative that took place to combat opioid pandemic in the United States.[54] Every state across the nation, with the exception of Missouri, currently has a PDPM overseen by each state's mandated policy.

CONCLUSION

Prevention has always been the cornerstone of public health and the National Action Plan[55] delineates several approaches to preventing ADE. While prevention of polypharmacy remains an approach for avoiding associated health hazards, appropriate management of polypharmacy is becoming the key to maintain quality of life in an older person with multimorbidity requiring multiple prescription drugs for health maintenance. Lack of adequately trained health care workers in managing polypharmacy in older adults is an ongoing challenge. However, public health educators can take the lead in developing and sharing evidence-based resources and tools with practitioners, institutions, and caregivers, along with the general public.

Continuing medical education credits for clinical prescribers can incorporate guidelines on quality prescribing, safe medication management, care planning, and patient assessment, in addition to monitoring and assessing health literacy level and engaging strategies to involve patients and their families. Patients and their families can be the focus of interventions and tools that empower them to take an active role in minimizing the risk of ADE. Like many other quality incentives, polypharmacy management can be a provider incentive that is aligned with the overreaching goal of preventing ADE and improving quality of life in older adults.

CASE STUDIES

Case Study 1: A Typical Scenario for an Older Adult and Polypharmacy Issues

A 76-year-old White woman with hypertension and migraine headaches presents to the clinic with dizziness. She started noticing the symptoms about six months ago and recent worsening, and had to see a physician because she is now unable get out of bed or drive without feeling dizzy. She is a caregiver for her husband and says that lately, she has been stressed as she is forgetting her husband's medication schedule as well as her own. Her current medication is propranolol (a beta-blocker), cyclobenzaprine (a muscle relaxant and is in the anticholinergic category), amitriptyline (tricyclic antidepressant), clonidine (an alpha-blocker), and lorazepam (benzodiazepine). She reports taking these medications for over 10 years and some for about 30 years.

Besides a good history, a physical examination revealed that the patient has orthostatic hypotension. She had not had any migraine headache in the past 30 years for which she was taking three medications (propranolol, cyclobenzaprine and amitriptyline); these medications were not part of the most up-to-date treatment for this medical condition. She did not have cognitive impairment but feels she is slow in her thinking process. Her blood pressure is very low and she may not need any medication to treat hypertension. She also lost about 50 pounds in the past 10 years without any active intervention. Sarcopenia and lower physiologic reserve due to the aging process may also be contributing to her altered metabolic rate that is changing the need for her medication doses at the current time. Medication reconciliation showed multiple inappropriate medications for the patient's age. (See Table 2-1 with Beers Criteria recommendation.)

Deprescribing following appropriate step-by-step direction since appropriate tapering of dose without any withdrawal symptoms is the key in managing this patient's symptoms. It seems the symptoms were mostly due to ADEs from inappropriate dosing and inappropriate use of medication in this patient. Other examples of tools for polypharmacy management that can be used to optimize current treatment plan and future prevention of ADE in this patient would be training of clinicians, interprofessional team involvement, etc. Most interventions are multifaceted and complex

Table 2-1. Medication Reconciliation and Matching Medications with Presenting Symptoms

Diseases	Medication taken	Dose	Side Effects	Beers Criteria (Recommendation Category)
Hypertension	Clonidine (alpha blocker)	0.1 mg by mouth three times a day	Dizziness due to orthostatic hypotension	Avoid (strong)
Migraine headache	Propranolol (beta blocker)	10 mg daily	Dizziness	None
	Cyclobenzaprine (skeletal muscle relaxant)	10 mg daily	Dizziness, fall	Avoid (Strong)
	Amitriptyline (tricyclic antidepressant)	30 mg daily	Dizziness, sedating, orthostatic hypotension	Avoid (Strong)
For sleep	Lorazepam (benzodiazepine)	1 mg daily	Risk of cognitive impairment, falls	Avoid (Strong)

Note: mg = milligrams.

along the care pathway. They include medication review, patient education, health professional training, medication adherence aids, and multi-disciplinary case conferences. Medicine labels can further be enhanced by increasing the font size of the drug name and dosage.

Case Study 2: A Social Welfare and Public Health Approach to Meeting the Needs of Rural Older Adults Facing Substance Use Disorders

Substance misuse among older adults is a growing concern in the fields of public health and social welfare. These concerns are increasingly significant among older adults residing in rural communities who are faced with limited access to care and heightened rates of social isolation. Moreover, the staggering rates of substance misuse resulting from the nationwide opioid crisis has had a profound impact on individuals living in economically marginalized and rural communities. The following presents a composite case illustrating concerns inherent among this population and offers considerations for delivering effective and age-specific care.

Mr. Smith is a 67-year-old White male residing in a rural community with his adult daughter and her husband. He was recently in a car accident that killed his wife, totaled his car, and resulted in a significant back injury. To help manage his back pain, Mr. Smith was prescribed an opioid which he has been misusing. He has a long history of undiagnosed alcohol misuse. Mr. Smith has limited supports and is grieving the loss of his wife. Although he was not responsible for the car accident, he is overwrought with grief resulting in increased substance misuse.

Mr. Smith's daughter encouraged him to contact an outpatient clinic specializing in substance use disorder treatment. Mr. Smith was open to treatment but without a car was concerned that he would not be able to attend treatment due to the clinic being 40 minutes away. Noting his lack of access to transportation, one of the clinic's social workers arranged to meet with Mr. Smith in his home to complete an intake assessment and connect him with transportation. During his intake, Mr. Smith was diagnosed with Alcohol and Opioid Use Disorders as well as Major Depressive Disorder. The social worker noted Mr. Smith's financial challenges, the limited social supports, and his recent back injury.

Mr. Smith was admitted to the clinic and his social worker arranged for him to have transportation to medical appointments, including counseling. This arrangement allowed Mr. Smith to attend individual and group counseling. Additionally, Mr. Smith began attending a virtual group counseling session that the clinic offered for those unable to attend in person. Early in treatment, Mr. Smith reported, that it was "helpful to talk with others dealing with the same issues." He reported that group meetings helped reduce the isolation he felt in his community.

During counseling Mr. Smith participated in cognitive behavioral therapy to help address the problematic thoughts and behaviors that have contributed to his continued substance use. At first, his cravings were so strong that he struggled to make progress. His social worker referred him to a medical specialist who prescribed him medication to reduce his opioid cravings and once his cravings were medically controlled, he found himself able to use his time in counseling to develop skills to help him advance his recovery goals. Overtime, his daughter and son-in-law joined him during therapy to help understand and support his recovery.

After six months of treatment, Mr. Smith had successfully maintained abstinence from alcohol and had used his pain medication only as prescribed. Mr. Smith's experienced a decrease in his depressive symptoms as a result of his sobriety and his improved social connections formed through group-based therapy. He continued to utilize medical transportation to access continued care. At present, Mr. Smith is preparing for discharge from his substance misuse treatment. He and his social worker are arranging for him to receive ongoing mental health treatment and he plans to regularly attend the clinic's alumni support group.

Mr. Smith's recovery was supported by his social worker's ability to understand his challenges from a biopsychosocial and public health perspective. In doing so, the multi-layered needs he faced were able to be addressed in tandem rather than in a fractured and siloed manner. Agencies seeking to adopt such approaches can benefit from interdisciplinary teams and cross-agency collaborations that are well versed in both a public health and social welfare treatment modalities. Further, in meeting the needs of rural residents with limited transportation, the ability to offer virtual and remote care is paramount. Older adults struggling with substance use disorders who may also be residing in rural communities are considered a vulnerable population. To meet the needs of these individuals, we must understand the importance of providing a custom-tailored multifaceted approach to treatment to help ensure successful treatment outcomes.

REFERENCES

1. Bowie MW, Slattum PW. Pharmacodynamics in older adults: a review. *Am J Geriatr Pharmacother.* 2007;5(3):263–303.

2. Dagli RJ, Sharma A. Polypharmacy: A global risk factor for elderly people. *J Int Oral Health.* 2014;6(6):i–ii.

3. Masnoon N, Shakib S, Kalisch-Ellett L, Caughey GE. What is polypharmacy? A systematic review of definitions. *BMC Geriatr.* 2017;17(1):230.

4. Welker KL, Mycyk MB. Pharmacology in the geriatric patient. *Emerg Med Clin North Am.* 2016;34(3):469–481.

5. Payne RA. The epidemiology of polypharmacy. *Clin Med (Lond)*. 2016;16(5):465–469.

6. Soni A. Agency for Healthcare Research and Quality. 2017. Statistical brief #498: Out-of-pocket expenditures for adults with multiple chronic conditions, US civilian noninstitutionalized population, 2014. Available at: http://www.meps.ahrq.gov/mepsweb/data_files/publications/st498/stat498.shtml. Accessed February 19, 2021.

7. Koroukian SM, Schiltz NK, Warner DF, et al. Multimorbidity: constellations of conditions across subgroups of midlife and older individuals, and related Medicare expenditures. *J Comorb*. 2017;7(1):33–43.

8. Aronson JK. In defence of polypharmacy. *Br J Clin Pharmacol*. 2004;57(2):119–120.

9. Cadogan CA, Ryan C, Francis JJ, et al. Development of an intervention to improve appropriate polypharmacy in older people in primary care using a theory-based method. *BMC Health Serv Res*. 2016;16(1):661.

10. Duerden M, Avery T, Payne R. *Polypharmacy and medicines optimisation: making it safe and sound*. London, United Kingdom: The King's Fund; 2013.

11. Hajjar ER, Cafiero AC, Hanlon JT. Polypharmacy in elderly patients. *Am J Geriatr Pharmacother*. 2007;5(4):345–351.

12. Sirois C, Lunghi C, Berthelot W, Laroche ML, Frini A. Benefits, risks and impacts on quality of life of medications used in multimorbid older adults: a Delphi study. *Int J Clin Pharm*. 2020;42(1):40–50.

13. Spencer-Bonilla G, Quiñones AR, Montori VM. Assessing the burden of treatment. *J Gen Intern Med*. 2017;32(10):1141–1145.

14. Quinn KJ, Shah NH. A dataset quantifying polypharmacy in the United States. *Sci Data*. 2017;4:170167.

15. Jirón M, Pate V, Hanson LC, Lund JL, Jonsson Funk M, Stürmer T. Trends in prevalence and determinants of potentially inappropriate prescribing in the United States. 2007 to 2012. *J Am Geriatr Soc*. 2016;64(4):788–797.

16. Charlesworth CJ, Smit E, Lee DS, Alramadhan F, Odden MC. Polypharmacy among adults aged 65 years and older in the United States: 1988-2010. *J Gerontol A Biol Sci Med Sci*. 2015;70(8):989–995.

17. Gnjidic D, Hilmer SN. Potential contribution of medications to frailty. *J Am Geriatr Soc*. 2012;60(2):401.

18. Agogo GO, Ramsey CM, Gnjidic D, Moga DC, Allore H. Longitudinal associations between different dementia diagnoses and medication use jointly accounting for dropout. *Int Psychogeriatr*. 2018;30(10):1477–1487.

19. Fabbietti P, Ruggiero C, Sganga F, et al. Effects of hyperpolypharmacy and potentially inappropriate medications (PIMs) on functional decline in older patients discharged from acute care hospitals. *Arch Gerontol Geriatr*. 2018;77:158–162.

20. Gnjidic D, Hilmer SN, Blyth FM, et al. Polypharmacy cutoff and outcomes: five or more medicines were used to identify community-dwelling older men at risk of different adverse outcomes. *J Clin Epidemiol.* 2012;65(9):989–995.

21. Porter B, Arthur A, Savva GM. How do potentially inappropriate medications and polypharmacy affect mortality in frail and non-frail cognitively impaired older adults? A cohort study. *BMJ Open.* 2019;9(5):e026171.

22. Lee EA, Brettler JW, Kanter MH, et al. Refining the definition of polypharmacy and its link to disability in older adults: Conceptualizing necessary polypharmacy, unnecessary polypharmacy, and polypharmacy of unclear benefit. *Perm J.* 2020;24:18.212.

23. Bushardt RL, Massey EB, Simpson TW, Ariail JC, Simpson KN. Polypharmacy: misleading, but manageable. *Clin Interv Aging.* 2008;3(2):383–389.

24. Institute of Medicine Committee on Quality of Health Care in America. *To Err is Human: Building a Safer Health System.* Washington DC: National Academies Press; 2000.

25. Nebeker JR, Barach P, Samore MH. Clarifying adverse drug events: a clinician's guide to terminology, documentation, and reporting. *Ann Intern Med.* 2004;140(10):795–801.

26. Parekh N, Ali K, Davies K, Rajkumar C. Can supporting health literacy reduce medication-related harm in older adults? *Ther Adv Drug Saf.* 2018;9(3):167–170.

27. Assiri GA, Shebl NA, Mahmoud MA, et al. What is the epidemiology of medication errors, error-related adverse events and risk factors for errors in adults managed in community care contexts? A systematic review of the international literature. *BMJ Open.* 2018;8(5):e019101.

28. Budnitz DS, Lovegrove MC, Shehab N, Richards CL. Emergency hospitalizations for adverse drug events in older Americans. *N Engl J Med.* 2011;365(21):2002–2012.

29. Levinson DR. *Adverse events in skilled nursing facilities: National incidence among Medicare beneficiaries.* Washington DC: US Department of Health and Human Services. 2014.

30. Coleman JJ, Pontefract SK. Adverse drug reactions. *Clin Med (Lond).* 2016;16(5):481–485.

31. World Health Organization. International drug monitoring: The role of national centres, report of a WHO meeting [held in Geneva, Switzerland from 20 to 25 September 1971]. *World Health Organ Tech Rep Ser.* 1972;498:1–25.

32. Oscanoa TJ, Lizaraso F, Carvajal A. Hospital admissions due to adverse drug reactions in the elderly. A meta-analysis. *Eur J Clin Pharmacol.* 2017;73(6):759–770.

33. Keine D, Zelek M, Walker JQ, Sabbagh MN. Polypharmacy in an elderly population: Enhancing medication management through the use of clinical decision support software platforms. *Neurol Ther.* 2019;8(1):79–94.

34. Sera LC, McPherson ML. Pharmacokinetics and pharmacodynamic changes associated with aging and implications for drug therapy. *Clin Geriatr Med.* 2012;28(2):273–286.

35. Sönnerstam E, Sjölander M, Lövheim H, Gustafsson M. Clinically relevant drug-drug inter-actions among elderly people with dementia. *Eur J Clin Pharmacol.* 2018;74(10):1351–1360.

36. Hanlon JT, Perera S, Newman AB, et al. Potential drug-drug and drug-disease interactions in well-functioning community-dwelling older adults. *J Clin Pharm Ther.* 2017;42(2):228–233.

37. Qato DM, Wilder J, Schumm LP, Gillet V, Alexander GC. Changes in prescription and over-the-counter medication and dietary supplement use among older adults in the United States, 2005 vs 2011. *JAMA Intern Med.* 2016;176(4):473–482.

38. Dunnenberger HM, Crews KR, Hoffman JM, et al. Preemptive clinical pharmacogenetics implementation: current programs in five US medical centers. *Annu Rev Pharmacol Toxicol.* 2015;55:89–106.

39. Fox C, Richardson K, Maidment ID, et al. Anticholinergic medication use and cognitive impairment in the older population: the medical research council cognitive function and age-ing study. *J Am Geriatr Soc.* 2011;59(8):1477–1483.

40. König M, Spira D, Demuth I, Steinhagen-Thiessen E, Norman K. Polypharmacy as a risk factor for clinically relevant sarcopenia: Results from the Berlin Aging Study II. *J Gerontol A Biol Sci Med Sci.* 2017;73(1):117–122.

41. Chaverneff F. Benzodiazepine and opioid prescribing in the elderly: What are the risks? Paper presented at: PAINWeek 2017; September 2017; Las Vegas, Nevada.

42. O'Brien MDC, Wand APF. A systematic review of the evidence for the efficacy of opioids for chronic non-cancer pain in community-dwelling older adults. *Age and Ageing.* 2020;49(2): 175–183.

43. Dahlhamer J, Lucas J, Zelaya C, et al. Prevalence of chronic pain and high impact chronic pain among adults—United States, 2016. *MMWR Morb Mortal Wkly Rep.* 2018;67(36):1001–1006.

44. Dowell D, Haegerich TM, Chou R. CDC guideline for prescribing opioids for chronic pain—United States, 2016. *JAMA.* 2016;315(15):1624–1645.

45. Pronovost PJ. Enhancing physicians' use of clinical guidelines. *JAMA.* 2013;310(23): 2501–2502.

46. Kim HS, McCarthy DM, Hoppe JA, Mark Courtney D, Lambert BL. Emergency department provider perspectives on nenzodiazepine-opioid coprescribing: A qualitative study. *Acad Emerg Med.* 2018;25(1):15–24.

47. Gellad WF, Grenard JL, Marcum ZA. A systematic review of barriers to medication adherence in the elderly: looking beyond cost and regimen complexity. *Am J Geriatr Pharmacother.* 2011;9(1):11–23.

48. The Joint Commission. 2021 National patient safety goals. 2021. Available at: https://www.jointcommission.org/standards/national-patient-safety-goals/. Accessed February 19, 2021.

49. Agency for Healthcare Research and Quality. Topic: Medication: Safety. Available at: https://www.ahrq.gov/topics/medication- safety.html. Accessed February 19, 2021.

50. American Geriatrics Society Beers Criteria® Update Expert Panel. American Geriatrics Society 2019 updated AGS Beers Criteria® for potentially inappropriate medication use in older adults. *J Am Geriatr Soc.* 2019;67(4):674–694.

51. Dharmarajan TS, Choi H, Hossain N, et al. Deprescribing as a clinical improvement focus. *J Am Med Dir Assoc.* 2020;21(3):355–360.

52. Hilmer SN, Gnjidic D, Le Couteur DG. Thinking through the medication list - appropriate prescribing and deprescribing in robust and frail older patients. *Aust Fam Physician.* 2012;41(12):924–928.

53. Reeve E, Gnjidic D, Long J, Hilmer S. A systematic review of the emerging definition of 'deprescribing' with network analysis: implications for future research and clinical practice. *Br J Clin Pharmacol.* 2015;80(6):1254–1268.

54. Centers for Disease Control and Prevention. Prescription drug monitoring programs (PDMPs): What states need to know. 2020. Available at: https://www.cdc.gov/drugoverdose/pdmp/states.html. Accessed February 19, 2021.

55. US Department of Health and Human Services. National Action Plan for Adverse Drug Event Prevention. Office of Disease Prevention and Health Promotion. 2014. Available at: https://health.gov/sites/default/files/2019-09/ADE-Action-Plan-508c.pdf. Accessed March 23, 2021.

Hearing Within Healthy Aging

Howard J. Hoffman, MA and Christa L. Themann, MA, CCC-A

INTRODUCTION

The senses play an important role in one's overall health, and of course, health outcomes. In this chapter as well as the next chapter the senses of hearing, sight, and taste (oral health) are addressed. Sensory loss is an important health problem that increases with aging, especially age-related hearing loss. Neary two-thirds of Americans older than 70 years currently suffer from hearing loss, which impacts on overall decline in the quality of life.

HEARING LOSS: PREVALENCE AND PUBLIC HEALTH IMPORTANCE

Background

Hearing is important. Our ability to hear connects us to other people, warns us of dangers, and provides pleasures such as music and laughter. Hearing influences how Americans of all ages learn, communicate, work, play, and interact with the world. It has a tremendous impact on overall health and well-being.

Our sense of hearing is quite amazing. The human ear contains the smallest bones and the smallest muscles in the body. The ear can sense vibrations that barely move the width of an atom and still withstand vibrations 10 million times stronger, though the tiny auditory structures can be ripped apart when sounds become dangerously loud. Our ears never rest; even when sleeping, our hearing is monitoring the sounds around us, though our brains generally take a break from processing what we hear. Perhaps because of its constant function—creating the auditory backdrop to our daily lives—our ability to hear is often taken for granted until it is lost. Perhaps because of its delicate nature, hearing is the easiest of our five senses to lose.

Millions of Americans live with hearing loss.[1-3] It has been called an "invisible" impairment because it often develops gradually and insidiously over time without any external signs of the damage that is done.[4,5] As a result, hearing loss often goes undetected for some time. People with hearing loss may assume others are just "mumbling." People around them frequently misinterpret the hearing loss as inattentiveness or cognitive decline. Even when identified and acknowledged, very few of those with mild or moderate hearing loss avail themselves of hearing aids and other rehabilitative therapies which could help.

Hearing loss has become an unrecognized public health crisis in the United States. There are more people with hearing loss than any other disability. Impaired hearing is the third most common chronic physical condition among adults in the United States, following hypertension and arthritis.[6,7] Addressing this public health problem will require a collaborative effort by public health professionals, hearing health care providers, health communication specialists, state, local and federal governments, professional organizations, the media, communities, families, and individuals—all working together to raise public awareness and increase access to care in order to minimize the impact of hearing loss.

Concepts

Hearing is a complex sense involving both the ear's ability to detect sounds in the environment and the brain's ability to interpret the auditory signal. Similarly, hearing loss is a complex impairment that can manifest differently across individuals depending on the point of damage in the auditory system; for example, some hearing losses primarily involve a reduction in volume (signals sound softer) while others involve a loss of clarity (signals sound distorted). Furthermore, similar hearing losses can have varying impact on different people, based on their other health conditions, communication needs, and available support.

Loss of hearing is not the only possible outcome to auditory damage. Tinnitus, or ringing in the ears, is a symptom that can become so bothersome as to be disabling. Hyperacusis, an abnormal sensitivity to sound, can make it difficult to tolerate even normal day-to-day sounds. Tinnitus and hyperacusis can occur alone or in conjunction with hearing loss.

Causes of Hearing Problems

Auditory dysfunctions have many causes. Hearing loss can be present at birth due to heredity, infections during pregnancy, complications in delivery during birth, or as part of a syndrome. It can result from diseases such as meningitis, mumps, measles, or chronic middle ear infections. Hearing problems can be caused by insults to the auditory system from noise, ototoxic drugs and chemicals, or physical trauma. As with other human sensory systems, hearing can undergo an exponential loss of function with aging.[8,9] Susceptibility to hearing problems from nearly all of these factors is further influenced by genetics and sociodemographic factors such as sex and race/ethnicity.[1,2,10,11] While some hearing losses due to medical conditions can be treated, most, including age-related hearing impairment, are permanent.

Measuring Hearing Loss

Hearing loss may be identified by the person involved (called "self-report"), report by friends and family, or identification by formal hearing (i.e., audiometric) testing. All of these measures are valuable for providing estimates of the prevalence of hearing loss and the burden of hearing loss on society.

Self-report of hearing loss and the report of friends and family are important because this information is relatively simple to obtain and provides a global assessment of the impact of the problem on individuals and on their social interactions. For some types of hearing trouble (e.g., tinnitus), self-report may be the only feasible approach. Yet, self-report is subjective and influenced by perceptions of how well peers in the same age group can hear. Compared with audiometric threshold exams, self-report of hearing loss may result in overestimation in younger individuals and underestimation in older individuals who may not always be aware of or acknowledge their hearing difficulty.[12]

Formal audiometric testing, on the other hand, provides more objective information about the softest sounds (called audiometric "thresholds") an individual can hear at various pitches (frequencies). Thresholds are measured on a decibel (dB) hearing level (HL) scale at single (pure tone) frequencies given in Hertz (Hz). Increasing decibels indicate louder sounds and increasing frequencies indicate higher pitch. Hearing loss is often defined by averaging thresholds across multiple frequencies. The frequencies included in the "pure tone average" (PTA) can vary. One traditional measure is the speech frequency PTA, which averages thresholds at 500, 1000, and 2000 Hz, and often correlates with an individual's ability to understand speech. The most common PTA found in epidemiological studies is the four-frequency average of thresholds at 500, 1000, 2000, and 4000 Hz.[13-16]

As the PTA increases, hearing ability decreases. There are differing standard classification schemes for defining hearing loss; normal hearing for speech in adults has been defined as a PTA of <20 dB HL or ≤25 dB HL. Pure tone averages of 20–35 dB HL are considered mild hearing loss and indicate a need for adaptive listening strategies (such as sitting closer to the source of sound) and possible amplification. With a PTA of 35–65 dB HL in both ears (moderate hearing loss), people are considered functionally impaired and are more likely to have difficulty with everyday communication without hearing aids or other assistive listening devices. Bilateral (both ears) speech frequency PTAs of 65–90 dB HL represent severe to profound hearing loss; with this degree of hearing loss, hearing aids provide limited benefit and cochlear implants may be considered. The term "deaf" is generally reserved for those with the greatest bilateral hearing loss (i.e., PTAs ≥90–95 dB HL).[13,14,17]

Prevalence of Hearing Loss

The World Health Organization estimates that 466 million people (6.1% of the world's population) have hearing impairment (≥35 dB HL); 93% of these (242 million males and 190 million females) are adults aged 15 years or older.[14,18] As the world's population ages and older individuals make up an increasing percentage, the numbers will grow considerably.[19] By 2050, the World Health Organization estimates the number with disabling hearing loss will reach 900 million.[18]

Data from the 2012 "National Health Interview Survey" indicate that 37.5 million US adults aged 18 and older have some degree of hearing impairment.[1] While the prevalence of hearing loss increases with age, it is not only a problem of older adults. Estimates of neonatal hearing loss in the United States range from 1.1 to about 2.5 per 1,000 infants who are deaf or hard of hearing.[20–22] See Figure 3-1 for key statistics on adult hearing loss in the US.[23] Approximately 3% of children under age 20 have mild or worse hearing impairment.[24] Among adults, disabling hearing loss occurs in about 2% of those aged

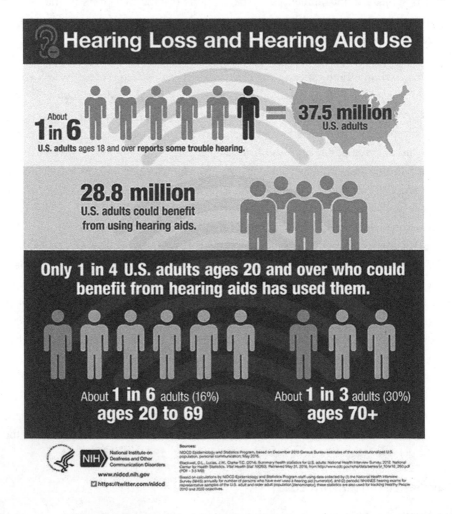

Source: Reprinted from The National Institute on Deafness and Other Communication Disorders, National Institutes of Health.[23]

Figure 3–1. Infographic Illustrating Key Statistics About Hearing Loss in the United States

45–54, 8.5%[22] of those aged 55–64, nearly 25% of those aged 65–74, and half of those aged 75 and older. During middle-age, hearing loss is more prevalent in men than in women. This disparity may be due to more extensive noise exposure from occupational and recreational (e.g., firearms use) sources.[2] Among older women and men, hearing loss prevalence is similar, as the effects of aging predominate.[25,26] Hearing loss is also more prevalent among non-Hispanic White people than Hispanic and non-Hispanic Black people.[27,28] Less than 20% of adults aged 20–69 and only about 30% of adults aged 70 and over who could benefit from a hearing aid actually use one (see Figure 3–1).[22,23,29]

Approximately 50 million Americans report tinnitus. About 10% of US adults (22 million) report prolonged (sustained) tinnitus that lasted five minutes or longer during the past 12 months.[30,31] Tinnitus, if present, is combined with the degree of hearing loss to derive disability weights for Global Burden of Disease estimates of burden.[32] About 3% (7.6 million) adults report their tinnitus is a "moderate, big, or very big" problem, whereas 1% (2 million) experience tinnitus so severe that it interferes with their daily life.[31] Of those with tinnitus, more than 72% (16 million) experience frequent tinnitus (i.e., weekly, daily, or nearly always). Tinnitus is most prevalent in the age range 40–75 years.[22,30]

Tinnitus is sometimes associated with a disabling condition of hyperacusis, a hypersensitivity to everyday sounds, that can have major impact on the quality of life.[33–35] Tinnitus and hyperacusis are symptoms rather than diseases and there are no universal cures. In rare cases, tinnitus can be resolved through management of the underlying condition. More frequently, it can be managed with success or with improved tolerance using masking, education and counseling, or retraining therapy.[33–38]

ISSUES

Hearing trouble results in a myriad of difficulties, including communication problems, difficulty at school or work, social isolation and/or stigmatization, and reduced quality of life. It is associated with accelerated cognitive decline, memory loss, depression, and poorer mental health. When noise exposure is a factor, cardiovascular disease and all-cause mortality increase.

Auditory Implications of Hearing Loss

Hearing loss affects everyone differently. Even when objective hearing test results are the same, the functional impact on the individual can vary considerably. In some cases, mild losses may not be noticed, and even moderate losses may not cause a problem for people with excellent perceptual abilities and good coping skills. Major determinants of the impact of hearing loss include the degree of loss and frequencies affected; whether the loss is only in one ear or both; the part of the auditory system where the dysfunction occurs (e.g., the ear canal, the sensory structures of the inner ear, the neural pathways, or the brain); the age of onset; comorbidities (e.g., diabetes or visual impairment); and access to treatment.

The auditory implications of hearing loss may seem obvious—difficulty hearing sound. However, the problems caused by hearing loss are more complex than just that. Hearing loss can make it difficult to hear in the presence of background noise, to localize the source of a sound, and to monitor the volume of one's own voice. Age-related hearing loss in particular leads to trouble hearing consonant sounds, such that the individual knows that something was said but cannot determine exactly what was said (e.g., Did the speaker just refer to a house, a mouse, or do they think someone is a louse?). Based on the 2014 National Health Interview Survey Hearing Supplement, 42% of older adults aged 70 years or more responded they often have difficulty following conversation amid noise (e.g., people talking in the background) compared with 13% of adults aged 18–39 years, a more than a three-fold difference.[35] The additional effort required to focus on the signal leads to fatigue and often results in the person withdrawing from social interactions and other daily activities.[39]

Association With Mental and Physical Health

A growing body of evidence is indicative of an association between hearing loss and cognitive decline (including dementia, memory loss, and thinking skills).[40-42] Hearing loss reduces input to the auditory areas of the brain, leading to a deterioration of associated brain functions. Additionally, research is finding an association between hearing loss, loneliness, and depression.[43-48] Tinnitus has also been found to be associated with depression, as well as anxiety.[49] Cognitive decline, depression, and anxiety all can have a detrimental effect on mental health.

Hearing loss has been associated with decrements in physical health as well. Untreated hearing loss has been linked to increased risk of falls, heart attack, and stroke.[50] Hearing loss is more prevalent among older adults with arthritis than those without.[51] Total health care costs over a 10-year period were reported to be 46% higher among hearing-impaired older adults than those without hearing loss; inpatient hospital stays and 30-day readmission rates were also higher for the hearing-impaired group.[52]

Mortality risk also increases with hearing loss. Population-based studies in Australia, Iceland, and Norway have consistently shown increased risk of all-cause mortality among individuals with hearing loss; some studies additionally have shown an increased risk of cardiovascular mortality.[53-55] Cardiovascular disease has been found to be independently associated with excessive noise exposure, which is a primary risk factor for adult-onset hearing loss.[56]

Quality of Life

The impact of hearing loss on quality of life can be discussed in a qualitative way by describing its effects in daily life. Many of these have already been discussed: communication difficulty, reduced environmental awareness, isolation from family and friends, loneliness, frustration, depression, and the loss of the emotional connections created through music and speech. Hearing loss often interferes with our ability to do our jobs or enjoy our hobbies.[57]

Impact on quality of life can also be quantified using measures of disease burden such as disability-adjusted life years (DALYs) and years lived with a disability (YLDs). DALYs represent the number of healthy years of life lost due to a disease or other health condition calculated using "disability weights" to assign relative values to the limitations caused by the severity of the condition.[32] YLDs represent the total number of years lived with a disability. The 2019 Global Burden of Disease Study reported that age-related hearing loss ranked among the top 10 contributors to DALYs in the 50–74 and >75 age categories.[7,58,59] Overall, the study estimated 40.2 million YLDs are lost worldwide due to hearing loss, ranking fourth among noncommunicable diseases.

Economic Burden

Globally, the annual cost of hearing loss is estimated at $750 billion, including health care costs (except for hearing aids), educational and vocational expenses, costs from lost productivity, and other societal costs.[60] In the United States, the economic cost of severe to profound hearing loss has been estimated to be $297,000 over the lifetime of every affected person.[61] Nationally, the cost of first-year hearing loss treatment is projected to increase five-fold between 2002 and 2030, from $8.2 billion to $51.4 billion.[62] The cost of health care in the United States for tinnitus is estimated to be at least $3.3 billion annually.[63]

At the individual level, hearing loss is associated with poorer employment rates, lower worker productivity, and higher health care costs. Adults with hearing loss are more likely to have low income (<$20,000/year) and be unemployed or underemployed (working less than 35 hours per week) than adults with normal hearing, even when adjusting for education and other factors.[64,65] Hearing loss can limit employability in hearing-critical jobs. Hearing loss can also be a workplace safety issue, leading to a higher risk of occupational injuries.[12] The number of older workers is increasing; people aged 65 and over represent the fastest-growing segment of the workforce.[66] The number of workers with hearing loss is therefore also expected to increase.

CHALLENGES

The World Health Organization estimates that at least 50% of hearing loss is preventable.[18] The impact of hearing loss and its sequelae is substantial. Strategies and technologies are available to manage hearing loss. Nevertheless, reducing the prevalence and burden of hearing loss, especially among older adults, remains a significant challenge. Several factors contribute to the problem.

Failure to Recognize Hearing Loss as a Public Health Problem

Public health efforts have been very effective in identifying hearing loss early in life and ensuring appropriate interventions. Nearly every baby born in the United States is screened for hearing loss at birth and screenings continue throughout the early elementary school years. But after early childhood, public health efforts to reduce the burden of hearing loss are sporadic; by adulthood, they are essentially nonexistent. Society in general and health care professionals in particular have not mustered the motivation to promote prevention among adults at risk of hearing loss due to age or exposures such as noise and ototoxins (e.g., lead, tobacco smoke, nonsteroidal anti-inflammatory drugs such as aspirin and ibuprofen, aminoglycoside antibiotics, diuretics, some cancer medications). The typically gradual development of hearing loss over time and poor recognition of its impact on quality of life may underlie the lack of attention to this problem. However, until we acknowledge hearing loss as the tremendous public health problem it is, we will not be able to make progress preventing it.

Undiagnosed Hearing Loss

Diagnosis is the first step toward addressing hearing loss and its consequences. Earlier identification of hearing loss can reduce its impact as well as the prevalence of associated conditions. Yet, despite the high prevalence of hearing loss among older adults, it often goes unrecognized. In a recent national study, nearly 25% of adults aged 20–69 who reported their hearing as "excellent" or "good" showed audiometric evidence of noise-induced hearing damage.[61]

Even among those who do report difficulty hearing, less than half report having discussed their hearing problem with their primary care physician.[67] Health care practitioners frequently fail to inquire about how their patients hear; the majority of primary care physicians do not ask patients about hearing or screen for hearing loss. Anecdotal stories abound of health care providers telling an older patient that their hearing "is fine for their age." Primary care physicians remain the gateway to most health services in the current US health care structure; increasing awareness of the ramifications of untreated hearing loss among these providers is an essential step in reducing the burden of hearing loss among older Americans.

Underutilization of Amplification and Rehabilitative Care

Hearing aids and other assistive devices can improve hearing ability and enhance quality of life for individuals with hearing loss. Hearing aid users report significantly greater communication performance and use of positive adaptive strategies than nonusers.[68] A Cochrane Systematic Review of hearing aid efficacy among adults with mild to moderate hearing loss found a large beneficial effect of hearing aid use on listening ability and hearing-related quality of life measures, as well as a smaller but significant beneficial effect on general health quality of life measures.[69]

Yet for a variety of reasons, many people with hearing loss do not seek out or receive hearing health care. Estimates indicate that 67%–86% of people who may benefit from hearing aids do not use them,[22] and many hearing assistive technologies as well as auditory rehabilitation services are not fully utilized.

One reason may be that US insurance coverage for adult hearing services and hearing aids is minimal. In general, Medicare does not pay for hearing tests, hearing aids, or aural rehabilitation services. Medicare Part B (Medical Insurance) will pay for hearing exams only when prescribed by a physician in order to determine the need for medical treatment. Medicare Part C (Medicare Advantage) may cover all or part of hearing care services (including hearing aids), but coverage varies by plan. Medicaid does not require states to cover hearing-related services for adults, so benefits differ by location. Most states offer some hearing benefits, but coverage is subject to limitations and frequently revised. The Veterans Administration provides hearing aids for military veterans who have a service-connected disability or meet other eligibility requirements (e.g., former prisoners of war and Purple Heart recipients); however, this benefit is not available for other veterans.

Costs and lack of insurance coverage are not the only obstacles to hearing aid uptake. Even in countries in which hearing aids are subsidized or provided at no charge through a national health care system, half or fewer among those who could benefit from amplification actually use it.[70] Other barriers to hearing aid use include perceptions that they are a sign of old age, that they don't really help, or that they aren't needed.[29] Increasing the acceptability of hearing aids is necessary to avoid the consequences of untreated hearing loss.

RELEVANT POLICIES AND LEGISLATION

Most hearing losses are permanent and yet, perhaps half of them are preventable.[18] Therefore, policies that help prevent hearing loss would go far to reduce the burden of hearing impairment on individuals and society. Prevention starts early in life, with proper prenatal care to prevent infections and birth complications that cause congenital hearing loss; childhood vaccinations against diseases that impair hearing; and diagnosis and management of chronic middle ear infections. In adulthood, regulations to reduce hazardous noise exposure (both on- and off-the-job), decreased exposure to or use of ototoxic medicines and chemicals, and policies to support access to hearing health care are key factors in minimizing adult-onset hearing loss.

For those who have already sustained a hearing loss, the Americans with Disabilities Act (ADA) of 1990 and the ADA Amendments Act of 2008 can provide assistance.

These Acts forbid discrimination against individuals with disabilities, including hearing loss, and ensure equal access to education, employment, and public services. This legislation requires employers, governments, and certain businesses (e.g., public transportation providers, health care facilities, and movie theaters) to offer reasonable accommodations that allow hearing-impaired individuals to participate fully in provided services and community events. Accommodations can include assistive listening systems that transmit signals directly to a user's hearing aids, closed captioning, and sign language interpreters. These services are frequently offered by entities not covered by the ADA (e.g., churches) as well, so individuals should ask about available assistive technologies whenever needed.

BEST PRACTICE INTERVENTIONS

In 2016, the National Academies of Sciences, Engineering, and Medicine (NASEM) released recommendations addressing the significant barriers to hearing health care for adults.[71] The report identified high cost of hearing aids, inadequate insurance coverage, lack of awareness of rehabilitative options, and the societal stigma tied to hearing loss as major obstacles to access to hearing care. Among the suggested solutions for overcoming these barriers, the report recommended the following:

- Eliminating the Food and Drug Administration (FDA) rule requiring adults to obtain medical clearance or sign a waiver before purchasing a hearing aid.
- Introducing a class of FDA-regulated over-the-counter hearing devices for mild to moderate hearing losses that would not fall under state hearing aid laws and could be purchased directly by the consumer without involving a hearing health professional.
- Evaluating options for expanded insurance coverage of hearing health care services by Medicare, Medicaid, and private health insurance plans.
- Increasing public awareness of hearing loss and rehabilitative and technological options for maximizing residual hearing.

The FDA ceased enforcing the medical clearance requirement for hearing aids shortly after the release of the NASEM report. The committee's other recommendations, including over-the-counter hearing devices (enacted legislatively but awaiting regulatory guidelines) and expanded insurance coverage, will take longer to implement.

SPECIAL CONSIDERATIONS AND SPECIAL POPULATIONS

Disparities have been documented for various subgroups (e.g., sex, race/ethnicity, educational attainment, family income, age, and disability status).[72] For example, the use of hearing aids is higher for individuals with higher educational attainment. Older men (aged 70 or older) with hearing loss are more likely to use hearing aids than older women (357 per 1,000 men vs. 291.0 per 1,000 women). Also, for older adults, the non-Hispanic White hearing aid use rate, 334.7

per 1,000, is higher than that of non-Hispanic Black use, 214.4 per 1,000 or of Hispanic use, 188.4 per 1,000. During the past two decades, the trend in hearing aid use has increased gradually for older adults, but no increase or trend has been shown for adults aged 20–69 years. Family income is also a factor as older adults whose income fell below the federal poverty rate (i.e., those with a poverty income ratio <1.0) had a lower percentage with their hearing tested in the past five years versus adults whose poverty income ratio was ≥2.0.

While there is a clear need to increase access to and utilization of hearing health care services among older adults, a shortage of practitioners is compounding the problem. Shifting demographics has led to increased numbers of older adults in need of hearing health care, while the number of hearing health care professionals is decreasing.[73]

The problem is particularly acute for certain segments of the population. Older adults are more likely to live in rural areas than in urban areas; however, the distribution of hearing health professionals is concentrated in metropolitan counties. Over 50% of US counties have no audiologist.[74] Another underserved segment of the population are the 1.4 million residents of long-term care facilities. Nursing home staff frequently lack training in recognizing hearing loss among residents, often assuming miscommunication stems from dementia, and in basic care and maintenance of hearing aids.[72,73]

One proposed solution for addressing the shortage of hearing health professionals is to train audiology assistants to manage routine tasks such as hearing screenings and basic hearing aid repair. The American Academy of Audiology and the American Speech-Language-Hearing Association have published position statements advocating support personnel; the latter has also released standards for training and certification of audiology assistants.[74–76] In time, this may help relieve the staff shortage; however, as audiology assistants are required to work under the supervision of an audiologist, it may not completely address the lack of practitioners in certain areas.

Another opportunity to expand hearing health care services to underserved populations is through partnerships with other professionals, such as community health workers. A pilot program in Arizona brought together audiology, public health, and community health workers to establish an outreach program for Spanish-speaking older adults. This program successfully led to over 75% of participants seeking follow-up hearing health care within a year.[77] See the "Case Study" section in this chapter for more information on this public health solution.

CONCLUSION: CHALLENGES AND OPPORTUNITIES FOR PUBLIC HEALTH

Untreated hearing loss among older adults is a significant public health problem. Several factors exacerbate the issue including inadequate early identification of hearing loss (both by individuals and health care practitioners), failure to recognize the impact of hearing loss on quality of life, and cultural acceptance of hearing risks such as loud noise exposure.

Partnerships with public health professionals are necessary to raise awareness of the issues surrounding hearing loss and promote available therapies and technologies that can ameliorate the problem. Providing information is necessary but seldom sufficient to change behavior. Establishing environments conducive to improved hearing health care and reducing the social acceptability of hearing risks is essential to lasting change.

The 2016 NASEM report on hearing health care for adults made a number of specific recommendations to this end.[71] The report suggested that health care providers and public health agencies promote hearing health during medical and wellness visits by encouraging patients to discuss concerns about their hearing and making appropriate referrals to hearing specialists. To facilitate this discussion, it recommended the development of hearing health care continuing education opportunities for primary care physicians. The NASEM report urged improving the affordability of hearing health care through increased coverage by health insurance plans, Medicare, and Medicaid, as well as improving access to care by removing barriers. The report encouraged the development of innovative models, such as telehealth, mobile health clinics, retail clinics, community health workers, and self-administered care that have the potential to increase access to and improve the affordability of hearing health care. People who need hearing health care services and technologies should be at the center of their own care, with the option to make decisions about what is most appropriate for them.

As with any public health effort, effective measures to assess and track the impact of hearing and public health interventions are crucial. Demonstration projects and other research studies that inform evidence-based practice are needed. Finally, using relevant communication channels to share success stories with other professionals is key to broader implementation of proven hearing health strategies.

CASE STUDY

A community-based outreach program has been successfully implemented in a rural Arizona county to bring hearing health services to an underserved population. The county is situated on the border between the United States and Mexico. At the time the program was developed, it was one of six counties in Arizona with no audiology services. The county population is 95% Hispanic and nearly 15% of residents are aged older than 65 years. Older Hispanic adults have the lowest hearing aid use rate among major racial/ethnic groups in the United States.

Lack of services was not the only barrier to hearing health care in this community. Residents lacked knowledge of available resources to improve hearing ability, believing both that hearing aids were the only possible solution and that they were too expensive to consider. Addressing hearing loss was considered a low priority when it was difficult to afford the expenses of food and shelter. Many people did not trust hearing aid dealers, suspecting they merely wanted to make a sale. Although some individuals perceived their hearing loss as a problem in need of an unattainable solution, others saw their hearing loss as an accomplishment in that they had survived to old age.

To address these barriers, audiologists from the University of Arizona established a collaboration with county community health workers to bring aural rehabilitative services to area residents. The American Public Health Association defines a community health worker as a lay person who has the same sociocultural characteristics as the community and is, therefore, trusted to provide public health services in a culturally relevant way. The community health workers were employed by the local federally qualified health center, which provides the majority of medical care to county residents. In their jobs at the health center, they had been previously trained in basic public health competencies including outreach and education.

The community health workers invited individuals known to them through other health promotion activities at the health center to participate in free hearing screenings. Ten individuals with hearing loss were recruited for a pilot program known as "*Oyendo Bien*" (Hearing Well), along with a family member or other communication partner. Participants attended five weekly sessions led by the community health workers which focused on rehabilitative strategies for hearing loss. Topics included communication strategies, using visual cues, coping with emotions, hearing protection, hearing health care pathways, self-advocacy, and the ADA. Information about hearing aids and other assistive devices was discussed, but the devices themselves were neither provided nor pushed for sale.

At the end of the five-week program, both the individuals with hearing loss and their communication partners reported improvement in speaking slowly and clearly to facilitate hearing, and an increase in planning activities in a way that facilitated participation by the hearing-impaired partner. One year later, 70% of participants had discussed their hearing loss with their family, 50% had discussed it with their primary care physician, and 30% had seen a hearing specialist. Of the eight participants who did not have hearing aids at the time of the program, four had obtained hearing aids or another assistive listening device. One participant reported, "You all taught us something new. Before attending the classes, I had almost no hearing. I now have one hearing aid and I have to go back in three weeks for a second."[77,78,79]

Disclaimer: The findings and conclusions in this chapter are those of the authors and do not necessarily represent the official position of their respective government agencies.

REFERENCES

1. Blackwell DL, Lucas JW, Clarke TC. Summary health statistics for US adults: National Health Interview Survey, 2012. National Center for Health Statistics. *Vital Health Stat.* 2014;10(260):1–61. Available at: https://www.cdc.gov/nchs/data/series/sr_10/sr10_260.pdf. Accessed February 20, 2021.

2. Zelaya CE, Lucas JW, Hoffman HJ. Self-reported hearing trouble in adults aged 18 and over: United States, 2014. *NCHS Data Brief.* 2015;(214):1–8.

3. Lin FR, Niparko JK, Ferrucci L. Hearing loss prevalence in the United States. *Arch Intern Med.* 2011;171(20):1851–1852.

4. Pacala JT, Yueh B. Hearing deficits in the older patient: "I didn't notice anything". *JAMA.* 2012;307(11):1185–1194.

5. Yueh B, Shapiro N, MacLean CH, Shekelle PG. Screening and management of adult hearing loss in primary care: scientific review. *JAMA.* 2003;289(15):1976–1985.

6. GBD 2016 Disease and Injury Incidence and Prevalence Collaborators. Global, regional, and national incidence, prevalence, and years lived with disability for 328 diseases and injuries for 195 countries, 1990–2016: a systematic analysis for the Global Burden of Disease Study 2016. *Lancet.*2017;390(10100):1211–1259.

7. Saunders JE, Rankin Z, Noonan KY. Otolaryngology and the global burden of disease. *Otolaryngol Clin North Am.* 2018;51(3):515–534.

8. Hinchcliffe R. Aging and sensory thresholds. *J Gerontol.* 1962;17(1):45–50.

9. Hinchcliffe R. The age function of hearing–aspects of the epidemiology. *Acta Otolaryngol Suppl.* 1991;476:7–11.

10. Gates GA, Couropmitree NN, Myers RH. Genetic associations in age-related hearing thresholds. *Arch Otolaryngol Head Neck Surg.* 1999;125(6):654–659.

11. Christensen K, Frederiksen H, Hoffman HJ. Genetic and environmental influences on self-reported reduced hearing in the old and oldest old. *J Am Geriatr Soc.* 2001;49(11):1512–1517.

12. Themann CL, Masterson EA. Occupational noise exposure: A review of its effects, epidemiology, and impact with recommendations for reducing its burden. *J Acoust Soc Am.* 2019;146(5):3879–3805.

13. Stevens GA, Flaxman SM, Mascarenhas M, et al. Global and regional hearing impairment prevalence. In: Newton V, Alberti P, Smith AW, eds. *Prevention of Hearing Loss.* Hauppauge, NY: Nova Science; 2012:21–50.

14. Stevens G, Flaxman S, Brunskill E, et al. Global and regional hearing impairment prevalence: an analysis of 42 studies in 29 countries. *Eur J Public Health.* 2013;23(1):146–152.

15. Cruickshanks KJ, Dhar S, Dinces E, et al. Hearing impairment prevalence and associated risk factors in the Hispanic Community Health Study/Study of Latinos (HCHS/SOL). *JAMA Otolaryngol Head Neck Surg.* 2015;141(7):641–648.

16. Hoffman HJ, Dobie RA, Losonczy KG, Themann CL, Flamme GA. Declining prevalence of hearing loss in US adults aged 20 to 69 years. *JAMA Otolaryngol Head Neck Surg.* 2017;143(3):274–285.

17. Olusanya BO, Davis AC, Hoffman HJ. Hearing loss grades and the International Classification of Functioning, Disability and Health. *Bull World Health Organ.* 2019;97(10): 725–728.

18. World Health Organization. Fact Sheet: Deafness and hearing loss. 2020. Available at: www.who. int/en/news-room/fact-sheets/detail/deafness-and-hearing-loss. Accessed February 20, 2021.

19. Olusanya BO, Davis AC, Hoffman HJ. Hearing loss: rising prevalence and impact. *Bull World Health Organ*. 2019;97(10):646–646A.

20. Vohr B. Overview: infants and children with hearing loss—part I. *Ment Retard Dev Disabil Res Rev*. 2003;9(2):62 64.

21. Centers for Disease Control and Prevention. Identifying infants with hearing loss - United States, 1999-2007. [published correction appears in *MMWR Morb Mortal Wkly Rep*. 2010:59(15):460]*MMWR Morb Mortal Wkly Rep*. 2010;59(8):220–223.

22. National Institute on Deafness and Other Communication Disorders. Statistics and epidemiology: charts and tables about hearing. National Institutes of Health. 2018. Available at: https://www.nidcd.nih.gov/health/statistics. Accessed February 20, 2021.

23. National Institute on Deafness and Other Communication Disorders. Hearing Loss and Hearing Aid Use. National Institutes of Health. 2017. Available at: https://www.nidcd.nih. gov/news/multimedia/hearing-loss-and-hearing-aid-use. Accessed May 28, 2021.

24. Mehra S, Eavey RD, Keamy DG Jr. The epidemiology of hearing impairment in the United States: newborns, children, and adolescents. *Otolaryngol Head Neck Surg*. 2009;140(4):461–472.

25. Li C-M, Zhao G, Hoffman HJ, Town M, Themann CL. Hearing disability prevalence and risk factors in two recent national surveys. *Am J Prev Med*. 2018;55(3):326–335.

26. Dobie RA. The burdens of age related and occupational noise-induced hearing loss in the United States. *Ear Hear*. 2008;29(4):565–577.

27. Hoffman HJ, Dobie RA, Ko CW, Themann CL, Murphy WJ. Hearing threshold levels at age 70 years (65–74 years) in the unscreened older adult population of the United States, 1959 1962 and 1999-2006. *Ear Hear*. 2012;33(3):437–40.

28. Flamme GA, Deiters KK, Stephenson MR, et al. Population-based age adjustment tables for use in occupational hearing conservation programs. *Int J Audiol*. 2020;59(sup1):S20–S30.

29. Fischer ME, Cruickshanks KJ, Wiley TL, Klein BE, Klein R, Tweed TS. Determinants of hearing aid acquisition in older adults. *Am J Public Health*. 2011;101(8):1449–1455.

30. Hoffman HJ, Reed GW. Epidemiology of tinnitus. In: Snow JB Jr, ed. *Tinnitus: Theory and Management*. Hamilton, Ontario, Canada: BC Decker, Inc. 2004;16–41.

31. Bhatt JM, Lin HW, Bhattacharyya N. Prevalence, severity, exposures, and treatment patterns of tinnitus in the United States. *JAMA Otolaryngol Head Neck Surg*. 2016;142(10):959–965.

32. Salomon JA, Haagsma JA, Davis A, et al. Disability weights for the Global Burden of Disease 2013 study. *Lancet Glob Health*. 2015;3(11):e712–e723.

33. Henry JA, Dennis KC, Schechter MA. General review of tinnitus: Prevalence, mechanisms, effects, and management. *J Speech Lang Hear Res*. 2005;48(5):1204–1235.

34. Jastreboff PJ, Jastreboff MM. Tinnitus Retraining Therapy (TRT) as a method for treatment of tinnitus and hyperacusis patients. *J Am Acad Aud*. 2000;11(3):162–177.

35. Zelaya CE, Lucas JW, Hoffman HJ. QuickStats: Percentage of adults with selected hearing problems, by type of problem and age group—National Health Interview Survey, United States, 2014. *MMWR Morb Mortal Wkly Rep*. 2015;64 (37):1058.

36. Henry JA, Stewart BJ, Griest S, Kaelin C, Zaugg TL, Carlson K. Multisite randomized controlled trial to compare two methods of tinnitus intervention to two control conditions. *Ear Hear*. 2016;37(6):e346-e359.

37. Jastreboff PJ. 25 years of tinnitus retraining therapy. *HNO*. 2015;63(4):307–311.

38. Phillips JS, McFerran D. Tinnitus Retraining Therapy (TRT) for tinnitus. *Cochrane Database Syst Rev*. 2010;2010(3):CD007330.

39. Themann C, Suter AH, Stephenson MR. National research agenda for the prevention of occupational hearing loss – Part 1. *Sem Hear*. 2013;34(3):145–207.

40. Lin FR, Yaffe K, Xia J, et al. Health ABC Study Group. Hearing loss and cognitive decline in older adults. *JAMA Intern Med*. 2013;173(4):293–299.

41. Lin FR. Hearing loss and cognition among older adults in the United States. *J Gerontol A Biol Sci Med Sci*. 2011;66(10):1131–1136.

42. Deal JA, Betz J, Yaffe K, et al. Health ABC Study Group. Hearing impairment and incident dementia and cognitive decline in older adults: The Health ABC Study. *J Gerontol A Biol Sci Med Sci*. 2017;72(5):703–709.

43. Hétu R, Getty L, Quoc HT. Impact of occupational hearing loss on the lives of workers. *Occup Med*. 1995;10(3):495–512.

44. Mener DJ, Betz J, Genther DJ, Chen D, Lin FR. Hearing loss and depression in older adults. *J Am Geriatr Soc*. 2013;61(9):1627–1629.

45. Li C-M, Zhang XZ, Hoffman HJ, Cotch MF, Themann CL, Wilson MR. Hearing impairment associated with depression in US adults, National Health and Nutrition Examination Survey 2005-2010. *JAMA Otolaryngol Head Neck Surg*. 2014;140(4):293–302.

46. Sung YK, Li L, Blake C, Betz J, Lin FR. Association of hearing loss and loneliness in older adults. *J Aging Health*. 2016;28(6):979–994.

47. Cosh S, Carriere I, Daien V, et al. The relationship between hearing loss in older adults and depression over 12 years: Findings from the Three-City prospective cohort study. *Int J Geriatr Psychiatry*. 2018;33(12):1654–1661.

48. Scinicariello F, Przybyla J, Carroll Y, Eichwald J, Decker J, Breysse PN. Age and sex differences in hearing loss association with depressive symptoms: analyses of NHANES 2011-2012. *Psychol Med*. 2019;49(6):962–968.

49. Shargorodsky J, Curhan GC, Farwell WR. Prevalence and characteristics of tinnitus among US adults. *Am J Med*. 2010;123(8):711–718.

50. Deal JA, Reed NS, Kravetz AD, Weinreich H, Yeh C, Lin FR, Altan A. Incident hearing loss and comorbidity: A longitudinal administrative claims study. *JAMA Otolaryngol Head Neck Surg*. 2019;145(1):36–43.

51. Fisher DE, Ward MM, Hoffman HJ, Li C-M, Cotch MF. Impact of sensory impairments on functional disability in adults with arthritis. *Am J Prev Med*. 2016;50(4):454–462.

52. Reed NS, Altan A, Deal JA, et al. Trends in health care costs and utilization associated with untreated hearing loss over 10 years. *JAMA Otolaryngol Head Neck Surg*. 2019;145(1):27–34.

53. Karpa MJ, Gopinath B, Beath K, et al. Associations between hearing impairment and mortality risk in older persons: The Blue Mountains Hearing Study. *Ann Epidemiol*. 2010;20(6): 452–9.

54. Fisher D, Li C-M, Chiu MS, et al. Impairments in hearing and vision impact on mortality in older persons: The AGES–Reykjavik Study. *Age Aging*. 2014;43(1):69–76.

55. Engdahl B, Idstad M, Skirbekk V. Hearing loss, family status and mortality - Findings from the HUNT study, Norway. *Soc Sci Med*. 2019;220:219–225.

56. Kerns E, Masterson EA, Themann CL, Calvert GM. Cardiovascular conditions, hearing difficulty, and occupational noise exposure within US industries and occupations. *Am J Ind Med*. 2018;61(6):477–491.

57. Campos JL, Launer S. From healthy hearing to healthy living: A holistic approach. *Ear Hear*. 2020;41 (Suppl 1):99S–106S.

58. GBD 2019 Diseases and Injuries Collaborators. Global burden of 369 diseases and injuries in 204 countries and territories, 1990–2019: a systematic analysis for the Global Burden of Disease Study 2019. *Lancet*. 2020; 96(10258):1204–1222.

59. Ramsey T, Svider PF, Folbe AJ. Health burden and socioeconomic disparities from hearing loss: a global perspective. *Otol Neurotol*. 2018;39(1):12–16.

60. World Health Organization. Global cost of unaddressed hearing loss and cost-effectiveness of interventions: a WHO report, 2017. Available at: https://apps.who.int/iris/handle/10665/254659. Accessed February 20, 2021.

61. Mohr PE, Feldman JJ, Dunbar JL, et al. The societal costs of severe to profound hearing loss in the United States. *Int J Technol Assess Health Care*. 2000;16(4):1120–1135.

62. Carroll YI, Eichwald J, Scinicariello F, et al. Vital Signs: Noise-Induced Hearing Loss Among Adults–United States 2011–2012. *MMWR Morb Mortal Wkly Rep*. 2017;66(5):139–144.

63. Goldstein E, Ho CX, Hanna R, et al. Cost of care for subjective tinnitus in relation to patient satisfaction. *Otolaryngol Head Neck Surg*. 2015;152(3):518–523.

64. Emmett SD, Francis HW. The socioeconomic impact of hearing loss in US adults. *Otol. Neurotol.* 2014;36(3):545–550.

65. Mamo S, Nieman CL, Lin FR. Prevalence of untreated hearing loss by income among older adults in the United States. *J Health Care Poor Underserved.* 2016;27(4):1812–1818.

66. US Bureau of Labor Statistics. Older workers: Labor force trends and career options. May 2017. Available at: https://www.bls.gov/careeroutlook/2017/article/older-workers.htm. Accessed February 20, 2021.

67. US Department of Health and Human Services. Healthy People 2030. Sensory and Communication Disorders. Office of Disease Prevention and Health Promotion. 2020. Available at: https://health. gov/healthypeople/objectives-and-data/browse-objectives/sensory-or-communication-disorders. Accessed February 20, 2021.

68. Dillon H, James A, Ginis J. Client oriented scale of improvement (COSI) and its relationship to several other measures of benefit and satisfaction provided by hearing aids. *J Am Acad Audiol.* 1997;8(1):27–43.

69. Ferguson MA, Kitterick PT, Chong LY, Edmondson-Jones M, Barker F, Hoare DJ. Hearing aids for mild to moderate hearing loss in adults. *Cochrane Database Syst Rev.* 2017;9(9): CD012023.

70. Fisher DE, Li CM, Hoffman HJ, et al. Sex-specific predictors of hearing-aid use in older persons: The Age, Gene/Environment Susceptibility - Reykjavik Study. *Int J Audiol.* 2015;54(9): 634–641.

71. National Academies of Science, Engineering, and Medicine. *Hearing Health Care for Adults: Priorities for Improving Access and Affordability. Consensus Study Report.* Washington, DC: The National Academies Press; 2016. Available at: https://www.nap.edu/catalog/23446/ hearing-health-care-for-adults-priorities-for-improving-access-and. Accessed March 23, 2021.

72. US Department of Health and Human Services. *Healthy People 2020. Progress Review–Hearing and Other Sensory or Communication Disorders & Vision* [webinar]. Office of Disease Prevention and Health Promotion. February 22, 2018. Available at: https://www.cdc.gov/ nchs/healthy_people/hp2020/hp2020_ent_vsl_and_v_progress_review.htm. Accessed February 20, 2021.

73. Freeman B. The coming crisis in audiology. *Audiology Today.* 2009;21(6):46–52.

74. Planey AM. Audiologist availability and supply in the United States: A multi-scale spatial and political economic analysis. *Soc Sci Med.* 2019;222:216–224.

75. American Academy of Audiology. *American Academy of Audiology Position Statement—Audiology Assistants.* September 2010. Available at: https://audiology- web.s3.amazonaws. com/migrated/2010_AudiologyAssistant_Pos_Stat.pdf_539978b1321499.80405268.pdf. Accessed February 20, 2021.

76. American Speech-Language-Hearing Association. Audiology assistants. Available at: https://www.asha.org/practice-portal/professional-issues/audiology-assistants. Accessed February 20, 2021.

77. Marrone N, Ingram M, Somoza M, Jacob DS, Sanchez A, Adamovich S, Harris FP. Interventional audiology to address hearing health care disparities: *Oyendo Bien* pilot study. *Semin Hear*. 2017; 38(2):198–211.

78. Ingram M, Marrone N, Sanchez DT, Sander A, Navarro C, de Zapien JG, Colina S, Harris F. Addressing hearing health care disparities among older adults in a US-Mexico Border Community. *Front Public Health*. 2016; 4:169.

79. Sánche D, Adamovich S, Ingram M, Harris FP, de Zapien J, Sánchez A, Colina S, Marrone N. The potential in preparing community health workers to address hearing loss. *J Amer Acad Audiol*. 2017; 28(6):562–574.

Oral and Vision Care for Healthy Aging

Jeananne Elkins, PhD, DPT, MPH, Michelle J. Saunders, DMD, MS, MPH, and Isis S. Mikhail, MD, DrPH, MPH

BACKGROUND

The senses play an important role in one's overall health, and of course, health outcomes. In this chapter, the senses of taste (oral health) and sight are addressed. Sensory loss is an important health problem that increases with aging, especially age-related vision impairment. These impairments have been associated with decreased function, cognitive decline, increased risk of falls, and an overall decline in the quality of life.

Poor dentition impacts all areas of a person's life, from chewing to smiling, from kissing to talking, and from social activities to eating. As soon as a person opens their mouth, poor dentition makes an impact. As people age, dental caries, particularly root caries, and periodontal disease exceed diabetes in prevalence. About 33% of older adults have diabetes, while more than 40% have oral pain and 46% have periodontal disease[1-4]; however, beyond the immediate impact to the individual, the impact in lost time due to oral and dental problems, especially in work time, costs the economy. In the United States, more than $124 billion are spent on problems related to dental care.[4] In addition, the correlation of periodontal disease to cardiovascular disease and diabetes is strong, as well as the link to other risk behaviors including tobacco use and consuming sugary beverages and foods.[1,3] Significant disparities are present in oral health in older adults. Thirty-six percent of older adults who are poor are edentulous as compared with only 9% of those older adults with incomes greater than $47,000 per year. One-third of older adults living in poverty have untreated dental caries.[3] Many disparities exist among minority older adults as well.

Oral health begins in the prenatal environment and extends across the life span; moreover, the oral cavity is a port into the human body.[5] Poor oral health in persons who are older reflects disparities of cost, quality, and access across the life span, not just in the time of aging.[3] However, we must also be concerned about the additional systemic diseases associated with poor oral health. Humphrey et al. published a systematic review with meta-analysis linking periodontal disease and coronary heart disease.[6] Periodontal disease increases the relative risk of cardiovascular disease 44% in older adults.[7]

Additionally, it is associated with other chronic diseases including impaired cognitive function, stroke, cancer, chronic kidney disease, respiratory diseases, rheumatoid arthritis, adverse pregnancy outcomes, and metabolic disease.[8]

Good oral health and prevention of periodontal disease begins in childhood. Approaches encouraged by the World Health Organization include good oral hygiene practices; a healthy diet; use of fluoride; use of antimicrobial mouthwashes; prevention and cessation of smoking and other use of tobacco products; and oral health screenings.[8] In 2000, the US Surgeon General issued a report, "Oral Health in America".[9] While many programs for children have emerged from this report, little attention has been given to the oral health of older people. The long-term success of programs for children will be better oral health of older adults. In the shorter term, the growing population of older adults have seen few changes in their ability to access oral and dental care, especially those people who live in long-term care facilities including nursing homes. To date, public health and public policy has largely ignored this segment of the population in oral health policy and programs; yet, in 2030, one in five Americans will be over the age of 65.[10]

Oral health begins in childhood and extends across the life span; thus, policies addressing oral health must address the life span instead of only focusing on the person who is older or younger. Dental sealants prevent more than 80% of caries in permanent molars; however, most children do not receive dental sealants. Children from lower income families are 20% less likely to have received dental sealants; and thus, are three times more likely to have caries in permanent molars than children who receive dental sealants. Dental caries, the most common chronic disease in children, does not disappear when the child ages.[3] Additionally, it is rare that dental sealants are used in older adults, even when indicated. Periodontal disease and subsequent root caries also increase among older adults in the absence of good oral hygiene and other preventive measures.

POLICIES AND LEGISLATION IMPACTING ORAL HEALTH

Fluorination of water, access to care in childhood, emergency care in older adults residing in nursing facilities under Medicaid, and oral health screenings all impact the oral health of older adults. Increasing the average number of teeth that adults move into older ages with provides a major benefit. In addition, economic prosperity is important to assure earlier access to good oral care.

Medicare does not cover most dental care, including dental procedures or dental supplies. Medicare does not cover cleanings, fillings, tooth extractions, dentures, dental plates, or other dental devices. In fact, at this time, Medicare only covers dental care connected to serious medical conditions, such as head and neck cancer, kidney transplant, and similar conditions.[11] Some Medicare Advantage programs have dental coverage, but this varies according to the insurance plan. Medicaid coverage in a limited number of states has some limited dental benefits, usually for nursing facility residents.

There is no question that both federal and state policies which recognize that oral health care is an integral part of primary care, and that are financed accordingly, for older Americans are needed. Given that the mouth is part of the body, mid-level practitioners should arise and be trained to improve access to oral health care for the aging disadvantaged, including poor rural and urban minority populations.[12]

Best Practice Interventions in Oral Care

Water fluorination and oral screenings as well as regular dental and oral care are the best practices. Of specific importance is to encourage cessation of risks related to oral health including tobacco use to preserve teeth and to decrease the impact of poor oral health on other human systems. Reducing barriers to oral care, including costs, is important to assure access to care.[13]

The Health Resources and Services Administration (HRSA) of the US Department of Health and Human Services funds 48 Geriatrics Workforce Enhancement Programs (GWEPs) across 35 states and two territories. Several of them have a focus on oral health, with accompanying resources for interprofessional trainees. An example is the Minnesota Northstar GWEP at the University of Minnesota. This program includes the Age Friendly Care and Education Collection, an online resource collection of educational and other training materials (available at: https://nexusipe.org/informing/resource-center/gwep-repository-home). These include geriatric education toolkits of modules, case studies, clinical tools, preceptor materials, patient education materials, journal articles, videos, and more.

VISION

Vision Impairment Among Older Adults

Approximately 18% of Americans 70 years and older suffer from vision impairment.[14] The most common vision impairments among older adults in the United States are age-related macular degeneration (AMD) and cataracts.

Age-related macular degeneration is an ocular disease that causes damage to the macula, the central part of the retina. Cataract causes cloudiness of the lens of the eye due to protein degenerative changes. Both reduce the person's central vision that impacts near vision activities such as reading.[15] Age-related macular degeneration affects about 30% of persons age 80 years and older, and 36% of persons older than 85 years old.[14] From 2000 to 2010, the number of people with AMD grew 18% from 1.75 million to about 2 million. It is anticipated that the number of persons with AMD will more than double by

2050 to exceed 5 million. Approximately 25% of individuals 65 years and older develop cataract, increasing to about 50% by age 75, and even further to about 70% in persons over 80 years of age. The prevalence of both AMD and cataract is higher among White adults compared with Black adults, and more common in women than in men.[16] Studies on sensory deficits have shown AMD being one of the leading causes of vision impairment and blindness among older adults.[17] Among cataract patients, cataract surgery has been successful in improving vision. Studies addressing improvement of cognitive function after cataract surgery have not been conclusive.[18]

Vision impairments results in depression, cognitive decline, mobility problems, increased falls and injuries, and overall decline in quality of life.[17] Few studies have shown an association between cognitive decline and dementia. However, studies addressing these differences are lacking. In a study of 6,112 women over the age of 69 years of age, Lin et al.[19] found that sensory impairment was associated with cognitive and functional decline in older women. They also suggested that studies were needed to determine whether treatment of vision and hearing impairment can decrease the risk for cognitive and functional decline.[19]

Harrabi et al.[20] used a sample of hospital-based, cross-sectional study of people aged 65 years or older from ophthalmology clinics to explore age-related eye disease and cognitive function. The authors found that people with vision loss due to three different age-related eye diseases (i.e., AMD, Fuch's corneal dystrophy, and glaucoma) had lower cognitive scores. Future research should focus on the reasons for this and this should be explored using longitudinal studies.[20]

The relationship between visual acuity and severe depressive symptoms also has empirical evidence to suggest that there is a connection between the two. Zheng et al.[21] examined this question using a population-based sample of participants aged 65–84 years in 1993–1995 assessed at baseline, and then again at two, six, and eight years later. It was found that depressive symptoms are associated with visual acuity cross-sectionally.[21] Persons with higher baseline depression scores were more likely to experience worsening visual acuity over time. There is a need for a continued effort to detect and treat both visual decline and depression in the older adult population.

Furthermore, vision loss has a substantial impact on activities of daily living, symptoms of depression and feelings of anxiety. Kempen et al.[22] examined the impact of low vision on activities of daily living, symptoms of depression, feelings of anxiety, and social support among community living older adults who sought vision rehabilitation services.[22]

Vision impairment is also associated with falls and falls risk. Hong et al. followed a cohort of older people for up to 15 years to explore the incidence of falls and fractures among older people.[23] In this older cohort, recent development of visual impairment was associated with increased likelihood of subsequent falls and fractures in the next five years, independent of other confounding variables.

Best Practice Interventions in Vision Care

Aging-related vision impairment and its effects on visual processing should be taken into consideration to reverse or minimize the progression of mobility dysfunction in older adults. There is a need for a continued effort to detect and treat both visual decline and depression in older adults. Clinicians and health care professionals assessing older adult individuals with a vision impairment should consider further evaluation and be aware of their increased risk of related health-related issues. Sensory decline is an emerging public health problem with the growing increase in the aging population.

SPECIAL CONSIDERATIONS AND SPECIAL POPULATIONS

Delivering care to institutionalized, economically disadvantaged older adults is difficult; however, alternative practices can be implemented to assure care to the most vulnerable populations, persons who live in residential care communities and especially those who are dual eligible Medicare/Medicaid beneficiaries. These practices include modeling practices after school-based care for children and implementing on-site dental clinics, as well as creating new models of care for advanced training of mid-level dental providers.

CONCLUSION: PUBLIC HEALTH CHALLENGES AND OPPORTUNITIES FOR SENSORY DEFECITS

Sensory decline is an emerging public health problem with the increase in the older adult population. Several descriptive studies are identified about sensory impairments. However, there is a need for more longitudinal studies for a comprehensive understanding of the mechanisms and to determine the genetic, epidemiological, and pathophysiological basis for sensory deficits, and examine gender, race, and ethnic differences. Translational studies and clinical trials are needed to inform clinical practice so the impact of sensory deficits in older adults can be identified and managed, leading to improved quality of life for this population. Clinicians and health care professionals assessing aging individuals with a sensory deficit should consider further evaluation and be aware of their increased risk of related health issues.

More studies on vision impairment in older adults are needed to address racial, genetic, and pathophysiologic factors on health outcomes, and quality of life. Physicians and health care providers need to focus on vision impairment among older adults and its association with cognitive deficits. There is a need for better communication and dissemination of information on vision care and the availability of interventions to improve mobility dysfunction and quality of life among visually impaired older adults. Interventions to reverse or minimize the progression of mobility dysfunction in older adults should take this common aging-related deficit in visual processing into account.

Further, decreasing accidents and preventable injuries among the older adult population can have an impact of health care system. There is a need for more longitudinal studies for a comprehensive understanding of the mechanisms and determine the genetic, epidemiological, and pathophysiological basis for vision impairment. These studies should also examine gender, race, and ethnic differences. Translational studies and clinical trials are needed to inform clinical practice so that the impact of vision impairment in older adults can be identified and managed, leading to improved quality of life for this population.

In 2016, the National Academies of Science and Engineering proposed a series of recommendations with the goal of making vision care a population health imperative. These recommendations include[24]

1. Facilitate public awareness through timeline access to accurate and locally relevant information,
2. Generate evidence to guide policy decisions and evidence-based actions,
3. Expand access to appropriate clinical care,
4. Enhance public health capacities to support vision-related activities, and
5. Promote community responses that encourage eye and vision healthy environments.

CASE STUDY FOR VISION PUBLIC HEALTH

Igor is an 88-year-old White male, currently living in his family home. He is a recent widower and has had macular degeneration for some years, and wears hearing aids. He worked as a bricklayer and miner earlier in his career, and during the timeframe of his employment, he did not utilize protective gear to address noise and other factors which could impact his hearing. Originally from Germany, his stoic nature and personality also prevented him from implementing measures during his working years to offer protection to his other sensory elements.

Igor's daughter (and only child) as well as his two grandchildren live close by and assist him with his household tasks. He prides himself on the use of headphones to hear his television and computer, and makes use of wide-screen devices for his computer monitor and his television. His cooking skills were always limited because his late wife insisted that meal preparation was part of her wifely duties. Now that he is living on his own, he enjoys simple meals prepared by his daughter or receives home delivered meals from the local senior center's meals on wheels program.

Igor recently was in a car accident, where it was discovered that he was driving despite his visual impairment. His girlfriend served as the co-pilot and instructed him on how to proceed on the country roads where he was driving. Unfortunately, he slipped into a ditch when she failed to instruct him on how to navigate a turn. Rural living for Igor posed problems with transportation since public transportation was very limited in his county, and nonexistent for the area where his family home was located.

The accident prompted local case management authorities to collaborate with the family to identify what supports would be needed in the community to support Igor's independence and meet his needs. Care for these community older adults is provided by an interprofessional team that includes dental providers. The team determines the care plan, which is individualized for each patient enrollee's individual and cultural needs. The care plan also considers the ability of each patient enrollee to tolerate and benefit from both preventive and restorative treatments. The goal is to maximize both function and quality of life.

CASE STUDY FOR INTEGRATED ORAL PUBLIC HEALTH

Another model of interprofessional oral health care delivery is the nonprofit On Lok Program of All-Inclusive Care for the Elderly (PACE), which began in San Francisco's Chinatown neighborhood. This 49-year-old program has since expanded to centers in Fremont and San José, California. On Lok provides quality, comprehensive care to its frail older adult population through a Centers for Medicare and Medicaid Services (CMS) reimbursement plan and a network of providers and appropriate technology. This community-based program came into being as community leaders in medicine, dentistry, nursing, social work, and government strove to address workforce issues and the needs of older adults in the community. Instead of investing significant funds in the development of a nursing facility, the organizers decided to develop a program that would provide for all the medical and dental needs of its enrollee patients through a waiver program with CMS, while enabling them to live in their own residences. It took fewer than ten years for On Lok to be able to provide all of its patient enrollees' medical care, including oral health care.

Since On Lok is financially structured as a capitation program, it does not bill Medicare or Medicaid. There is no fee-for-service payment for on-site providers; and no pre-authorization is required for dental services. Outcomes, cost, and other quality measures are evaluated quarterly using randomly selected patient records. There is an electronic health record for each patient enrollee which tracks encounters and specific care provided, as well as the respective ICD-10 diagnostic codes and costs per enrollee patient per month and per visit.

Staff and contract dentists provide oral care on site. Care by off-site dental specialty providers is predetermined in the interdisciplinary care plan. There is no additional cost for patient enrollees because of the Medicare waiver structure. Private practitioners are encouraged to participate because reimbursement rates are higher than state Medicaid rates. Two dental schools in the area provide onsite training for pre- and post-doctoral students at On Lok and at the schools for oral surgery and radiology services.

Each patient enrollee receives an initial oral exam and annual evaluation. This helps to identify disease early and provide continuity of care. A range of preventive, restorative, and emergency procedures are provided as determined by the interdisciplinary care team. These limit the need for more costly and extensive procedures in this frail population.

On Lok's oral health care goals are to enable patient enrollees to maintain freedom from discomfort, function, and quality of life with dignity by providing medically necessary oral health care services; this includes restoring function tailored to the individual's needs, relieving any discomfort, maintaining oral health, and preventing new or recurring disease. This model is now used at other PACE programs across the country.[13]

REFERENCES

1. Corriere M, Rooparinesingh N, Kalyani R. Epidemiology of diabetes and diabetes complications in the elderly: An emerging public health burden. *Curr Diab Rep.* 2013;13(6):805–813.

2. Eke PI, Thornton-Evans GO, Wei L, Borgnakke WS, Dye BA, Genco RJ. Periodontitis in US adults: National Health and Nutrition Examination Survey 2009-2014. *J Am Dent Assoc.* 2018;149(7):576–588.

3. Griffin SO, Barker LK, Griffin PM, Cleveland JL, Kohn W. Oral health needs among adults in the United States with chronic diseases. *J Am Dent Assoc.* 2009;140(10):1266–1274.

4. Centers for Disease Control and Prevention. *Oral Health Surveillance Report: Trends in Dental Caries and Sealants: Tooth Retention, and Edentulism, United States, 1999–2004 to 2011–2016.* Atlanta, GA: US Department of Health and Human Services; 2019.

5. Coppes MJ, Fisher-Owens SA. Oral health: A critical piece to develop into a healthy adult. *Pediatr Clin North Am.* 2018;65(5):xvii–xix.

6. Humphrey L, Fu R, Buckley D, Freeman M, Helfand M. Periodontal disease and coronary heart disease incidence: A systematic review and meta-analysis. *J Gen Intern Med.* 2008;23(12):2079–2086.

7. Janket S-J, Baird AE, Chuang S-K, Jones JA. Meta-analysis of periodontal disease and risk of coronary heart disease and stroke. *Oral Surg Oral Med Oral Path Oral Radiol Endod.* 2003;95(5):559–569.

8. Nazir MA. Prevalence of periodontal disease, its association with systemic diseases and prevention. *Int J Health Sci.* 2017;11(2):72–80.

9. National Institute of Dental and Craniofacial Research. Oral Health in America: A Report of the Surgeon General. Rockville, MD: US Department of Health and Human Services, National Institutes of Health; 2000.

10. US Census Bureau. Older people projected to outnumber children for the first time in US history. 2018. Available at: https://www.census.gov/newsroom/press-releases/2018/cb18-41-population-projections.html. Accessed on February 21, 2021.

11. Centers for Medicare and Medicaid Services. *Medicare & You.* Baltimore, MD: US Department of Health and Human Services; 2021.

12. Becerra K, Nguyen V. The Gary and Mary West Senior Dental Center: An integrated model of dental health, and wellness care for older adults. *Generations.* 2016;40(3):100–103.

13. Chávez EM and Lederman B. On Lok PACE: Where Oral Healthcare Is an Integral Part of Healthcare. *Generations.* 2016;40(3):104–106.

14. Jonasson F, Arnarsson A, Eiríksdottir G, et al. Prevalence of age-related macular degeneration in old persons: Age, Gene/environment Susceptibility Reykjavik Study. *Ophthalmology.* 2011;118(5):825–830.

15. Eichenbaum JW. Geriatric vision loss due to cataracts, macular degeneration, and glaucoma. *Mt Sinai J Med.* 2012;79(2):276–294.

16. National Eye Institute. Eye Health Data and Statistics. 2019. Available at: https://www.nei.nih.gov/learn about-eye-health/resources-for-health-educators/eye-health-data-and-statistics. Accessed February 21, 2021.

17. Heine C, Browning C. Dual sensory loss in older adults: A systematic review. *Gerontologist.* 2015;55(5):913–928.

18. Hall TA, McGwin G Jr, Owsley C. Effect of cataract surgery on cognitive function in older adults. *J Am Geriatr Soc.* 2005;53(12):2140–2144.

19. Lin MY, Gutierrez PR, Stone KL, et al. Vision impairment and combined vision and hearing impairment predict cognitive and functional decline in older women. *J Am Geriatr Soc.* 2004;52(12):1996–2002.

20. Harrabi H, Kergoat MJ, Rousseau J, et al. Age-related eye disease and cognitive function. *Invest Ophthalmol Vis Sci.* 2015;56(2):1217–1221.

21. Zheng DD, Bokman CL, Lam BL, et al. Longitudinal relationships between visual acuity and severe depressive symptoms in older adults: the Salisbury Eye Evaluation study. *Aging Ment Health.* 2016;20(3):295–302.

22. Kempen GI, Ballemans J, Ranchor AV, van Rens GH, Zijlstra GA. The impact of low vision on activities of daily living, symptoms of depression, feelings of anxiety and social support in community-living older adults seeking vision rehabilitation services [published correction appears in *Qual Life Res.* 2012 Oct;21(8):1413]. *Qual Life Res.* 2012;21(8):1405–1411.

23. Hong T, Mitchell P, Burlutsky G, Samarawickrama C, Wang JJ. Visual impairment and the incidence of falls and fractures among older people: longitudinal findings from the Blue Mountains Eye Study. *Invest Ophthalmol Vis Sci.* 2014 Nov 4;55(11):7589–93.

24. National Academies of Sciences, Engineering, and Medicine. *Making Eye Health a Population Health Imperative: Vision for Tomorrow.* Washington, DC: National Academies Press; 2016.

Mental Health and Healthy Aging

William Cabin, PhD, MPH, MSW and Shana D. Stites, PsyD, MS, MA

BACKGROUND

Mental health disorders, regardless of age, are recognized as major contributors to the global disease burden.[1-4] Mental health is a major burden worldwide and in the United States, with an estimated 1 billion people globally affected by mental and addictive disorders in 2016, causing 7% of all global burden of disease, as measured by Disability Adjusted Life Years (DALYS), and 19% of all years lived with disabilities.[4] The World Health Organization (WHO)[5] estimates that 25% of the world's population experiencing a mental or behavioral illness sometime in their lifetime. Mental illnesses are expected to increase their proportion of total global burden of disease from 10.5% in 1990 to 15% by 2020.[2,3] The WHO also indicates 15% of adults aged 60 and older suffer from a mental disorder, and their neurological and mental disorders account for 6.6% of the global burden of disease.[5] The WHO has stated that mental health and physical health are interrelated, so much so that they have adopted the proposition that there can be "no health without mental health".[6-8]

In addition to the measure of burden of illness by the years of life and health lost to death and disability, mental illnesses have high financial costs. The National Alliance on Mental Health[9] estimates the direct and indirect costs of untreated mental disorders in the United States is $300 billion annually. About 80% of the indirect costs derive from lost or reduced productivity at the workplace, school, and home, reflecting the relatively low mortality and early age of onset for most mental illnesses.[10] Unützer et al.[11] found that Medicare patients with depression were almost twice as costly as those without depression.

In the United States, an estimated 22% of the adult population has one or more diagnosable mental disorders in a year.[12-14] The estimated lifetime prevalence for mental disorders among the US adult population is as follows: 29% for anxiety disorders; 25% for impulse control disorders; 21% for mood disorders; 15% for substance abuse disorders; and 46% for any one of these disorders.[15]

Mental health among older Americans (i.e., persons 65 years or older) is also a significant problem, with mental illness prevalence estimated at 20%.[12-14] Conditions vary, including early-onset conditions (i.e., schizophrenia and recurrent major affective disorders) which continue into old age; later-onset conditions (i.e., depression), which often complicate or occur as a result of a medical illness; and various dementias.[16]

The National Comorbidity Survey Replication found 7% of adults aged 65 and older met criteria for experiencing an anxiety disorder in a 12-month period.[15] Another study found the proportion of older adults who experienced any past-year anxiety disorder was 11.4%.[17] The same study found 6.8% of older adults experienced any past-year mood disorder; 3.8% had past-year substance use disorder; and 14.5% had one or more personality disorders. Depp et al.[18] found 62% of adults aged 60–95 report experiencing at least one panic attack in 2005. The average number of panic attacks in 2004 was 3.23. Grenier et al.[19] found a 12–month prevalence rate of 1.5% among adults aged 65 years and older for obsessive compulsive disorder.

Chronic mental illness among the older adult population is substantially augmented by later-onset conditions, such as cognitive impairment, depression, and various forms of dementia. For purposes of this chapter, it is worth noting an estimated 50 million people are living with dementia.[20] These numbers are projected to reach 82 million by the year 2030 and 152 million by 2050.[5,20] Within the United States, approximately 5.7 million people are living with dementia.[21–23] These numbers are expected to rise as life expectancy increases. More broadly, cognitive impairment may display in various forms and be mild, moderate, or severe. Mild cognitive impairment (i.e., without dementia) may affect 16%–25% of older adults.[24–26]

Depression among the older adult population in the United States is also a significant problem, though there is wide variation in estimates and types of depression. One estimate is that 1%–5% of all community dwelling older adults have clinically defined major depression, with the rate rising to 7%–36% among older adult medical outpatients, 11%–40% among hospitalized older adults, up to 50% in residents of long-term care facilities, and including 13.5% of older persons receiving home health care.[27–30] One home care study found a 27.5% prevalence rate of severe depressive symptomatology.[31,32] The estimates are considered conservative because depression is often underdiagnosed and untreated among the older adult population.[33]

Additionally, older populations experience subsyndromal depression, which are symptoms falling short of meeting the full clinical definition of major depression.[34–36] For example, among American community dwelling older adults, who represent about 90% of all older adults, an additional 8%–20% are estimated to have minor depression, and another 2.1% to have dysthymia, a less severe type of depression, or bipolar disorder.[33] Estimates place the prevalence of late-life depression in adults over age 65 at approximately 15%.[37] Additionally, estimates run as high as 37% of all geriatric primary care patients having some type of depression.[38,39]

The negative consequences of depression in older adults are significant. Depression is considered a major contributor to functional disability, a cause of diminished productivity, and an increased use of health care services.[40] In fact, a meta-analysis of 78 studies exploring risk factors for functional decline in community dwelling older adults found depression as one of the risk factors with the highest strength of evidence.[41] In addition to increased physical disability, studies have found older adult depression associated with increases in nursing home placement, burden on caregivers, utilization of medical services, perceptions of poor health, and health care costs.[42-46] Estimates indicate only 10% of depressed older adults obtain formal evaluation or treatment for the condition.[47] Prognosis is often poor, even with effective treatment.[48]

Despite their adverse impact on disability, care needs, and costs, older Americans' mental illnesses are less commonly recognized, diagnosed, and treated than those of younger patients.[49] This is despite the fact that evidence from both clinical trials and practice-based research that mental health care is effective for older Americans and can reduce costs and improve daily functioning.[50-55]

Stigma is a major factor in limiting older adults from seeking mental health treatment, particularly Black and Hispanic adults.[56-59] Other studies indicate that primary care physicians and other health care providers may discriminate against older adults, often assuming that mental health behaviors are part of the normal aging process instead of assessing and treating older adults directly or by referral.[60] Burnes et al.[61] have found significant negative effects of ageism generally on the risks of older adults mental and physical health, while also identifying interventions effective in reducing ageism.

Public policy places a limited emphasis on mental health among older adults. Medicare showed that only 4.2% of total Medicare spending went to mental health services and 8.5% went to additional medical spending associated with mental illness, for a total of 12.7% of total Medicare spending being associated with mental health disorders.[62-68]

CHALLENGES IN HEALTHY AGING AND MENTAL HEALTH

There has been policy-level recognition that a public health model for mental health is needed, and yet limited progress has been made in setting priorities in research, policy, or practice to establish such a model. In fact, several US Surgeon General reports suggest that the disconnection between public health and mental health undermines the "wellness" of Americans by placing an enormous burden on society and the economy; imposing debilitating burdens on sick individuals and their families; and contributing to premature morbidity and mortality.[12,69-71]

MENTAL HEALTH CONDITIONS

The interaction at the neighborhood, individual, and system levels impacts the nature and extent of mental health conditions and available interventions which, in turn, impacts health, mental health, and economic outcomes. Those outcomes, in turn, affect neighborhood- and individual-level characteristics, as noted in Figure 5–1.

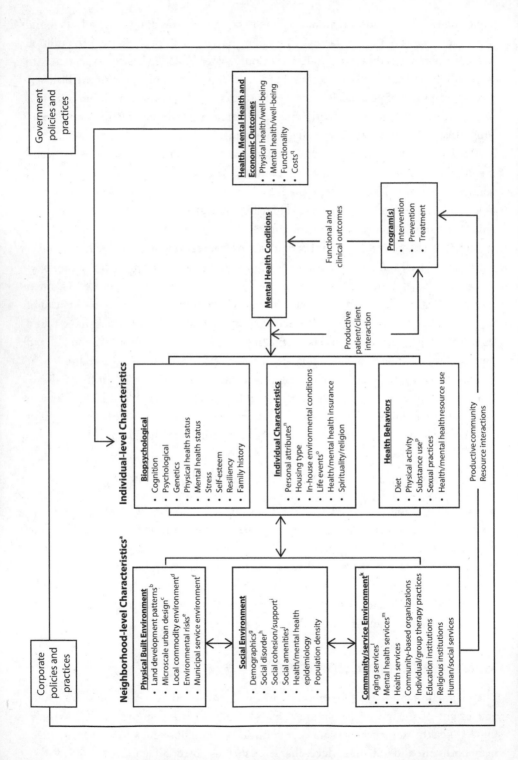

Note: [a] Neighborhood characteristics, definitions, and measures will vary. [b] Land development patterns include land-use mix, residential density, housing (type and condition), green layer space, and educational facilities. [c] Microscale urban design includes street connectivity, sidewalks, walking, infrastructure, walkability, bike lanes, pedestrian safety, and streetlights. [d] Local commodity environment includes distribution of, types of, and access to commercial and retail establishments, including food, alcohol, and tobacco outlets. [e] Environmental risks include air, water, and ground pollution, distribution of risk producing facilities/plants, and noise levels. [f] Municipal services environment includes police, fire, and sanitation (public and private) facilities. [g] Demographics include distribution of age, gender, education level, income level, homelessness, and employment. [h] Social disorder includes crime rate, juvenile delinquency, graffiti, violence, and drug use. [i] Social cohesion includes social networks and social support. [j] Social amenities include libraries, museums, parks, and other recreational activities. [k] Community service environment includes private and public entities. Aging services include senior centers, adult day care services, other services by local area agencies on aging, and community-based organizations serving older adults. [m] Mental health services include inpatient, outpatient, and community-based. [n] Personal attributes include age, gender, income level, education level, marital status, sexual orientation, family size, ethnicity/race employment status, and immigration status. [o] Life events include adverse childhood experiences, caregiver burden, care recipient burden, loss/grief/bereavement (i.e., death, major injury), and divorce/separation. [p] Substance abuse includes drugs, alcohol, and tobacco use. [q] Costs include both direct and indirect costs including productivity.

Figure 5–1. Conceptual Framework for Public Health, Mental Health, and Older Adults

There are varying definitions of mental health conditions, with some being clinically defined using professional guidelines, such as the *Diagnostic and Statistical Manual or International Classification of Diseases*; others by an array of signs and symptoms defined or if a patient is observed to be subsyndromal; and yet others defined by measurement scales.[3,35]

As noted throughout the chapter, the primary health, mental health, and economic outcomes affected by mental health conditions are physical health and well-being; mental health and well-being; functionality (i.e., activities and instrumental activities of daily); and individual and societal costs.

RELEVANT GOVERNMENT LEGISLATION AND PROGRAMS

Government legislation, regulations and programs at the local, state, and federal level are broadly considered government policies and represent the system level factors in the Fahs, Cabin, and Gallo model,[72] which focuses specifically on older adults, public health and mental health. The most significant policies affecting healthy aging and mental health are federal programs, particularly Medicare, Medicaid, and grants through the Substance Abuse and Mental Health Services Administration.

Despite being the primary payer for mental health services for older Americans, Medicare coverage is limited.[73,74] Medicare home health provides limited social work coverage to homebound older Americans with significant mental health issues[51,53] and Medicare does not cover most evidence-based, home, and community-based mental health interventions.[63,75] Medicare historically has required older Americans to pay higher copays for outpatient mental health and substance use care than for physical health care and set lower payment rates to mental health providers, until recent mental health parity and equity legislation.[76] There are other federal policies which do not exclusively focus on the mental health of older Americans which, nevertheless, impact the physical and mental health of older Americans by impacting the social determinants of health.

Availability of mental health services for older adults is further compounded by the limited role of states and local departments of public health in mental health. Purtle et al.[77] found that there were eight types of mental health activities provided by local health departments (LHDs), with the highest being assessing access to gaps to mental health services (39.3%) and implementing strategies to increase access to mental health services (32.8%). However, for four of the activities the proportion of LHDs providing the activity was below 20%; being involved in policy/advocacy activities to address metal health (18.5%); performing population-based primary prevention activities to address mental illness (16.4%); providing mental health services (14%); and addressing access gaps through the provision of mental health services (13.9%).

BEST PRACTICE INTERVENTIONS

There is significant literature on evidence-based practices in geriatric mental health care, including several systematic reviews and meta-analyses.[78-86] Among the major categories of evidence-based interventions are physical exercise and a variety of non-pharmacological interventions related to different conditions, including social support, physical exercise, social activities, multicomponent interventions, reminiscence therapy, problem-solving therapy, cognitive behavioral therapy, and skills-training.[3,87-93]

Despite the existence of best practices and evidence-based interventions, the Medicare program has no process for assessing and approving coverage of evidence-based mental health/psychosocial interventions in home or community-based settings.[94,95] As a result, for example, many evidence-based home and community-based psychosocial interventions for persons with Alzheimer's disease and their caregivers, tested in multiple randomized controlled trials, are not covered by Medicare.[96] These include noncoverage of evidence-based interventions for older Americans with depression recommended by the Centers for Disease Control and Prevention such as IMPACT, PEARLS, & Healthy IDEAS.[96]

SELECTED POPULATION CONSIDERATIONS

There is a need to accommodate vulnerable populations, particularly based on literature-based documentation of health disparities, particularly focused on factors such as community dwelling,[97-99] senior housing,[100] assisted living,[101,102] public housing,[103] being in a nursing homes,[104-106] gender,[107-110] sexual identity,[111-113] race and ethnicity,[114-116] being a veteran,[117,118] being incarcerated,[119,120] and income and wealth.[121-125] Racial and ethnic disparities in access to physical and mental health have been well documented. A 2015 Population Reference Bureau report[123] underscored the projected increase in racial and ethnic diversity among older Americans and corresponding issues in terms of health care access and outcomes. More specifically, the report noted

- The older population is becoming more racially and ethnically diverse. Between 2018 and 2060, the share of the older population that is non-Hispanic White is projected to drop from 77%–55%.
- Despite the increased diversity in the older adult population, the more rapidly changing racial/ethnic composition of the population under age 18 relative to those ages 65 and older has created a diversity gap between generations.
- Wide economic disparities are evident across different population subgroups. Among adults ages 65 and older, 18% of Latinx and 19% of Black populations lived in poverty in 2014, which is more than twice the rate among older non-Hispanic White adults (8%).[125]

CONCLUSION: CHALLENGES AND OPPORTUNITIES FOR PUBLIC HEALTH

The three major challenges for healthy aging and mental health in the United States are lack of adequate income and wealth among older Americans; limited federal funding for mental health; and failure of federal programs to address social determinants of health. A 2017 Commonwealth Fund International Policy Survey of Older Adults in 11 countries found that 43% of American older adults are high need older adults and nearly 31% skip care (physical and mental health) because of costs.[126] Federal funding for older Americans' mental health remains limited, even though Medicare is the largest single payer for older Americans' mental health. Multiple authors have found that although the United States spends more per capita on health care than other major industrial countries, the United States' failure to spend sufficiently for social care has resulted in the United States ranking low on many important health care outcomes compared with other major industrial countries.[127–130]

There are opportunities to address all three major challenges to healthy aging and mental health. Improvements in income and wealth among older persons have had the least progress and are not evident in any Congressional proposals. However, creation of the Affordable Care Act's Medicaid Expansion option has assisted many low-income older adults to improve their income indirectly through Medicaid eligibility. Medicaid Expansion has increased federal funding in mental health in the 37 states participating in the program. Multiple studies have found that Medicaid Expansion states have increased Medicaid beneficiaries' access to mental health services and, as a result, their health outcomes.[131–133] The Medicaid expansion is important to older adult Americans' mental health because 11% of all Medicaid beneficiaries are older persons.[134]

In the private sector, The Institute of Medicine has documented progress in integrating and increasing cooperation between primary care and public health.[73] The National Academies of Sciences, Engineering, and Medicine[135] has documented progress and encouraged expansion of integrating social care into health care delivery and in interventions to decrease social isolation among older adults. Some hospitals already have a variety of initiatives to focus on addressing housing and other social needs in addition to medical needs.[136–139] Taylor et al. conducted a meta-analysis of 32 studies of investments in either social services or integrated models of health care and social services which found positive health outcomes, health care costs, or both in 82% of the investments.[140]

Challenges remain despite these opportunities and current limited progress. As a result, it is imperative that senior citizen advocacy groups advocate for increased health insurance coverage, and public health advocacy organizations remain vigilant in pursuing the expanded coverage of social determinants and preserving Medicaid expansion.

CASE STUDY

Ms. V is a 67-year-old Black woman who lives by herself in Philadelphia, Pennsylvania. Ms. V is a retired receptionist. She is estranged from her husband, who became abusive after losing his job. Her daughter checks on Ms. V a few times each week and helps with grocery shopping. The younger of her two sons visits monthly and occasionally helps with yard and home maintenance. The eldest son was killed in a neighborhood shooting four years ago.

Ms. V has participated in the neighborhood Baptist church and volunteered at a local food pantry and women's shelter for many years. More recently, Ms. V has become a homebody, with the exception of Sunday church services. Ms. V complains that she's lonely because her daughter does not visit enough and because she no longer watches her grandchildren, ages two and four. Ms. V had often helped her daughter by caring for her daughter's two young children, but her daughter found alternative childcare after she arrived one evening to pick them up and found her mother had left the stove on after making lunch. The situation strained Ms. V's relationship with her daughter.

When the time arrived, Ms. V and her daughter attended Ms. V's annual medical visit together. Ms. V's doctor began Ms. V's examination by asking her a routine set of questions. The doctor also asked questions to Ms. V's daughter. The doctor conducted a complete exam, which included a medical history and tests to screen for common problems for older adults.

The doctor concluded that Ms. V showed symptoms of depression and age-related changes in cognition. The doctor recommended to Ms. V that she set up an appointment with a psychologist. The doctor also suggested that Ms. V consider becoming involved in activities at the local senior center, which could help her be socially connected and get regular exercise. The doctor prescribed a low dose antidepressant.

Ms. V told the doctor she was worried about the financial costs and how others might treat her if they find out her diagnosis or that she was going to a senior center. The doctor talked with Ms. V about her concerns about being stigmatized and helped Ms. V feel comfortable accessing care. The doctor also confirmed for Ms. V that her Medicare insurance covers the costs of her care while the local senior center programming is covered by government benefit programs under the Older Americans Act. Ms. V decided to move forward with the treatment plan.

Summary: The case illustrates a common scenario. Older adults often experience depression, isolation, and cognitive changes that interact with family and social dynamics. In the case study, Ms. V's cognitive and depressive symptoms may be attributable to social determinants of health (i.e., social isolation and stress, health risk behaviors, trauma, racism, etc.), one or more underlying pathologies or genetic susceptibilities, or some combination thereof.

In addition, the specific ways Ms. V's symptoms interfere with daily life and her clinician's ability to identify those symptoms and their impacts are also both moderated by social dynamics. In the case study, the cognitive and motor skills Ms. V practiced over years working as a receptionist and the activities she does and does not do during her retirement may all impact Ms. V's cognitive and emotional symptoms. Moreover, her daughter's participation in her routine wellness visit is also an example of family and social dynamics impact symptom identification. Although didactic visits like this are a best practice in memory centers and other clinical services focused on older adults, several social factors (i.e., employment, stigma, gender roles, and other factors) can impact an adult daughter's and other care partner's participation in routine clinical visits. This can in turn can impact the data that are used to assess the older adult's wellbeing and functioning.

Many social factors can also determine who serves as the family doctor for an older adult. These factors can include insurance and economic drivers, geographic features, and macro-level system factors that influence training and licensure as a clinician. The family doctor in the case study leads the clinical assessment and demonstrates best practices. She acts as gate keeper to services and conducts a multicomponent intervention that consists of primary and secondary prevention strategies. This is done through appropriate screenings that identify common problems and addressing barriers to accessing services and treatment fidelity.

For Ms. V's family doctor to be successful at screening and intervention, Ms. V had to be willing to seek services. Moreover, Ms. V's family doctor needed to have access to evidence-based tools for prevention. In addition, effective public policies and funds made available and accessible the resources that Ms. V needed.

As we consider our aging population, we must undertake several steps to achieve the multipronged approach that's needed to address mental health.

Action Steps

- Educate older adults, their families, and general public to address stigma that impedes seeking appropriate mental, medical, and social care.
- Develop a workforce that is trained on screening and prevention of common problems faced by older adults, particularly general medicine physicians, who are the frontline in identifying mental health problems in older adults, and mental health practitioners who provide specialty care needed to treat many of the most common mental health problems encountered by older adults.
- Advocate for public policies and funding that makes available and ensures access to services, programs, and other resources.
- Support research to develop and disseminate culturally competent and evidence-based practices for mental health treatment for older adults. In this model, public health

practitioners demonstrate multicultural competence in attributing mechanisms of health and disease and operating public health programs that function as intended within often complex and interrelated systems.

- Support research and social programming that promotes mental, physical, and social wellbeing for older adults.

REFERENCES

1. Shultz JM, Sullivan LM, Galea S. *Public Health: An Introduction to the Science and Practice of Population Health*. New York, NY: Springer Publishing; 2020.

2. Murray CJL, Lopez AD (Eds.). "The Global Burden of Disease: A Comprehensive Assessment of Mortality and Disability From Diseases, Injuries, and Risk Factors in 1990 and Projected to 2020: Summary." World Health Organization, World Bank, and Harvard School of Public Health; 1996.

3. World Health Organization. "Promoting Mental Health: Concepts, Emerging Evidence, & Practice, Summary Report." Geneva, Switzerland: World Health Organization; 2004

4. Rehm J, Shield, KD. Global burden of disease and the impact of mental and addictive disorders. *Curr Psychiatry Rep*. 2019;21(2):10.

5. World Health Organization. Mental health of older adults. 2017. Available at: https://www.who.int/news-room/fact-sheets/detail/mental-health-of-older-adults. Accessed February 21, 2021.

6. Trautmann S, Rehm J, Wittchen H-U. The economic costs of mental disorders: Do our societies react appropriately to the burden of mental disorders? *EMBO Reports*. 2016;17(9):1245–1249.

7. Ohrnberger J, Fichera E, Sutton M. The relationship between physical and mental health: A mediation analysis. *Soc Sci Med*. 2017;195:42–49.

8. Prince M, Patel V, Saxena S, et al. No health without mental health. *Lancet*. 2007;370(9590): 859–877.

9. National Alliance on Mental Illness. Medicaid Expansion. Available at: https://www.nami.org/Advocacy/Policy-Priorities/Improve-Care/Medicaid-Expansion. Accessed February 21, 2021.

10. Rupp, DE, Vondanovich, SJ, Credé M. The multidimensional nature of Ageism: construct validity and group differences. *J Soc Psychol*. 2005;145(3):335–362.

11. Unützer J, Schoenbaum M, Katon WJ, et al. Healthcare costs associated with depression in medically Ill fee-for-service Medicare participants. *J Am Geriatr Soc*. 2009;57(3):506–510.

12. US Department of Health and Human Services. Mental health: A report of the Surgeon General. Rockville, MD: US Department of Health and Human Services, Substance Abuse and

Mental Health Services Administration, Center for Mental Health Services, National Institutes of Health, National Institute of Mental Health; 1999.

13. US Department of Health and Human Services. Healthy People 2020. Washington, DC: US Government Printing Office; 2020.

14. Administration for Community Living. 2019 Profile of Older Americans. US Department of Health and Human Services. 2020. Available at: https://acl.gov/sites/default/files/Aging%20 and%20Disability%20in%20America/2019ProfileOlderAmericans508.pdf. Accessed April 5, 2021.

15. Kessler RC, Bergland P, Demler O, Jin R, Merikangas KR, Walters E. Lifetime prevalence and age-of-onset distributions of DSM-IV disorders in the national comorbidity survey replication. *Arch Gen Psychiatry*. 2005;62(6):593–602.

16. Federal Interagency Forum on Aging Related Statistics. 2016 Older Americans key indicators of well-being. Washington DC: US Government Printing Office; 2016. Available at: https://agingstats.gov/docs/LatestReport/Older-Americans-2016-Key- Indicators-of-WellBeing.pdf. Accessed February 21, 2021.

17. Reynolds K, Pietraza RH, El-Gabalawy R, Mackenzie C, Sareen J. Prevalence of psychiatric disorders in US older adults: findings from a nationally representative survey. *Psychiatry*. 2015;14(1):74–81.

18. Depp C, Woodruff-Borden J, Meeks S, Gretarsdottir E, DeKryger N. The phenomenology of non-clinical panic in older adults in comparison to younger adults. *J Anxiety Disord*. 2005;19(5):503–519.

19. Grenier S, Preville M Boyer R, O'Connor K. Prevalence and correlates of obsessive-compulsive disorder among older adults living in the community. *J Anxiety Disord*. 2009;23(7):858–865.

20. Alzheimer's Disease International. World Alzheimer Report 2020: The global impact of dementia. 2020. Available at: https://www.alzint.org/resource/world-alzheimer-report-2020. Accessed April 5, 2021.

21. Alzheimer's Association. 2020 Alzheimer's disease facts and figures. Available at: https://alz-journals.onlinelibrary.wiley.com/doi/full/10.1002/alz.12068. Accessed April 5, 2021.

22. Plassman BL, Langa KM, Fisher GG, et al. Prevalence of Dementia in the United States: The Aging, Demographics, and Memory Study. *Neuroepidemiology*. 2007;29(1–2):125–132.

23. National Institute on Aging. Why Population Aging Matters. 2017. Available at: https://www.nia.nih.gov/sites/default/files/2017-06/WPAM.pdf. Accessed February 21, 2021.

24. Grenier S, Preville M Boyer R, O'Connor K. Prevalence and correlates of obsessive- compulsive disorder among older adults living in the community. *J Anxiety Disord*. 2009;23(7):858–865.

25. Lopez OL, Jagust WJ, DeKosky ST, et al. Prevalence and classification of mild cognitive impairment in the Cardiovascular Health Study Cognition Study. *Arch Neurol*. 2003;60(10):1385–1389.

26. Unverzagt FW, Gao S, Baiyewu O, et al. Prevalence of cognitive impairment: Data from the Indianapolis Study of Health and Aging. *Neurology*. 2001;57(9):1655–1662.

27. Bruce ML, McAvay GJ, Raue PJ, et al. Major depression in elderly home health care patient. *Am J Psychiatry*. 2002;159(8):1367–1374.

28. Butler RN, Lewis M, Sunderland T. *Aging and Mental Health: Positive Psychosocial and Bio-medical Approaches*. New York: Merrill/Macmillan Publishing Company; 1991.

29. Hybels CF, Blazer DG. Epidemiology of late-life mental disorders. *Clin Geriatr Med*. 2003;19(4):663–696.

30. National Institute of Mental Health. Older Adults: Depression and suicide facts. 2009. Available at: https://mental-health-matters.com/older-adults-depression-and-suicide-facts. Accessed February 21, 2021.

31. Gellis ZD, Kim J. Confirmatory factor analysis of the CES-D Short form as a screening measure of depression in an elderly home health care population. Paper presented at: The 57th Gerontological Society of America Annual Conference; 2004;Washington, DC.

32. Gellis ZV, Kim JC. Predictors of depressive mood, occupational stress, and propensity to leave in older and younger mental health case managers. *Community Ment Health J*. 2004;40(5):407–421.

33. Gellis ZD. Mental and emotional disorders in older adults. In: Berkman B, ed. *Handbook of Social Work in Health and Aging*. New York, NY: Oxford University Press; 2006:129–139.

34. Gallagher-Thompson D, Steffen AM, Thompson LW, eds. *Handbook of Behavioral and Cognitive Therapies with Older Adults*. New York, NY: Springer; 2008.

35. American Psychiatric Association. *Diagnostic and Statistical Manual of Mental Disorders (DSM-5)*, 5th ed. Arlington, VA: American Psychiatric Association; 2013.

36. Horwath E, Johnson J, Klerman GL, Weissman MM. Depressive Symptoms as Relative and Attributable Risk Factors for First-Onset Major Depression. *Arch Gen Psychiatry*. 1992;Oct;49(10):817–23.

37. Geriatric Mental Health Foundation. Depression in Late Life: Not A Natural Part Of Aging. Available at: https://www.aagponline.org/index.php?src=gendocs&ref=depression&category–Foundation. Accessed February 21, 2021.

38. Garrard J, Rolnick SJ, Nitz NM, et al. Clinical detection of depression among community-based elderly people with self-reported symptoms of depression. *J Geront Biol Sci Med Sci*. 1998;53(2):M92–M101.

39. Glasser M, Gravdal JA. Assessment and treatment of geriatric depression in primary care settings. *Arch Fam Med*. 1997;6(5):433–438.

40. B Birrer RB, Vermuri SP. Depression in later life: A diagnostic and therapeutic challenge. *Am Fam Physician*. 2004;69(10):2375–2382.

41. Stuck AE, Walthert JM, Nikolaus T, Bula CJ, Hohmann C, Beck JC. Risk factors for functional status decline in community-living elderly people: A systematic literature review. *Soc Sci Med.* 1999;48(4):445–469.

42. Charney DS, Nemeroff CB, Lewis L, et al. National depressive and manic-depressive association consensus statement on the use of placebo in clinical trials on mood disorders. *Arch Gen Psychiatry.* 2002;59(3):262–270.

43. Katon V, Bush L, Ormel J. Adequacy and duration of anti-depressant treatment in primary care. *Medical Care.* 1992;30(1):67–76.

44. Unützer J, Patrick DL, Simon G, et al. Depressive symptoms and the cost of health services in HMO patients aged 65 years and older. A 4-year prospective study. *JAMA.* 1997;277(20):1618–1623.

45. Wells KB, Rogers W, Burnam A, Greenfield S, Ware JE Jr. How the medical comorbidity of depressed patients differs across health care settings: Results from the Medical Outcomes Study. *Am J Psychiatry.* 1991;148(12):1688–1696.

46. Blazer DG. Depression in late life: Review and commentary. *J Gerontol.* 2003;58(3):249–265.

47. Weisman MM, Bruce ML, Leaf PJ, Florio LP, Holzer CE. Affective disorders. In: Robins LN, Regier DA, eds. *Psychiatric Disorders in America: The Epidemiologic Catchment Area Study.* New York, NY: The Free Press; 1991: 53–80.

48. Kohn, R., Epstein-Lubow, G. Course and outcomes of depression in the elderly. *Curr Psychiatry Rep.* 2006;8(1):34–40.

49. Bor, JS. Among the elderly, many mental illnesses go undiagnosed. *Health Affairs.* 2015; 34(5):727–731.

50. Borson S, McDonald GJ, Gayle T, Deffebach M, Lakshminarayan S, VanTuinen C. Improvement in mood, physical symptoms, and function with nortriptyline for depression in patients with chronic obstructive pulmonary disease. *Psychosomatics.* 1992;33(2):190–201.

51. Cabin W. Social workers assert Medicare home care ignores social determinants of health. *Home Health Care Manag Pract.* 2020;32(4)199–205.

52. Oslin DW, Streim J, Katz IR, Edell WS, TenHave T. Change in disability follows inpatient treatment for late life depression. *J. Amer. Gerontological Soc.* 2000;48(4):357–362.

53. McEvoy, P. and Barnes, P. Using the chronic care model to tackle depression among older adults who have long-term physical conditions. *J Psychiatr Nurs Ment Health Serv.* 2007;14(3):233–238.

54. Rabins PV. Barriers to diagnosis and treatment of depression in elderly patients. *Am J Geriatr Psychiatry.* 1996;4(suppl 1):S79–S83.

55. Schneider LS. Efficacy of clinical treatment for mental disorders among older persons. In: Gantz M, ed. *Emerging Issues in Mental Health and Aging*. Washington, DC: American Psychological Association; 1995:19–71.

56. Alliance for Aging Research. Alliance Exposes Widespread Ageism in US Healthcare. Available at: https://www.agingresearch.org/press-release/alliance-exposes-widespread-ageism-in-u-s-healthcare. Accessed February 21, 2021.

57. Corrigan P. Ben Zeev D. The Particular Role of Stigma. In: Cohen N, Galea S, eds. *Population Mental Health: Evidence, Policy, and Public Health Practice*. New York, NY: Routledge; 2011.

58. Graham JE, Rockwood K, Beattie BL, et al. Prevalence and severity of cognitive impairment with and without dementia in an elderly population. *Lancet*.1997;349(9068):1793–1796.

59. Sirey JA, Franklin AJ, Mckenzie SE, Ghosh S, Raue PJ. Race, stigma, and mental health referrals among clients of aging services who screened positive for depression. *Psychiatr Serv*. 2014;65(4):537–40.

60. Ben-Harush A, Shiovitz-Ezra S, Doron I, et al. Ageism among physicians, nurses, and social workers: findings from a qualitative study. *Eur J Ageing*. 2017;14(1):39–48.

61. Burnes D, Sheppard C, Henderson CR, et al. Interventions to reduce ageism against older adults: A systematic review and meta-analysis. *Am J Public Health* 2019;109(8):e1 e9.

62. Figueroa JF, Phelan J, Orav J, Patel V, Jha AK. Association of mental health disorders with health care spending in the Medicare population. *JAMA Network Open*. 2020;3(3):1–12.

63. Cabin W. "Less is better" philosophy decreases home health aide utilization to increase reimbursement in Medicare home health. *Home Health Care Manag Pract*. 2019;32(2):105–109.

64. Marmot M, Goldblatt P, Allen J, et al. *Fair Society, Healthy Lives: The Marmot Review- Strategic Review of Health Inequalities in England Post-2010*. London, England: Institute of Health Equity; 2010.

65. Marmot M. "Health Inequities in the EU: Final report of a consortium." European Commission-General for Health and Consumers; 2013.

66. Marmot M. *The Health Gap. The Challenge of an Unequal World*. London, England: Bloomsbury; 2015.

67. Marmot D. The health gap: Doctors and the social determinants of health. *Scan J Public Health*. 2017;45(7):686–693.

68. Bradley E. Taylor L. *The American Health Care Paradox: Why Spending More Is Getting Us Less*. New York, NY: Public Affairs Press; 2013.

69. Bradley E, Elkins BR, Herrin J, Elbel B. Health and social services expenditures: Associations with health outcomes. *BMJ Qual Saf*. 2011;20(10):826–831.

70. US Department of Health and Human Services. Report of the Surgeon General's conference on children's mental health: Developing a National Action Agenda. Washington, DC: US

Department of Health and Human Services, US Department of Education, US Department of Justice; 2000.

71. US Substance Abuse and Mental Health Services Administration. Mental health: culture, race, and ethnicity: a supplement to mental health: a report of the Surgeon General. Rockville, MD: Substance Abuse and Mental Health Services Administration, Center for Mental Health Services, National Institute of Mental Health; 2001.

72. Fahs M, Cabin W, Gallo W. Healthy Aging and Mental Health: A Public Health Challenge for the 21st Century. In: Cohen N, Galea S, eds. *Population Mental Health: Evidence, Policy, and Public Health Practice.* New York, NY: Routledge; 2011.

73. Institute of Medicine. Primary care and public health: Exploring integration to improve public health. Washington, DC: The National Academies Press; 2012.

74. Ley DJ. The Medicare behavioral health failure. *Psychol Today.* 2015. Available at: https://www.psychologytoday.com/us/blog/women-who-stray/201510/the-medicare-behavioral-health-failure. Accessed February 21, 2021.

75. Gitlin L. Testimony before the United States Senate Special Committee on Aging. Hearing on Until There's A Cure: How to Help Alzheimer's Patients and Families Now. December 8, 2010. Available at: https://www.aging.senate.gov/imo/media/doc/1282010.pdf. Accessed February 21, 2021.

76. Lê Cook B, Flores M, Zuvekas SH, Newhouse JP, et. al. The impact of Medicare's mental health cost-sharing parity on use of mental health care services. *Health Aff (Millwood).* 2020;39(5):819–827.

77. Purtle J, Klassen AC, Kolker J, Buehler JW. Prevalence and correlates of local health departments activities to address mental health in the United States. *Prev Med.* 2016;82:20–27.

78. Bartels SJ, Dums AR, Oxman TE, et al. Evidence-based practices in geriatric mental health care: An overview of systematic reviews and meta-analyses. *Psychiatr Clin North Am.* 2003;26(4):971–990.

79. Klug G, Gallunder M, Hermann G, Singer M, Schulter M. Effectiveness of multidisciplinary psychiatric home treatment for elderly patients with mental illness: a systematic review of empirical studies. *BMC Psychiatr.* 2019;19:382.

80. Zhang A, Kong D, Jiang L, Sun F, Dunkle RE, Liu C. Understanding the effectiveness of psychosocial services for anxiety and depression in Chinese older adults: A systematic review and meta-analysis of controlled trials. *Gerontologist.* 2020;60(1):e76–e92.

81. MacCourt P, Wilson K, Tourigny-Rivard M-F. Guidelines for comprehensive mental health services for older adults in Canada. Ottawa, Ontario, Canada: Mental Health Commission of Canada; 2011.

82. Niclasen J, Lund L, Obel C, Larsen L. Mental health interventions among older adults: A systematic review. *Scand J Public Health.* 2019;47(2):240–250.

83. Windle G, Hughes D, Linck P, Russell I, Woods B. Is exercise effective in promoting mental well-being in older age? A systematic review. *Aging Ment Health.* 2010;14 (6):652– 669.

84. Madeelah TA, Mohd T, Yunus RM, Hairi F, Hairi NN, Choo WY. Social support and depression among community-dwelling older adults in Asia: A systematic review. *BMJ Open.* 2019;9(7):e026667.

85. Leggett A, Zarit SH. Prevention of mental disorder in older adults: Recent innovations and future directions. *Generations.* 2014;8(3):45–52.

86. National Prevention Council. Healthy aging in action. Washington, DC: US Department of Health and Human Services, Office of the Surgeon General; 2016.

87. De Oliveira M, Radanovic M, Homem de Mello PC, et al. Nonpharmacological interventions to reduce behavioral and psychological symptoms of dementia: A systematic review. *Biomed Res Int.* 2015:2015:218980.

88. Cohen-Mansfield, J. Nonpharmacologic interventions for inappropriate behaviors in Dementia: A review, summary, and critique. *Am J Geriatr Psychiatry.* 2001;9(4):361.

89. Na R, Yang J, Yeom Y, Kim YJ, Byun S, Kim K, Kim KW. A systematic review and meta-analysis of nonpharmacological interventions for moderate to severe dementia. *Psychiatry Investig.* 2019;16(5):325–335.

90. Hendriks GJ, Oude Voshaar RC, Keijsers GP, Hoogduin CA, van Balkom AJ. Cognitive-behavioural therapy for late-life anxiety disorders: a systematic review and meta-analysis. *Acta Psychiatr Scand.* 2008;117(6):403–411.

91. Apostolo J, Bobrowicz-Campos E, Rodrigues M, Castro I, Cardoso D. The effectiveness of non-pharmacological interventions in older adults with depressive symptoms: A systematic review. *Int J Nurs Stud.* 2016;58:59–70.

92. Chen Y, Li X, Pan B, et al. Non-pharmacological interventions for older adults with depressive symptoms: a network meta-analysis of 35 randomized trials. *Aging Ment Health.* 2019; 27:1–14.

93. Cohen-Mansfield J, Libin A, Marx MS. Nonpharmacological treatment of agitation: A controlled trial of systematic individualized treatment. *J Gerontol Med Sci.* 2007;62A(8):908–916.

94. England MJ, Butler AS, Gonzalez ML, eds. *Psychosocial Interventions for Mental and Substance Use Disorders: A Framework for Establishing Evidence-based Standards.* Washington, DC: The National Academies Press; 2015.

95. Hirschman KB, Hodgson, NA. Evidence-based interventions for transitions in care for individuals living with dementia. *Gerontologist.* 2018;58(suppl 1):S129–S140.

96. Centers for Disease Control and Prevention and National Association of Chronic Disease Directors. Issue brief #1: What does the data tell us. 2020. Available at: https://www.cdc.gov/aging/pdf/mental_health.pdf. Accessed February 21, 2021.

97. Garrido MM, Kane RL, Kaas M, Kane RA. Perceived need for mental health care among community-dwelling older adults. *J Gerontol B Psychol Sci Soc Sci.* 2009;648(6):704–712.

98. Lee SY, Franchett MK, Imanbayev A, Gallo JJ, Spira AP, Lee HB. Non-pharmacological prevention of major depression among community-dwelling older adults: a systematic review of the efficacy of psychotherapy interventions. *Arch Gerontol Geriatr.* 2012;55(3)522–529.

99. Snowden M, Steinman L, Mochan K, et al. Effect of exercise on cognitive performance in community-dwelling older adults: Review of intervention trials and recommendations for public health practice and research. *JAGS.* 2011;59:704–716.

100. Jeste DV, Glorioso D, Lee EE, et al. Study of independent living residents of a continuing care Senior housing community: Sociodemographic and clinical associations of cognitive, physical, and mental health. *Am J Geriatr Psychiatry.* 2019;27(9):895–907.

101. Marx KA, Duffort N, Scerpella DL, Samus QM, Gitlin LN. Evidence-based non- pharmacologic interventions for managing neuropsychiatric symptoms and mental health issues in residents in assisted living. *Seniors Hous Care J.* 2017;25(1):71–83.

102. Silveira A. Depression in Assisted Living Facilities. Available at: https://www.jhsph.edu/offices-and-services/student-assembly/student- groups/SPHI/Depression%20in%20Assisted%20Living%20Facilities_Silveira.pdf. Accessed February 21, 2021.

103. Simning A, van Wijngaarden E, Fisher SG, Richardson TM, Conwell Y. Mental health care need and service utilization in older adults living in public housing. *Am J Geriatr Psychiatry.* 2012;20(5):441–451.

104. Grabowski DC, Aschbrenner KA, Rome VF, Bartels SJ. Quality of mental health care for nursing home residents: A literature review. *Med Care Res Rev.* 2010;67(6):627–656.

105. Camp CJ, Cohen-Mansfield J, Capezuti EA. Use of nonpharmacologic interventions among nursing home residents with dementia. *Psychiatr Services.* 2002;53(11):1397.

106. Vernooij-Dassen M, Vasse E, Zuidemo S, England J, Moyle, W. Psychosocial interventions for dementia patients in long-term care. *Int Psychogeriatr.* 2010;22(7):1121– 1128.

107. Cassidy K, Kotynia-English R, Flicker L, Lautenschlager NT, Almeida OP. Association between lifestyle factors and mental health measures among community-dwelling older women. *Aust N Z J Psychiatry.* 2004;38(11–12):940–947.

108. Mackenzie CS, Gekoski WL, Knox VJ. Age, gender, and the underutilization of mental health services: The influence of help-seeking attitudes. *Aging & Mental Health.* 2006;10(6):574–582.

109. Girgus JS, Yang K, Ferri CV. The gender difference in depression: Are elderly women at greater risk for depression than elderly men? *Geriatrics (Basel).* 2017;2(4):35.

110. Kiely KM, Brady B, Byles J. Gender, mental health and ageing. *Maturitas.* 2019;129:76–84.

111. Brown GR, Jones KT. Mental health and mental health disparities in 5135 transgender veterans receiving healthcare in the Veterans Health Administration: A Case-Control study. *LGBT Health.* 2016;3(2):122–131.

112. National LGBT Health Education Center. Promoting the behavioral health of LGBT older adults. 2019. Available at: https://www.lgbthealtheducation.org/publication/promoting-the-behavioral-health-of-lgbtq-older-adults. Accessed February 21, 2021.

113. Hoy-Ellis CP, Ator M, Kerr C, Milford J. Innovative approaches address aging and mental health needs in LGBTQ communities. *Generations.* 2016;40(2):56–62.

114. Fuentes D, Aranda MP. Depression interventions among racial and ethnic minority older adults: A systematic review across 20 years. *Am J Geriatr Psychiatry.* 2012;20(11):915–931.

115. Cook BL, Hou SS-H, Lee-Tauler Y, Progovac AM, Samson F, Sanchez MJ. A review of mental health and mental health care disparities research: 2011–2014. *Med Care Res Rev.* 2018;76(6):683–710.

116. Alegría M, Alvarez K, Ishikawa RZ, DiMarzio K, McPeck S. Removing obstacles to eliminating racial and ethnic disparities in behavioral health care. *Health Aff (Millwood).* 2016; 35(6):991–999.

117. American Public Health Association. Removing barriers to mental health services for veterans. 2014 Available at: https://www.apha.org/policies-and-advocacy/public-health-policy-statements/policy-database/2015/01/28/14/51/removing-barriers-to-mental-health-services-for-veterans. Accessed February 21, 2021.

118. O'Malley KA, Vinson L, Kaiser AP, Sager Z, Hinrichs K. Mental health and aging veterans: How the Veterans Health Administration meets the needs of aging veterans. *Public Policy & Aging Report.* 2020:30(1):19–23.

119. Fazel PS, Hayes AJ, Bartellas K, Clerici M, Trestman R. The mental health of prisoners: a review of prevalence, adverse outcomes and interventions. *Lancet Psychiatr.* 2016;3(9):871–881.

120. Maschi T, Kaye A. Incarcerated older adults. Grantmakers in Aging. Available at: https://www.giaging.org/issues/incarcerated-older-adults. Accessed February 21, 2021.

121. Patel V, Burns JK, Dhingra M, Tarver L, Kohrt BA, Lund C. Income inequality and depression: a systematic review and meta-analysis of the association and a scoping review of mechanisms. *World Psychiatry.* 2018;17(1):76–89.

122. Khullar D, Chokshi DA. Health Policy Brief: Culture of health: Health, income, and poverty: Where we are and what could help. *Health Affairs.* 2018. Available at: https://www.healthaffairs.org/do/10.1377/hpb20180817.901935/full. Accessed February 21, 2021.

123. Herbert J. The scandal of inequality and its effect on mental health. Psychology Today. 2008. Available at: https://www.psychologytoday.com/us/blog/hormones-and-the- brain/201811/the-scandal-inequality-and-its-effect mental-health. Accessed February 21, 2021.

124. Lincoln KD. Economic Inequality in Later Life. *Generations.* 2018;42(2):6–12.

125. Mather M, Jacobsen LA, Pollard KM. Aging in the United States. *Popul Bull.* 2015;70(2):1–20.

126. Osborn R, Doty MM, Moulds D, Sarnak DO, Shah A. Older Americans were sicker and faced more financial barriers to health care than counterparts in other countries. *Health Aff (Millwood).* 2017;36(12):2123–2132.

127. Kamal R. What are the current costs and outcomes related to mental health and substance use disorders. Peterson-KFF: Health System Tracker. 2017. Available at: https://www.healthsystemtracker.org/chart-collection/current-costs-outcomes-related-mental-health-substance-abuse-disorders. Accessed February 21, 2021.

128. Papanicolas I, Woskie LR, Jha AK. Health care spending in the United States and other high-income countries. *JAMA.* 2018;319(10):1024–1039.

129. Papanicolas I, Woskie LR, Orlander D, Orav EJ, Jha AK. The relationship between health spending and social spending in high-income countries: How does the US compare? *Health Aff (Millwood).* 2019;38(9):1567–1575.

130. Bradley EH, Canavan M, Rogan E, et al. Variation in health outcomes: The role of spending on social services, public health, and health care, 2000–2009. *Health Aff (Millwood).* 2016;35(5):760–768.

131. Huang C-C. Unfinished Business From the 2017 Tax Law. Testimony before the House Ways and Means Subcommittee on select revenue measures. March 12, 2019. Available at: https://www.cbpp.org/federal-tax/unfinished-business-from-the-2017-tax-law. Accessed February 21, 2021.

132. Dey J, Rosenoff E, West K. Benefits of Medicaid expansion for behavioral health. Washington DC: US Department of Health and Human Services, Assistant Secretary for Planning and Evaluation; 2016.

133. Guth M, Garfield R, Rudowitz R. The effects of Medicaid expansion under the ACA: Updated findings of from a literature review. San Francisco, CA: Kaiser Family Foundation; 2020.

134. Maxwell J, Bourgoin A, Lindenfeld Z. Battling the mental health crisis among the underserved through state Medicaid reforms. February 10, 2020. Available at: https://www.healthaffairs.org/do/10.1377/hblog20200205.346125/full. Accessed February 21, 2021.

135. Solomon LS, Kanter MH. Health care steps up to social determinants of health: current context. *Perm J.* 2018;22:18–139.

136. Keith K. Supreme Court denies expedited review of Texas. *Health Affairs.* 2020. Available at: https://www.healthaffairs.org/do/10.1377/hblog20200121.699161/full. Accessed February 21, 2021.

137. Brady M. GOP states to swerve as Medicaid work requirements hit legal wall. Modern Health Care. November 2019. Available at: https://www.modernhealthcare.com/medicaid/gop-states-swerve-medicaid-work- requirements-hit-legal-wall. Accessed February 21, 2021.

138. Center on Budget and Policy Priorities. Taking away Medicaid for not meeting work requirements harms older Americans. March 2020. Available at: https://www.cbpp.org/research/health/taking-away-medicaid-for-not-meeting-work- requirements-harms-older-americans. Accessed February 21, 2021.

139. Ramesh T. Undermining Medicaid: How block grants would hurt beneficiaries. Center For American Progress. August 2019. Available at: https://www.americanprogress.org/issues/healthcare/reports/2019/08/07/472879/undermining-medicaid-block-grants-hurt-beneficiaries. Accessed February 21, 2021.

140. Taylor LA, Tan AX, Coyle CE, et al. Leveraging the social determinants of health: What works? *PLoS One.* 2016;11(8):e0160217.

II. NEIGHBORHOOD AND BUILT ENVIRONMENT

This section on neighborhood and the built environment addresses the impact that neighborhood and different types of built and living situations have on the health and social outcomes of older adults. Neighborhoods and the type of livable communities available to one as they grow older will play a major role in one's health, well-being, and functioning. This section addresses the issues which make up this social determinant of health: access to quality housing, transportation, neighborhoods, and availability of specific resources (e.g., healthy food, quality air, and water).

The built environment, the topic of the lead chapter in this section, influences all levels of the social determinants of health. As discussed in Chapter 6, the built environment influences not only older adults' perceptions of safety and walkability but also their access to healthy food and appropriate programming. The chapter also addresses how public health practitioners should work to inform their nonaging focused colleagues on how to ensure their programming is accessible to all.

Chapter 7 addresses housing options for people growing older, and articulates how the continuum of options will contribute to healthy aging. Housing strategies to promote health, and the various options associated are also discussed.

The section concludes with Chapter 8, on the World Health Organization's International Classification of Functioning, Disability, and Health (ICF). This framework serves to help classify both the condition (disease) and the environment (community) in relation to disability and health, and helps tie the entire section of this book segment together.

Built Environments for Healthy Aging: A Social Determinants Approach

Elizabeth G. Hunter, PhD, OTR/L and M. Aaron Guest, PhD, MPH, MSW

INTRODUCTION TO BUILT ENVIRONMENTS

Health starts in our homes, schools, workplaces, neighborhoods, and communities. Neighborhoods and the built environment are important components of the social determinants of health since they contribute to overall health outcomes. The context people grow up and age in strongly influence health and quality of life outcomes. The field of environmental gerontology, defined as "the description, explanation, and modification or optimization of the relation between the person and their environment"[1] seeks to further understand these relationships. This concept of environment entails access to social and economic opportunities, resources to support our homes, neighborhoods and schools, and our social interactions among other factors.[2]

In addition to the more material components of the term environment, the patterns of social engagement and sense of security and well-being are also affected by where people live.[3] Resources that enhance quality of life can have a significant influence on population health outcomes for all people, but particularly on people during the last few decades of their life. Within this chapter, the authors will discuss these resources and how they enhance the health outcomes of people growing older. Examples of these resources include the quality of housing, safety, availability of healthy foods, access to health services, and environments free of life-threatening toxins.[2]

Social determinant factors encompass social as well as physical environmental factors. Social factors include the availability of support for community living and opportunities for recreation and leisure activities. Transportation and public safety are also important social factors. Physical environmental factors include green space, buildings, sidewalks, roads, recreational settings, physical barriers, good lighting, trees, and benches. This is a very broad category, with important factors that influence health, safety, and quality of life. In this chapter we will describe many of these environmental determinants of health and provide examples to show the types of programs that currently exist. There are a number of important organizations working on issues related to environmental social determinants of health and older adults. The World Health Organization (WHO), the Centers for Disease Control and Prevention (CDC), and AARP provide useful information and interventions.

AGING IN PLACE

Critical to understanding the built environment in aging is the concept of "aging in place." Approximately 90% of adults age 65 or older want to age in place. The CDC defines aging in place as the "ability to live in one's own home and community safely, independently, and comfortably, regardless of age, income, or ability level."[3] In recent years, some scholars have opted to focus on "aging in community," with the recognition it is not the physical structure the individual lives in that matters but the supportive community and resources that allow individuals to live comfortably.[4] Policies that promote aging in place are based on the premise that there are social and financial benefits to programs that support the desire of older people, especially those who are frail, to live in their own homes and apartments located in familiar neighborhoods and communities.[5] These policies face a number of barriers, including inaccessible and unsupportive housing, which hinder aging in place, and pushing frail older people towards less desirable and more restrictive settings, such as nursing homes. The challenges for the future are to create policies that better link housing with services, modify existing housing to accommodate aging in place, create new types of housing based on principles of universal design, and provide a range of housing options in age-friendly or "livable" communities.[6]

NEIGHBORHOODS

Residential neighborhoods are an important space for older adults, as they spend more time in their neighborhoods than do employed younger adults. Neighborhoods are highly segregated by race and socioeconomic status, and neighborhood socioeconomic status is associated with mortality, disability, and self-assessed health. The conditions that are likely to affect older adults in lower income neighborhoods include determinants of health such as fewer grocery stores and alternatives to fast food. Low-income communities also have fewer and lower quality sources of medical care, higher crime rates, lower quality housing, and weaker social support networks.[7]

The neighborhood-health literature has long highlighted four categories of association among neighborhood and health outcomes: overall mortality,[8–10] chronic condition mortality or disease prevalence,[11–13] mental health outcomes,[14–16] and health behaviors (e.g., diet, physical activity).[17–20] Environmental determinants may be accentuated among older adults due to combinations of physical/mobility and mental decline associated with age, reduction in social networks and social support, and increased fragility.[20]

Neighborhood characteristics affect people of all ages, but older adults may be influenced more than other groups. As the aging population is growing in the United States, it is becoming more and more important to focus on older adults.[21] However, for the last seven decades, the dominant focus has been on meeting the perceived needs of families with children. This is illustrated through the predominant development of single-family detached homes, requiring automobiles to navigate, and are largely separated from commercial and industrial uses.[22] Due to this type of community planning, we are currently faced with longer and more costly commutes, social isolation, and dependency on automobiles for independence. All of these can be particularly negative influences on the community aging experience. The following are some specific environmental factors that can influence the experience of health and quality of life for older adults.

Environmental Health

In addition to neighborhood development, older adults are at significant risk related to exposure to negative environmental factors.[23] Many older adults live in older neighborhoods. It is quite common for them to spend decades in a particular neighborhood. Two critical points emerge from this. First, if their community has negative environmental conditions, they may have been exposed to them for long periods of time (e.g., mold or asbestos leading to respiratory problems). Long-term exposure to stress in disadvantaged neighborhoods may lead to "weathering," a cumulative biological impact of being chronically exposed to and having to cope with socially structured stressors.[24] This is a specific area where public health practitioners can play a role, especially environmental health officers. Second, neighborhoods can change over time. They age and this may result in old buildings, unsafe environments, and the loss of social and service supports. Neighborhoods can age around an older adult and the resident may not want or be able to move away from their neighborhood.

Social Isolation

We know that the built environment in which older adults live can influence health and is associated with weak social ties, problems accessing health care and other services, reduced physical activity, health problems, mobility limitations, and high stress. These factors directly influence health. Social connections are important for all human beings and older adults are at significant risk of having weak social connections. Social isolation is a social determinant of health, and negatively influences health in the same way as health behaviors such as smoking. In fact, it has been found that social isolation poses the same risk to one's health as smoking up to 15 cigarettes a day.[25] Social isolation, with or without loneliness, can have as large effect on mortality risk as smoking, obesity, sedentary lifestyle and high blood pressure.[26] Thus, these factors, dependent upon the social connections within neighborhoods plays a significant role on the health outcomes and well-being of an older adult.

Social isolation is expensive; an estimated $6.7 billion in annual federal spending is attributable to social isolation among older adults. Poor social relationships were associated with a 29% increase in risk of coronary heart disease and a 32% rise in the risk of stroke.[27] Authorities expect the financial and public health impact of loneliness to increase as the nation's population ages.[27,28] Living alone, being unmarried (i.e., single, divorced, or widowed), limited or no participation in social groups, fewer friends, and strained relationships are not only all risk factors for premature mortality but also for increased risk for loneliness.[28] Of course, as we age our networks begin to shrink.[29] Retirement can lead to a loss of social connections and early mortality, and post-retirement relocation can also reduce lifelong connections.[30] The past few decades we have created places that inhibit, or even prevent older adults from interacting with others as they age. This is influenced by a loss of mobility or poor home design.[22] Some neighborhood designs enable or encourage community connections, whereas others do not. Neighborhood designs most likely to promote social networks are those that are mixed use and pedestrian oriented, enabling residents to perform daily activities without the use of a car.[31] Finally, the availability of parks and civic spaces also increases the potential for social interaction.[32]

Transportation

Many older adults lack access to transportation. Nearly 600,000 older adults stop driving each year. Due to this, they can find their access to services such as stores and health care is reduced and may spend a higher proportion of their resources on transport.[33] They are likely to be especially vulnerable in areas where a private car is required.[34] Transportation is one of the most common supports provided by family caregivers. In fact, 80% of caregivers provide or arrange for rides for their loved ones.[35] Still, older adults who live a long distance from family or who need frequent rides (e.g., individuals receiving chemotherapy or renal dialysis) depend on more formal services to meet their needs. While the health impact of reduced access to needed medical services is obvious (i.e., missed appointments, emergency hospital visits, lack of continual care), social isolation due to lack of transportation can have an equally negative effect on health and mental health. Without accessible, reliable, and affordable transportation, many older adults could face the possibility of placement in a long-term care facility.[36]

While public transit is available to many older adults in urban environments, the same is not true for their suburban and rural counterparts. Providing mass transportation services is important, but auto-based travel and walking have emerged as the most realistic and preferred transportation options.[37] In these communities, programs such as dial-a-rides, volunteer transportation programs, and even ridesharing services such as Uber/Lyft have become primary modes of transportation for older adults. These programs are funded with a combination of governmental and personal funds. The Federal Transit Administration's Section 5310 Program and Title III B of the Older Americans Act are two federal funding sources that frequently support such programs.[36]

Access to Food

Neighborhoods can affect individuals' health by influencing the food that residents eat. Access to fruits, vegetables, and low-fat food results in lower risk of developing high blood pressure.[38] Alternatively, living in an unhealthy food environment, like a high density of fast food restaurants, is associated with increased risk of stroke and malnutrition. Older adults may also live in food deserts, that is, areas where access to healthy foods, fresh fruits, and vegetables are extremely limited. In these areas, there may be limited to no options to access healthy foods.[39] Barriers to transportation can prevent older adults from being able to leave food deserts to access healthier foods, leaving them dependent on others for their food, or dependent on unhealthy and expensive options.

Neighborhood Safety

A sense of safety is key for older adults to have healthy activity levels.[40] This is particularly true for older adults with disabilities. Research shows that interventions, such as those proposed in developing aging-friendly communities aimed at encouraging older adults with mobility limitations to be active within their neighborhood, may contribute to physical function.[41] However, these programs designed to increase physical activity must consider neighborhood safety concerns as barriers to participation.[40]

Accessibility

Accessibility has been defined as the complete use of a dwelling and immediate environment. Older adults are most likely to experience accessibility problems and these increase with age. Accessibility problems have been linked with low subjective well-being, poor perceived health, and poor psychological well-being.[42] The concept of design for life acknowledges the changing needs of building occupants throughout their lives and ensures that homes are accessible and adaptable for people with mobility problems, whether the accessibility limitations are temporary or permanent.[43]

Accessibility encompasses people with different levels of functional ability being able to access the built environments they need. This can pertain to their own homes. As one ages, functional changes can create new difficulties for people to negotiate their own personal environments. Some of these difficulties directly influence safety and injury. Common injuries include specifically falls that often result in hip fractures, along with other types of home injuries.[44,45]

In the past, studies related to older adult housing were focused on senior housing, nursing homes, and shared community living rather than private housing.[46,47] Today it is well known that the vast majority of older adults in the United States plan to age in place. They do not plan to move to supported or congregate living.

BEST PRACTICE INTERVENTIONS

Identifying age-appropriate services and resources for communities can be a challenge. Building codes, planned developments, and cultural and community expectations result in multiple types of environments for aging. By working to establish policies that positively influence social and economic conditions and those that support changes in individual behavior, we can improve health for large numbers of people in ways that can be sustained over time. Policies, such as the American with Disabilities Act of 1990, were passed to prohibit discrimination on the basis of ability and increase accessibility. It, along with the Architectural Barriers Act of 1968 and Fair Housing Act of 1968, which sought to prevent discrimination and increase accessibility in building design and prevent discrimination in land use, were powerful tools in increasing accessibility and livability of communities for older adults.

Age-Friendly Cities and Communities Framework

Improving the conditions in which we live, learn, work, and play, and the quality of our relationships, will create a healthier population, society, and workforce. To provide guidance to localities, the WHO has established the Age-Friendly City Framework to guide the development of appropriate environments for aging.[47] These guidelines assist local communities in developing policies and programs that improve the lives of individuals across the life span.

The Age-Friendly City Framework focuses on eight interrelated domains and example of possible community programing. These are the following:

- Community and health care
  - Example: Ensuring access to health care for all ages through community-based programming and services.
- Transportation
  - Example: Mass transit systems that encourage participation and use.
- Housing
  - Example: Accessibility of affordable housing.
- Social Participation
  - Example: Programs encourage the use of services by all ages.
- Outdoor Spaces and Buildings

- ○ Example: Outdoor spaces and buildings that encourage social participation and use by all ages.
- Respect and Social Inclusion
  - ○ Example: Development of intergenerational and community programming that promote inclusion.
- Civic Participation and Employment
  - ○ Example: Opportunities for all ages to be engaged in civic projects and the availability of jobs for all ages.
- Communication and Information
  - ○ Example: Targeted communication that is accessible in a variety of modalities.

In each of these domains, the WHO provides a checklist of activities, community programming, and policy opportunities to guide the development of age-friendly communities. Age-friendly environments are meant to be designed for all ages, not only focusing on older adulthood. In this sense, they apply the principles of universal design (i.e., the use of design principles to make things accessible to all people, regardless of ability level). Since 2017, the Age Friendly City Initiatives has expanded to include Age Friendly Cities, Communities, and States. In 2019, the WHO announced the launch of the Age-Friendly World Initiative, with the aim of making the Age-Friendly principles part of long-term planning.[48]

In the United States, AARP and the WHO have partnered to encourage American communities to better meet the needs of their older residents. AARP is the official sponsor of the Age-Friendly initiative in the United States and is responsible for promoting the Global Network of Age-Friendly Cities and Communities in the United States. As of 2021, six states (Colorado, Michigan, New York, Maine, Massachusetts, Florida), one territory (the US Virgin Islands), and 471 communities have joined the AARP Network of Age-Friendly States and Communities.

Age-Friendly communities are inclusive and considerate of the perspectives of all residents, of all ages, and all persuasions. They encourage and benefit from diverse citizen engagement by including residents in a process to identify the community needs, and develop and implement an action plan to address those needs.[48] Typical practices to evaluate and develop a livable environment for aging adults at the individual level include home adaptation, connecting people to needed social services, and education. At the community level, evaluation of available services, housing, walkability, and safety among others are common methods to assess the environment and target points for intervention. Important factors include expanding and professionalizing the caregiver workforce, improving transportation access and services, and making delivery reforms within Medicaid programs.

The Age-Friendly Cities effort, led by the WHO and embodied in a number of US initiatives, provides a series of policy-level analyses for how communities can provide a context that promotes healthy aging through policies across multiple sectors.[22,42] In the United States, this has been discussed as prioritizing "health in all policies." These efforts show how policymakers and others who shape the life spaces of older adults need to improve their health literacy to promote health equity for older adults.

Universal Design

Underlying the Age-Friendly initiatives are the principles of universal design. Environmental design has focused on a variety of ideas related to accessibility. Initially, the focus was on developing specific designs for specific people, resulting in isolating those with accessibility problems. The next step was to develop adaptable house design.[49,50] This allowed a house to be set up to be easily adapted should the homeowner need it. Today there is more of a focus for "design for all" as a tool for ensuring physical accessibility for aging homeowners.[46] This approach is much more holistic and is based out of the universal design school of thought. The idea is to design for the broadest segment of people possible. From the conception of a building plan, steps will be taken to include design factors that will enhance accessibility for as many people as possible.[51] This is an approach that needs to be systematically and consistently developed during the design process. Find the seven principles of universal design in Table 6-1.

Public health practitioners in aging often use the principles of universal design in their work without even realizing it. In these situations, universal design principles are used to ensure public health and aging programming is accessible to all individuals, regardless of demographic of social categories. Through naming the principles, public health and aging practitioners can be more attentive and purposeful in their use.

Table 6-1. Principles of Universal Design

Principles	Description
1. Equitable use	The design is useful and marketable to people with diverse abilities.
2. Flexibility in use	The design accommodates a wide range of individual preferences and abilities.
3. Simple and intuitive use	Use of the design is easy to understand, regardless of the user's experience, knowledge, language skills or current concentration level.
4. Perceptible information	The design communicates necessary information effectively to the user, regardless of ambient conditions or the user's sensory abilities.
5. Tolerance for error	The design minimizes hazards and the adverse consequences of accidental or unintended actions.
6. Low physical effort	The design can be used efficiently and comfortably and with a minimum of fatigue.
7. Size and space for approach and use	Appropriate size and space is provided for approach, reach, manipulation and use, regardless of the user's body size, posture, or mobility.

Source: Reprinted from Demirkan.[46]

Considerations for Practice and the Built Environment

Socioeconomic Status

A growing body of research shows that living in high poverty neighborhoods is associated with weak social ties, problems accessing health care and other services, reduced physical activity, health problems, mobility limitations, and high stress. Neighborhood economic status is often measured by median household income. For older adults living in neighborhoods with people living below the poverty line, there is a greater likelihood that they will have chronic health and mobility issues and die at younger ages compared with older adults living in more affluent neighborhoods.[52,53] The environment is closely related to factors such as income, location, and ability.

Rural

Older adults in rural communities will face dramatically different issues than those living in urban or suburban communities. Not only are there higher concentrations of older adult residents in rural areas than in urban areas, but rural, older adults are poorer, have more complex health conditions, and experience the impact of health-related social factors such as lack of housing, transportation, and food more acutely than their urban peers.[54] Rural adults are more likely to be older (>85), female, and White, compared with their urban counterparts. Finally, rural older adults are also less likely to use home- and community-based services and more likely to use nursing facility services.[55] These factors, combined with provider shortages in rural areas, make it difficult for older adults to remain in their homes and communities as they age.

Marginalized and Underrepresented Communities

It is well documented that marginalized communities experience some of the most adverse health outcomes as they age.[56] Black adults have lower life expectancies and higher health care cost than their White counterparts.[57] Gay men report higher rates of social isolation than their heterosexual peers.[58] Immigrant populations face greater barriers to access health care services. In part, these health outcomes are associated with the physical location the individual lives, works, and ages.[59,60] The adage that "one's zip codes tells more than one's genetic code" is perhaps even more true when looking at marginalized communities. Marginalized aging individuals often find themselves living in more resource poor and health poor environments than their counterparts. They have fewer opportunities overall to access health and community resources throughout their lives, and these opportunities only diminish as they age. The factors discussed throughout this chapter (e.g. transportation, nutrition, neighborhood safety) can pose even greater challenges to aging marginalized communities.

CONCLUSION: CHALLENGES AND OPPORTUNITIES FOR PUBLIC HEALTH

Public health practitioners have the opportunity to fulfill a vital role in the development of age-friendly communities. The variety of specialization within public health, from epidemiology to health promotion to health management, positions the field well to serve individuals across the life course. In older age, this includes the development of age-appropriate interventions, programs, and health promotion strategies that target the specific health needs of older populations. Through the WHO Age-Friendly Community Framework, public health professionals have the opportunity to intervene and develop more just built environments.

As the center of multiple local-community efforts, community public health departments can shape the adoption and delivery of age-friendly and livable community frameworks. Public health departments also have the capacity to encourage the development of programs and activities in line with the WHO Age-Friendly Community Initiative. In connection with the local Area Agencies on Aging, public health departments have the opportunity to develop truly novel community-based programming that can encourage healthy activity among our aging community. Those not in public health departments have the chance to apply Age-Friendly and Universal Design principles in their work and to extend the reach of age-friendly initiatives through bringing in unique collaborators from multiple sectors.

The built environment influences all levels of the social determinants of health. The fact is, there are built environments that are conducive to aging and there are those that are not. As discussed in this chapter, the built environments influence older adults' perceptions of safety and walkability, but also their access to healthy food and age-appropriate community programming. Public health practitioners who focus on aging should look to engage colleagues in diverse fields such as architecture, land developers, community planners, and local policymakers to encourage an approach to development grounded in healthy aging principles. They should also work to inform their non-aging-focused colleagues on how to ensure their programming is accessible to all.

CASE STUDY

Interventions to Increase Transportation Options for Individuals Using Age-Friendly and Universal Design Principles

As discussed earlier, transportation can be a major barrier for older adults. Policy developed interventions can also be used to increase access to transportation among older adults. Tennessee enacted legislation in 2015 to limit the liability of volunteer drivers who provide rides for older residents through a charitable organization or human services organization. The state's Commission on Aging and Disability worked to facilitate the formation of these programs, which offer rides to medical appointments as well as for other purposes, such as going to grocery stores. Among these programs are MyRide TN, which is sponsored by the Tennessee Commission on Aging and Disability and serves multiple counties in the state, including eight rural counties. The volunteer programs leverage the legislation when recruiting volunteer drivers. They also leverage Older Americans Act funding. In addition, riders, who must be at least 60 years of age, pay a small fee for rides. According to state officials, 40% of the trips provided by the volunteer services are for doctor visits.[61]

A solution for transportation problems is to modify the built environment. One common example of modifying the built environment is making communities more walkable. The Complete Streets Initiative[62] encourages transportation planners to consider road users of all modes, ages, and abilities. Another opportunity for improving the built environment is to have "senior-friendly" transportation services that are available, accessible, acceptable, affordable, and adaptable.[63]

Other programs that exist to help address the gap in transportation for older adults are things like the Fixing America's Surface Transportation Act (FAST Act),[64] which authorized funding from 2016–2020 to address transportation infrastructure planning and investment. This involved block grants to develop trails and pedestrian and bicycle facilities, along with metropolitan planning for public transportation, and statewide and nonmetropolitan planning for public transportation.

REFERENCES

1. Wahl HW, Weisman GD. Environmental gerontology at the beginning of the new millennium. Reflections on its historical, empirical, and theoretical development. *Gerontologist.* 2003;43(5):616–627.

2. US Department of Health and Human Services. Healthy People 2030. Office of Disease Prevention and Health Promotion. 2020. Available at: https://health.gov/healthypeople/objectives-and-data/social-determinants-health. Accessed October 20, 2020.

3. Centers for Disease Control and Prevention. Healthy Places Terminology. 2009. Available at: https://www.cdc.gov/healthyplaces/terminology.htm. Accessed February 22, 2021.

4. Golant SM. *Aging in the Right Place.* Baltimore, MD: Health Professions Press; 2015.

5. Scharlach A, Diaz-Moore K. Aging-In-Place. In: Bengston VL, Settersten RA, eds. *Handbook of Theories of Aging.* 3rd ed. New York, NY: Springer Publishing; 2016:407–425.

6. Ahn M, Kang J, Kwon HJ. The concept of aging in place as intention. *Gerontologist.* 2019;60(1):50–59.

7. Valtorta NK, Moore DC, Barron L, Stow D, Hanratty B. Older adults' social relationships and health care utilization: A systematic review. *Am J Public Health.* 2018;108(4):e1–e10.

8. Yen IH, Kaplan GA. Neighborhood social environment and risk of death: multilevel evidence from the Alameda County Study. *Am J Epidemiol.* 2009;149(10):898–907.

9. Borrell LN, Diez Roux AV, Rose K, Catellier D, Clark BL. Neighbourhood characteristics and mortality in the Atherosclerosis Risk in Communities Study. *Int J Epidemiol.* 2004;3(2):398–407.

10. Winkleby MA, Cubbin C. Influence of individual and neighbourhood socioeconomic status on mortality among black, Mexican-American, and white women and men in the United States. *J Epidemiology Community Health.* 2003;57(6):444–452.

11. Reijneveld SA. Neighbourhood socioeconomic context and self reported health and smoking: a secondary analysis of data on seven cities. *J Epidemiology Community Health.* 2002; 56(12):935–942.

12. Sundquist K, Winkleby M, Ahlen H, Johansson SE. Neighborhood socioeconomic environment and incidence of coronary heart disease: a follow-up study of 25,319 women and men in Sweden. *Am J Epidemiol.* 2004;159(7):655–662.

13. Cubbin C, Winkleby MA. Protective and harmful effects of neighborhood-level deprivation on individual-level health knowledge, behavior changes, and risk of coronary heart disease. *Am J Epidemiol.* 2005;162(6):1–10.

14. Lofors J, Sundquist K. Low-linking social capital as a predictor of mental disorders: A cohort study of 4.5 million Swedes. *Soc Sci Med.* 2007;64(1):21–34.

15. Galea S, Ahern J, Nandi A, Tracy M, Beard J, Vlahov D. Urban neighborhood poverty and the incidence of depression in a population-based cohort study. *Ann Epidemiol.* 2007;17(3):171–179.

16. Truong KD, Ma S. A systematic review of relations between neighborhoods and mental health. *J Ment Health Policy Econ.* 2006;9(3):137–154.

17. Papas MA, Alberg AJ, Ewing R, Helzlsouer KJ, Gary TL, Klassen AC. The built environment and obesity. *Epidemiol Rev.* 2007;29:129–143.

18. Saelens BE, Handy SL. Built environment correlates of walking: a review. *Med Sci Sports Exerc.* 2008;40(suppl 7):S550–S566.

19. Sallis JF, Glanz K. Physical activity and food environments: solutions to the obesity epidemic. *Milbank Quarterly.* 2009;87(1):123–154.

20. Shaw BA, Krause N, Liang J, Bennett J. Tracking changes in social relations throughout late life. *J Gerontol B Psychol Sci Soc Sci.* 2007;62(2):S90–S99.

21. Ortman J, Velkoff V, Hogan H. *An Aging Nation: The Older Population in the United States.* Washington, DC: US Census Bureau; 2014:28.

22. Arigoni, D. Preparing for an Aging Population. 2018. AARP. Available at: https://www.aarp.org/livable-communities/about/info-2018/aarp-livable-communities-preparing-for-an-aging-nation.html. Accessed February 22, 2021.

23. Kim M, Clarke P. Urban social and built environments and trajectories of decline in social engagement in vulnerable elders: findings from Detroit's Medicaid home and community-based waiver population. *Res Aging*. 2015;37(4):413–435.

24. Geronimus AT, Pearson JA, Linnenbringer E, et al. Race/ethnicity, poverty, urban stressors and telomere length in a Detroit community-based sample. *J Health Soc Behav*. 2015;56(2):199–224.

25. Health Resources and Services Administration. The "Loneliness Epidemic". 2019. Available at: https://www.hrsa.gov/enews/past-issues/2019/january-17/loneliness-epidemic. Accessed February 22, 2021.

26. Cacioppo JT, Hawkley LC, Norman GJ, Berntson GG. Social isolation. *Ann NY Acad Sci*. 2011;123(11):17–22

27 Holt-Lunstad J, Robles TF, Sbarra DA. Advancing social connection as a public health priority in the United States. *The American Psychologist*. 2017; 72(6): 517–530.

28. Holt-Lunstad J, Smith TB, Layton JB. Social relationships and mortality risk: A meta-analytic review. *PLoS Medicine*. 2010;7(7):e1000316.

29. Carstensen, L. Social and emotional patterns in adulthood: Support for socioemotional selectivity theory. *Psychol Aging*. 1992;7(3):331–338.

30. Kemperman A, van den Berg P, Weijs-Perrée M, Uijtdewillegen K. Loneliness of older adults: Social network and the living environment. *Int J Environ Res Public Health*. 2019;16(3):406.

31. Leyden KM. Social capital and the built environment: The importance of walkable neighborhoods. *Am J Public Health*. 2003;93(9):1546–1551.

32. de Vries S, Verheij RA, Groenewegen PP, Spreeuwenberg P. Natural environments—healthy environments? An exploratory analysis of the relationship between greenspace and health. *Environ Plan A*. 2003;35(10):1717–1731.

33. Acheson D. *Independent Inquiry into Inequalities and Health Report*. London, England: London Stationary Office; 1998.

34. Bascom GW, Christensen KM. The impacts of limited transportation access on persons with disabilities' social participation. *J Transp Health*. 2017;7(B):227–234.

35. National Alliance for Caregiving. Caregiving in the US. 2020. Available at: https://www.caregiving.org/caregiving-in-the-us-2020. Accessed February 22, 2021.

36. National Aging and Disability Transportation Center. Unique issues related to older adults and transportation. Available at: https://www.nadtc.org/about/transportation-aging-disability/unique-issues-related-to-older-adults-and-transportation. Accessed February 22, 2021.

37. Rosenbloom S. The travel and mobility needs of older persons now and in the future. In D'Ambrosio L, Coughlin JF, eds. *Aging in America and Transportation: Personal Choices and Public Policy.* New York, NY: Springer Publishing; 2012:39–54.

38. Kaiser P, Diez Roux AV, Mujahid M, et al. Neighborhood environments and incident hypertension in the multi-ethnic study of atherosclerosis. *Am J Epidemiol.* 2016;183(11):988–97

39. Larsen K, Gilliland J. A farmers' market in a food desert: Evaluating impacts on the price and availability of healthy food. *Health Place.* 2009;15(4):1158–1162.

40. Tucker-Seeley RD, Subramanian SV, Li Y, Sorensen G. Neighborhood safety, socioeconomic status, and physical activity in older adults. *Am J Prev Med.* 2009; 37(3):207–213.

41. Latham K, Clarke P. The role of neighborhood safety in recovery from mobility limitations: Findings from a national sample of older Americans (1996–2008). *Res Aging.* 2013;35(4): 481–502

42. World Health Organization, Europe. The Fourth Ministerial Conference on Environment and Health. Budapest, Hungary. 2004. Available at: https://www.euro.who.int/__data/assets/ pdf_file/0005/88214/RC54_edoc10.pdf?ua=1#:~:text=The%20Fourth%20Ministerial%20 Conference%20on%20Environment%20and%20Health%20took%20place,broader%20 context%20of%20sustainable%20development.&text=It%20was%20also%20agreed% 20to,and%20Health%20Committee%20(EEHC). Accessed February 22, 2021.

43. Lavin T, Higgins C, Metcalfe O, Jordan A. *Health Impacts of the Built Environment: A Review.* Institute of Public Health in Ireland. 2006.

44. Camilloni L, Farchi S, Rossi PG, et al. A case-control study on risk factors of domestic accidents in an elderly population. *Int J Inj Contr Saf Promot.* 2011;18(4):269–276.

45. Chan WC, Law J, Seliske P. Bayesian spatial methods for small area injury analysis: a study of geographical variation of falls in older people in the Wellington-Dufferin-Guelph health region of Ontario, Canada. *Inj Prev.* 2012;18(5):303–308.

46. Demirkan H. Housing for the aging population. *Eur Rev Aging Phys Act.* 2007;4:33–38.

47. Beard JR, Montawi B. Age and the environment: The global movement towards age-friendly cities and communities. *J Soc Work Pract.* 2015;29(1):5–11.

48. Garner IW, Holland CA. Age-friendliness of living environments from the older person's viewpoint: development of the Age-Friendly Environment Assessment Tool. *Age Ageing.* 2019;49(2):193–198.

49. Peloquin A. *Barrier-free Residential Environments.* New York, NY: McGraw-Hill, New York; 2002.

50. Scheidt RJ, Windley PG. Environmental gerontology: Progress in the post-Lawton era. In: Birren J, Schale KW, eds. *Handbook of the Psychology of Aging.* 6th edition. Amsterdam, The Netherlands: Elsevier; 2006:105–125.

51. Steinfeld E, Maisel J. *Universal design: Creating Inclusive Environments*. Hoboken, NJ: John Wiley and Sons; 2012.

52. Freedman V, Grafova I, Rogowski J. Neighborhoods and chronic disease onset in later life. *Am J of Public Health*. 2011;101(1):79–86.

53. Freedman V, Grafova IB, Schoeni RF, Rogowski J. Neighborhoods and disability in later life. *Soc Sci Med*. 2008;66(11):2253–2267.

54. Pew Research Center. Shrinking share of Americans in rural communities, 2018. Pew Research Center's Social & Demographic Trends Project. Available at: https://www.pewresearch.org/social-trends/2018/05/22/demographic-and-economic-trends-in-urban-suburban-and-rural-communities/psd_05-22-18_community-type-01-00. Accessed February 22, 2021.

55. Coburn AF, Griffin E, Thayer D, Croll Z, Ziller EC. Are Rural Older Adults Benefiting from Increased State Spending on Medicaid Home and Community Based Services? 2016. Maine Rural Health Research Center. Available at: http://muskie.usm.maine.edu/Publications/rural/Medicaid-Home-Community-Based-Services-Rural.pdf. Accessed February 22, 2021.

56. Ferraro KF, Shippee TP. Aging and cumulative inequality: how does inequality get under the skin? *Gerontologist*. 2019;49(3):333–343.

57. Menkin JA, Guan SA, Araiza D, et al. Racial/ethnic differences in expectations regarding aging among older adults. *Gerontologist*. 2017;57(suppl 2):S138–S148.

58. Fredriksen-Goldsen, K. I. Dismantling the silence: LGBTQ aging emerging from the margins. *Gerontologis*. 2017;57(1):121–128.

59. Margolis R, Verdery AM. Older adults without close kin in the United States. *J Gerontol B Psychol Sci Soc Sci*. 2017;72(4):688–693.

60. Salma J, Salami B. "We are like any other people, but we don't cry much because nobody listens": The need to strengthen aging policies and service provision for minorities in Canada. *Gerontologist*. 2020;60(2):279–290.

61. Cothron A. The Tennessee Commission on Aging and Disability transportation for older adults. Tennessee Public Health Association Newsletter. 2018. Available at: https://tnpublichealth.org/docs/tpha-march-2018-newsletter.pdf. Accessed March 19, 2021.

62. Lynott J, Haase J, Nelson K, et al. Planning complete streets for an aging America. Washington, DC: AARP Public Policy Institute; 2009.

63. Kerschner H. Transportation transitions and older adults. *Top Geriatr Rehabil*. 2009;25(2):173–178.

64. Fixing America's Surface Transportation Act, 23 USC §101 note (2015).

Housing

M. Aaron Guest, PhD, MPH, MSW and Elaine T. Jurkowski, PhD, MSW

Shelter is one of the most basic human needs. Appropriate shelter allows for individuals to grow and adapt while inappropriate shelter can lead to poorer health outcomes. The importance of shelter, or housing, across the life course cannot be understated. Poor housing can lead to a host of adverse health outcomes.[1-4] The same, of course, is also true in older age. Housing is a critical downstream social determinant of health that can have multiple upstream outcomes for individuals.[5-8] Yet, while a basic need, housing is not one-size fits all. Misconceptions of housing for older populations abound. This chapter aims to address some of those misconceptions around housing for older adults. The importance of an appropriate environment for aging has been discussed elsewhere in this book (Chapter 6) as have programs, considerations, and policies for older adults aging in community (Chapters 8, and 18, respectively). Rather than repeat these here, this chapter describes the housing continuum available to individuals as they age and the most important aspects for public health practitioners.

WHERE DO OLDER ADULTS LIVE?

It is wrongly assumed the majority of older adults live in some type of nursing care facility. In fact, only 4.5% of older adults live in nursing homes. A further 2% live in assisted living facilities. The vast majority of older adults (93.5%) are community dwelling. Overall, the number of older adults in institutionalized care has declined over the last twenty years while the number of older adults living in the community has increased. At the same time, the percentage of Medicare recipients classified as nondisabled has risen, meaning more older adults are entering older age in better health.[9,10]

The results are that more older adults are living in the community they aged in, but in new ways. One such way has been the growth of cohabitation among individuals aged 50 and over. Since 2007, there has been a 75% increase in cohabitation among unmarried individuals age 50 and over.[11] Multigenerational vertical, or beanpole, households have also become more common, rising from 14% in 1990 to 20% in 2016. These multigenerational housing units generally consist of at least three generations, including older adults, living together.[12] Even so, in the United States, older adults are far more likely to live alone than anywhere else in the world. In the United States, roughly 27% of individuals over age 60 live alone.[13] The needs of these populations are covered in more detail in Chapter 10. Furthermore, less than 10% of homes in the United States are considered to be aging-ready.[14] This means the vast majority of the homes in the United States are not conducive to a healthy aging experience. It is in these environments that adverse events may occur that result in individuals moving to other housing options.

THE HOUSING CONTINUUM

The housing continuum describes the variety of environmental living options available to individuals throughout the life course. The housing continuum is primarily organized around the functional status of the individual and their ability to self-manage. The housing continuum moves from the least restrictive (i.e., living in one's own home) to most restrictive (i.e., living in a medical environment).[15] This mirrors the level of dependence of the individual, from independent to completely dependent as well as the overall cost of the type of housing option.[16]

Below we describe several of the options along the housing continuum, highlighting the ones most commonly available to older adults. The exact availability, type, and cost will vary from state to state. The funding source for payment ranges from self-pay to Medicare. While Medicaid is the largest payer of nursing home care, it does not cover many of the other options discussed in the next section, leaving the responsibility to the individual, their family, or other insurance options.

Overview of Housing Continuum Options

To the novice, the myriad of options within the long-term care and housing sectors for older adults can be daunting. Trying to identify which is the best option can be a challenge without an understanding of what the options are or how they are designed to meet the needs of people growing older. As illustrated in Figure 7-1, the more independent an

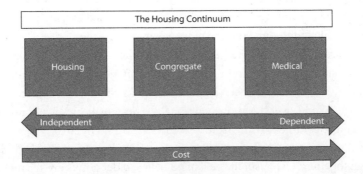

Figure 7–1. The Housing Continuum

older adult is, the less the cost, while the more dependent an older adult is, the more medical care is needed and the cost increases. This section will identify these options and articulate some of the key features of each model.

Independent Living and Living In One's Own Home

In this framework, people remain living within either the community they raised their family in, or a community which meets their needs for home maintenance and care. Within this framework, usually the older adult resident does not need additional supports to live independently.

Age-Segregated Communities (55+)

Senior apartments or 55+ housing can either be apartment based or a condominium community designed for residents over the age of 55. Within this framework, one can also find service coordinators on staff to help care for needs of the residents, activities, and some services to minimize the amount of work required by the older adult.

Assisted Living

Assisted living facilities are congregate care settings where there are individual apartment units equipped with appliances in order to prepare light meals and a congregate dining area where at least one main meal is served daily. Residents have the opportunity to be as independent as possible, or to take advantage of activities held in house. Residents must be independent and able in most cases to take care of their own medications and activities of independent living (e.g., shopping, transportation, financial, laundry, and personal care).

Rehabilitation and Short-Term Care

Rehabilitation and short-term care is offered through facilities to people who need some post-acute care to meet their medical and rehabilitation needs. At the outset, people generally are given a specific time period for which they undergo an assessment to determine that their rehabilitation needs can be met by the facility/program. People who may have experienced strokes or medical interventions, such as knee or hip replacements, may be examples of the type of conditions which would take advantage of this type of housing option as they prepare to transition back to their home.

Pioneer Facilities

A residential facility for older adults and people with disabilities is termed "a pioneer facility" when they follow principles established by the National Pioneer Coalition movement. The Pioneer movement is based upon principles defined by Dr. Bill Miller, Founder of the Eden Alternative movement. Facilities are designed with the principles of "least restrictive environment," "person first," and maximizing personal choice for the resident. These homes take into consideration who the resident is and what personal preferences have been a part of their culture and lifestyle.[17]

Skilled Nursing Facility

A long-term care facility provides nursing and medical care to the extent needed to residents. Generally, people living in this level of care provided cannot handle their Instrumental Activities of Daily Living and need help with feeding, bathing, dressing, grooming, toileting, and transferring (i.e., Activities of Daily Living).[18] (See Table 7-1.)

SPECIALIZED POPULATIONS

As we have discussed throughout the chapter, housing is a basic need. The type of housing and the associated supportive services vary with age and level of need. Inequalities exist in who is able to access these services. Cost is a major decision driver for movement along the housing continuum. Economic barriers prevent individuals from always accessing the most appropriate level of housing and delivery of care they may need. In these situations, families, communities, and public health practitioners may be required to step in to ensure appropriate levels of care. Some populations face additional challenges in accessing the appropriate level of housing and care. We discuss a few of these in the following sections.

Table 7-1. Need for Help With Activities of Daily Living Within Care Facilities

Year	Gender	No ADLs	1–3 ADLs	4–6 ADLs
1985	Male	8.8	28.8	62.5
	Female	3.8	25.3	70.9
1995	Male	3.0	25	72
	Female	3.8	25.3	70.9
1997	Male	5.0	25.7	74.4
	Female	1.8	20.4	77.8
1999	Male	5.0	20.7	74.3
	Female	2.4	19.6	78.0
2013	Male	9.0	18.4	76.6
	Female	13.9	21.3	79.0

Source: Adapted from the National Nursing Home Survey.[19]

Note: Numbers represent percentages. The six activities of daily living (ADLs) included are bathing, dressing, eating, toileting, and transferring in and out of bed or chairs. Requiring assistance refers to assistance from nursing home facility staff. Help received from family members or friends is not included. Data refer to individuals living in long-term care facilities, rather than personal care, foster care, or domiciliary care homes.

Aging Unhoused Populations

There is an increasing number of unhoused older adults over the age of 65.[20] Many of these individuals have experienced precarious housing situations throughout their lives, leading to an increase in certain chronic health conditions. As they age, they are faced with increasing medical and health needs in order to ensure a healthy aging experience.[21,22] Many of the homeless shelters and supportive services are unprepared to deal with older homeless individuals, resulting in difficulty for these individuals to access resources or to locate appropriate care. They are often unlikely to be able to afford many of the medical and supportive options along the housing continuum. Public health must continue to advocate for an end to the housing crisis through the development of novel solutions, while also developing programs that assist the aging unhoused population.

Aging LGBTQ Populations

Research has shown that many lesbian, gay, bisexual, transgendered, and queer (LGBTQ) older adults are fearful of entering assisted living and nursing home environments.[23–25] There is a predominant, and well-founded, fear that in these environments they will be forced back into the closet, will not have access to activities that match their interest, or that they will be ostracized from the community due to their sexual identity.[26,27] In many instances, staff at these facilities are unaware of the specific needs of aging LGBTQ populations.[28] They have not been trained or informed, and they may not even think about these populations in their daily work. In response to this housing crisis, there have been developments of competencies and trainings to support nursing home and assisted living staff in creating supportive and affirming LGBTQ environments for older adults in these medical settings.[29] Furthermore, over the last decade there has been an increase in LGBTQ-oriented senior housing, assisted living, and nursing home facilities.[30,31] These housing options are developed with LGBTQ populations in mind and work to cater to their needs. As public health practitioners, we must continue to advocate for all of our aging populations and encourage continuing education on emerging topics.

Aging Rural Populations

Individuals want to age in their community. They want to age around those they know and in geographic environments they are familiar with.[32] For older adults in rural environments, this can be problematic. Often, there is a lack of housing options, particularly towards the end of the housing continuum.[33] While rural older adults may self-report that they want to age in their community, and plan to do so, the reality is often much different.[34] The lack of housing infrastructure results in individuals being required to leave their communities to seek care and access supportive housing services. For these individuals, public health must work to not only identify realistic goals and services that can allow people to age in appropriate communities, but also to identify necessary transition assistance if that is not possible.

CONCLUSION: CHALLENGES AND OPPORTUNITIES FOR PUBLIC HEALTH

Housing is one of the basic needs for everyone, regardless of age, but becomes even more important as one grows older. Increasingly, we are finding that people growing older are more apt to be consumer conscious. They are challenging traditional models of institutional care so that they can "age in place" with as few restrictions as possible, and with as much independence as possible. The independent living paradigm[35] was a philosophy that helped people with disabilities be functional within environments with as few restrictions as possible, and has now impacted the housing market and housing initiatives for older adults. The concepts of "aging in place" and "within the least restrictive environment" will remain important, and likely gain momentum in the future.

Another alternative to home health care, which transfers the power of hire/fire to the person as opposed to an agency, is a strategy for older adults to have their preferences respected. They are able to maintain control over those coming to provide home health services or personal services that enable them to remain living in their home. This approach to consumer control will also remain important as time moves forward.

Alternative models of care and living models, which tend to be licensed and regulated/ overseen by public health authorities, will pose challenges in the future to this regulatory process. Most regulations have been developed and based upon a medical model of institutional care. Models such as the "Pioneer Coalitions" and the "Least Restrictive Environment" attempt to integrate culture and personal preferences into place, while housing options such as assisted living, skilled nursing care, and long-term care nursing facilities tend to follow regulations inspired by the hospital and medical care system. These different models will find public health at the center, trying to reconcile how to maintain regulatory standards for both.

Specialized populations will also pose a challenge for public health in the future because there will be an increased demand for housing options and communities to meet the needs of these specialized groups. In addition to the groups discussed within this chapter, housing for grandparents raising grandchildren will be an issue for public health to consider, as well as people with histories of incarceration. Currently, neither group can take advantage of licensed housing options due to regulatory conditions in most states.

Housing and quality housing will remain an important need which public health will need to assure is met. We know that housing is a critical factor as one of the social determinants of health, the built environment and community context, and plays a role in health outcomes for older adults. Public health advocacy for safe, affordable options will be necessary as we strive to ensure equity, and safe, healthy housing options for people growing older.

CASE STUDY

Louise

Louise is a 96-year-old woman who has survived the Holocaust and currently lives in Fort Myers, Florida. Louise moved into an assisted living facility two years ago when she lost her driving privileges and had been reported to be falling within her home. Louise manages her own breakfast within her suite but receives soup/sandwich items for lunch and a hot dinner from the facility. She manages her own laundry within her suite. A facility van helps out by providing transportation to a local shopping mall for groceries and sundries.

Louise recently tripped on a carpet when entering her apartment within the assisted living facility. She was hospitalized and sustained a broken arm, a broken leg, and badly bruised herself. She was not using a cane or walker, and had assessments with physical and occupational therapy during her hospitalization. Due to the assessments, it was decided that she should enter a facility designated to provide rehabilitation care and assist her to be able to regain balance and walk safely. Although Louise prided herself in being able to get around without a cane, she accepted that, at her age, she should be utilizing a tripod cane once her breaks healed. In the meantime, she should take advantage of a walker when able to bear weight. Additionally, she was not able to take care of many of her personal care needs because of her broken arm and inability to bear weight on her broken leg in the short-term.

When Louise was getting ready to move from the hospital to the rehabilitation care setting, a case conference was held and Louise's daughter and son attended. They voiced concerns about their mother potentially continuing to fall and requested that she move directly into a nursing home setting where her activities could be more closely monitored. Louise protested and was indignant, insisting that she should be able to eventually return to her home at the assisted living facility, resuming her activities including her bridge club, movie, and book clubs.

REFERENCES

1   McCartney G, Hearty W, Arnot J, Popham F, Cumbers A, McMaster R. Impact of Political economy on population health: A systematic review of reviews. *Am J Pub Health.* 2019;109(6):e1–e12.

2. Scheibl F, Farquhar M, Buck J, et al. When frail older people relocate in very old age, who makes the decision? *Innov Aging.* 2019;3(4).

3. Ahn M, Kang J, Kwon HJ. The concept of aging in place as intention. *Gerontologist.* 2019;60(1): 50–59.

4. Gobbens RJJ, van Assen M. Associations of environmental factors with quality of life in older adults. *Gerontologist.* 2018;58(1):101–110.

5. Pynoos J. Housing for older adults: A personal journey in environmental gerontology. *Annu Rev Gerontol Geriatr.* 2018;38(1):147–164.

6. Iwarsson S. From occupational therapy to environmental gerontology. *Annu Rev Gerontol Geriatr.* 2018;38(1):109–130.

7. Stephens C, Szabó Á, Allen J, Alpass F. Livable environments and the quality of life of older people: An ecological perspective. *Gerontologist.* 2018;59(4):675–685.

8. Ferraro KF, Shippee TP. Aging and cumulative inequality: how does inequality get under the skin? *Gerontologist.* 2009;49(3):333–343.

9. Harris-Kojetin L SM, Lendon JP, Rome V, Valverde R, Caffrey C. Long-term care providers and services users in the United States, 2015–2016. National Center for Health Statistics. *Vit Health Stat.* 2019;3(43).

10. Federal Interagency Forum on Aging-Related Statistics. *Older Americans 2016: Key Indicators of Wellbeing.* Washington, DC: US Government Printing Office; 2016.

11. Gibson WE. Far More 50+ Couples Shacking Up. AARP. 2017. Available at: https://www.aarp.org/home-family/friends-family/info-2017/older-couples-cohabitation.html#:~:text=%E2%80%9CIn%202016%2C%204%20million%20adults,2016%2C%20up%20from%207.2%20million. Accessed February 23, 2021.

12. Cohn D, Passel J. A record 64 million Americans live in multigenerational households. Pew Research Center. 2018. Available at: https://www.pewresearch.org/fact-tank/2018/04/05/a-record-64-million-americans-live-in-multigenerational-households. Accessed February 23, 2021.

13. Ausubel J. Older people are more likely to live alone in the US than elsewhere in the world. Pew Research Center. 2020. Available at: https://www.pewresearch.org/fact-tank/2020/03/10/older-people-are-more-likely-to-live-alone-in-the-u-s-than-elsewhere-in-the-world. Accessed February 23, 2021.

14. Vespa J, Engelberg J, He W. *Old Housing, New Needs: Are US Homes Ready for an Aging Population? Current Population Reports.* US Census Bureau. Washington, DC: US Government Printing Office; 2020.

15. Rowles GD. Housing for Older Adults. In: Devlin AS, ed. *Environmental Psychology and Human Well-Being.* Amsterdam, The Netherlands: Elsevier: 2018:77–106.

16. Wiles JL, Leibing A, Guberman N, Reeve J, Allen RE. The meaning of "aging in place" to older people. *Gerontologist.* 2012;52(3):357–366.

17. Jurkowski ET. *Changing the Culture of Long Term Care: Strategies and Benchmarks.* New York, NY: Springer Publishing; 2013.

18. Jurkowski ET. Housing and Long-Term Care. In: Jurkwoski ET, ed. *Policy and Program Planning for Older Adults and People With Disabilities.* 2nd Edition. New York, NY: Springer Publishing; 2018:257–272.

19. Centers for Disease Control and Prevention. National Center for Health Statistics. National Nursing Home Survey. 2015. Available at: https://www.cdc.gov/nchs/nnhs/index.htm. Accessed May, 28, 2021.

20. Grenier A, Barken R, Sussman T, Rothwell D, Bourgeois-Guerin V, Lavoie JP. A Literature Review of Homelessness and Aging: Suggestions for a policy and practice-relevant research agenda. *Can J Aging*. 2016;35(1):28–41.

21. Kaplan-Weisman L, Tam J, Crump C. Utilization of advance care planning for homeless adults: Case studies. *J Urban Health*. 2019;96(5):726–733.

22. Watkins JF, Hosier A. Conceptualizing Home and Homelessness: A Life Course Perspective. In: Rowles GD, Chaundhry H, eds. *Home and Identity in Late Life International Perspectives*. New York: Springer Publishing; 2005:197–215.

23. Daley A, MacDonnell JA, Brotman S, St Pierre M, Aronson J, Gillis L. Providing health and social services to older LGBT adults. *Annu Rev Gerontol Geriatr*. 2017;37:143–160.

24. Hiedemann B, Brodoff L. Increased risks of needing long-term care among older adults living with same-sex partners. *Am J Public Health*. 2013;103(8):e27–33.

25. Stein GL, Beckerman NL, Sherman PA. Lesbian and gay elders and long-term care: identifying the unique psychosocial perspectives and challenges. *J Gerontol Soc Work*. 2010;53(5):421–435.

26. Porter KE, Brennan-Ing M, Chang SC, et al. Providing competent and affirming services for transgender and gender nonconforming older adults. *Clin Gerontol*. 2016;39(5):1–24.

27. Dentato MP, Craig SL, Lloyd MR, Kelly BL, Wright C, Austin A. Homophobia within schools of social work: the critical need for affirming classroom settings and effective preparation for service with the LGBTQ community. *Soc Work Educ*. 2016;35(6):672–692.

28. Portz JD, Retrum JH, Wright LA, et al. Assessing capacity for providing culturally competent services to LGBT older adults. *J Gerontol Soc Work*. 2014;57(2–4):305–321.

29. Fredriksen-Goldsen KI, Hoy-Ellis CP, Goldsen J, Emlet CA, Hooyman NR. Creating a vision for the future: key competencies and strategies for culturally competent practice with lesbian, gay, bisexual, and transgender (LGBT) older adults in the health and human services. *J Gerontol Soc Work*. 2014;57(2–4):80–107.

30. King A, Stoneman P. Understanding SAFE Housing – putting older LGBT people's concerns, preferences and experiences of housing in England in a sociological context. *Hous Care Support*. 2017;20(3):89–99.

31. Larson B. Intentionally Designed for Success: Chicago's first LGBT-friendly senior housing. *Generations*. 2016;40(2):106–107.

32. Golant SM. *Aging in the Right Place*. Baltimore, MD: Health Professions Press; 2015.

33. Skemp LE, Maas ML, Umbarger-Mackey M. Doing it my way. *Gerontologist*. 2014;54(4):693–703.

34. Rowles GD. Place attachment among small town elderly. *J Rural Community Psychol*. 1990;11(1):103–120.

35. DeJong G. Independent living: from social movement to analytic paradigm. *Arch Phys Med Rehabil*. 1979;60(10):435–46.

International Classification of Functioning, Disability, and Health

Kristine A. Mulhorn, PhD, MHSA

BACKGROUND

Several clinical fields use the International Classification of Functioning, Disability, and Health (ICF) as part of their standard practice training (e.g., physical therapy, occupational therapy, speech and language therapy, clinical social work) and it provides a framework for thinking about the role of society in the experience of disability. So, it is very important to understand the vocabulary and perspective that the ICF brings. Those in public health should recognize the efforts made to create a conceptual model of disability that eliminates subjective terms that continue the negative perceptions of disability and functioning such as "impairment" and "handicap" and replace them with objective terms such as "participation" and "activities." The purpose of the ICF is outlined in the introductory document published in 2001 by the World Health Organization.[1] A critical purpose of this effort is to develop a conceptual model that could allow better communication about functioning and disability across all cultures so that measurement of functioning would be based on the same concepts (see Figure 8-1).[2] The ICF is critical for the training of various clinical professions, and for each of them, there are recommendations for how ICF can be integrated into the goal planning for the particular populations they serve. Some examples for three of these clinical fields, physical therapy, occupational therapy, and speech and language therapy, can be found in the Case Studies discussed at the end of this chapter. Selected examples are based on possible cases among those who are 65 and older. The Practical Manual for the ICF,[3] published by the World Health Organization, provides an overall strategy for various professions, and then each of these professions require the application of concepts such as "barriers" and "facilitators" to create goals for each patient. In public health, our goal relates to how aging populations can more fully participate in society and continue to engage in activities that positively affect health. Applying these concepts from the ICF, especially those concepts that relate to environmental factors, can prepare public health professionals to better communicate with other health care professionals about improving healthy aging.

The ICF framework addresses the relationship between functioning and health. It also allows us to think of functioning in the context of environmental factors, which is where public health practice can be influential. Considering areas of functioning for those over

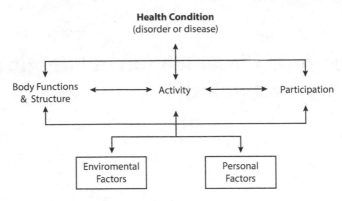

Source: Adapted from the World Health Organization.[2]

Figure 8-1. Overview of the ICF Model for Disability and Health

65, the fastest growing subpopulation in the United States, ICF addresses both the factors associated with physiological matters as well as environmental factors (e.g., legal structures, accessibility of services, accessibility of transportation, policies affecting housing and other services). These factors are closely related to the realm of public health. The ICF provides a framework for considering whether or not various factors about health services delivery is either a barrier or a facilitator for better functioning.[4]

POLICIES AND RELEVANT GOVERNMENT PROGRAMS

Policies that enhance full participation in community activities for older adults include better transportation, more mechanisms for mobility, and social participation. These are all ways that seniors can be healthier; however, if we see health only around physical functioning, we miss opportunities for social functioning and participation, which enhance health and longevity, and delay cognitive decline.

Currently, reimbursement mechanisms such as Medicare and Medicaid do not directly apply the ICF framework, but the emphasis on reimbursement is moving towards population health measures and structural barriers, and the ways public health can remove barriers or facilitate better health outcomes.

BEST PRACTICE INTERVENTIONS

Interpreting disability and functioning in the context of body structure and functioning includes participation in activities, along with environmental and personal factors. The implication is that interventions require considerations of the extent to which individuals can participate in everyday activities, when they are unable to participate, and what help they require to get there. It also creates a framework that encourages public health advocates to consider environmental factors such as legislation and other supports that can be a facilitator, or barrier, to functioning.

One call for development is to collaborate with major technology companies to integrate the guidelines into apps, data platforms, etc. This is an example of creating facilitators, or strategies, for healthy living and healthy aging that can affect environmental factors such as perceptions of what is healthy. Another call is to develop a road map for integrating physical activity prescriptions into payment systems and delivery of care with the Prescription for Activity Task Force.[5] There is evidence that the ICF model has clearly demonstrated that it has applications for healthy aging and for conceptualizing the notion of healthy aging.[5] Beyond regular screening, individuals can be prescribed mechanisms for increasing physical activity.

Special Considerations and Special Populations

The ICF framework allows for those considerations around environmental factors that can facilitate or be a barrier to functioning. For example, environmental factors such as the training of health care professionals may affect the health outcomes of Black seniors if health care professionals are trained to consider their implicit bias towards Black people and/or those who are aging. This means that as different subpopulations are targeted for particular interventions, members of that population can help define what measures, policies, or activities are beneficial and which ones create barriers.

CONCLUSION: CHALLENGES AND OPPORTUNITIES FOR PUBLIC HEALTH

Many challenges exist within the implementation of the ICF framework for the aging/disability/health arena for public health in North America. An initial challenge is the lack of integration of the ICF language in addressing the neighborhoods and built environment. One way that public health entities can address aging in a positive way is to consider the ICF framework as they integrate services for seniors. Also, they can provide services that match the supports that are needed so that seniors can more fully participate in community events and community activities. It is important for public health professionals to recognize how those over 65 are impacted by particular policies and interventions. The ICF framework presents an opportunity to find ways to affect functioning most positively by applying the terminology that can be common among various health professionals, and consider what policies create facilitators for improving functioning.

ICF CASE STUDY 1

A 75-year-old woman with fall history and fall risk in the home.

Population Health Evaluation and Considerations

The professionals using ICF (e.g., physical therapists, occupational therapists) will consider the ICF when focusing on targets for recovery and changes to reduce the patient's risk of falling. All members of the team will address particular interventions to move towards these goals.

At the population health level, there should be consideration of the services and evaluations that can be done in the home to reduce risks of falls. Community organizations and the Area Agencies on Aging may have resources for home maintenance or repairs to address considerations of what was raised by the health care team.

Due to balance issues, osteopenia, and osteoporosis as well as general poor bone health, many women 65 and older are at risk for falls. The ICF provides a mechanism to conceptualize the situation in a way that considers not only the clinical factors, but the environmental factors in her neighborhood and in her home.

Ms. Mori's Assessment

Akiko Mori first fell with some injury in 2017. She later received an assessment by her primary care provider, her physical therapist, and a bone specialist. There was also an assessment of the fall risks within her home from an occupational therapist. The assessment from the health care professionals also included the perspective of Ms. Mori herself.[6] (See Table 8-1.)

ICF CASE STUDY 2

An 85-year-old woman living at home with symptoms of dementia affecting her health.

Population Health Evaluation and Considerations

The professionals using ICF will be considering the living conditions in the home and risk factors for higher level of care. As a conceptual model, ICF is not an assessment tool itself; however, others have used ICF to develop assessment models. For example, Bharucha et. al.[10] developed a guide for using ICF items to assess technology needs for those with dementia. Also, the American Speech-Language-Hearing Association has a guide to use the ICF to gather assessment data.[11]

At the population health level, there should be consideration of the services and evaluations that can be done. Community organizations, and the Area Agencies on Aging may have resources for assessments of health care needs, companion care needs, respite care volunteers to support family caregivers, and adult day services that may be available in their area.

Ms. James' Assessment

Viola James takes medication for high blood pressure, and is in general good health, but recently has symptoms of significant memory loss. There was an assessment conducted to identify the supports she needs to remain healthy.[6] (See Table 8-2.)

Table 8-1. Ms. Mori's Assessment by Health Care Professionals

ICF Code	Description	Barriers	Facilitators
Activities/Participation			
d2401	Handling stress	Lack of mental health resources; lack of awareness of level of stress or effects of stress on health	Awareness of stress levels and available to mental health services
d470	Transportation	Poor access to transportation needed for getting medical services or social activities	Access to transportation through family members or public transportation
Maintaining health			
d5702	Meeting physical therapy and occupational therapy targets	No access to physical therapy assessment or occupational therapy assessment or assessment of other home health needs; lack of careful follow-up after post-acute services; lack of support from caregiver or family members; lack of transportation to services	Appropriate physical therapy assessment or occupational therapy assessment; appropriate assessment of home health needs; advocacy by caregiver to receive in-depth follow-up after post-acute services; supportive family members or caregiver; access to transportation to services
d5702	Weight bearing exercises	Physician may not approve of assessment leading to insurance not covering physical therapy; lack of access to weights or proper instruction; ineffectual or nonexistent encouragement from caregiver or others	Appropriate instruction and guidance; insurance coverage; access to home health care; encouragement by family members or caregiver
d5702	Other exercise as recommended	Lack of instruction, supervision or monitoring; lack of encouragement; lack of self-efficacy	Access to instruction, guidance by physical therapist with monitoring and encouragement by family member or caregiver; other services may be available in the community if patient has access and transportation
d5702	Taking medications (i.e., calcium)	Medicare prescription program unavailable	Prescription benefits available; Medigap insurance covers
d630-d649	Household tasks	No family available to help during rehabilitation at home	Other resources available such as Area Agency on Aging volunteers
d710-d479	Interpersonal inter-actions and relationships	Family miscommunications; widow, therefore no spouse; estranged from children	Family relationship allows for regular family visits
d840-d859	Work employment; volunteering	Poor or no access to transportation limits access to work or volunteering	Access to transportation; public transportation which reaches locations for work or volunteer opportunities
d910-d998	Community life	Few local activities; lack of internet or wi-fi; lack of knowledge about programs; not linked to community groups	Many local activities; newsletter (hardcopy or email); shuttle or other transportation available to reach community events; strong social ties in the community; electronic bulletin board or website with available information about events

(Continued)

Table 8–1. (Continued)

ICF Code	Description	Barriers	Facilitators
d999	Social life	Lack of access to information about social activities such as limited social network, no nearby family or friends, lack of internet; not a member of community group or organization	Access to information about social activities in the community; ready access to transportation or social activities with transportation available for those who do not drive; social activities within close proximity; access to internet; membership in various social organizations or regular attendee to other groups to stay socially engaged; volunteer or other role in social organizations with weekly activities
d999	Civic life	Lack of communication about civic organizations; lack of information or outreach to older individuals living in the community; lack of internet; limited transportation options outside of neighbors or friends	Regular participation in civic organizations; available information from civic organizations; volunteer for civic organizations or government activities such as elections; other engagement or participation; access to internet; access to transportation to attend and/or participate in events
d999	Human rights	Lack of access to legal information; legal services	Clear information available in easy-to-find locations or other access to legal aid
Environmental Factors			
e115	Products and technology	Resources; lack of accessibility	Available resources needed to follow up physical therapy exercises
e1101	Medications	Access to drug coverage (Medicare Part D)	Drug coverage; convenient way to see the primary care physician or bone specialist
e235	Support and relationships	Poor or no access to information; no membership in local organizations; limited social network outside of the family; no regular activities or classes outside of the home; no access to the internet and online programs	Access to transportation; accessible home for visitors; source of information such as internet access; membership to local organizations; social network with regular meetings or gatherings; classes available in the community
e340	Direct support staff	Doctor's orders or physical therapy orders may not call for this need, yet individual needs help at home	Available through visiting nurses and Medicare coverage for up to 90 days
e310/e315	Family caregivers	Family caregivers not available for various reasons	Available/visiting often; caregiving on a regular basis; assisting with health care services management/ social services/home maintenance
e320	Friends	Absent or unavailable to help	Available; actively caring or checking in
e410	Attitudes of family members	Beliefs about disability discourage participation	Support and encourage engagement in community

(Continued)

Table 8-1. (Continued)

ICF Code	Description	Barriers	Facilitators
e410-e499	Communication Services, Systems, Policies	Internet difficulties; no Wi-Fi access	Access to patient portal due to Wi-Fi/internet access
e535-e599	Transportation services	Without independent transportation resources might be harder to access, such as rural areas	Some transportation available
Personal Factors			
Personal factors such as age, gender, and race do not currently have ICF codes.		Bone Loss (osteoporosis) Disparity	COVID-19 Disparity
	Age	The age-adjusted prevalence of osteoporosis at either the femur neck or lumbar spine or both was 12.6% among adults aged 50 and over and was higher among adults aged 65 and over (17.7%) compared with those aged 50–64 (8.4%).[7]	Concern is that COVID-19 restrictions are causing delays or cancellations of testing for bone loss, such as DXA testing.
	Gender	In 2017–2013, low bone mass prevalence was higher among women than men. In 2017–2018, the age-adjusted prevalence of osteoporosis at either the femur neck or lumbar spine or both among adults aged 50 and over was 12.6% and was higher among women (19.6%) compared with men (4.4%).[7]	Men have experienced greater severity of symptoms of COVID-19 and more hospitalizations than women.[8]
	Race	During 2017–2018, the age-adjusted prevalence of osteoporosis among adults aged 50 years and older was 12.6%. A lower percentage of non-Hispanic Black adults (6.8%) had osteoporosis compared with non-Hispanic White adults (12.9%), non-Hispanic Asian adults (18.4%), and Hispanic adults (14.7%). The observed differences among non-Hispanic White, non-Hispanic Asian, and Hispanic adults did not reach statistical significance.[9]	We cannot change these factors; however, due to other inequalities associated with the social determinants of health, disparities of the severity of COVID-19 are experienced by older adults, Black people, and men.[8]

Table 8–2. Ms. James' Assessment by Health Care Professionals

ICF Code	Description	Barriers	Facilitators
Environmental Factors			
e115	Products and technology for personal use in daily living	Lack of assessment; lack of resources; no access to Wi-Fi (Assessment using ICF Core Set).[12] Family members or health care professionals are not trained in products and technology that could enhance communication/understanding.[13]	Available resources needed to follow up physical therapy exercises; training family caregivers in cuing system for facilitating communication; memory wallets and conversation notebooks.[13]
e1101	Medications	No access to drug coverage (Medicare Part D); or poor health literacy around drug coverage and effectiveness of medication options	Drug coverage; convenient way to see the primary care physician or bone specialist
e210–e299	Natural environment and human-made changes to environment: physical geography; flora and fauna; natural events; human-caused events; air quality	(Note: Considerations of COVID-19 can be found below under "Personal Factors and Dementia" in this table)	Facilitators for functioning during the COVID-19 pandemic include allowing personal assistants to enter the home while following mask-wearing; as vaccinations become available, the patient, home health aides, and other caregivers should be vaccinated to minimize risk of contracting the virus
e320–e5900	Support and relationships	Barriers to support such as isolation, long distance from family or friends, acquaintances; technology barriers preventing communication	Support services; availability of family relations; caregivers; mechanisms for social participation in the community or online
e340	Direct support staff	Diagnosis may not be available for various reasons; therefore, Medicare will not cover support	Available through visiting nurses and Medicare coverage for up to 90 days
e310/e315	Family caregivers	Family caregivers not available for various reasons; family members or health care professionals not trained in effective communication	Available/visiting often; caregiving on a regular basis; assisting with health care services management/social services/home maintenance; speech-language professionals can train family caregivers in effective communication
e320	Friends	Absent or unavailable to help	Available/actively caring or checking in
e355	Health care professionals	Level of training in geriatrics and dementia and care of dementia patients	Special training in geriatrics and dementia for primary care providers, nurses, nurse practitioners, speech-language professionals, physical therapist, physician assistants, etc.

(Continued)

Table 8-2. (Continued)

ICF Code	Description	Barriers	Facilitators
e410-e499	Attitudes of immediate family members, extended family members, of people in authority, of people in subordinate positions, personal assistants, health care professionals, societal attitudes	Lack of available training about strategies for communication, mitigation of agitation; lack of resources regarding easing stress linked to memory loss; lack of support for medication management	Research shows those with dementia retain a sense of self which should be respected in caring; societal shift towards thinking of those with dementia as persons rather than a disease process.[11]
e535	Communication Services, Systems, Policies	Internet difficulties; no Wi-Fi access	Access to patient portal due to Wi-Fi/internet access
e540	Transportation services	Without independent transportation resources might be harder to access; such as rural areas.	Some transportation available

Personal Factors and Dementia

Personal factors	Dementia Disparity		Risk of COVID-19
Such as age, gender, and race do not currently have ICF codes.	Age	The prevalence of dementia increases with age. It is known that 5.6 million among those of the over 65 years of age have a dementia as of 2014.[12]	The severity of COVID-19 increases with age.[12]
	Gender	In the United States women experience disability (27.2%) at a higher prevalence than men (24.7%).[14]	Men have experienced greater severity of symptoms of COVID-19 and more hospitalizations than women.[8]
	Race	Black adults have the highest prevalence of Alzheimer's and related dementias (13.8%) compared with Hispanic adults (12.2%) and non-Hispanic White adults (10.3%), followed by Native American and Alaska Natives (9.1%), and Asian and Pacific Islanders (8.4%).[14]	Black adults have the highest prevalence and deaths from COVID-19.[8]
	Age of Onset	Not always known; varies based on when dementia or mild cognitive impairment was first diagnosed	Assessment unavailable; no regular source of care; suspicion of health care system; fear of seeking care; no or limited access to social activities in or outside the home to improve cognitive functioning

REFERENCES

1. World Health Organization. Towards a Common Language for Functioning, Disability and Health: ICF. 2002. Available at: https://www.who.int/classifications/icf/training/icfbeginnersguide.pdf. Accessed February 23, 2021.

2. World Health Organization. International classification of functioning, disability and health: ICF. World Health Organization. 2001. Available at: https://apps.who.int/iris/handle/10665/42407. Accessed April 9, 2021.

3. World Health Organization. How to use the ICF: A practical manual for using the International Classification of Functioning, Disability, and Health (ICF). Exposure draft for comment. 2013. Available at: https://www.who.int/classifications/drafticfpracticalmanual.pdf. Accessed February 23, 2021.

4. Welch Saleeby P. Applications of a capability approach to disability and the International Classification of Functioning, Disability, and Health (ICF) in social work practice. *J Soc Work Disabil Rehabil.* 2006;6(1–2):217–232.

5. Prescription for Activity Task Force. Available at: https://www.prescriptionforactivity.org. Accessed February 23, 2021.

6. The ICF-based Case Studies Project. ICF assessment sheets. 2018. Available at: https://www.icf-casestudies.org. Accessed February 23, 2021.

7. Sarafrazi N, Wambogo EA, Shepherd JA. Osteoporosis or low bone mass in older adults: United States, 2017–2018. NCHS Data Brief, no 405. National Center for Health Statistics. March 1, 2021. Available at: https://stacks.cdc.gov/view/cdc/103477. Accessed June 22, 2021.

8. Centers for Disease Control and Prevention. Identify strategies to reduce spread of COVID-19: Sample training plan. 2020. Available at: https://www.cdc.gov/coronavirus/2019-ncov/php/contact-tracing/strategies-to-reduce-spread.html. Accessed on February 23, 2021.

9. Wambogo E, Sarafrazi N. QuickStats: Percentage of Adults Aged ≥50 Years with Osteoporosis, by Race and Hispanic Origin — United States, 2017–2018. *MMWR Morb Mortal Wkly Rep.* 2021;70:731.

10. Bharucha, AJ, Anand V, Forlizzi J, et al. Intelligent assistive technology applications to dementia care: current capabilities, limitations, and future challenges. *Am J Geriatr Psychiatry.* 2009;17(2):88–104.

11. American Speech-Language-Hearing Association. International Classification of Functioning, Disability, and Health (ICF). Available at: https://www.asha.org/slp/icf. Accessed February 23, 2021.

12. Centers for Disease Control and Prevention. What is dementia? 2019. Available at: https://www.cdc.gov/aging/dementia/index.html. Accessed February 23, 2021.

13. Byrne K, Orange JB. Conceptualizing communication enhancement in dementia for the family caregivers using the WHO-ICF framework. *Adv Speech Lang Pathol.* 2005;7(4):187–202.

14. Matthews KA, Xu W, Gaglioti AH, et al. Racial and ethnic estimates of Alzheimer's disease and related dementias in the United States (2015–2060) in adults aged ≥65 years. *Alzheimers Dement.* 2019;15(1):17–24.

III. SOCIAL AND COMMUNITY CONTEXT

This section incorporates the social factors of the social determinants of health that affect aging within a social and community context. The chapters within this section integrate topics such as cohesion within civic participation, discrimination, and contexts within which people live, learn, work, and recreate. These concepts are woven through the chapters and help the reader understand the connection between these concepts and healthy aging.

This section is led by a chapter on social support. It is well documented that there is a strong correlation between social support and health outcomes. Chapter 9 provides the reader with an appreciation of the role social support plays in health, health outcomes, and healthy aging.

Mobility is also a factor as one ages, impacted by bodily changes, frailty, and falls. Chapter 10 addresses both mobility factors and transportation factors that impact people as they grow older. The chapter addresses the linkage between civic participation, mobility, falls, and interventions to serve as protective factors for older adults.

Caregiving is an important factor in the lives of people advancing in age and healthy aging. Paid and unpaid caregivers contribute widely to the health and well-being of older adults. The role caregivers play and the impact formal and informal caregiving has on healthy aging are addressed in Chapter 11.

This section concludes with a chapter on end-of-life considerations. It reiterates the connection between one's well-being as they depart and their relationships with others through work, play, and relations throughout their life span.

Social Support and Aging

Stephanie T. Child PhD, MPH, Emily J. Nicklett, PhD, MSW,
Donna Beth Stauber, PhD, and Danielle Ward, PhD, MPH

INTRODUCTION

Social support is a widely recognized aspect of physical health and mental well-being, and an increasingly important factor for successful aging.[1,2] Social support has been studied since the late 1970s when it was described as "information leading one to believe that [they are] cared for, loved, esteemed, and a member of a network of mutual obligations."[3] As the description suggests, humans are inherently social beings and thrive on positive interactions with others. Feeling supported can be especially crucial for coping with stressful experiences, such as periods of transition (e.g., retirement, moving) or during acute, stressful events (e.g., loss of a spouse). In addition to being a key resource for buffering stressful experiences,[4,5] research has consistently shown social support to be an important factor in everyday life. Social support is directly linked with health outcomes and behaviors, and more broadly, successful aging via physiological, psychological, and behavioral mechanisms. In this chapter, we explore the many facets of social support, from how it is measured to the challenges older adults may face in maintaining support, programs, and institutions that are essential to providing support to older adults.

What is Social Support?

Social support can be described in a number of ways. Table 9-1 from Gottlieb and Bergen[6] provides a list of definitions to help distinguish between many support-related concepts.

The literature on social support has largely measured perceived support. Perceived support is the subjective evaluation of support available to an individual (i.e., "I have someone who could drive me to the doctor's office if I am sick"). This evaluation may differ substantially from objective support, or actual support received. However, perceived support is important because it represents resources that can be leveraged, or mobilized, during a time of need. The ability to depend on support from social networks, or conversely, the realization that support is not available during stressful events is an important factor related to the appraisal of stress and its ability to affect health.

Table 9-1. Support-Related Concepts and Definitions

Support-Related Concepts	Definitions
Social support	The social resources that persons perceive to be available or that are actually provided to them by nonprofessionals in the context of both formal support groups and informal helping relationships.
Social network	A unit of social structure composed of the individual's social ties and the ties among them.
Social integration	The extent to which an individual participates in private and public social interactions.
Functional support	The varied kinds of resources that flow through the network's social ties.
Structural support	The number and pattern of direct and indirect social ties that surround the individual.
Types of support	Emotional, instrumental, informational, companionate, and esteem support.
Perceived support	The individual's beliefs about the availability of varied types of support from network associates.
Received support	Reports about the types of support received.
Support adequacy	Evaluations of the quantity and/or quality of received support.
Directionality of support	Determination of whether support is unidirectional or bidirectional (mutual).

Source: Reprinted with permission from Gottlieb and Bergen.[6]

Social support is also divided into different types. Emotional support is often in the form of a confidant or someone to share intimate details of our lives and feelings with. Emotional support often comes from people we have known the longest and increasingly may come from people who live at a distance, and is associated with reduced feelings of loneliness. Instrumental support, in contrast, is often in the form of having someone close by who can provide assistance, such as someone to deliver groceries and provide care while sick. Instrumental support is important for older adults who may be isolated and at risk of self-neglect. Informational support is the provision of information, advice, or guidance, which can influence how decisions are made. Companionate support again comes from someone who is close by, but the focus is on a shared activity or interest, such as someone to play cards, and can increase feelings of social belonging. Unlike instrumental support, which can sometimes trigger anxiety by feeling that one is burdensome to another, companionate support is often a reciprocal relationship. As such, older adults may feel more comfortable receiving companionate-type support. Esteem support is similar to emotional support, but is often specific to promoting an individuals' abilities and value, and is important for behavior modification.

Inadequate Levels of Support: Prevalence of Loneliness and Social Isolation

It is hard to estimate the prevalence of social support itself. Instead, researchers and practitioners interested in social support often examine outcomes experienced when social support is lacking or inadequate, namely loneliness and social isolation. Social isolation and loneliness are risk factors for poor physical, mental, and cognitive health outcomes[7-9] such as cardiovascular disease,[10] cognitive decline,[11] and mortality.[12,13]

Though similar, the two concepts are distinct. Social isolation is characterized by a physical lack of social connectivity and is often measured objectively by assessing a person's living arrangements, their frequency of communication with others, and community involvement.[14] Social isolation is likely to occur when an older adult lives alone, has limited mobility or transportation options for engaging in their community, and/or has limited physical contact with relatives, friends, and neighbors. In 2020, approximately 28% (or 13.8 million) of adults over the age of 65 lived alone.[15] Similarly, 24% (7.7 million) of older adults reported being socially isolated.[16] However, the link between living alone, being socially isolated, and feeling lonely is tenuous at best, as "these are three distinct conditions, and experiencing one (living alone) does not necessarily mean experiencing one or both of the others (being isolated or feeling lonely)."[13]

Loneliness comes from the subjective assessment of one's social relationships,[17] and often occurs when one's expectations for support are not matched in reality. A person can have ample opportunities for social engagement and yet still feel lonely if they perceive that no one understands or cares about them. While loneliness is perceived to be a common circumstance among older adults, it is not considered a normal part of aging. In fact, loneliness continues to decrease until adults reach age 75, after which rates of loneliness begin to increase. Moreover, recent evidence on the prevalence of loneliness suggests there has not been an increase in the severity of loneliness, but rather that the number of older adults experiencing loneliness or isolation is increasing as Baby Boomers age into their later 70s and beyond.[18] Notably, poor health is a strong indicator of loneliness among older adults,[18,19] suggesting that health conditions may limit positive social interactions. Moreover, it suggests a cyclical relationship between health and social support, such that decreases in one aspect may predict decreases in another.

Why is Social Support Important for Health?

Social support is a function of having good social relationships. Humans are hardwired for successful and meaningful interactions. Individuals who experience prolonged social isolation and who are less socially integrated are at higher risk for cardiovascular disease and mortality.[12,20] This is because social isolation is viewed as a threat to the human mind and body, likely an adaptive trait that helped humans forge meaningful alliances and survive against predators in early human history.[21] Indeed, the threat of isolation was such a meaningful predictor of human survival that even today a chronic sense of rejection or isolation can impair cellular processes that allow our immune system to function properly. Social support is also associated with changes in our cardiovascular and neuroendocrine systems[22] and is linked to physiological aging. Individuals with less support tend to age faster biologically,[23,24] which can lead to the early onset of many chronic disease conditions and mortality.

Social support is linked to health via three primary pathways: (1) relationships provide social influence and support for health behaviors (e.g., medication adherence, physical activity), (2) social embeddedness offers instrumental support, information sharing, and other resources, and (3) social connection enhances feelings of belongingness, as well as emotional and moral support. Social support is also important in the stress appraisal process,[25] meaning social support can reduce physiological responses associated with stressful circumstances or events. For example, having a partner who can be relied upon during troubled times and who also provides a source of companionship during normal times, is considered to be beneficial for health and well-being.

Finally, social support helps to enhance self-esteem and provides a sense of stability, which may engender positive emotional affect and reduce the negative effects of stress.[26] Social support may also be related to life satisfaction, which is also known to drive health and well-being. People often define themselves in terms of their friendships and the support roles they provide and receive (e.g., a mother/father, sister/brother, advisor/confidant), many of which are often central to our identities.

Tools for Measuring Social Support Among Older Adults

One difficulty with social support is how best to measure it. Early literature defines support as "an exchange of resources between at least two individuals perceived … to enhance the well-being of the recipient,"[27] suggesting support must be recognized by the recipient and be helpful. Some have suggested that resources exchanged can have either a negative or positive effect[28]; others have noted that objective support, a measure of actual support received, may be more useful.[29] Additionally, there are different perspectives about how social support operates. These issues include the direct versus buffering nature of support, the appropriateness of the type of support received as compared with what may be needed, and the potential reciprocal effects of social support and health. The most commonly used scales are discussed in the following sections.

The Multidimensional Scale of Perceived Social Support

The Multidimensional Scale of Perceived Social Support consists of 12 items across three subscales. It asks participants to rate the extent to which they agree with each statement on a seven-point Likert scale (very strongly agree to very strongly disagree).[30,31] It is one of the first scales to ask about three distinct sources of support (i.e., a significant other, family, and friends). However, each of the subscales may not be appropriate for certain populations. For example, the "significant other" subscale could take on a number of different meanings for adults who are not partnered. When added together as a scale, the MSPSS prescribes what social support *should* look like, but may not look like for every older adult.

Lubben Social Network Scale

The Lubben Social Network Scale (LSNS) assesses social networks that likely provide social support, rather than support itself. Individuals at lower ranges of the scale are described as being at risk of social isolation.

The LSNS uses 10 items to assess an individuals' likeliness of finding support if and when it is needed.[32] Three items ask about frequency of contact with family members, and how many family members a person feels close to. The same three questions are asked about friends. Two items ask about giving and receiving support from a confidant (i.e., "When you have an important decision to make, do you have someone you can talk to about it?"). One item asks about *providing* instrumental support to others based on the notion of reciprocity. The final item asks about living arrangements, awarding the most points to those living with a spouse. Scales such as the LSNS-6 are a practical choice for practitioners seeking to screen older adults to identify those at increased risk for social isolation.

Objective Support via Name Generators

Objective measures of support are often assessed using something called a "name generator." The most commonly used name generator asks respondents to list the names of people with whom they discuss important personal matters as part of the General Social Survey. The Short Form Social Support Questionnaire is similar and asks respondents to name up to nine different people for each of six different questions.[33] The number of names generated by these types of questions often serves as an objective measure of support, with higher numbers of names indicating greater levels of support. Other items might ask respondents to name the number of people who have, for example, provided assistance recently or could be relied on for transportation in an emergency. In general, the more names provided, the better. However, there is some evidence to suggest diminishing returns at higher levels of names. Because of this, and to reduce participant burden and recall bias, name generators are often limited to naming five or so individuals.

Social Engagement and Frequency of Communication

Other factors that can help assess social support include levels of social engagement, such as participation in social groups and the frequency and mode (i.e., face to face, telephone) of communication with friends and family. The Social Engagement and Activities Questionnaire is a 10-item scale used to assess social group, interpersonal interaction, and solitary activities among low-income, depressed, homebound older adults.[34] The scale is comprised of two components: (1) a general social-group activities engagement component, positively correlated with perceived social support, and (2) a low level of socialization. Additionally, mode and frequency of communication with friends and family may help to identify potential gaps in social support. Thus, while an older adult may telephone with friends or family frequently throughout the week, it is important to consider how often they are visited by someone face to face, or whether they have someone close by who can be called upon in an emergency or for tangible support.

COMMON ISSUES AND CHALLENGES

Social Relationships and Cognition

The basis of social relationships and the ability to confer support relies heavily on communication. For older adults with cognitive decline, it can be hard to maintain conversations or communicate in meaningful or engaging ways. Subsequently, deep relationships could deteriorate or cease when an individual experiences dementia, memory loss, or other cognitive decline. The loss of friendships and other relationships due to cognitive decline is a topic that deserves more attention, especially as it relates to consequent losses in companionate support.

While the loss of cognition is likely to lead to the loss of social relationships, there is evidence to suggest the reverse may also be true: the loss of social relationships can lead to, and even exacerbate cognitive decline.[35,36] Both providing and receiving social support increases life satisfaction and decreases depression, which may play a role in the link between support and cognition.[2,37] Contact with family and friends, emotional and informational support, and anticipated support are all associated with better cognition.[38] Conversely, poor social connections, infrequent participation in social activities, and social disengagement all predicted the risk of cognitive decline in a longitudinal study of community dwelling adults.[39]

This empirical evidence has important implications for current practices with regards to adults experiencing cognitive decline. Because the loss of social relationships may contribute to and further exacerbate cognitive decline, it remains imperative for older adults with memory loss and other forms of dementia to continue to be socially engaged in thoughtful, meaningful, and respectful ways by those providing care for them.

Life Events and Resulting Disruption in Support Systems

There are several major life events that can lead to the disruption of social support for an individual. Retirement often marks a transition to a new phase of life and can often result in drastically reduced contact with coworkers and associated opportunities for socializing.[40] Moving or relocating is another major life event that leads to the disruption or loss of social support systems. Moving may be particularly disruptive for older adults who have lived in their communities for several years, possibly decades, and are likely to have well-established connections with neighbors, local businesses and organizations, their local faith community, and so on. As such, they are socially embedded across multiple levels of social relationships, and moving represents a major upheaval across these various types of support mechanisms.

Other events leading to the disruption of social support can arise from the death of friends, relatives, and other close ties, which become increasingly common as people grow older. Older adults have fewer opportunities to build new social relationships, especially for ties they have known for several years or decades, so the death of a close friend is often an irreplaceable loss of support. The death of friends and relatives serves to amplify social disparities. For example, individuals lower in socioeconomic resources, which are risk factors for poor health, are also more likely to experience the death of social ties, resulting in the loss of health-supporting resources. Widowhood is a particularly salient event that can result in the disruption of social support, including the loss of relationships that were more closely maintained by the spouse who died. The new widow/widower may not speak to and socialize with their in-laws as much, and they may not spend as much time with other couples as they previously did. As such, these relationships and the support they previously provided may fade over time.[40]

The interruption or loss of social support stemming from life events and periods of transition is an important issue to consider. Public health policymakers and practitioners should pay particular attention to major life events and transitions among older adults that may trigger the loss or disruption of social support to identify individuals who may be at risk of loneliness, isolation, and other health issues.

Social Support and Neglect

Low social support has been found to significantly increase the risk of virtually all forms of mistreatment among older adults.[41,42] A rising public health concern, however, is the risk of self-neglect among older adults who live alone. One of the many important functions of social relationships and the support they provide is the influence they have on behaviors, and in particular, health-related behaviors including self-care. The National Center on Elder Abuse defines older adult self-neglect as behavior that threatens a person's own health and safety. This often manifests itself as "a refusal or failure to provide himself/herself with adequate food, water, clothing, shelter, personal hygiene, medication (when indicated), and safety precautions."[43] Lack of support is believed to be a primary risk factor for self-neglect,[44] with older adults who live alone and without adequate support and resources from family, friends, and religious affiliations at higher risk.[45] Subsequently, lack of support, cognitive decline, and self-neglect often compound together among at-risk older adults,[46] resulting in severe declines in health, accidents, and mortality. Given a rising trend in older adults who choose to "age in place," practitioners and policymakers should seek to implement strategies for identifying self-neglect among older adults who live alone.

Relevant Policies and Legislation

The Older Americans Act

In 1965, Congress passed the Older Americans Act (OAA) establishing programs and services which currently serve about 11 million older adults in the United States. The major focus of the Older Americans Act includes the organization and delivery of nutritional and social services of older adults and their caregivers. One example of the multipronged benefit of the programs supported by the OAA is Meals on Wheels, which provides home-delivered meals to over 1.5 million older adults in the United States, many of whom live alone and experience physical and/or social vulnerabilities.[47] Clients experience social as well as nutritional benefits from the program, including the exchange of pleasantries and exchanges of information about other supports older adults might need. Prior studies have also found that the Meals on Wheels program provides an excellent opportunity to integrate screenings and interventions for diverse concerns, including depression[48] and falls.[49]

Government Agencies

Senior Corps, a government agency that operates in the Corporation for National and Community Service, uses an intergenerational and intragenerational service model to engage adults aged 55 or older as volunteers for individuals, and community, faith-based, and nonprofit organizations. Senior Corps addresses community needs through three distinct programs: Foster Grandparents, Senior Companions, and the Retired and Senior Volunteer Program, which creates opportunities for skilled seniors to apply their knowledge and skills to meet the needs of communities and organizations. In addition to providing social support and tangible assistance to older adult recipients of the Senior Companions Program, Senior Corps programs also benefit the volunteers themselves. Studies evaluating the impact of Senior Corps suggest a positive impact on the health and well-being of volunteers, particularly for women and older seniors.[50,51]

Government-Related Programs

It is estimated that a lack of social contacts among older adults results in an additional $6.7 billion in Medicare health care costs.[52] Medicare is uniquely positioned to identify and provide social support resources for older adults. There are several health services organizations that work with Medicare specifically to reduce loneliness and social isolation among seniors. In 2018, the US Centers for Medicare and Medicaid Services granted Medicare Advantage plans greater flexibility in establishing creative supplemental benefits. Many plans now offer an array of benefits that can reduce social isolation, such as home delivery of meals; ride-sharing services from companies such as Uber and Lyft; and new technology start-ups offering volunteer services including companionship, taking seniors to the grocery store or doctor's appointments, help with chores, and teaching seniors how to set up a new smartphone.[53]

Medicare and other health care plans are also an essential tool for identifying at-risk older adults. CareMore Health (available at: https://www.caremore.com), an integrated health plan for Medicare and Medicaid patients, created their Togetherness Program that identifies lonely and socially isolated older adults. This program engages its members via phone calls, home visits, and by connecting their older members with community-based programs. An evaluation of the Togetherness Program showed that hospital admissions for program participants are 20.8% lower than nonparticipants, and that emergency room visits decreased by 3.3% for participants.

Efforts to address loneliness and social isolation can be seen in other government-related programs across the globe. In 2018, the United Kingdom launched a loneliness campaign which included appointing a Minister of Loneliness. The Campaign to End Loneliness (available at: https://www.campaigntoendloneliness.org), a national campaign, included cross sector and cross ministry partnerships. Elements of the campaign include partnering with the Royal Mail to have mail carriers to check in on those who are socially isolated. In France, through the program Veiller Sur Mes Parents (translated as Watch Over My Parents), people can pay a monthly fee for a postal worker to make weekly house calls, deliver a monthly newsletter to an aging parent, and even provide a daily report (except Sunday) to their family via a mobile phone app (available at: https://www.laposte.fr/particulier/veiller-sur-mes-parents). Similar postal programs that check in on older adults are available in Japan, South Korea, and Finland.

BEST PRACTICE INTERVENTIONS

The coronavirus pandemic of 2020 led to physical distancing guidelines, stay-at-home orders, and the shuttering of many local institutions that typically provide older adults with various sources of social support. Given the risk for social isolation among older adults, the pandemic highlighted the need for community based organizations to search for unique solutions to maintain the provision of services and programs for engaging and supporting older adults during this time. The following is a discussion of a few examples.[54]

Numerous interventions have documented the benefit of social support-focused interventions on behavioral and mental health outcomes of older adults, including chronic disease self-management,[55] nutrition, and frailty.[56] Yet, relatively few studies have investigated interventions to address social connectedness, support, and loneliness among older adults. While it is generally recognized that increasing support is beneficial, there remains a lack of understanding regarding which types of interventions are most useful to address which problems and for whom.[57] In a comprehensive scoping review, O'Rourke, Collins, and Sidani identified 39 studies that examined interventions to address social connectedness and loneliness for older adults, of which 17 were conducted in the United States.[58] The authors identified nine intervention types across the 39 studies, with One-to-One Personal Contact and Group Activity examined most frequently. Across studies, increasing social contact appeared to be the most influential component of interventions examined. In particular, further evidence is needed to identify specific interventions that are effective in increasing social support among diverse older adult populations.

Special Considerations and Special Populations

Migrant Communities

Special consideration should be given to aging migrant communities who represent a fast-growing demographic within the United States. In 2018, 13.9% of the total older population (7.3 million) were foreign-born people over the age of 65. By 2060, this is expected to increase to 22 million or almost a quarter of the total older population.[59]

Public health practitioners should have an awareness that migration, especially later in life, is a stressful life event and a major disruption to an individual's social support system, and could result in increased risk for loneliness in particular.[60] Practitioners should also note there is considerable heterogeneity within the foreign-born population regarding socioeconomic status, culture, and health. Older foreign-born individuals have the potential to arrive at different points in their life course and will have varying levels of acculturation. The needs, challenges, and perceptions of those who arrived early in their life course are likely substantial different from those who arrived later in their life course, with respect to language, documentation, or refugee status. Although the literature describes a healthy immigrant effect, there is still a substantial and negative effect of foreign birth status on access to insurance and preventative health care.

Public health practitioners should be aware of factors that can boost or add to the healthy aging of migrant communities (e.g., social connections and religious or spiritual beliefs). Additionally, it is important to know the mechanisms through which they work. Knowing how migrant communities view healthy aging can go a long way in helping public health policymakers and practitioners assist this segment of the population.

Public health practitioners should collaborate with specific migrant advocacy groups, faith communities, sympathetic legal clinics, and senior centers existing within migrant communities. Practitioners should try to enter these communities with respect, and have the understanding that they are invited guests who have been given the privilege to enter these spaces. Collaborators should first seek to understand their perceptions towards health and healthy aging and how social support operates within the different immigrant communities.

CONCLUSION: CHALLENGES AND OPPORTUNITIES FOR PUBLIC HEALTH

In summary, social support is a crucial factor for the continued physical and mental well-being of older adults. Social support includes both actual and perceived resources provided by others that enable a person to feel cared for, valued, and part of a network of communication. Social support can be especially critical for older adults who rely on family, friends, or organizations to assist them with daily living activities, provide companionship, and care for their well-being. Older adulthood represents a period of transition in which the sources of and need for social support can change rapidly, stemming from major events such as retirement, loss of a spouse, and declines in health and mobility. Major challenges include identifying and targeting adults who live alone; those who are socially isolated due to mobility issues; those who are underserved, under-resourced, or uninsured; and those who may otherwise need additional forms of support, including older adults who are managing chronic diseases. Further, social isolation and limited mobility may limit older adults' social interactions, increasing their risk for self-neglect and cognitive decline.

Yet, opportunities abound for ensuring older adults' social support needs are met. There is a tremendous opportunity for public health practitioners to work with community based organizations to increase opportunities to provide support for older adults. By working together to provide opportunities for social interaction and support for aging adults, these programs can extend the quality of life for older populations.

CASE STUDY

Integrating the Medical and Faith Communities to Combat Loneliness

Ms. Case was a 78-year-old recently discharged emergency department patient who lived alone with no family or friends in the area. Upon returning home, Ms. Case became overwhelmed and confused by her discharge paperwork, causing her to forget to take her medication and schedule follow-up appointments. Most of her time was spent alone in her living room. After weeks of isolation, Ms. Case returned to the emergency department, partially because she was ill, but mainly because she desired social interaction.

Need and Intervention

Loneliness is a burden that affects every stage of life and negatively affects the comprehensive health of an individual. In order to alleviate the isolation often felt within older adults, Faith Community Health (FCH) provides support that benefits the health outcomes of individuals (available at: https://www.texashealth.org/en/About-Texas-Health/Faith-and-Spirituality/Faith-Community-Health). Through weekly one-hour visits, Faith Community Caregivers (trained congregational volunteers) help patients adhere to their medical plan of care by providing transportation to local medical appointments, assisting with medication adherence, connecting patients to community resources (e.g., food pantries, community clinics), and more. Volunteers educate patients on the following four principles:

1. Right Door: utilization of the appropriate health care door, rather than the emergency department.
2. Right Time: equipping individuals with preventative information to help recognize health issues early.
3. Ready to be Treated: helping individuals be prepared for medical appointments.
4. Reassured (Not Alone): providing a "ministry of presence" (physical and spiritual support) to alleviate loneliness and isolation.

Faith Community Health Successes

Faith Community Health began in Texas in 2015 through the Faith in Action Initiatives in the Office of Mission & Ministry at Baylor Scott and White Health (BSWH). It represents a growing movement of health care that helps isolated individuals reach optimal health by integrating faith communities, health care, and community resources. Eight communities throughout Texas are operated by FCH, having served over 300 patients. While ministering to those of all ages and backgrounds (with an average age of 74.5), FCH has reduced emergency department utilization and hospital admission rates within program participants by 30% and 40%, respectively. Additionally, the program has produced assumed savings of $5 million for the BSWH system.

Collaborative partnerships with health care professionals, faith communities, and community-oriented functionality creates relationships that are long-lasting with multi-faceted benefits and successes. Faith Community Health has collaborated with over 150 faith communities across Texas.

How Can Others Implement?

To initiate a faith health program, begin by utilizing community conversations and community health needs assessments to determine the highest needs of the community.

Thereafter, develop the program to be community-oriented by training faith community volunteers to help combat the health needs identified. Collaborate with local health care professionals to identify socially isolated patients to be paired with trained volunteers. Through the pairings, keep the program community and patient centric, thus helping all involved leverage the resources available to better the health of engaged participants.

REFERENCES

1. Berkman LF, Glass T. Social Integration, Social Networks, Social Support, and Health. In: Kawachi I, Berkman L, eds. *Social Epidemiology*. New York, NY: Oxford University Press; 2000.

2. Gow AJ, Pattie A, Whiteman MC, Whalley LJ, Deary IJ. Social support and successful Aging. *J Individ Differ*. 2007;28(3):103–115.

3. Cobb S. Social support as a moderator of life stress. *Psychosom Med*. 1976;38(5):300–314.

4. Cohen S, Wills TA. Stress, social support, and the buffering hypothesis. *Psychol Bull*. 1985;98(2):310–357.

5. Dean A, Lin N. The stress-buffering role of social support. *J Nerv Ment Dis*. 1977;165(6):403–417.

6. Gottlieb BH, Bergen AE. Social support concepts and measures. *J Psychosom Res*. 2010;69(5):511–520.

7. Cacioppo JT, Cacioppo S. Older adults reporting social isolation or loneliness show poorer cognitive function 4 years later. *Evid Based Nurs*. 2014;17(2):59–60.

8. Courtin E, Knapp M. Social isolation, loneliness and health in old age: A scoping review. *Health Soc Care Community*. 2017;25(3):799–812.

9. Shovestul B, Han J, Germine L, Dodell-Feder D. Risk factors for loneliness: The high relative importance of age versus other factors. *PLoS One*. 2020;15(2):e0229087.

10. Hawkley LC, Thisted RA, Masi CM, Cacioppo JT. Loneliness predicts increased blood pressure: Five-year cross-lagged analyses in middle-aged and older adults. *Psychol Aging*. 2010;25(1):132–141.

11. Boss L, Kang D-H, Branson S. Loneliness and cognitive function in the older adult: a systematic review. *Int Psychogeriatr*. 2015;27(4):541–553.

12. House JS. Social isolation kills, but how and why? *Psychosom Med*. 2001;63(2):273–274.

13. Klinenberg E. Social Isolation, loneliness, and living alone: Identifying the risks for public health. *Am J Public Health*. 2016;106(5):786–787.

14. Wenger GC, Davies R, Shahtahmasebi S, Scott A. Social isolation and loneliness in old age: Review and model refinement. *Ageing Soc*. 1996;16(3):333–358.

15. US Health Resources & Services Administration. The "Loneliness Epidemic." 2019. Available at: https://www.hrsa.gov/enews/past-issues/2019/january-17/loneliness-epidemic. Accessed February 23, 2021.

16. Cudjoe TKM, Roth DL, Szanton SL, Wolff JL, Boyd CM, Thorpe RJ. The epidemiology of social isolation: National health and aging trends study. *J Gerontol Ser B*. 2020;75(1):107–113.

17. Cacioppo JT, Hawkley LC. Perceived social isolation and cognition. *Trends Cogn Sci*. 2009;13(10):447–454.

18. Hawkley LC, Wroblewski K, Kaiser T, Luhmann M, Schumm LP. Are US older adults getting lonelier? Age, period, and cohort differences. *Psychol Aging*. 2019;34(8):1144–1157.

19. Solway E, Piette J, Kirch M, Singer D, Kullgren J, Malani P. Loneliness and health among older adults: Results from the University Of Michigan National Poll On Healthy Aging. *Innov Aging*. 2019;3(Suppl 1):S600–S601.

20. House JS, Landis KR, Umberson D. Social relationships and health. *Sci Wash*. 1988;241(4865):540.

21. Cacioppo JT, Patrick W. *Loneliness: Human Nature and the Need for Social Connection*. London, United Kingdom: WW Norton and Co; 2008:xiv, 317.

22. Uchino BN. Social support and health: A review of physiological processes potentially underlying links to disease outcomes. *J Behav Med*. 2006;29(4):377–387.

23. Seeman T. How Do Others Get under Our Skin? In: Ryff CD, Singer BH, eds. *Emotion, Social Relationships, and Health*. New York, NY: Oxford University Press; 2001.

24. Brooks KP, Gruenwald T, Karlamanga A, Hu P, Koretz B, Seeman TE. Social relationships and allostatic load in the MIDUS Study. *Health Psychol Off J Div Health Psychol Am Psychol Assoc*. 2014;33(11):1373–1381.

25. Thoits PA. Social support as coping assistance. *J Consult Clin Psychol*. 1986;54(4):416–423.

26. Pearlin LI, Menaghan EG, Lieberman MA, Mullan JT. The stress process. *J Health Soc Behav*. 1981;22(4):337–356.

27. Shumaker SA, Brownell A. Toward a theory of social support: Closing conceptual gaps. *J Soc Issues*. 1984;40(4):11–36.

28. Cohen S, Syme SL. Issues in the study and application of social support. In: Cohen S, Syme SL, eds. *Social Support and Health*. Cambridge, MA: Academic Press; 1985:3–22.

29. Lin N. Conceptualizing social support. In: Lin N, Dean A, Ensel WM, eds. *Social Support, Life Events, and Depression*. Cambridge, MA: Academic Press; 1986:17–30.

30. Zimet GD, Dahlem NW, Zimet SG, Farley GK. The multidimensional scale of perceived social support. *J Pers Assess*. 1988;52(1):30–41.

31. Stanley MA, Beck JG, Zebb BJ. Psychometric properties of the MSPSS in older adults. *Aging Ment Health*. 1998;2(3):186–193.

32. Lubben JE. Assessing social networks among elderly populations. *Fam Community Health J Health Promot Maint.* 1988;11(3):42–52.

33. Sarason BR, Shearin EN, Pierce GR, Sarason IG. Interrelations of social support measures: Theoretical and practical implications. *J Pers Soc Psychol.* 1987;52(4):813–832.

34. Marti CN, Choi NG. Measuring social engagement among low-income, depressed homebound older adults: Validation of the Social Engagement and Activities Questionnaire. *Clin Gerontol.* 2020;15:1–14.

35. Ellwardt L, van Tilburg TG, Aartsen MJ. The mix matters: Complex personal networks relate to higher cognitive functioning in old age. *Soc Sci Med.* 2015;125:107–115.

36. Kelly ME, Duff H, Kelly S, et al. The impact of social activities, social networks, social support and social relationships on the cognitive functioning of healthy older adults: a systematic review. *Syst Rev.* 2017;6(1):259.

37. Gow AJ, Corley J, Starr JM, Deary IJ. Which social network or support factors are associated with cognitive abilities in old age? *Gerontology.* 2013;59(5):454–463.

38. La Fleur CG, Salthouse TA. Which aspects of social support are associated with which cognitive abilities for which people? *J Gerontol Ser B.* 2017;72(6):1006–1016.

39. Zunzunegui M-V, Alvarado BE, Del Ser T, Otero A. Social networks, social integration, and social engagement determine cognitive decline in community-dwelling Spanish older adults. *J Gerontol Ser B.* 2003;58(2):S93–S100.

40. Rook KS. Gaps in social support resources in later life: An adaptational challenge in need of further research. *J Soc Pers Relat.* 2009;26(1):103–112.

41. Cooper C, Livingston G. Intervening to reduce elder abuse: challenges for research. *Age Ageing.* 2016;45(2):184–185.

42. National Research Council (US) Panel to Review Risk and Prevalence of Elder Abuse and Neglect. Elder Mistreatment: Abuse, Neglect, and Exploitation in an Aging America. In: Bonnie RJ, Wallace RB, eds. Washington, DC: National Academies Press; 2003.

43. National Center on Elder Abuse. Types of abuse. Available at: https://ncea.acl.gov/Suspect-Abuse/Abuse-Types.aspx#self. Accessed on February 23, 2021.

44. Dyer CB, Goodwin JS, Pickens-Pace S, Burnett J, Kelly PA. Self-neglect among the elderly: A model based on more than 500 patients seen by a geriatric medicine team. *Am J Public Health.* 2007;97(9):1671–1676.

45. Burnett J, Regev T, Pickens S, et al. Social networks: a profile of the elderly who self- neglect. *J Elder Abuse Negl.* 2006;18(4):35–49.

46. Dong X, Simon MA, Mosqueda L, Evans DA. The prevalence of elder self-neglect in a community-dwelling population: Hoarding, hygiene, and environmental hazards. *J Aging Health.* 2012;24(3):507–524.

47. Thomas KS, Gadbois EA, Shield RR, Akobundu U, Morris AM, Dosa DM. "It's not just a simple meal. It's so much more": Interactions between meals on wheels clients and drivers. *J Appl Gerontol.* 2020;39(2):151–158.

48. Choi NG, Lee A, Goldstein M. Meals on Wheels: exploring potential for and barriers to integrating depression intervention for homebound older adults. *Home Health Care Serv Q.* 2011;30(4):214–230.

49. Demons JL, Chenna S, Callahan KE, et al. Utilizing a meals on wheels program to teach falls risk assessment to medical students. *Gerontol Geriatr Educ.* 2014;35(4):409–420.

50. McDonald TW, Chown EL, Tabb JE, Schaeffer AK, Howard EKM. The impact of volunteering on seniors' health and quality of life: An assessment of the retired and senior volunteer program. *Psychology.* 2013;04(03):283–290.

51. Tan EJ, Georges A, Gabbard SM, et al. The 2013–2014 Senior Corps Study: Foster grandparents and senior companions. *Public Policy Aging Rep.* 2016;26(3):88–95.

52. Flowers L, Houser A, Noel-Miller C, et al. Medicare Spends More on Socially Isolated Older Adults. 2017. AARP Public Policy Institute. Available at: https://www.aarp.org/ppi/info-2017/medicare-spends-more-on-socially-isolated-older-adults.html. Accessed February 23, 2021.

53. Davis A. Addressing Loneliness and Social Isolation in the Medicare Population. HIT Consultant. 2020. Available at: https://hitconsultant.net/2020/04/09/medicare-population-loneliness-social-isolation-sdoh. Accessed February 23, 2021.

54. Smith ML, Steinman LE, Casey EA. Combatting social isolation among older adults in a time of physical distancing: The COVID-19 social connectivity paradox. *Front Public Health.* 2020;8:403.

55. van Dam HA, van der Horst FG, Knoops L, Ryckman RM, Crebolder HFJM, van den Borne BHW. Social support in diabetes: a systematic review of controlled intervention studies. *Patient Educ Couns.* 2005;59(1):1–12.

56. Luger E, Dorner TE, Haider S, Kapan A, Lackinger C, Schindler K. Effects of a home-based and volunteer-administered physical training, nutritional, and social support program on malnutrition and frailty in older persons: A randomized controlled trial. *J Am Med Dir Assoc.* 2016;17(7):671.e9-671.e16.

57. Hogan BE, Linden W, Najarian B. Social support interventions: Do they work? *Clin Psychol Rev.* 2002;22(3):381–440.

58. O'Rourke HM, Collins L, Sidani S. Interventions to address social connectedness and loneliness for older adults: a scoping review. *BMC Geriatr.* 2018;18(1):214.

59. Mizoguchi N, Walker L, Trevelyan E, Ahmed B. *The Older Foreign-Born Population in the United States: 2012-2016.* Washington, DC: US Census Bureau; 2019:42.

60. Treas J. Four myths about older adults in America's immigrant families. *Generations.* 2008;32(4):40–45.

10

Mobility and Falls Among Older Adults

Caroline D. Bergeron, DrPH, MSc, Steven A. Cohen, DrPH, MPH, and Matthew Lee Smith, PhD, MPH

BACKGROUND

Mobility is the ability of an individual to move or transfer as needed, and is an integral component of healthy aging.[1] Nearly 15 million adults older than 65 years of age in the United States have mobility limitations, affecting approximately 30% of the older adult population.[2] While medical and public health advances in assistive technologies designed to improve mobility among older adults reduced the prevalence of mobility limitations leading up to the year 2000, the prevalence of mobility limitations has plateaued and has since begun to increase over the past two decades.[3] These increases, in part, may be attributed to the rising prevalence of obesity among older adults[4] as well as the increasing prevalence of chronic diseases (e.g., diabetes, hypertension) among the baby boomer population.[5,6] Although exact costs of mobility limitations are difficult to estimate, one study suggests that among Medicare beneficiaries, the costs of mobility limitations to Medicare alone were as high as $103 billion annually.[7,8]

Mobility and falls are interrelated concepts. Mobility impairments are associated with an increased risk of falls.[9] Conversely, experiencing a fall may further reduce a person's mobility.[10] A fall is defined as "inadvertently coming to rest on the ground, floor or other lower level, excluding intentional change in position to rest in furniture, wall, or other objects."[11] One in four older adults experiences a fall every year, affecting approximately 30 million older Americans.[12,13] Having a fall can lead to future falls.[14] The risk and frequency of falls also increase with age.[15] One in five falls causes a serious injury, such as bone fractures or head injuries,[13] and approximately 30,000 people die every year as a result of a fall.[12] Falls, including its associated injuries and costs, are largely preventable.[16,17] Improving physical mobility is one of many effective interventions to help prevent future falls.[18]

MOBILITY AS A MULTIDIMENSIONAL CONCEPT

Mobility is key to healthy aging. Optimal mobility is defined by Satariano and colleagues[19] as the ability to "go where you want to go, when you want to go, and how you want to get there," a critical aspect of successful and healthy aging.[20] The definition of mobility is broad, and includes movement in all forms, such as transferring (i.e., the movement of a person from one place or surface to another, such as from the bed to a chair) and ambulation (i.e., the ability to walk from place to place independently).[19] Mobility becomes an issue for older adults particularly when it is absent or declining. It is intrinsically tied to almost all aspects of health and well-being, including general health status,[21] mental health,[22] quality of life,[23,24] and social participation.[25,26] Therefore, researchers, clinicians, and practitioners are interested in understanding those factors that drive mobility and ways to prevent the declines in mobility that occur throughout the aging process.[27]

The concept of mobility can take many forms and exists on multiple levels, and is inherently tied to life space. Life space is the area through which a person travels over a given time period,[28,29] and tends to decline with age.

Mobility, Health, and Well-Being

Mobility is the subject of a growing body of research in public health and gerontology. The ecological model for the enhancement of mobility, personal care, and instrumental tasks has been used to identify environmental, behavioral, and biological factors that predict mobility and ability to conduct instrumental tasks.[30] Mobility can also impact health and other aspects of life through a number of pathways. The health impacts of mobility can be categorized into five broad categories of determinants: cognitive, psychosocial, physical, environmental, and financial. Each of these may be altered by culture and sociodemographic characteristics.[31]

Cognition is closely linked to mobility. A systematic review and meta-analysis of the relationship between cognition and mobility found that, overall, older adults with better mobility had better global cognition, executive function, memory, and processing speed.[32] A study of the Baltimore Longitudinal Study of Aging found that the relationship between cognition and mobility was bidirectional for most of the measures assessed, and therefore, one does not necessarily cause the other.[33] Mobility and cognitive function are both associated with well-being, and mobility is also associated with health-related quality of life.[34] Depression, and related conditions, and suicidality can result from physical isolation and loss of social ties resulting from reduced mobility.[22,35,36] One study found a dose-response, with greater levels of trait anxiety symptomatology and anxiety disorder linked to increased incidence of activity limitations, even after controlling for other mental health issues such as depression.[37] Driving cessation, for example, is an important event that substantially limits mobility in older adults, and is linked to negative psychosocial outcomes, including depression[38,39] and social integration (i.e., the number and frequency of social contacts).[40]

Physical health is associated with mobility through direct and indirect means. Older adults with limited mobility are more likely to have worse overall health, seek more health care,[41] and become institutionalized.[42] Limited mobility may also reduce the ability of affected older adults to procure fresh foods and medical care that promote health,[43] which may be exacerbated among racial and ethnic populations and those living in poorer neighborhoods.[44]

Neighborhood characteristics and environmental factors are also related to mobility. Walkability, or the ability to safely move around one's neighborhood or community, is one such example. Older adults living in more walkable neighborhoods had higher levels of mobility and physical activity compared to those living in less walkable neighborhoods.[45,46] Diversity of amenities, including easy access to retail services, health care, and civic spaces, plays a significant role in promoting mobility among older adults, although the precise mechanisms through which this occurs is unclear.[47] Findings from one study suggest that associations between neighborhood characteristics and mobility are stronger for Black older adults than for older adults of other races and ethnicities,[48] but further study is needed for validation.

Financial resources are also tied to mobility among older adults. For example, poorer older adults living in their own homes are less financially able to purchase assistive devices, such as canes and walkers, and make home modification designed to improve personal mobility than their wealthier counterparts.[49] Related to environmental and neighborhood characteristics, wealthier older adults are more likely to live in communities in which there is a greater diversity of amenities and walkability, which influences community mobility and related functional limitations.[50] Regardless of socioeconomic status, mobility limitations leading to falls and other injuries pose an economic threat to older adults. The cost of a fall requiring hospitalization averages over $26,000 in the United States.[51]

LIMITATIONS IN MOBILITY RESEARCH

Despite the abundance of research into mobility and aging, there are clear research gaps. Current research is limited by differences in how mobility is measured and the overall prominence of cross-sectional study designs, as opposed to longitudinal research.[45] Several measures of individual and community mobility exist, such as measuring activities of daily living (ADLs; i.e., basic activities for functional living, such as feeding, dressing, bathing, and walking) and instrumental activities of daily living (IADLs; i.e, activities that allow an individual to live independently, such as cooking, cleaning, transportation, laundry, and managing finances).[52,53] One of the fundamental issues with these and other related measures of mobility is that they measure a person's mobility at a point in time and do not generally consider how these activities manifest in that person's everyday life.[54]

RISK FACTORS FOR FALLS

As mentioned above, mobility tends to decline with age.[55] Lack of physical activity resulting from decreasing mobility can result in loss of muscle mass and bone density. Sarcopenia is the age-related loss of skeletal muscle mass and strength beginning around age 30.[56] Up to 50% of muscle mass may be lost by age 70.[57] The loss of muscle mass from sarcopenia is one of the main drivers of adverse health outcomes and chronic conditions among older adults, including disability and frailty.[58] Loss of bone density through osteoporosis can result in increased bone fragility, decreased balance, and decreased lower limb strength, further limiting mobility.[59] Osteoporosis and sarcopenia are often observed together in older adults. However, physical decline is only one of several possible factors that increase the risk of falling.

In the World Health Organization's falls risk factor model, falls are the result of a combination of modifiable and non-modifiable biological, behavioral, environmental, and socioeconomic factors.[18] (See Figure 10-1.) Biological risk factors refer to age, gender, and race/ethnicity. These risk factors can be associated, for example, with physical and cognitive decline. Behavioral risk factors are related to actions and decisions, and include sedentary behavior, malnutrition, medication use, and alcohol use.[18] Environmental risk factors refer to items or hazards in the physical surroundings of the older person that can cause a fall. Examples include slippery floor, loose rugs, uneven sidewalks, and poor lighting. Socioeconomic risk factors for falls refer to the social and economic status of the individual in the community. The main socioeconomic risk factors include income, education, housing, access to health care, and access to community resources. Older adults with higher socioeconomic status and better access to resources tend to report

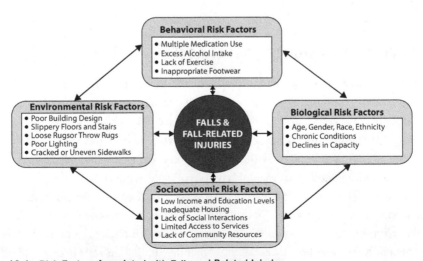

Figure 10-1. Risk Factors Associated with Falls and Related Injuries

better health and healthy behaviors, ability to install needed home modifications and acquire assistive technologies, greater access to health care, and fewer falls.[60,61] These factors are interconnected.[18] For example, while additional safety features can be set up in the environment to prevent a fall (e.g., installing a grab bar in the shower), an older person with low income or living in a rented apartment may not have the financial ability or the control to make this change.[62] Similarly, while vision loss worsens with age,[63] not everyone has the means to consult with an optometrist and purchase glasses to better see and prevent future falls.[62]

Rather than using the World Health Organization's ecological model, the Centers for Disease Control and Prevention's Stopping Elderly Accidents, Deaths, and Injuries (STEADI) initiative refers to intrinsic or extrinsic risk factors that contribute to falling.[64] This initiative, largely based on Wagner's Chronic Care Model,[65] utilizes an algorithm to guide health care teams' screening, treatment, referral, and follow-up activities to address falls risk.[66,67] Intrinsic factors, those related directly to the older person, may include advanced age, previous falls, muscle weakness, gait and balance problems, poor vision, postural hypotension (i.e., when the blood pools in the legs when a person stands up after sitting or lying down), chronic conditions, and fear of falling. Extrinsic factors, which are outside of this individual, may refer to the lack of stair handrails, poor stair design, lack of bathroom grab bars, dim lighting or glare, physical obstacles and tripping hazards, slippery or uneven or unsafe surfaces, and improper use of assistive devices such as canes or walkers.[64] The greater the number and severity of risk factors, the greater the likelihood of experiencing a fall.[64]

Finally, in their comprehensive literature review, Poh and Shorey[68] refer to additional factors that were not previously mentioned, including demographic information such as marital status (e.g., people who are divorced were more often admitted to the hospital for fall-related injuries)[69] and literacy and health literacy (e.g., those with limited literacy had higher risks of hip fractures),[70] intrinsic factors (e.g., body mass index), and additional extrinsic factors (e.g., time of day, location, mechanism of the fall). Fall risk factors have been the subject of a growing body of research in gerontology with the goal of better understanding these risk factors, evaluating which factors are modifiable, and preventing future falls. Among all the above mentioned fall risks, specific factors associated with mobility deserve further attention.

Fear of Falling

Fear of falling is defined as an ongoing anxiety, concern or belief related to experiencing a fall.[71-73] Fear of falling can be observed in people with or without a previous fall experience,[74,75] although fear of falling can be up to 6.41 times higher among those with a history of falling compared with those without such experience.[76] Fear of falling has long been associated with mobility restrictions,[75] including reduced activities of daily living[77] and physical activity.[78] In Lee and colleagues' study on factors associated with fear of falling, they found that fear of falling was strongly associated with experiencing some discomfort in the neighborhood environment, including in any of the living areas at home (e.g., entrance and stairs), when going outside (e.g., getting on and off buses, walking up and down slopes), and in the community (e.g., at the supermarket, bank, medical facilities).[79] Fear of falling in both indoor and outdoor environments makes older adults reluctant to engage in mobility-related activities, such as walking, ascending stairs, and performing IADLs.[79,80]

Mechanism of the Fall

In a study by Poh and Shorey,[68] the fall mechanism refers to the mobility activity leading up to the fall (e.g., whether the person was walking up or down the stairs, getting in or out of bed, or ambulating). The risks of experiencing a fall are higher when the center of mass and the center of gravity of a person move outside of the base of support covered by the feet.[16,81] Different conditions that occur as people age, such as diminished depth perception, decreased proprioception, and sarcopenia, may impact postural stability.[82,83] For example, older adults with chronic low back pain, a common condition, may move their center of gravity posterior to the center to reduce the pain, which may increase body sway to maintain a balanced position.[84-86] Greater body sway is associated with an increased risk of falls.[83] In addition, when there is an external perturbation to the center of mass (e.g., being pushed) or to the base of support (e.g., tripping), a weaker postural control system is less able to compensate and stabilize the body to prevent a fall.[87,88] Therefore, the mechanism of a fall is a complex system which includes an older person's static and dynamic balance with a reduced base of support,[89] gait (velocity and stride length),[90,91] and muscle strength (lower extremity, core).[89,91-93]

Assessment of Falls

To prevent falls and maintain mobility among older adults, systematic, multifactorial geriatric fall risk assessments and other screening tools are recommended to identify modifiable risk factors to address as part of subsequent interventions.[94] A comprehensive assessment can be conducted by geriatricians and can include an in-depth physical exam to assess postural hypotension, medications, feet and footwear, use of mobility aids, visual acuity, and cognition.[94-97] Other health care professionals can also conduct risk assessments using the following tools: the Fall Risk Assessment Tool (FRAT),[98] the Hendrich II Fall Risk Model™,[99] the St Thomas's Risk Assessment Tool in falling older adult inpatients,[100] the Peter James Centre Fall Risk Assessment Tool,[101] and the Resident Assessment Instrument,[102] with each having its strengths and drawbacks. One of the central critiques of these tools is that they take too much time to administer properly in clinical settings.[103] Some tools, such as the FRAT, have been modified and shortened without substantial loss of validity and reliability.[104] There are also tools and instruments such as the Falls Efficiency Scale-International [105,106] that are used to assess fear of falling, described previously, as an important aspect of mobility among older adults.

Reliable and valid fall risk screening tools, including the Tinetti Performance Oriented Mobility Assessment,[107,108] the Berg Balance Test,[109] and the Timed Up-and-Go Test,[95,110–112] may also be used to assess gait and balance, which are important predictors of falls. A specific assessment may be chosen based on the desired duration of administration and the setting (e.g., acute care, outpatient, extended care, primary care setting).[94,103] Once the risks have been identified, older adults may be guided to evidence-based interventions as part of a comprehensive multifactorial approach to address these risk factors and prevent falls.[103] The Centers for Disease Control and Prevention details the general screening, assessment, and intervention process through its STEADI algorithm for community-dwelling adults 65 years and older, available online at: www.cdc.gov/steadi/pdf/STEADI-Algorithm-508.pdf.[113]

Based on Hogue's falls and mobility ecological model[30] and Yen and Anderson's conceptual framework of factors that promote mobility in older adults,[114] Figure 10-2 provides an overview of this preceding background section. In this model, health is determined by interrelated factors, mobility and falls, and generally are the result of some sort of activity, such as walking. Both mobility and falls are also influenced by the environment, including the interconnected social, economic, and physical environments that impact one's individual and community mobility. All of these factors need to be considered to better understand mobility and falls among older adults.

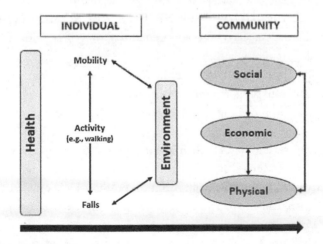

Source: Based on Hogue[30] and Yen and Anderson.[114]

Figure 10-2. Continuum of Falls Risk

RELEVANT POLICIES AND LEGISLATION

Several national and state policies impact mobility and falls among older adults in the United States. The main relevant policies at the national level are the Older Americans Act (OAA) of 1965 and the Americans with Disabilities Act (ADA) of 1990. The OAA was passed to provide community social services to older Americans. For the past 55 years, the OAA promotes the delivery of service programs including evidence-based falls prevention programs. The ADA, including its guidelines for buildings and facilities, requires modifications to the built environment to ensure universal access to all.[115,116] The implementation of these standards in public spaces, transportation, and new housing help enhance mobility of older adults and individuals with disabilities, while also reducing potential fall hazards.[116,117]

Government-Related Programs

Several government programs support falls prevention and mobility of older adults. As part of the enrollment into Medicare Part B program, a "Welcome to Medicare" visit is organized, which includes a single preventive physical exam to help detect frailty and mobility issues that could result in a fall.[118] In this visit, patients also receive education and counseling on falls prevention. Those enrolled for longer than 12 months can also access the free Annual Wellness Visit where they are screened for falls risk.[118]

Free transportation to and from medical appointments is also offered to Medicaid beneficiaries through the Medicaid nonemergency medical transportation (NEMT) program.[119] State Medicaid programs can also decide to cover nonmedical community transportation for their clients. In 2010, 28 states provided optional transportation services to their older adults.[120] The ridesharing company Lyft has also partnered with NEMT providers across the United States to provide NEMT services for enrolled Medicaid recipients.[121] Older rural residents have especially benefitted from these ridesharing options to attend their medical appointments.[121]

The Federal Transit Administration's Enhanced Mobility of Seniors and Individuals with Disabilities program supports transportation mobility options from large urbanized areas to rural areas by providing funding to support special transportation needs of seniors and individuals with disabilities.[122]

At the state level, several states have innovative programs to support mobility among older adults. In Pennsylvania[123] and Rhode Island,[124] for example, adults 65 years of age or older have access to free public transportation on their local public transit systems. Older Pennsylvanians can also benefit from the shared-ride, curb to curb program where they only pay 15% of the fare.[123] In Vermont, the statewide online trip planner "Go! Vermont" provides improved access to transit information, including to and from rural settings, and hail-a-ride options.[121]

BEST PRACTICE INTERVENTIONS

The Administration for Community Living (ACL) endorses a variety of evidence-based fall prevention programs delivered nationwide in diverse settings to assist older adults prevent and manage falls.[125] Each of these programs has demonstrated ability to reduce falls and fall-related risk in their own respective efficacy or effectiveness trials. Over the last decade, ACL has supported an implementation infrastructure to sustain these evidence-based programs, which are eligible for OAA Title III-D funding.[126] Delivered primarily through the aging services network and health care system, these programs were designed to meet the varying levels of fall-related risk and mobility experienced among older adults. Many of these fall prevention programs address fear of falling and self-efficacy while incorporating exercises to increase lower limb strength, balance, and flexibility.[127] Facilitated by trained lay leaders or allied health professionals, these programs can be integrated in clinical and community settings to complement other efforts to mitigate fall risk and improve mobility among older adults as part of the larger evidence-based movement.[128]

SPECIAL CONSIDERATIONS AND SPECIAL POPULATIONS

The issues of mobility and falls among older adults is especially important when considering special populations, such as older adults in poverty, those living in rural areas (including those without access to public transportation), and older adults living alone without family present or nearby. Economic factors such as low socioeconomic status and poverty impact older adult mobility on multiple levels. On the individual level, those experiencing mobility limitations and/or falls as a result of those limitations are less likely to be able to afford home modifications, assistive technologies, and high-quality health care than wealthier older adults, which makes those individuals at a higher risk of complications and mortality from limited mobility and falls, even among Medicare and Medicaid dual-eligible beneficiaries.[129] Many low-income older adults live in public housing, which is associated with a higher prevalence of a litany of diseases and conditions compared with those dwelling elsewhere.[130] On the community level, poorer older adults, as lower income populations in general, tend to live in neighborhoods where crime is higher and safety, or perceived safety, is minimal, further hindering neighborhood or community mobility.[131]

Another important population to consider when promoting mobility and reducing the risk of falls is older adults living in rural areas. Rural older adults face unique challenges, including geographic isolation, lack of transportation, poor area resources (i.e., lack of retail facilities and fresh foods),[132] and lack of access to high-quality health care.[133,134] Older adults in rural areas experience higher levels of social isolation as well,[135] as rural older adults are less likely to cohabitate with other people compared with older adults in urban and suburban areas.[136] Demographic changes over the past several decades have left rural areas with a higher concentration of older adults compared to more urban areas, which leaves rural older adults less likely to have family nearby. All of these factors contribute to rural older adults having reduced community mobility. Recent research suggests that rural residents benefit more from effective interventions to improve mobility compared with urban older adults.[137] Any programs designed to improve mobility and reduce falls should take into account the geographic and contextual factors inherent to where older adults live.

CONCLUSION: CHALLENGES AND OPPORTUNITIES FOR PUBLIC HEALTH

Mobility issues and falls continue to be a major public health challenge and burden for older adults, family systems, and the health care system. Diverse older adults across the socioeconomic, demographic, and geographic spectra face different barriers at the individual and community levels, which can significantly impact their quality of life. Ideally, public health practitioners and other medical and allied health professionals would work together in integrated teams to engage in detection and early intervention of older adults to address known multifactorial risks for mobility and falls. Coordinated efforts related to falls prevention and mobility can drive research, practice, and policy initiatives to advance older adult health and reduce health disparities among this population.

CASE STUDY

A case study of mobility and falls can be found in Contra Costa County, California, a county in the San Francisco-Oakland metropolitan area of just over a million residents, approximately 16% of which are aged 65 and over.[138] A recent study by Ragland et al.[139] surveyed 510 older adults living in the county and found that several factors contributed to the limited mobility of its older residents. These included poor public transit infrastructure in the county and resultant infrequent use of it by older adults. Accordingly, the results revealed that most of the older adults in the county are car dependent, which can have notable effects on community mobility as residents age. Common to many other communities and counties in the United States, rideshare services are available in Contra Costa County, but older residents reported low use of it. The study also found that lack of transportation led to decreased community mobility which, in turn, resulted in older adults missing activities. To improve mobility and, more generally, quality of life for older adults, the study authors suggest that efforts should be made to develop mobility solutions beyond private vehicles. The authors cite the Coordinated Public Transit-Human Services Transportation Commission of the

San Francisco Bay Area as an agency whose task is to provide cost-effective and comprehensive mobility options for older adults with mobility disabilities as is the case in other parts of the San Francisco Bay Area.

REFERENCES

1. De Silva NA, Gregory MA, Venkateshan SS, Verschoor CP, Kuspinar A. Examining the association between life-space mobility and cognitive function in older adults: A systematic review. *J Aging Res*. 2019;2019:1–9.

2. Musich S, Wang SS, Ruiz J, Hawkins K, Wicker E. The impact of mobility limitations on health outcomes among older adults. *Geriatr Nur (Lond)*. 2018;39(2):162–169.

3. Freedman VA, Kasper JD, Spillman BC, et al. Behavioral adaptation and late-life disability: A new spectrum for assessing public health impacts. *Am J Public Health*. 2014;104(2):e88–e94.

4. Vincent HK, Vincent KR, Lamb KM. Obesity and mobility disability in the older adult: Obesity, old age and disability. *Obes Rev*. 2010;11(8):568–579.

5. Gregg EW, Li Y, Wang J, et al. Changes in diabetes-related complications in the United States, 1990–2010. *N Engl J Med*. 2014;370(16):1514–1523.

6. Odden MC, Coxson PG, Moran A, Lightwood JM, Goldman L, Bibbins-Domingo K. The impact of the aging population on coronary heart disease in the United States. *Am J Med*. 2011;124(9):827–833.e5.

7. Brown CJ, Flood KL. Mobility limitation in the older patient: A clinical review. *JAMA*. 2013;310(11):1168–1177.

8. Hoffman JM, Ciol MA, Huynh M, Chan L. Estimating transition probabilities in mobility and total costs for Medicare beneficiaries. *Arch Phys Med Rehabil*. 2010;91(12):1849–1855.

9. Barker AL, Nitz JC, Low Choy NL, Haines TP. Mobility has a non-linear association with falls risk among people in residential aged care: an observational study. *J Physiother*. 2012;58(2):117–125.

10. Dionyssiotis Y. Analyzing the problem of falls among older people. *Int J Gen Med*. 2012:805–813.

11. World Health Organization. *A Global Report on Falls Prevention: Epidemiology of Falls*. Geneva, Switzerland: World Health Organization; 2007:40.

12. Bergen G, Stevens MR, Burns ER. Falls and fall injuries among adults ≥ 65 years—United States, 2014. *MMWR Morb Mortal Wkly Rep*. 2016:993–998.

13. Centers for Disease Control and Prevention. Keep on your feet—Preventing older adult falls. 2019. Available at: www.cdc.gov/injury/features/older-adult-falls/index.html. Accessed February 25, 2021.

14. Tinetti ME, Speechley M. Prevention of falls among the elderly. *N Engl J Med.* 1989;320(16):1055–1059.

15. Jin J. Prevention of falls in older adults. *JAMA.* 2018;319(16):1734.

16. Florence CS, Bergen G, Atherly A, Burns E, Stevens J, Drake C. Medical costs of fatal and nonfatal falls in older adults: Medical costs of falls. *J Am Geriatr Soc.* 2018;66(4):693–698.

17. Stevens JA, Lee R. The potential to reduce falls and avert costs by clinically managing fall risk. *Am J Prev Med.* 2018;55(3):290–297.

18. World Health Organization. *WHO Global Report on Falls Prevention in Older Age.* Geneva, Switzerland: World Health Organization; 2007.

19. Satariano WA, Guralnik JM, Jackson RJ, Marottoli RA, Phelan EA, Prohaska TR. Mobility and aging: New directions for public health action. *Am J Public Health.* 2012;102(8):1508–1515.

20. World Health Organization. Global age-friendly cities: A guide. 2007. Available at: www.who.int/ageing/publications/Global_age_friendly_cities_Guide_English.pdf. Accessed February 25, 2021.

21. Brennan DS, Singh KA. Dietary, self-reported oral health and socio-demographic predictors of general health status among older adults. *J Nutr Health Aging.* 2012;16(5):437–441.

22. Lampinen P, Heikkinen E. Reduced mobility and physical activity as predictors of depressive symptoms among community-dwelling older adults: An eight-year follow-up study. *Aging Clin Exp Res.* 2003;15(3):205–211.

23. Groessl EJ, Kaplan RM, Rejeski WJ, et al. Health-related quality of life in older adults at risk for disability. *Am J Prev Med.* 2007;33(3):214–218.

24. Stubbs B, Schofield P, Patchay S. Mobility limitations and fall-related factors contribute to the reduced health-related quality of life in older adults with chronic musculoskeletal pain. *Pain Pract.* 2016;16(1):80–89.

25. Rosso AL, Taylor JA, Tabb LP, Michael YL. Mobility, disability, and social engagement in older adults. *J Aging Health.* 2013;25(4):617–637.

26. Rasinaho M, Hirvensalo M, Leinonen R, Lintunen T, Rantanen T. Motives for and barriers to physical activity among older adults with mobility limitations. *J Aging Phys Act.* 2007;15(1):90–102.

27. Webber SC, Porter MM, Menec VH. Mobility in older adults: A comprehensive framework. *Gerontologist.* 2010;50(4):443–450.

28. Baker PS, Bodner EV, Allman RM. Measuring life-space mobility in community-dwelling older adults. *J Am Geriatr Soc.* 2003;51(11):1610–1614.

29. May D, Nayak USL, Isaacs B. The life-space diary: A measure of mobility in old people at home. *Int Rehabil Med.* 1985;7(4):182–186.

30. Hogue CC. Falls and mobility in late life: An Ecological Model. *J Am Geriatr Soc.* 1984;32(11):858–861.

31. DiPietro L. Physical activity in aging: Changes in patterns and their relationship to health and function. *J Gerontol A Biol Sci Med Sci.* 2001;56(suppl 2):13–22.

32. Demnitz N, Esser P, Dawes H, et al. A systematic review and meta-analysis of cross-sectional studies examining the relationship between mobility and cognition in healthy older adults. *Gait Posture.* 2016;50:164–174.

33. Tian Q, An Y, Resnick SM, Studenski S. The relative temporal sequence of decline in mobility and cognition among initially unimpaired older adults: Results from the Baltimore Longitudinal Study of Aging. *Age Ageing.* 2017;46(3):445–451.

34. Davis JC, Bryan S, Li LC, et al. Mobility and cognition are associated with wellbeing and health related quality of life among older adults: a cross-sectional analysis of the Vancouver Falls Prevention Cohort. *BMC Geriatr.* 2015;15(1):75.

35. Barry LC, Coman E, Wakefield D, Trestman RL, Conwell Y, Steffens DC. Functional disability, depression, and suicidal ideation in older prisoners. *J Affect Disord.* 2020;266:366–373.

36. Thompson JL, Bentley G, Davis M, Coulson J, Stathi A, Fox KR. Food shopping habits, physical activity and health-related indicators among adults aged ≥70 years. *Public Health Nutr.* 2011;14(9):1640–1649.

37. Norton J, Ancelin ML, Stewart R, Berr C, Ritchie K, Carrière I. Anxiety symptoms and disorder predict activity limitations in the elderly. *J Affect Disord.* 2012;141(2–3):276–285.

38. Windsor TD, Anstey KJ. Interventions to reduce the adverse psychosocial impact of driving cessation on older adults. *Clin Interv Aging.* 2006;1(3):205–211.

39. Windsor TD, Anstey KJ, Butterworth P, Luszcz MA, Andrews GR. The role of perceived control in explaining depressive symptoms associated with driving cessation in a longitudinal study. *Gerontologist.* 2007;47(2):215–223.

40. Mezuk B, Rebok GW. Social integration and social support among older adults following driving cessation. *J Gerontol B Psychol Sci Soc Sci.* 2008;63(5):S298–S303.

41. Hardy SE, Kang Y, Studenski SA, Degenholtz HB. Ability to walk 1/4 mile predicts subsequent disability, mortality, and health care costs. *J Gen Intern Med.* 2011;26(2):130–135.

42. Luppa M, Luck T, Weyerer S, Konig H-H, Brahler E, Riedel-Heller SG. Prediction of institutionalization in the elderly. A systematic review. *Age Ageing.* 2010;39(1):31–38.

43. Gardner P. The role of social engagement and identity in community mobility among older adults aging in place. *Disabil Rehabil.* 2014;36(15):1249–1257.

44. Cagney KA, Browning CR, Wen M. Racial disparities in self-rated health at older ages: What difference does the neighborhood make? *J Gerontol B Psychol Sci Soc Sci.* 2005;60(4):S181–S190.

45. Rosso AL, Auchincloss AH, Michael YL. The urban built environment and mobility in older adults: A comprehensive review. *J Aging Res.* 2011;2011:1–10.

46. King AC, Sallis JF, Frank LD, et al. Aging in neighborhoods differing in walkability and income: Associations with physical activity and obesity in older adults. *Soc Sci Med.* 2011;73(10):1525–1533.

47. Rosso AL, Grubesic TH, Auchincloss AH, Tabb LP, Michael YL. Neighborhood amenities and mobility in older adults. *Am J Epidemiol.* 2013;178(5):761–769.

48. Rosso AL, Tabb LP, Grubesic TH, Taylor JA, Michael YL. Neighborhood social capital and achieved mobility of older adults. *J Aging Health.* 2014;26(8):1301–1319.

49. Mathieson KM, Kronenfeld JJ, Keith VM. Maintaining functional independence in elderly adults. *Gerontologist.* 2002;42(1):24–31.

50. Levasseur M, Généreux M, Bruneau J-F, et al. Importance of proximity to resources, social support, transportation and neighborhood security for mobility and social participation in older adults: results from a scoping study. *BMC Public Health.* 2015;15(1):503.

51. Davis JC, Robertson MC, Ashe MC, Liu-Ambrose T, Khan KM, Marra CA. International comparison of cost of falls in older adults living in the community: A systematic review. *Osteoporos Int.* 2010;21(8):1295–1306.

52. Granger CV, Gresham GE. Functional assessment in rehabilitation medicine. *Phys Med Rehabil Clin N Am.* 1993;4(3):417–423.

53. Lawton MP, Moss M, Fulcomer M, Kleban MH. A research and service oriented multilevel assessment instrument. *J Gerontol.* 1982;37(1):91–99.

54. Peel C, Baker PS, Roth DL, Brown CJ, Bodner EV, Allman RM. Assessing mobility in older adults: The UAB Study of Aging Life-Space Assessment. *Phys Ther.* 2005;85(10):1008–1019.

55. Rantakokko M, Mänty M, Rantanen T. Mobility decline in old age: *Exerc Sport Sci Rev.* 2013;41(1):19–25.

56. Walston JD. Sarcopenia in older adults: *Curr Opin Rheumatol.* 2012;24(6):623–627.

57. Metter EJ, Conwit R, Tobin J, Fozard JL. Age-associated loss of power and strength in the upper extremities in women and men. *J Gerontol A Biol Sci Med Sci.* 1997;52A(5):B267–B276.

58. Marsh AP, Rejeski WJ, Espeland MA, et al. Muscle strength and BMI as predictors of major mobility disability in the Lifestyle Interventions and Independence for Elders Pilot (LIFE-P). *J Gerontol A Biol Sci Med Sci.* 2011;66A(12):1376–1383.

59. Mousa SM, Rasheedy D, El-Sorady KE, Mortagy AK. Beyond mobility assessment: Timed up and go test and its relationship to osteoporosis and fracture risk. *J Clin Gerontol Geriatr.* 2016;7(2):48–52.

60. Gill T, Taylor AW, Pengelly A. A population-based survey of factors relating to the prevalence of falls in older people. *Gerontology.* 2005;51(5):340–345.

61. Fabre JM, Ellis R, Kosma M, Wood RH. Falls risk factors and a compendium of falls risk screening instruments. *J Geriatr Phys Ther*. 2010;33(4):184–197.

62. Ontario Neurotrauma Foundation. How socioeconomic status affects fall risk. 2015. Available at: www.fallsloop.com/discussions/10199. Accessed February 25, 2021.

63. Centers for Disease Control and Prevention. Vision impairment and older adult falls. 2019. Available at: www.cdc.gov/visionhealth/resources/features/vision-loss-falls.html. Accessed February 25, 2021.

64. Centers for Disease Control and Prevention. Fact sheet: Risk factors for falls. 2017. Available at: www.cdc.gov/steadi/pdf/Risk_Factors_for_Falls-print.pdf. Accessed February 25, 2021.

65. Wagner EH. Chronic disease management: What will it take to improve care for chronic illness? *Eff Clin Pract*. 1998;1(1):2–4.

66. Stevens JA, Phelan EA. Development of STEADI: A fall prevention resource for health care providers. *Health Promot Pract*. 2013;14(5):706–714.

67. Stevens JA, Smith ML, Parker EM, Jiang L, Floyd FD. Implementing a clinically based fall prevention program. *Am J Lifestyle Med*. 2020;14(1):71–77.

68. Poh FJX, Shorey S. A literature review of factors influencing injurious falls. *Clin Nurs Res*. 2020;29(3):141–148.

69. Coutinho ES, Fletcher A, Bloch KV, Rodrigues LC. Risk factors for falls with severe fracture in elderly people living in a middle-income country: a case control study. *BMC Geriatr*. 2008;8(1):21.

70. Ravindran RM, Kutty VR. Risk factors for fall-related injuries leading to hospitalization among community-dwelling older persons: A hospital-based case-control study in Thiruvananthapuram, Kerala, India. *Asia Pac J Public Health*. 2016;28(suppl 1):70S–76S.

71. Gazibara T, Kurtagic I, Kisic-Tepavcevic D, et al. Falls, risk factors and fear of falling among persons older than 65 years of age: Falls in the older population. *Psychogeriatrics*. 2017;17(4):215–223.

72. Young WR, Mark Williams A. How fear of falling can increase fall-risk in older adults: Applying psychological theory to practical observations. *Gait Posture*. 2015;41(1):7–12.

73. Tinetti ME, Powell L. 4 fear of falling and low self-efficacy: A cause of dependence in elderly persons. *J Gerontol*. 1993;48(Special_Issue):35–38.

74. Jung D. Fear of falling in older adults: Comprehensive review. *Asian Nurs Res*. 2008;2(4):214–222.

75. Delbaere K, Crombez G, van Haastregt JCM, Vlaeyen JWS. Falls and catastrophic thoughts about falls predict mobility restriction in community-dwelling older people: A structural equation modelling approach. *Aging Ment Health*. 2009;13(4):587–592.

76. Kim S, So W-Y. Prevalence and correlates of fear of falling in Korean community-dwelling elderly subjects. *Exp Gerontol*. 2013;48(11):1323–1328.

77. Cumming RG, Salkeld G, Thomas M, Szonyi G. Prospective study of the impact of fear of falling on activities of daily living, SF-36 scores, and nursing home admission. *J Gerontol A Biol Sci Med Sci*. 2000;55(5):M299–M305.

78. Murphy SL, Williams CS, Gill TM. Characteristics associated with fear of falling and activity restriction in community-living older persons. *J Am Geriatr Soc*. 2002;50(3):516–520.

79. Lee S, Oh E, Hong G-R. Comparison of factors associated with fear of falling between older adults with and without a fall history. *Int J Environ Res Public Health*. 2018;15(5):982.

80. Gaxatte C, Nguyen T, Chourabi F, et al. Fear of falling as seen in the multidisciplinary falls consultation. *Ann Phys Rehabil Med*. 2011;54(4):248–258.

81. Institute of Medicine. Falls in older persons: Risk factors and prevention. In: Berg RL, Cassells JS, eds. *The Second Fifty Years: Promoting Health and Preventing Disability*. Washington, DC: National Academies Press; 1992.

82. Maki BE, McIlroy WE. Postural control in the older adult. *Clin Geriatr Med*. 1996;12(4): 635–658.

83. Jančová Všetečková J, Drey N. What is the role body sway deviations and body sway velocity play in postural stability in older adults? *Acta Medica Hradec Kralove Czech Repub*. 2013;56(3):117–123.

84. Kim D-H, Park J-K, Jeong M-K. Influences of posterior-located center of gravity on lumbar extension strength, balance, and lumbar lordosis in chronic low back pain. *J Back Musculo-skelet Rehabil*. 2014;27(2):231–237.

85. Stubbs B, Binnekade T, Eggermont L, Sepehry AA, Patchay S, Schofield P. Pain and the risk for falls in community-dwelling older adults: Systematic review and meta-analysis. *Arch Phys Med Rehabil*. 2014;95(1):175–187.e9.

86. Leveille SG. Chronic musculoskeletal pain and the occurrence of falls in an older population. *JAMA*. 2009;302(20):2214.

87. Alexander NB. Postural control in older adults. *J Am Geriatr Soc*. 1994;42(1):93–108.

88. Winter DA, Patla AE, Frank JS. Assessment of balance control in humans. *Med Prog Technol*, 16(1–2):31–51.

89. Muir SW, Berg K, Chesworth B, Klar N, Speechley M. Balance impairment as a risk factor for falls in community-dwelling older adults who are high functioning: A prospective study. *Phys Ther*. 2010;90(3):338–347.

90. Salzman B. Gait and balance disorders in older adults. *Am Fam Physician*. 2010;1(82): 61–68.

91. Sinaki M, Brey RH, Hughes CA, Larson DR, Kaufman KR. Balance disorder and increased risk of falls in osteoporosis and kyphosis: significance of kyphotic posture and muscle strength. *Osteoporos Int*. 2005;16(8):1004–1010.

92. Granacher U, Gollhofer A, Hortobágyi T, Kressig RW, Muehlbauer T. The importance of trunk muscle strength for balance, functional performance, and fall prevention in seniors: A systematic review. *Sports Med.* 2013;43(7):627–641.

93. Ishigaki EY, Ramos LG, Carvalho ES, Lunardi AC. Effectiveness of muscle strengthening and description of protocols for preventing falls in the elderly: a systematic review. *Braz J Phys Ther.* 2014;18(2):111–118.

94. Perell KL, Nelson A, Goldman RL, Luther SL, Prieto-Lewis N, Rubenstein LZ. Fall risk assessment measures: An analytic review. *J Gerontol A Biol Sci Med Sci.* 2001;56(12):M761–M766.

95. Welch V, Ghogomu E, Shea B. Evidence-Based Screening Tools and Fall Risk Assessment in Continuing Care: A Bruyère Rapid Review. 2016. Bruyère Research Institute. Available at: www.bruyere.org/uploads/Falls%20assessment%20in%20continuing%20care.pdf. Accessed February 25, 2021.

96. Beauchet O, Montero-Odasso M. Comprehensive Falls Assessment: Cognitive Impairment Is a Matter to Consider. In: Montero-Odasso M, Camicioli R, eds. *Falls and Cognition in Older Persons: Fundamentals, Assessment and Therapeutic Options.* Cham, Switzerland: Springer International Publishing; 2020:87–106.

97. Hunter SW, Speechley M. Evidence, Recommendations, and Current Gaps in Guidelines for Fall Prevention and Treatments. In: Montero-Odasso M, Camicioli R, eds. *Falls and Cognition in Older Persons: Fundamentals, Assessment and Therapeutic Options.* Cham, Switzerland: Springer International Publishing; 2020:263–272.

98. MacAvoy S, Skinner T, Hines M. Fall risk assessment tool. *Appl Nurs Res.* 1996;9(4):213–218.

99. Hendrich AL, Bender PS, Nyhuis A. Validation of the Hendrich II Fall Risk Model: A large concurrent case/control study of hospitalized patients. *Appl Nurs Res.* 2003;16(1):9–21.

100. Oliver D, Britton M, Seed P, Martin FC, Hopper AH. Development and evaluation of evidence based risk assessment tool (STRATIFY) to predict which elderly inpatients will fall: case-control and cohort studies. *BMJ.* 1997;315(7115):1049–1053.

101. Haines TP, Bennell KL, Osborne RH, Hill KD. A new instrument for targeting falls prevention interventions was accurate and clinically applicable in a hospital setting. *J Clin Epidemiol.* 2006;59(2):168–175.

102. Hawes CH, Morris JN, Phillips CD, Fries BE, Murphy K, Mor V. Development of the nursing home resident assessment instrument in the USA. *Age Ageing.* 1997;26(suppl 2):19–25.

103. Phelan EA, Mahoney JE, Voit JC, Stevens JA. Assessment and management of fall risk in primary care settings. *Med Clin North Am.* 2015;99(2):281–293.

104. Hnizdo S, Archuleta RA, Taylor B, Kim SC. Validity and reliability of the modified John Hopkins Fall Risk Assessment Tool for elderly patients in home health care. *Geriatr Nur (Lond).* 2013;34(5):423–427.

105. Yardley L, Beyer N, Hauer K, Kempen G, Piot-Ziegler C, Todd C. Development and initial validation of the Falls Efficacy Scale-International (FES-I). *Age Ageing*. 2005;34(6):614–619.

106. Greenberg SA. Assessment of fear of falling in older adults: the Falls Efficacy Scale-International (FES-I). *Disabil Rehabil*. 2011;29(2):155–162.

107. Tinetti ME. Performance-oriented assessment of mobility problems in elderly patients. *J Am Geriatr Soc*. 1986;34(2):119–126.

108. Leading Age Minnesota. Tinetti Performance Oriented Mobility Assessment (POMA). Available at: www.leadingagemn.org/assets/docs/Tinetti-Balance-Gait--POMA.pdf Accessed February 25, 2021.

109. Berg K. Balance and its measure in the elderly: A review. *Physiother Can*. 1989;41(5):240–246.

110. Bohannon RW. Reference values for the Timed Up and Go Test: A descriptive meta-analysis. *J Geriatr Phys Ther*. 2006;29(2):64–68.

111. van Hedel HJ, Wirz M, Dietz V. Assessing walking ability in subjects with spinal cord injury: Validity and reliability of 3 walking tests. *Arch Phys Med Rehabil*. 2005;86(2):190–196.

112. Vaught SL. Gait, balance, and fall prevention. *Ochsner J*. 2001;3(2):94–97.

113. Centers for Disease Control and Prevention. STEADI—Older adult fall prevention: Materials for healthcare providers. 2020. Available at: www.cdc.gov/steadi/materials.html. Accessed February 25, 2021.

114. Yen IH, Anderson LA. Built environment and mobility of older adults: Important policy and practice efforts. *J Am Geriatr Soc*. 2012;60(5):951–956.

115. US Architectural and Transportation Barriers Compliance Board. Americans with Disabilities Act: Accessibility guidelines for buildings and facilities. 2003. Available at: https://www.access-board.gov/files/ada/adaag-2002.pdf. Accessed February 25, 2021.

116. Farber N, Shinkle D, Lynott J, Fox-Grage W, Harrell R. Aging in place: A state survey of livability policies and practices. AARP. 2011. Available at: www.ncsl.org/documents/transportation/Aging-in-Place-2011.pdf. Accessed February 25, 2021.

117. National Council on Aging. Falls Free: 2015 National Falls Prevention Action Plan. 2015. Available at: https://www.ncoa.org/wp-content/uploads/FallsActionPlan_2015-FINAL.pdf. Accessed February 25, 2021.

118. Special Committee on Aging. Falls prevention: National, state, and local solutions to better support seniors. US Senate. October 2019. Available at: www.aging.senate.gov/imo/media/doc/SCA_Falls_Report_2019.pdf. Accessed February 25, 2021.

119. Centers for Medicare & Medicaid Services. Medicaid non-emergency medical transportation booklet for providers. April 2016. Available at: www.cms.gov/medicare-medicaid-coordination/fraud-prevention/medicaid-integrity-education/downloads/nemt-booklet.pdf. Accessed February 25, 2021.

120. Fox-Grage W, Lynott J. Expanding specialized transportation: New opportunities under the Affordable Care Act. January 2015. Available at: www.aarp.org/content/dam/aarp/ppi/2015/AARP-New-ACA-Transportation-Opportunities.pdf. Accessed February 25, 2021.

121. Godavarthy R, Hough J, Libberton S, Koff R. Opportunities for state DOTs (and Others) to encourage shared-use mobility practices in rural areas. December 2019. Available at: http://onlinepubs.trb.org/onlinepubs/nchrp/2065/Task76Report.pdf. Accessed February 25, 2021.

122. US Department of Transportation. Enhanced mobility of seniors & people with disabilities fact sheet (Chapter 53 Section 5310). 2020. Available at: www.transit.dot.gov/sites/fta.dot.gov/files/docs/funding/grants/37971/5310-enhanced-mobility-seniors-and-individuals-disabilities-fact-sheet.pdf. Accessed February 25, 2021.

123. Pennsylvania Department of Transportation. Seniors and persons with disabilities. 2020. Available at: www.penndot.gov/TravelInPA/PublicTransitOptions/Pages/Seniors-and-Persons-With-Disabilities.aspx#sharedride. Accessed February 25, 2021.

124. Executive Office of Health and Human Services, State of Rhode Island. Rhode Island's non-emergency medical transportation services. 2020. Available at: www.eohhs.ri.gov/Consumer/TransportationServices.aspx. Accessed February 25, 2021.

125. National Council on Aging. Evidence-based falls prevention programs. 2019. Available at: https://www.ncoa.org/article/evidence-based-falls-prevention-programs. Accessed July 21, 2021.

126. Boutaugh ML, Jenkins SM, Kulinski KP, Lorig KL, Ory MG, Smith ML. Closing the disparity: The work of the Administration on Aging. *Generations*. 2014;38(4):107–118.

127. Smith M, Towne S, Herrera-Venson A, et al. Delivery of fall prevention interventions for at-risk older adults in rural areas: Findings from a national dissemination. *Int J Environ Res Public Health*. 2018;15(12):2798.

128. Ory MG, Smith ML. Research, practice, and policy perspectives on evidence-based programming for older adults. *Front Public Health*. 2015;3.

129. Wright KD, Pepper GA, Caserta M, et al. Factors that influence physical function and emotional well-being among Medicare-Medicaid enrollees. *Geriatr Nur (Lond)*. 2015;36(2):S16–S20.

130. Parsons PL, Mezuk B, Ratliff S, Lapane KL. Subsidized housing not subsidized health: health status and fatigue among elders in public housing and other community settings. *Ethn Dis*. 2011;21(1):85–90.

131. McFadden ES, Lucio J. Aging in (privatized) places: Subsidized housing policy and seniors. *J Hous Elder*. 2014;28(3):268–287.

132. Cohen SA, Greaney ML, Sabik NJ. Assessment of dietary patterns, physical activity and obesity from a national survey: Rural-urban health disparities in older adults. *PloS One*. 2018;13(12):e0208268.

133. Durazo E, Jones M, Wallace S, Van Arsdale J, Aydin M, Stewart C. The health status and unique health challenges of rural older adults in California. UCLA Center for Health Policy Research. June 2011. Available at: https://escholarship.org/uc/item/0ds8j0w9. Accessed February 25, 2021.

134. Smith M, Prohaska T, MacLeod K, et al. Non-emergency medical transportation needs of middle-aged and older adults: A rural-urban comparison in Delaware, USA. *Int J Environ Res Public Health*. 2017;14(2):174.

135. Cudjoe TKM, Roth DL, Szanton SL, Wolff JL, Boyd CM, Thorpe RJ. The epidemiology of social isolation: National Health and Aging Trends Study. Carr D, ed. *J Gerontol Ser B*. 2020;75(1):107–113.

136. Eshbaugh EM. The role of friends in predicting loneliness among older women living alone. *J Gerontol Nurs*. 2009;35(5):13–16.

137. Smith ML, Ahn SN, Sharkey JR, Horel S, Mier N, Ory MG. Successful falls prevention programming for older adults in Texas: Rural–urban variations. *J Appl Gerontol*. 2012;31(1):3–27.

138. US Census Bureau. QuickFacts: Contra Costa County, California. 2019. Available at: https://www.census.gov/quickfacts/contracostacountycalifornia. Accessed February 25, 2021.

139. Ragland DR, McMillan T, Doggett S. Mobility challenges facing older adults: A Contra Costa County case study. *Univ Carlifornia Inst Transp Stud*. 2019. Available at: https://escholarship.org/uc/item/6j47524x#main. Accessed June 1, 2021.

Caregiving

Talha Ali, PhD, MS, Godfred O. Boateng, PhD, MPhil, Andrea P. Medeiros, MPH, and Minakshi Raj, PhD, MPH

BACKGROUND AND DESCRIPTION

Caregiving is an important need in the lives of people advancing in age. Formal and informal caregivers contribute widely to the health and well-being of older adults. Most countries are experiencing population aging with longer life expectancies accompanied by increasing prevalence of chronic conditions. This makes the demand and cost of caregiving in both formal and informal sectors both urgent and arduous. The scope, duration, and intensity of caregiving needs vary by the age, physical, and cognitive functional status of the care recipient. Older adults less than 65 years of age, especially those with pre-existing health conditions, are more likely to require high intensity long-term care. More than half of the individuals aged 85–89 years need a family caregiver due to health problems or functional limitations, with three out of four older adults aged less than 90 years requiring advanced forms of care through home health and institutional settings (e.g., nursing homes).[1] Due to the underfunded and fragmented health and social support systems, most of these services have now become the responsibility of informal caregivers.[1] Despite the increased demand for caregivers, there is a shortage in the supply of caregivers due to the uneven distribution of the young and old in the population.

CURRENT LITERATURE

Ontology and Typology of Caregiving

Caregivers are typically categorized as formal or informal. Formal caregivers are individuals within the health care system who are trained and paid to give care, whereas informal caregivers are individuals outside the health care system who are typically not trained or paid for their caregiving services. Informal caregivers include family caregivers (e.g., adult children, grandchildren, in-laws, spouse/partner, siblings) and other informal caregivers, such as friends or neighbors.[2] Family caregivers can be classified further as sandwich generation and non-sandwich generation caregivers. Sandwich generation caregivers, mostly women, play a dual role between caring for their children and their older parents or relatives concurrently.

Caregiving in either formal or informal settings takes multiple forms. Formal care needs may include allopathic services (i.e., use of medications to suppress disease symptoms), dental and vision care; nursing care; physical, occupational and speech therapy; medical social services; care from home health aides; nutritional support; imaging (e.g., X-ray); and pharmaceutical services.[3] Informal caregivers may help with everyday activities such as transportation; bathing; meal preparation; and health care activities, including assistance with physician visits, transitioning between settings of care, and making medical decisions. Increasingly, complex medical tasks such as medication management and those that are typically performed by nurses, such as administering injections and wound care, are being performed by informal caregivers.[4,5]

Demographic Profiles of Caregivers

Over 40 million informal caregivers supported an adult aged 50 or older in 2020 and 26% of family caregivers supported a relative with dementia.[6] Family caregivers represent all ages, genders, and socioeconomic and racial/ethnic groups, including immigrant communities. A majority of family caregivers are women. Although one in four family caregivers are millennials, a large proportion of family caregivers are supporting a spouse/partner and many are themselves older than 65 years of age.[5]

Nearly half of informal caregivers (42%) support a parent and about 7% support a parent-in-law.[5] About 7% care for a grandparent or grandparent-in-law, and roughly 15% support a friend, neighbor, or another nonrelative.[5] Currently, more than 11 million Americans are considered sandwich generation family caregivers. The typical sandwich generation caregiver is, on average, 41 years old.[7] Just over one-third of caregivers live in the same home as their care recipient, and others live in a different household while their care recipient lives in their own home, an assisted living, or skilled nursing facility.[5] While some caregivers may live within driving distance of their care recipient, many are considered "remote" or "long-distance," meaning they may live in another state, region, or country.

The number of informal caregivers and the economic value of their unpaid contributions has been increasing. In the United States, in 2017, about 41 million informal family caregivers provided an estimated 34 billion hours of care, worth $470 billion in economic value to care recipients.[8] The economic value of caregiving is even more striking when considering that more than half of informal caregivers are employed either part-time or full-time.[9] The stress associated with caregiving while employed is tremendous; more than one-third of caregivers leave the workforce or reduce their hours worked, with women more likely to leave their jobs.[10] Among employed individuals, those who were caregivers were more likely to have fair or poor health than those who are not caregivers.[11]

OVERVIEW OF THE MAIN CONCEPTS, ISSUES, AND CHALLENGES

Concepts

Table 11-1 provides definitions of key concepts relevant for practitioners supporting caregivers.

A Caregiving Socioecological Model

Caregivers face many challenges both in their interpersonal interactions as well as system-level barriers. Here, we draw upon the socioecological model as a helpful framework for explaining: (1) demand for caregiving (i.e., factors increasing the need for caregiving), (2) threats to caregiving (i.e., factors making it difficult to carry out caregiving responsibilities), and (3) cost/consequences of caregiving (i.e., effects of caregiving). These factors occur at multiple levels of influence including individual, interpersonal, institutional, and policy levels.[15] The socioecological model examines health outcomes, behaviors, and risks stemming from the social and physical environment, and suggests that different environmental and social factors codetermine health outcomes. We adopt a variation of the ecological model to explain the multilevel influences of caregiving (see Figure 11-1).

Demand for Caregiving

The increasing demand for caregiving can be examined at the individual, interpersonal, organizational/institutional, community, and public policy level.

At the individual level, the demand for caregiving is driven by aging. As individuals are living longer, they are also living more years of life with chronic conditions, cognitive impairments, and functional disabilities, increasing the individual-level demand for caregiving.[16,17] For instance, the number of older Americans living with Alzheimer's dementia, one of the top conditions requiring informal care, is projected to double by 2050.[18,19]

At the interpersonal level, social networks of families, neighbors and friends play a key role in caregiving. Due to a shortage of health care providers trained in supporting older adults, in addition to efforts encouraging older adults to "age in place" in their community rather than in institutional environments, social networks of older adults are increasingly expected to step in and provide informal care. Additionally, paid caregiving can be expensive. However, the competing demands of employment, other personal and family responsibilities, and changes in family dynamics make it difficult for families to play such roles.

At the institutional level, there is a growing shortage of health care providers including physicians and nurses, which is expected to intensify as the health care needs of older

Table 11-1. Summary of Key Concepts Relevant for Practitioners Supporting Caregivers

Concept	Definition
Activities of Daily Living (ADLs)	Everyday tasks related to personal care usually performed for oneself in the course of a normal day, including bathing, dressing, grooming, eating, walking, taking medications, and other personal care activities.
Caregiver Burden	Emotional, social, and financial stresses caregiving imposes on the caregiver.[12] Caregiver burden can be categorized into objective and subjective burdens. Objective burden consists of the symptoms and behavior of the patient and their consequences that lead to the disruption of social, financial, and occupational functioning of the caregiver. Subjective burden refers to the psychological consequences of caregiving such as stress, anxiety, distress, and burnout.[13]
Chronic Conditions	According to the Centers for Disease Control, chronic conditions can be defined broadly as conditions that last more than one year and require ongoing medical attention or limit activities of daily living, or both. These can include diseases such as heart disease, cancer, and diabetes.
Family Caregiver	Informal caregivers who are supporting a relative, usually a spouse and children of the person in need of care.
Family Caregiver Assessment	A systematic process of gathering information about a family caregiving situation to identify the specific problems, needs, strengths, and resources of the family caregiver, as well as the caregiver's ability to contribute to the needs of the care recipient. A family caregiver assessment asks questions of the family caregiver. It does not ask questions of the care recipient about the family caregiver.[8]
Formal Caregiver	A provider associated with a formal service system, whether a paid worker or a volunteer.
Informal Caregiver	Refers to any unpaid, nonprofessional relative, partner, friend, or neighbor who has a significant personal relationship with, and who provides a broad range of assistance for, an older person or an adult with a chronic, disabling, or a serious health condition.
Instrumental Activities of Daily Living (IADLs)	Activities related to independent living, such as preparing meals, managing money, shopping for groceries or personal items, performing light or heavy housework, and using a telephone.
Long-Term Services and Supports (LTSS; also referred to as Long-Term Care)	The broad range of day-to-day help needed by people with long-term conditions, disabilities, or frailty. This includes personal care (such as bathing and dressing); complex care (such as with medications or wound care); help with housekeeping, transportation, paying bills, and meals. LTSS may be provided in the home, in assisted living and other supportive housing settings, in nursing facilities, and in integrated settings such as those that provide both health care and supportive services. LTSS also includes supportive services provided to family members and other unpaid caregivers.[8]
Long-Distance Caregiving	Care provided by a caregiver living more than an hour away from the care recipient. Caring from a distance is emotionally and logistically difficult, and is most common in situations where adult children and their parents do not live in the same area. In these cases, the caregiver's role is not as much "hands-on" as it is gathering information about available resources, coordinating services and putting together a "team" of family, friends, and paid help that can meet the care recipient's needs.
Respite Care	The provision of short-term relief (respite) from the tasks associated with caregiving. Respite services encompass traditional home-based care, such as hiring an attendant, as well as care provided to the care recipient in out-of-home care settings, such as adult day services and short-term stays in a nursing home or other care facility. Respite can vary in duration from a few hours to several weeks.
Sandwich Generation Caregiver	Family caregivers who find themselves in the position of caring for younger children and their older parents or other family members.[14] They are usually in their mid-forties, married, and employed.

Source: Based on Reinhard et al.,[8] George and Gwyther,[12] Baruch et al.[13] and Steiner and Fletcher.[14]

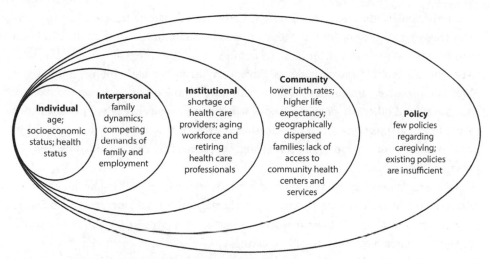

Figure 11-1. Caregiving Socioecological Model Showing Factors Increasing Demand for Care

adults increase. Nursing schools across the country are struggling to expand capacity to meet the rising demand for care.[20] In 2018, US nursing schools turned away more than 75,000 qualified baccalaureate and graduate nursing applicants due to insufficient resources.[20] A shortage in formal caregivers, such as nurses and home health aides, leads to an increase in demand for informal caregivers.

At the national or policy levels, there are very few local, state, or federal policies and support programs in the United States that incorporate the needs of informal caregivers. Some examples of current policies include the national RAISE Family Caregivers Act[21] and the Supporting Grandparents Raising Grandchildren Act.[22] However, additional policies are needed to secure the well-being of informal caregivers.

Threats to Caregiving

The threats to caregiving are complex and should be examined from a multilevel perspective.

At the individual level, several social determinants of health affect both the caregiver and care recipient. Low socioeconomic status threatens independent living; for instance, an individual living in poverty has limited access to paid caregiving services and is forced to rely on family members and friends for support, who may be compelled by cultural or familial obligations to provide unpaid care. Additionally, lower socioeconomic status of the caregivers places a limitation on the quality and quantity of care that they can provide, and may limit their access to good quality health care and respite care to help them manage the stresses associated with caregiving. Further, the current generation of older adults is more likely to be unmarried or divorced, presenting a threat to their likelihood of having a spouse or partner informal caregiver.[23]

Interpersonally, the changes in family structure and dynamics pose a threat to informal caregiving. American families today are smaller and more geographically dispersed than in previous generations, limiting the family's capacity to provide care for older relatives with disabilities.[8] Increasingly, caregivers are caring for both young children and older adult relatives, and are forced to provide care from a distance. Having to balance rising work and other personal obligations with caring for older relatives poses a major threat to caregiving. This threat is exacerbated as informal caregivers are expected to perform more complex aspects of caregiving, supplementing care provided by licensed providers but without sufficient training and resources.

At the institutional level, an aging health care workforce and retiring health care professionals threaten caregiving by creating a shortage of formal care providers. Future projections show that by 2040 there will be a shortfall of nearly 350, 000 direct care workers and 11 million family and friends, creating a major barrier to caregiving.[24]

At the community level, lack of access to community health centers, especially in poorer neighborhoods, poses a threat to caregiving. The situation is particularly dire in rural regions, where access to health care services is scarce. Caregivers living in remote areas and in communities designated as health professional shortage areas have difficulty finding care for their care recipient and for themselves. Rural older adults require more assistance from informal caregivers with transportation to medical visits and in emergency situations.

At the policy level, publicly funded programs such as Medicaid, Medicare, and state programs that provide support for home and community-based services are now at maximum utility and need expansion. In 2015, 1.4 million people received Medicaid support for nursing home residence and 3.2 million for home care. However, in 2014 across 39 states, 582,000 people were on wait-lists for home-based and community-based services.[24,25] As the population continues to age and more people are placed on the wait-list for these services, relying on a smaller population of working adults to contribute to services, sustainability of Medicaid and Medicare programs is threatened. Without private long-term care insurance, more aging adults will have to finance their health through out-of-pocket payments or depend on families for care, which increases the financial burden on family members.

Consequences of Caregiving: Health Effects of Caregiving

The strain associated with caregiving can affect caregivers' physical, emotional, environmental, financial, and social wellness.[26] While Table 11-2 provides examples of some of the negative experiences' caregivers may have across dimensions of wellness, it is important to note that caregivers also have many positive experiences with caregiving. A better understanding of the various challenges faced by caregivers can help inform evidence-based interventions to reduce the burden of caregiving. The effects of caregiving are complex and operate at multiple levels, including individual, interpersonal, institutional, and public policy.

At the individual and interpersonal levels, caregivers experience challenges with their physical health. Caregivers may need to lift older adults, offer support with standing and walking, as well as assist with falls, which can be physically exhausting. Additionally, caregivers, between work and caring for their older adults, often work long hours without additional support, and with little or no time left for their own social and physical activity. The health consequences of these include marked sleep deprivation and increased risk of chronic conditions among caregivers, which could lead to temporary and permanent disability or premature death.[27,28]

Caregivers experience mental and emotional health challenges in trying to understand where to seek help and how to support their older adult with complex health care needs. Feelings of frustration and helplessness ultimately lead to stress, anxiety, vicarious trauma, and depression among caregivers.[8,27,28] Among informal caregivers, caregiving distress can additionally lead to strains on individual and family relationships.[27]

Economically, caregivers suffer huge losses in income. Most caregivers are forced to take unpaid leave, reduce work hours, or rearrange their work schedules to assume care responsibilities.[29] In some cases, caregiving leads to frequent absenteeism, decreases productivity while at work, and increases early retirement and exit from paid work which culminates in financial losses for informal caregivers.[8,29]

Socially, informal caregivers suffer from loneliness and social isolation. In a national survey examining social connections, 42% of family caregivers reported feeling lonely compared with non-caregivers (34%) in midlife and older ages.[8] Generally, demands of caregiving have the capacity to disrupt social activities. Among formal caregivers, feelings of isolation and alienation from important family and friend social gatherings are common (see Table 11-2).

At the institutional level, care commitments lead to loss of workplace productivity and full-time workers. This could lead to a loss of expertise and mentoring and increase the need to retrain new workers, which comes at a high cost to institutions.

At the national or policy level, an increase in caregiving, both formally and informally, puts pressure on the limited health care facilities, programs, and personnel. It also means an allocation of a higher proportion of budgets to health care which may lead to budget deficits. The cost of Medicare and Medicaid may not be sustainable for governments if the current trend of aging and prolonged chronic conditions continues.

RELEVANT POLICIES AND LEGISLATION

The Family and Medical Leave Act requires employers to provide employees with 12 weeks of unpaid leave within a 12-month period for their spouse, child, or parents for serious health matters, without risk of losing their job or their health insurance.[30] Fifteen states (California, Colorado, Connecticut, Hawaii, Maine, Maryland, Massachusetts, Minnesota, New Jersey, New York, Oregon, Rhode Island, Vermont, Washington, Wisconsin) and the District of Columbia have expanded the definition of family for caregiving purposes to

Table 11-2. Summary of Health Effects of Caregiving with Relevant Examples

Dimensions of wellness	Dunn 1961 Definition	Relevant examples of challenges for caregivers
Physical	Physical activity, healthy foods, and sleep	Musculoskeletal injuries, physical exhaustion, lack of exercise, poor sleep, and poor diet due to lack of time for personal wellness/self-care
Mental/Emotional	Coping effectively with life and creating satisfying relationships	Inability to cope effectively with life stressors and form healthy relationships result in anxiety, depression, and burnout from caregiving
Economical/Financial	Satisfaction with current and future financial situations	Financial burden as a result of supporting health care costs of the care recipient and lower income if forced to take unpaid leave to care for the older relative
Social	Developing a sense of connection, belonging, and a well-developed support system	Isolation and loneliness from friends as a result of increased caregiving responsibilities that take time away from other relationships; potentially conflictual relationship with care recipient especially as a result of changing roles
Intellectual	Recognizing creative abilities and finding ways to expand knowledge and skills	Postponing education and other intellectual endeavors to care for the older adult
Spiritual	Sense of purpose and meaning in life	Losing sense of purpose because caregiving responsibilities leave little time for hobbies and other meaningful activities
Environmental	Good health by occupying pleasant, stimulating environments that support well-being	Lack of personal space and privacy for caregivers that co-reside with the care recipient and other household members
Occupational	Personal satisfaction and enrichment from one's work	Workplace absenteeism due to caregiving responsibilities might reduce workplace satisfaction and may even lead to loss of employment

Source: Based on Dunn.[26]

include grandparents, a sibling, or an in-law.[31] Although it is difficult to plan a leave in advance, the law requires that employees give their supervisors at least a 30-day notice.

The Recognize, Assist, Include, Support and Engage (RAISE) Family Caregivers Act requires the US Secretary of Health and Human Services (HHS) to develop an integrated national family caregiving strategy to support family caregivers. Led by the Administration for Community Living,[21] The RAISE Act directed the establishment of the Family Caregiving Advisory Council to provide recommendations to HHS on effective models for family and support caregivers along with improving coordination across federal government programs.

The Supporting Grandparents Raising Grandchildren Act directs HHS to create a federal advisory council as a one-stop shop of information and resources to support grandparents raising grandchildren.[22,32] This includes information on navigating the school system, planning for their families' future, addressing mental health issues for themselves and their grandchildren and building social support networks.[32]

The Caregiver Advise, Record, Enable (CARE) Act helps family caregivers support older adults upon discharge from the hospital. It was developed to provide a tool for education of family caregivers of individuals who have been hospitalized. The law requires that hospitals (1) record the name of the family caregiver on the medical record, (2) inform the caregiver on the patient's discharge time, and (3) provide the caregiver with education of the medical tasks needed to be performed.[33]

In addition to the aforementioned provisions, policymakers must address workplace flexibility, long-term care improvements, and offer a national infrastructure to support care provided for all ages.

GOVERNMENT-RELATED PROGRAMS

Personal care services which allow participants to self-direct their own care and hire the caregiver of their choosing vary by state.[34] Informal caregivers can become paid caregivers through their state's plan if they are eligible. Policymakers should consider the expansion of Medicaid's ability to compensate family caregivers from a few to all states.

The Eldercare Locator is a nationwide public service through the US Administration on Aging connecting older Americans and their caregivers with local support resources.[35] Individuals can speak with an information specialist and also visit the Caregiver Corner for resources on getting paid to be a caregiver, legal assistance, transportation, and more.

The National Family Caregiver Support Program was established to provide grants to states and territories to fund a range of supports that help informal caregivers care for older adults in their homes for as long as possible.[36]

The Lifespan Respite Care Program was authorized in Congress in 2006.[37] The program is for family caregivers of children and adults of all ages with special needs. Grants are directed to the states in order to provide environmental scanning of family caregiver needs, marketing and outreach campaigns for caregivers about respite care and accessing services, along with training of respite providers.

BEST PRACTICE INTERVENTIONS

The nature and scope of caregiving and its associated burdens is variable. In the same vein, caregiving interventions vary in scope and target, with some interventions being more efficacious than others for specific types of caregivers and caregiving situations. Interventions may focus on group-based or individual-based solutions and may or may not use technology.

Group-based solutions provide information and social support to caregivers in a group setting and help manage psychosocial and health consequences of caregiving.[38]

This approach allows caregivers to share experiences and learn from each other. Group-based solutions take two forms: in-person and internet-based support groups usually facilitated by a professional. These approaches have been shown to improve caregiver self-efficacy, promote coping strategies, and lower stress.[8,39]

Individual-based solutions include one-to-one meetings, usually between a clinician and primary caregiver either in person or online, as well providing caregiver training (e.g. identifying health needs of care recipients and making environmental modifications aimed at stress reduction).[40] Interactive interventions targeting the unique needs of caregivers are considered most valuable.[40]

Technology-based solutions (TBS) can reduce the burden on family caregivers and help them coordinate multiple demanding tasks through the use of technology. Computer or web-based applications may be used to deliver health information, social support, and behavioral change materials to caregivers.[41] The TBS approach is considered best practice because it (1) offers caregivers access to information in different formats (i.e. video, audio, text, infographics), (2) can be accessed at one's convenience, (3) is a low-cost solution, and (4) facilitates efficient decision-making.[41] TBS also facilitates social connection and support between caregivers. Innovations in TBS include task management apps and assistive technologies that help with day-to-day caregiving by coordinating family tasks in the context of other family activities; wearable technologies (i.e. devices worn on or placed in the body to help monitor a person's overall health); and technologies that provide better connections between family caregivers and health professionals, enabling them to work more effectively as a team to provide care to older adults.[42]

Other best practices include the implementation of cognitive reframing, mindfulness techniques, stress management strategies, and physical activity for caregivers who express anxiety, stress, and depressive symptoms.[39] Within the formal setting, the use of specially designated and trained professionals who attend to specific diseases have been found to be beneficial to both the caregiver and patient. Taken together, these best practices present useful alternatives and evidence-based practices that can ease the burden on caregivers and promote health.

SPECIAL CONSIDERATIONS AND SPECIAL POPULATIONS

Informal caregivers come from increasingly diverse backgrounds with different cultural expectations and values that must be considered when developing intervention programs.

Minority Populations

Caregivers may experience different types of sociocultural expectations, support, or circumstances that must be considered in understanding their experience as caregivers. For instance, compared to Hispanic caregivers, Black caregivers are older and more likely to be single and therefore, may also need support as they age. Caregivers who are not native English speakers may face language barriers when communicating with doctors or social service providers.[43] In the United States, Hispanic older adults are expected to comprise 20% of the older adult population in 2050,[44] and their caregivers may benefit from language resources. Minority caregivers often face specific cultural expectations such as familial or filial obligation in providing care.[45] These expectations are associated with heightened caregiver depression (e.g., among Asian caregivers).[45] Minority caregivers facing cultural expectations may also be less likely to identify as a caregiver and subsequently seek support related to caregiver distress.

Geographic Considerations

In addition to minority caregivers, individuals providing care from a distance also face unique challenges. Long-distance caregivers may need to choose an in-home caregiver or develop a routine for checking in on their relative.[46] They may also require additional avenues for communicating with their care recipient's health care providers (e.g., through follow-up phone calls). For instance, caregivers of individuals living in rural areas have to provide care from a distance. Although 25% of rural caregivers live in the same household as the care recipient, 60% live at least an hour away.[47] Rural caregivers have fewer support services, financial resources, health and social services, and public transportation options. Rural caregivers have to traverse greater distances between themselves and the services they need compared with their counterparts, putting rural caregivers and their care recipients at a higher risk for adverse outcomes.

Young Caregivers

Millennials (i.e., generation of people born in the 1980s or 1990s) and Generation Z (i.e., the generation of people born in the late 1990s and early 2000s) represent an emerging group of caregivers.[6] Roughly 70% of child caregivers are supporting a parent or grandparent with the most common conditions being Alzheimer's disease or dementia, heart, lung, or kidney disease, arthritis, and diabetes.[48] Child caregivers require different services than those provided for adult caregivers with many agencies not prepared to support child caregivers. Steps need to be taken to build a research, practice, and policy agenda that includes child caregivers.

CONCLUSION: CHALLENGES AND OPPORTUNITIES FOR PUBLIC HEALTH

Professional practitioners will need to learn about diverse populations and their respective needs as we work on addressing caregiving challenges. The increasing need for caregivers as a result of population aging will create new opportunities in caregiving employment and an increase in various specializations related to caregiving.

One of the biggest challenges in public health research is the accurate identification of caregivers. Many individuals do not self-identify as caregivers because they do not realize their actions as being a part of caregiving; caregiving is what they do naturally. There is a need for public health professionals to collaborate with other allied health fields to identify caregivers using information from different medical systems and organizations. Accurate identification of caregivers is key to accurately assessing caregivers' needs and providing adequate support.

National conversations continue on paid family and medical leave, universal childcare, and the need to expand long-term support services (LTSS). There is additionally a need to invest in workplace flexibility and a robust national infrastructure that can support and supplement care for friends and families of care recipients. Sustainable solutions such as expanding LTSS and investing in workplace flexibility and a national infrastructure will reduce caregiver burden, while also enhancing healthy aging.

CASE STUDY

A Case Study of Caregiver Family Therapy

Hugo and Paula are both recently retired. At his latest medical appointment, Hugo's primary care provider (PCP) diagnosed Hugo with Type 2 diabetes and chronic obstructive pulmonary disease. The news of her husband's diagnosis caused Paula to be stressed and afraid of the future. At a doctors' visit, Paula learned of a therapist at a health clinic who offered Caregiver Family Therapy (CFT) and reached out to him. Paula attended multiple CFT sessions which helped her to adjust to her husband's illness and become more comfortable in her role as his caregiver. During CFT, Paula's therapist worked with her to focus on the following:

1. Addressing the care recipient's problem: At her appointment with the CFT therapist, Paula was encouraged to speak with Hugo's PCP to conduct further tests to help them "name the problem." Upon receiving the test results, Hugo and Paula together with his PCP, developed a plan for him to stop smoking, walking for exercise, and maintain a strict new diet. Armed with a better understanding of the problem and lifestyle changes needed to manage Hugo's health, Paula felt less worried.

2. Establishing the caregiving role structures: As Paula's caregiving demands increased, her CFT therapist encouraged her to reach out to her family for support. With help from her therapist, Paula drew a family genogram to determine the current caregiving structure within her family. Paula and Hugo's adult children were invited to a CFT session, where they worked with Paula, Hugo, and the therapist to create a schedule that involved having someone visit Paula and Hugo on a daily basis, assist with grocery shopping and meal preparation on a weekly basis, and do home repairs as needed.

3. Addressing the caregiver's self-care: Although Paula settled into a routine in which she became comfortable with her new role as Hugo's caregiver, she could not find time and energy to attend church or visit her friends. Paula brought up her concerns with the

therapist who helped her identify her daughter Maria as an available resource to help her. Paula talked with Maria, who offered to have Hugo over to her home for brunch on the weekends as a way of spending time with her father and also encouraging her mother to go back to her church services.[49]

Caregivers and care recipients are often afraid of what lies ahead as they struggle with their changing roles. This can lead to burnout in both caregivers and care recipients. Caregiver family therapy is a treatment model that guides families through the developmental transitions of later-life.[49] Therapists help to create family-level shifts in roles that position families to meet the needs of the care recipient. Three distressing processes of family caregiving are the focus of CFT: (1) addressing the care recipient's problem, (2) establishing the caregiving role structures, and (3) addressing the caregiver's self-care. The needs of caregivers and care recipients can be successfully addressed by CFT because, unlike other interventions focused on a single caregiver, CFT includes the family as a system. It addresses a wide array of needs of the caregiver, care recipient, and their families dealing with a range of diseases and disabilities within the context of their unique families.[49] Caregivers Family Therapy is designed to be implemented in clinicians' practices across a variety of settings and across the full range of the caregiving process from early, to middle, and to late stages.[49]

REFERENCES

1. Schulz, R. Older adults who need caregiving and the family caregivers who help them. In: Schulz R, Eden J, eds. *Families Caring for an Aging America*. Washington, DC: National Academies Press 2016.

2. Schulz R, Beach SR, Czaja SJ, Martire LM, Monin JK. Family caregiving for older adults. *Annu Rev Psychol*. 2020;71:635-659.

3. John Hopkins Medicine. Types of Home Health Care Services. 2019. Available at: https://www.hopkinsmedicine.org/health/caregiving/types-of-home-health-care-services. Accessed February 25, 2021.

4. Wolff JL, Spillman BC, Freedman VA, Kasper JD. A national profile of family and unpaid caregivers who assist older adults with health care activities. *JAMA Intern Med*. 2016;176(3):372–79.

5. National Alliance for Caregiving and the AARP Public Policy Institute. "Caregiving in the US: 2015 Report." Washington, DC: Greenwald & Associates; 2015. Available at: https://www.aarp.org/content/dam/aarp/ppi/2015/caregiving-in-the-united-states-2015-report-revised.pdf. Accessed June 1, 2021.

6. AARP. Caregiving in the U.S–2020 Report. 2020. Available at: https://www.aarp.org/content/dam/aarp/ppi/2020/05/full-report-caregiving-in-the-united-states.doi.10.26419-2Fppi.00103.001.pdf. Accessed February 25, 2021.

7. National Alliance for Caregiving. Burning the candle at both ends: Sandwich generation caregiving in the US. 2019. Available at: https://www.caregiving.org/wp-content/uploads/2020/05/NAC-CAG_SandwichCaregiving_Report_Digital-Nov-26-2019.pdf. Accessed February 25, 2021.

8. Reinhard SC, Feinberg LF, Houser A, Choula R, Evans M. Valuing the invaluable 2019 Update: Charting a path forward. AARP Public Policy Institute. 2019.

9. Edwards VJ, Bouldin ED, Taylor CA, Olivari BS, McGuire LC. Characteristics and health status of informal unpaid caregivers–44 States, District of Columbia, and Puerto Rico, 2015–2017. *MMWR Morb Mortal Wkly Rep*. 2020;69(7):183.

10. Evercare and National Alliance for Caregiving. Evercare study of family caregivers — What they spend, what they sacrifice. 2007. Available at: http://www.advancingstates.org/sites/nasuad/files/hcbs/files/129/6408/CaregiverCost.pdf. Accessed February 25, 2021.

11. Adler R, Mehta R. Catalyzing technology to support family caregiving. National Alliance for Caregiving. 2014. Available at: https://www.caregiving.org/wp-content/uploads/2010/01/Catalyzing-Technology-to-Support-Family-Caregiving_FINAL.pdf. Accessed February 25, 2021.

12. George LK, Gwyther LP. Caregiver well-being: A multidimensional examination of family caregivers of demented adults. *Gerontologist*. 1986:26(3):253–59.

13. Baruch E, Pistrang N, Barker C. Psychological interventions for caregivers of people with bipolar disorder: A systematic review and meta-analysis. *J Affect Disord*. 2018;236:187–98.

14. Steiner AM, Fletcher PC. Sandwich generation caregiving: A complex and dynamic role. *J Adult Dev*. 2017;24 (2):133–43.

15. Bronfenbrenner, U. Toward an experimental ecology of human development. *Am Psychol*. 1977;32(7):513-522.

16. Bedaf S, Gelderblom GJ, Syrdal DS, et al. 2014. Which activities threaten independent living of elderly when becoming problematic: Inspiration for meaningful service robot functionality. *Disabil Rehabil Assist Technol*. 2014:9(6):445–52.

17. Boateng GO, Adams EA, Boateng MO, Luginaah IN, Taabazuing M-M. Obesity and the burden of health risks among the elderly in Ghana: A population study. *PLoS One*. 2017;12(11):e0186947.

18. Alzheimer's Association. 2020 Alzheimer's disease facts and figures. Chicago, IL: Alzheimer's Association; 2020.

19. Hebert LE, Weuve J, Scherr PA, Evans DA. Alzheimer disease in the United States (2010–2050) estimated using the 2010 census. *Neurology*. 2013;80(19):1778–83.

20. Rosseter R. Nursing shortage fact sheet. American Association of Colleges of Nursing. 2019. Available at: https://www.aacnnursing.org/Portals/42/News/Factsheets/Nursing-Shortage-Factsheet.pdf. Accessed February 25, 2021.

21. RAISE Family Caregiving Advisory Council. Administration for Community Living. 2021. Available at: https://acl.gov/programs/support-caregivers/raise-family-caregiving-advisory-council. Accessed March 22, 2021.

22. Supporting Grandparents Raising Grandchildren. Administration for Community Living. 2020. Available at: https://acl.gov/programs/support-caregivers/supporting-grandparents-raising-grandchildren-0. Accessed March 22, 2021.

23. Mather M, Scommegna P, Kilduff L. Fact sheet: Aging in the United States. Population Reference Bureau. 2019. Available at: https://www.prb.org/aging-unitedstates-fact-sheet. Accessed February 25, 2021.

24. Osterman P. The landscape of long-term care in the United States. In: Osterman P, ed. *Who Will Care For Us? Long-Term Care and the Long-Term Workforce*. New York, NY: Russell Sage Foundation; 2017:16–25.

25. Kaiser Family Foundation. Medicaid's role in nursing home care. 2017. Available at: https://www.kff.org/infographic/medicaids-role-in-nursing-home-care/. Accessed February 25, 2021.

26. Dunn HL. *High-Level Wellness: A collection of twenty-nine short talks on different aspects of the theme "High-Level Wellness for Man and Society"*. Arlington, VA: RW Beatty; 1961.

27. Boateng GO, Schuster RC, Boateng MO. Uncovering a health and wellbeing gap among professional nurses: Situated experiences of direct care nurses in two Canadian cities. *Soc Sci Med*. 2019;242:112568.

28. Reinhard SC, Given B, Petlick NH, Bemis A. Supporting family caregivers in providing care. In Hughes RG, ed. *Patient Safety and Quality: An Evidence-Based handbook for Nurses*. Rockville, MD: Agency for Healthcare Research and Quality; 2008.

29. Stone RI, Short PF. The competing demands of employment and informal caregiving to disabled elders. *Med Care*. 1990;28(6):513–26.

30. Family and Medical Leave Act. US Department of Labor. Available at: https://www.dol.gov/agencies/whd/fmla. Accessed March 22,2021.

31. Keister K. Family and medical leave: How to tell your boss you need to take time off. AARP. 2019. Available at: https://www.aarp.org/caregiving/financial-legal/info-2019/workers-family-medical-leave-act.html. Accessed February 25, 2021.

32. US Senate Special Committee on Aging. Collins, Casey urge HHS to swiftly implement new law to support grandparents raising grandchildren. US Senate. September 14, 2018. Available at: https://www.aging.senate.gov/press-releases/collins-casey-urge-hhs-to-swiftly-implement-new-law-to-support-grandparents-raising-grandchildren. Accessed February 25, 2021.

33. Escobedo M. States enacting CARE Act provide needed support to caregivers and their loved ones. The John A. Hartford Foundation. 2016. Available at: https://www.johnahartford.org/blog/view/states-enacting-care-act-provide-needed-support-to-caregivers-and-their-lov. Accessed February 25, 2021.

34. American Council on Aging. How to receive financial compensation via Medicaid to provide care for a loved one. 2019. Available at: https://www.medicaidplanningassistance.org/getting-paid-as-caregiver. Accessed February 25, 2021.

35. Eldercare Locator. US Administration on Aging. Available at: https://eldercare.acl.gov/Public/Index.aspx. Accessed February 25, 2021.

36. Administration for Community Living. National Family Caregiver Support Program. 2021. Available at: https://acl.gov/programs/support-caregivers/national-family-caregiver-support-program. Accessed February 25, 2021.

37. Administration for Community Living. Lifespan Respite Care Program. 2019. Available at: https://acl.gov/programs/support-caregivers/lifespan-respite-care-program. Accessed February 25, 2021.

38. Thompson CA, Spilsbury K, Hall J, Birks Y, Barnes C, Adamson J. Systematic review of information and support interventions for caregivers of people with dementia. *BMC Geriatr.* 2007;7(1):18.

39. Piersol CV, Canton K, Connor SE, Giller I, Lipman S, Sager S. Effectiveness of interventions for caregivers of people with Alzheimer's disease and related major neurocognitive disorders: A systematic review. *Am J Occupl Ther.* 2017;71(5):7105180020p1.

40. Wasilewski MB, Stinson JN, Cameron JI. Web-based health interventions for family caregivers of elderly individuals: A scoping review. *Int J Med Inform.* 2017;103:109–38.

41. Godwin KM, Mills WL, Anderson JA, Kunik ME. Technology-driven interventions for caregivers of persons with dementia: A systematic review. *Am J Alzheimer's Dis Other Demen.* 2013;28(3):216–22.

42. Adler R, Mehta R. Catalyzing technology to support family caregiving. National Alliance for Caregiving. 2014. Available at: https://www.caregiving.org/wp-content/uploads/2010/01/Catalyzing-Technology-to-Support-Family-Caregiving_FINAL.pdf. Accessed on February 25, 2021.

43. Metlife Mature Market Institute. The Metlife study of caregiving costs to working caregivers. 2011. Available at: https://www.caregiving.org/wp-content/uploads/2011/06/mmi-caregiving-costs-working-caregivers.pdf. Accessed February 25, 2021.

44. Villa VM, Wallace SP, Bagdasaryan S, Aranda MP. Hispanic baby boomers: Health inequities likely to persist in old age. *Gerontologist.* 2012;52(2):166–176.

45. Bastawrous M. Caregiver burden—A critical discussion. *Int J Nurs Stud.* 2013;50(3):431–441.

46. National Alliance for Caregiving and AARP. Caregiving in the US: A focused look at those caring for the 50+. 2009. Available at: https://assets.aarp.org/rgcenter/il/caregiving_09.pdf. Accessed February 25, 2021.

47. Metlife Mature Market Institute. Miles away: The MetLife Study of Long-distance Caregiving. 2004.

48. Easter Seals and National Alliance for Caregiving. Caregiving in rural America. 2006. Available at: https://secure.easterseals.com/site/DocServer/Caregiving_in_Rural-saveas-compress.pdf;jsessionid=00000000.app276a?docID%5Cu003d49463&NONCE_TOKEN=ED-763122CEC9C327400916E0035C95CB. Accessed February 25, 2021.

49. Qualls SH, Williams AA. *Caregiver family therapy: Empowering families to meet the challenges of aging.* Washington DC: American Psychological Association; 2013.

The Intersection of End-of-Life and Grief

Rachael D. Nolan, PhD, MPH, CPH, Jon Agley, PhD, MPH,
Charles R. Doarn, MBA, and Amy Funk, PhD

The present lack of emphasis on end-of-life experiences, including death, dying, and bereavement, truly constitutes a disparity—once an individual enters end-of-life, there is a real possibility that needs and wants, including pain and symptom management, will not be understood or serviced.[1-3] End-of-life is also unique in that all of us, at least for a short period of time, will eventually experience this disparity directly, and most of us will also experience ambiguous and concrete loss related to our friends, family, and other loved ones. Attainment of affirmative health and well-being among the dying provides valuable benefits to society[4] and is a shared responsibility between national, state, local, tribal, and community entities, including the public, private, and nonprofit sectors.

A NEW ERA OF END-OF-LIFE

The longer I live, the more beautiful life becomes.
–Frank Lloyd Wright[5]

The US population is growing older. With senescence, there is the inevitable end-of-life and grief. End-of-life is a public health issue. Grief advocacy and management are prevention. Although public health and allied fields may perceive that end of life issues and grief are beyond their scope of practice, core public health values and principles have much to offer to people who are dying, their families, and their communities. In 1948, the World Health Organization defined health as "… a state of complete physical, mental and social well-being and not merely the absence of disease or infirmity."[6] Especially when end-of-life circumstances make the absence of infirmity impossible, public health still has much to offer in the way of facilitating well-being for individuals. Many end-of-life experiences result in multiple grievers besides the individual, both in the face of clear loss, such as death itself, and ambiguous loss, such as cognitive decline.[7] As the primary causes of death have shifted from infectious disease to chronic illness,[8] it has been estimated that for every death in a community, approximately 4–30 people are left to cope with and mourn the loss.[9,10]

Traditionally, the public health response to death has been one of specialization consisting of embalmers, coroners, and funeral directors. However, faces of end-of-life care, death, and grief have evolved, with community health care workers now identifying as death specialists, death doulas (roughly described as death midwifery), and thanatologists (those who study the nature of death itself).[11] Technology has extended, and sometimes unnecessarily prolonged, life through advanced medical interventions, while the essence of many loved ones lives on forever in social media.[12] By acknowledging death and loss, and incorporating education and support into public health practice, we ensure that end-of-life care promotes well-being for the individual and their family.

We Are Growing Older

The US Census Bureau estimates that by 2035, older Americans aged 65 and up will be more populous than children under the age of 18.[13] By other accounts, the oldest Americans, persons older than 85 years of age, are expected to number more than 14 million by the year 2040.[14] This growing number of older adults, unprecedented in the United States, will lead to more individuals living with chronic disease and more people dying each year. The Centers for Disease Control and Prevention reported that the deaths per 100,000 US residents in 2018 doubled between the 55–64 age bracket (886.7/100,000) and the 65–74 bracket (1,783.3/100,000), and was more than 15 times higher for ages 85 and older (13,450.7/100,000).[15] These individuals will need to make crucial end-of-life decisions, but often do not express their preferences to health care proxies who tend to make these choices on their behalf. As a result, end-of-life courses are often medically and ethically complex; medical care that may prolong life may not provide for quality of life.[16] Furthermore, there may not be enough caregivers available to provide services as the population expands,[17] and, with the growing availability of technology, individuals are remaining in the community longer, and with more complicated health needs and support structures.[18] These changing trends will impact all aspects of daily life from caregiving to city planning efforts, to working adults needing to simultaneously provide for their children and parents (sometimes called the sandwich generation).[19] On the basis of these numbers, the potential for grief is tremendous. But in the face of death and loss, informed public health professionals can provide comfort and dignity, as well as quality support and education for end-of-life care.

We Are Afraid of Death, But More Likely to Live

Within the last 20 years, there has been a substantial shift in the causes of death from infectious disease or sudden deaths to chronic, long-term, and degenerative disease processes.[20] As a result, public health professionals have been forced to face a new set of challenges; how do we appropriately frame death and dying, especially at the end-of-life, as a public health issue? How best can we provide care in the community for those suffering with life limiting and terminal illness? How best can we support the dying and those who love them in living their grief?

Physician and author H. Warraich writes, "...contrary to general perception, never has death been more feared than it is today."[21] Warraich attributes this fear to the number of aging people living through long periods of debilitation due to multiple, chronic, and life-threatening conditions.[21] Because of their prolonged and weakened state, these individuals become more cloistered as end-of-life grows near, making the reality of death more terrifying not only to those affected by debilitating and/or chronic disease, but also their family members and communities affected by loss. Further, among those expected to die within the next few decades are people suffering from maladaptive coping responses, which are notably preceded by trauma and loss, and may result in premature, psychogenic death.[22]

The groundbreaking report from the Institute of Medicine (2015), "Dying in America," highlights five key recommendations, including the need for a collaborative effort in public education and engagement in understanding how best to care for the seriously ill; understanding the advance care planning process; and how to make informed decisions about end-of-life care.[23] This report also calls for increased use of media and other educational methods to promote informed choices and counter misinformation about dying, such as the erroneous belief in "death panels," or that the government has the authority to make decisions about end-of-life care for people on Medicare.[23]

The Public Health Response at the End-of-Life

Public health practitioners in the 21st century can work to reduce the burden of poor health outcomes associated with end-of-life and loss. Whereas grief has been described as the normal and natural response to loss and death, bereavement is known as the period of mourning following loss and death.[9,11,15-18,21,22] Across these interrelated axes of grief, bereavement, and death, multiple disciplines of public health respond to loss though interdisciplinary care, health information, health literacy, health communication, agenda setting, surveillance, and advocacy.[24,25]

Public health also has a responsibility to braid best practices with individuals' and families' preferences for end-of-life experiences. Most people choose to die at home and prefer less aggressive care at end-of-life,[26] although such opportunities are not equally distributed. It is important to educate the public and provide community-level instruction on how to avoid unnecessary and futile care during the critical transitional period between life and death.[27] Equally important to these efforts is the promotion of increased, accessible, and high-quality palliative care, which is an interdisciplinary and holistic approach to improving the quality of life and symptom management for persons and their families facing life-threatening illness.[28] Also necessitated is improved advocacy for a greater match between dying persons' wishes and their actual receipt of care so that individual choice is honored, and less burden is experienced by surviving caregivers.[29] This, too, is key, because grieving caregivers may take up to nine or ten months following the death of a loved one to return to a pre-death level of health and quality of life, if they ever do.[30]

At the same time, multiple barriers exist to accomplishing these aims. First, while progress has been made, many clinicians are not proficient in assisting individuals and their loved ones with end-of-life choices, bereavement, and grief. "It is a catastrophic failure in medical training to not deliver a proper end-of-life education," explains the Association for Palliative Medicine's Dr. Amy Proffitt.[31] Newly trained physicians who have never had to deal with death find themselves having to deal with the newly deceased, as well as the newly bereaved.[32,33] Further, health care workers whose patients die may themselves experience grief and emotional vulnerability, potentially impacting their work in a variety of ways.[34] Second, information systems are not currently configured in ways that facilitate honoring individual decisions related to end-of-life. These problems include, but are not limited to, inadequate interoperability of electronic health records between health care systems; inconsistent methods of documenting end-of-life choices into the medical record; inconsistent procedures for alerting staff to end-of-life preferences upon admission or transfer to another setting; and limited preservation of choices once the individual returns home.[35,36] Third, current end-of-life preparation rarely includes discussion about the financial costs of death. Beginning in 1986, the Consumer Price Index for All Urban Consumers began tracking funeral expenses. In the decades since then, the price of funerals in the United States has risen almost twice as fast (227.1%) as consumer prices for all items (123.4%).[37] Attributed to these rising costs was the increased production and pricing for burial caskets, which rose 230% within the last several decades.[37] Prioritizing public health-based financial preparations for an aging and dying population are critical as well, especially among resource-poor families, to prevent poor secondary outcomes due to the immediate financial impact of death. To some degree, though, technological advances may serve to mitigate these concerns to support a public health approach to dying.

The Promise of Technology

Though technology has been underutilized in end-of-life care, public health is well-positioned to meet the unmet needs of the dying population and their caregivers through technological adoption and advancement.[38] There has been a growing interest in and demand for telemonitoring, telehealth, digital communications, and mobile applications to improve health outcomes. For example, in older adult populations with chronic and life-limiting disease, particularly those in rural areas, remote technology services have offered a lifeline for the provision of quality comfort care.[38] These services, however, are often limited in their scope and reach, particularly in geographically isolated regions, due to insufficient accessibility, reliability, and bandwidth, as well as ineffective reimbursement models to minimize costs to the consumer.[38] Parallel to the increased demand in telemedicine and telehealth services, telepalliative care became widely adopted in 2019, and even more rapidly in early 2020 due to the COVID-19 pandemic.[39,40] Moreover, virtual learning communities have been used by public health and clinical practitioners for continuing professional development, and for developing skills and competencies, potentially leading to improvements in end-of-life care and public health outcomes. A notable model for digital case-based learning in palliative care is the Extension for Community Healthcare Outcomes program, which has been replicated successfully on an international level.[41] To ensure adoption of best practices, as well as policy implementation that mirrors state-of-the-science approaches to end-of-life care, more research is needed to understand the benefits, risks, barriers, and facilitators to the adoption and use of these technologies near end-of-life, as well as to determine the cost-effectiveness and best practices for technological acquisition and implementation.

Beyond medical expansion and virtual training, technology-based industry partners and organizations have also begun innovating in the areas of death, dying, and grief. At a basic level, podcasts and social media sites have been used to provide education and social support near end-of-life,[42] voice command technology has been explored for symptom assessment and pain management,[43] and smart home technology has been used for diagnostic assessment and treatment.[44] More recently, the field has seen proliferation of grief-related apps, online grief sharing platforms, and support networks though MyDeathSpace.com, FaceBook ghosts,[45] augmented-eternity programs, consciousness cloud computing and uploading start-ups (i.e. Nectome), digital death-planning, artificial intelligence (AI) chatbots, autonomous androids of the deceased (i.e. Robo-C),[46] and legacy afterlife services such as Afternote, Soul Machines, Lifenaut, Virtual Eternity, and Replika.[47] Though most, if not all, of these services aim to preserve the memory of those who have died through digital-afterlife technology, the ability to assign ownership and preservation of these remembrance services has remained complex relative to morals, ethics, and social norms.[21] There has also been increased development of deathcentric, daily engagement technology known as WeCroak,[48] which received inspiration from the Bhutanese saying that, "to be a happy person, one must contemplate death five times daily."[48,49] Accordingly, the app sends five daily invitations to users' devices in the form of quotes and sayings that ponder death and dying. Even the body art (i.e., tattoo) industry has developed the technology to produce sound wave tattoos, which can be used to memorialize the voice of deceased loved ones and can be played using a smartphone.[50]

In this collision of technology and culture, Americans have begun to incorporate death and dying into their everyday lives. Largely as a result of the current cultural interest in digitizing and sharing every aspect of life (e.g., smartphone selfies), American society has begun to shift from a death-denying society to a death-accepting society, reminiscent of the Victorian era.[51] In an unexpected turn of events, this interest has manifested in a dramatic resurgence of home death photography.[52] Cancer patients and others with terminal illnesses have long used photos and videos to bear witness to their suffering and make visible that which is considered off limits (e.g., on blogs, Twitter, and now TikTok), and have encouraged family members and friends to do so on their behalf, when they are no longer able to do so, pushing visual and emotional boundaries well beyond what may be considered comfortable. Of course, these advancements will also need to be researched to be fully understood and for public health and allied professions to understand the implications for assessment, policy development, and assurance, as well as how best to incorporate these ideas into existing practice.

The Acknowledgement of Grief

Grief long has been considered an adjunct to death and dying, but is not always understood as a public health or clinical problem in and of itself, especially when a death or loss cannot be acknowledged, or occurs among the socially marginalized.[53,54] Recognized as a powerful, sometimes pathogenic event, both psychologically and physically, grief commonly is exemplified by emotional distress, physical symptoms, and loss of social functionality. For others, grief can be characterized by the excessive mortality, morbidity, and use of health services following loss.[55] Due to growing recognition that the grieving process has no set duration, and that symptomatology may be experienced throughout the life course, sustainable and long-term solutions to help mitigate the burden of grief within populations are necessitated.[56] This belief has been accompanied by calls from researchers to abandon the prescriptive "stages of grief" approach,[57] which may unduly limit a therapeutic response to grief because of the misunderstood nature and mislabeling of grief as linear process. Instead, the concept of grief can be described as a unique constellation of emotions and reactions for which there are no predetermined phases or endpoints.

Along with these shifts, American society has undergone several changes that have impacted the circumstances of death and what are considered typical courses of bereavement. For instance, while most persons report a gradual return to function and adaptation to loss with time, the intensity, magnitude, and consequences of grief are significant enough to attract the attention of a variety of institutions, resulting in technological advances described in this chapter and elsewhere.[9,22,30,32–34,42,54,55,57] Geographic mobility has had a profound influence on the availability and accessibility of social supports from interpersonal and community networks.[58] With the dawn of compassionate communities and promotion of grief advocacy as a means of prevention, more cities are facilitating death cafes; positive grieving art and poetry exhibitions; open mic grief stories and podcasts; book clubs and public forums on grief, death, and loss; as well as hosting community events like Death over Dinner[59] or The Dinner Party.[60] These initiatives may be implemented by experienced laypeople, who typically have been bereaved, or by certified and/or licensed professionals from public health, medicine, nursing, social work, psychology, or the ministry, who may have received specialized training in grief and bereavment.[61,62] Therefore, continued education, training, and experience of public health practitioners in processes of bereavement and loss may serve to mitigate the growing concern about the ability and capacity of health care to best support and meet the needs of grievers.

Importantly, while most of these initiatives are designed to facilitate the normal grieving process, others are intended to help people having, or who are at high risk of having, more intense or complicated grief reactions. Some opportunities are directed to the loss experience itself (e.g., loss of a parent), while others focus on people who have particular grief-related circumstances in common (e.g., trauma).[61-63] The majority of these programs, however, are designed to help alleviate the burden of grief experienced by individuals, families, and/or communities. They are increasingly being implemented in institutional settings such as hospitals, churches, long-term care facilities, and community health centers. Finally, as with the wide variety of available technological solutions for grief, the effectiveness of most community and individually based grief-related programming has not been established; nor have the main theoretical frameworks of these interventions been empirically articulated or evaluated.[62]

IMPORTANT POLICIES AND LEGISLATION

> Well, everyone can master a grief but he that has it.
> —William Shakespeare[64]

Support for individuals providing end-of-life care, or experiencing bereavement, is difficult to access and is often inadequate. At a national level, the US Family and Medical Leave Act and the US Fair Labor Standards Act provide limited support for end-of-life care.[65,66] One must work for a covered employer (i.e., most large private employers, plus public agencies and all elementary and secondary schools) and must also be eligible, which includes having worked for a covered employer for at least 12 months, for at least 1,250 hours, and at a location with at least 50 employees within 75 miles.[67] If these conditions are met, allowance is made for 12 weeks of unpaid, but job-protected, time off to care for an immediate family member (limited to parents, children, and spouses) who has a serious health condition.[67] No provisions are made for bereavement or other circumstances when care is no longer being provided because the family member has died. Further, the policies do not mandate paid leave, nor do they include grandparents, in-laws, siblings, cousins, friends, domestic partners, extended family, or pets. In addition, only one state (Oregon) has a law requiring employers to provide bereavement leave, though individual employers may choose to provide paid or unpaid leave.[68] The United States is one of only a handful of industrialized nations that does not have national bereavement legislation.[69]

Advance Directives have been a strategy to promote end-of-life planning for people nearing the end of their journey.[70] Other policy relevant to end-of-life adds a voluntary option to give patients' control over when and how they die, while ensuring safeguards to prevent misuse and abuse of the procedures.[71] This legislation, known as "Right to Die," or "Death with Dignity," allows mentally competent adults with a life expectancy of six or fewer months to request a prescription medication to accelerate their death.[71] So far, this legislature only has been passed by eight states (California, Colorado, Hawaii, Maine, New Jersey, Oregon, Vermont, Washington) and Washington D.C.

COMMUNITY RESOURCES RELATED TO END-OF-LIFE CARE

> *I navigated as best I could the role of end-of-life shepherd – a journey I had never taken before. I have to forgive myself for what I did not know.*
> –Lisa Shultz[72]

Government agencies and programs often center on resource location and supportive information rather than participatory activities near end-of-life. Of such available resources, there continues to be widespread misunderstanding about the importance of advance care planning prior to a critical emergency. Focused on discussing, documenting, and sharing preferences for life-sustaining treatments, advance care planning aims to ensure that individual choices for end-of-life care are honored in the chance of an actual life-threatening event. Unfortunately, no standardized process for implementing advance care planning currently exists in the United States. Lack of coordination within electronic medical records, as well as poor communication between patients, families, and their providers have led to many advance directives not being honored within health care systems. To address these challenging issues, many local, state and national programs are being widely used to promote advance care planning among the public. Moreover, as a testament to its effectiveness, Medicare now pays health care providers to facilitate advance care planning sessions in physician offices and hospital settings,[70] positioning public health as an instrumental mode of advance care-related communication, planning, education, and outreach. Medicare pays for voluntary advanced care planning under the Medicare Physician Fee Schedule and the Hospital Outpatient Prospective Payment System (available at: https://www.medicare.gov/coverage/advance-care-planning).

At the same time, there is a growing body of evidence that suggests participation in a grief-related program could be a necessary and effective component of the healing process after significant loss. Yet, to date, few grief-related programs have been empirically evaluated for their effectiveness. Of the programs that do appear in the research literature, one has been found to be theoretically effective, providing a framework for how and why grief-related improvements have been reported with program participation.[62] In the program, grievers are exposed to evidence-based curricula designed to influence variables of grief described as knowledge, attitudes, beliefs, and behaviors.[62] Other programs, for which increasing amounts of anecdotal evidence support implementation, use combinations of techniques and innovative technological approaches to support those experiencing grief or grappling with end-of-life care. Selected grief-related programs identified by the authors are briefly described later in the chapter and include: Actively Moving Forward, Outward Bound, Grief Resource Network, The Grief Recovery Method, Tragedy Assistance Program for Survivors, Traditions Program, National Alliance for Grieving Children, GriefShare, Good Grief, and A Safe Place to Grieve. For palliative and end-of-life care discourse: Death over Dinner, The Conversation Project, The Dinner Party, Five Wishes, Compassion & Choices, the National Provider Orders for Life-Sustaining Treatment (POLST) Paradigm, and VitalTalk.

AVAILABILITY OF BEST PRACTICES

Research here is exploration and discovery. It's investigating [something that] no one knows or understands.
–Neil Armstrong[73]

Individuals nearing end-of-life, or whose prognosis is uncertain, often receive inconsistent information about their care.[74] Because of this ambiguity, patients and their families may experience psychological distress due to a combination of factors including clinical uncertainty, poor communication, and lack of discussion about core issues (e.g., preferences for location of death).[75] End-of-life decision-making has been further complicated by advanced technology,[75] with many dying individuals and their families lacking the medical knowledge required to make informed decisions about clinical interventions that best support end-of-life care. The gold standard for establishing a best practice clinical approach (i.e., a randomized controlled trial), can be difficult to implement for educational and supportive programs at end-of-life.[76] Although, some organizations have worked to provide clusters of information on best practices for end-of-life care, such as the American Association of Family Physicians (available at: https://www.aafp.org/afp/topicModules/viewTopicModule.htm?topicModuleId=57).

With community and population based grief-related programming, best practices begin with the mitigation of disruptive group dynamics that are commonly experienced with implementation and participation.[77] For example, some participants may believe that their loss is more important than others; others may take on inappropriate roles such as moralist, advice giver, or interrupter.[78] Therefore, customization of community and population based initiatives may be needed to manage group characteristics.[77,78] It is equally imperative that all community- and population-based grief-related programming be grounded in theory. Grief-related programming grounded in theory possesses a systematic understanding for how programmatic components lead to desirable outcomes.[58,79] Framed this way, theory considers the forces that shape the grieving process, including social and physical environments, and can be used to identify suitable audiences, methods for fostering change, and concrete outcomes to evaluate for improvement in grief-related symptomatology. For these reasons, programs based in theory are more likely to succeed than those developed without the benefit of a theoretical perspective.[58,79]

VULNERABILITY AT THE END-OF-LIFE

One of the most important things you can do on this earth is to let people know they are
not alone.
–Shannon L. Alder[80]

Enrollment in palliative (i.e., holistic symptom management for those seriously ill but not necessarily dying) and hospice care (i.e., holistic care for the actively dying) at end-of-life can increase quality of life for patients and families, but not all patients are equally likely to receive such care. Variables such as race and ethnicity, likely moderated by geographical variation (e.g., county and availability of resources), can affect hospice use,[81] as can the surviving spouse's education level, when the decedent is partnered at the time of death.[82] Care must therefore be taken to minimize the influence of structural factors on access to end-of-life care, as well as to provide culturally-appropriate knowledge and education to patients and their families. For example, Black adults often receive less medical attention than others throughout the life course, so providers who recommend hospice care in lieu of aggressive medical treatment may be perceived as trying to deny necessary life-sustaining treatment.[83]

Further, there are cultural variations in what is defined as grief and loss, as well as how people cope with end-of-life situations. Not all mourners, nor each among the dying, needs grief-related programming[84]; therefore, a one size fits all approach is not the most practical solution given the subjective nature of the grieving and end-of-life processes. Empirically, those who benefit the most from grief-related programming are younger, female, and those who have experienced a longer passage of time since the loss.[58] Additional studies have shown that men grieve more instrumentally, approaching end-of-life through problem based solutions, fact-finding, and rationalization.[58,85] Women, on the other hand, grieve more intuitively and for longer periods of time, focusing on feelings and the expression of loss.[58,85] Therefore, before accommodations should be made with respect to the appropriateness of specific programs given a particular circumstance (i.e. demographic or population characteristic), a considerable amount of research is needed.

CONCLUSION: CHALLENGES AND OPPORTUNITIES FOR PUBLIC HEALTH

When we least expect it, life sets us a challenge to test our courage and willingness to change; at such a moment, there is no point in pretending that nothing has happened or in saying that we are not yet ready.

–Paulo Coelho[86]

While public health long has focused on well-being, and not merely an absence of disease, "well-being" may often be interpreted as resulting from efforts to control communicable or chronic disease with the goal of establishing healthy environments and populations. Issues related to death, dying, and grief do not fit neatly into this conceptualization, such as the inherent right of all individuals to die with their dignity intact,[87] or the ability for dying persons to have autonomy over their own dying processes, as well as the ability to make decisions as to where and how they prefer to die.[87] In fact, achieving the preferred manner and place of death is many times a hallmark of a "good death," one that is in concordance with the wishes of both the dying and the grieving.[88]

Another serious challenge, and opportunity for the future, is the lack of agreement about what constitutes normal or abnormal outcomes following loss, as well as the absence of reliable criteria and valid instrumentation for assessing those outcomes.[58] Scholars have proposed a variety of different ways to determine whether someone has "returned to normal" after grieving a loss, such as a reduction of depression-like symptoms; the return to a level of social functioning similar to the period pre-grief/loss; a reduction in the frequency of distressing memories; the capacity to form new relationships and undertake new social roles; and functional outcomes, such as the return to work.[58] Numerous scales and indices have been used to measure these concepts, but their reliability and validity rarely have been studied.[58] Other challenges exist with the measures themselves, especially those that assess relationships and social roles following a loss event, which can never be fully reestablished because of the irreversibility of the loss experience.[89] To this end, perhaps one of the most hotly contested issues concerning grief and loss stemmed from the bereavement exclusion criterion for Major Depressive Disorder in the latest version of the *Diagnostic and Statistical Manual of Mental Disorders*. Supporters for the exclusion argued that while typical responses to grief and loss may include some depressive symptomatology, these characteristics tend to lessen with time; whereas a depressed mood is more sustained.[84,90] Alternatively, opponents of the exclusion argued that although it is difficult to distinguish manifestations of grief from depression, grief and bereavement can still be considered a depressive qualifier.[84,90]

Moreover, public health professionals and allies such as thanatologists, psychologists, and population grief researchers have described a number of processes associated with poor outcomes following a loss event, including absent, delayed, anticipatory, masked, disenfranchised, prolonged, or chronic grief.[90] However, due to the expected variation in individuals' responses to loss, there is currently no universally accepted standard for the amount of grief that is too much or too little, nor for whether grief is normal or abnormal in terms of health and well-being.[90] Further, there has been controversy regarding the appropriateness of considering the constellation of depression-like symptoms common in grief as an illness. This issue was first raised by Engel in his seminal 1961 paper, "Is Grief a Disease?", where he argues that although persons experiencing grief are distressed, they are not ill or diseased and should not be treated as such in clinical practice.[91] Later research showed that pharmacological interventions used to treat grief-related symptomatology have little to no effect on the grieving situation, leading to the hypothesis that grief is not a pathological outcome, but rather a normal and natural reaction to loss.[92] Although it is true that grieving persons may seek clinical care to alleviate some forms of grief-related symptomatology, pharmacological treatments such as tranquilizers, sleeping pills, and sedatives seldom improve the grief experience itself, and may inhibit the natural process of grieving.[93] The importance of and preparation for grief-related symptomatology and advance care planning prior to a life-limiting event are critical public health issues that need to be addressed for the health and well-being of all populations. These issues will require partnership with numerous partners, such as social workers, physicians, nurses, pharmacists, and other members of allied health fields.

CASE STUDY: THE STORY OF ROMAN AND EUGENIA

This case study is a narration of the life of Eugenia Kuyda, developer of Replika (A Virtual Reality Application).[94] The story shares how a person, devastated by the death of her friend, used technology to mitigate her grief by developing a new therapeutic invention. This novel intervention uses AI to create a digital character who represents a person who has died. The character is programmed to sound and talk like the deceased person, and people can interact with the character through text messaging and photographs. People who have interacted with the avatars have reported being comforted and finding a sense of peace.[94]

Roman was considered an unusually serious child who had a fascination with life and death. At the age of eight, he wrote a letter to his deceased relatives discussing his values of wisdom and justice. During his years studying abroad, Roman developed a passion for computer science, art, and design. After college graduation, Roman met Eugenia while exploring the Moscow nightlife. The two became close friends and cofounded Luka, an AI startup. As an adult, Roman became known for openly contemplating his own mortality. He often told people that upon his death, he planned to have pieces of his will divided and given away to people who did not know each other. Thus, to read his will, complete strangers would have to come together and meet for the first time. To those who knew him best, Roman's intent was to bring people together in death, just as he did in life. In the summer of 2015, Roman became inspired by what he understood as a growing resistance for traditional funerals. This notion led him to develop an idea for a new kind of cemetery where the dead would be buried in biodegradable capsules, eventually turning into trees, creating what he referred to as "memorial forests." At the bottom of each tree would lie a digital display that offered information about the deceased.

Later that same year, Roman was crossing a busy street in central Moscow and was accidentally struck by a car. Although he was rushed to the nearest hospital, Roman later died of his injuries. Devastated by the loss of her best friend and longing to speak with him again, Eugenia began collecting text messages sent by Roman to her and to others prior to his death. After gathering several years of text messages and posts on social media, Eugenia felt that she had acquired enough data to build a chatbot that mimicked Roman's speech patterns. By creating what she referred to as a "digital estate" of Roman's essence, Eugenia thought it might help her and others to cope with his loss. After several years of private beta tasting, Eugenia made the decision to publicly launch the chatbot enhanced by AI technology. Since that time, interacting with the chatbot has been reported to have a therapeutic effect for not only Eugenia, but also other friends and family members of Roman, and complete strangers. Talking about her creation, Eugenia has said that the chatbot has allowed her to gain a sense of peace about Roman's death, in part, because she had built a place where she could direct her grief. The chatbot also serves as a symbolic, safe place where she, Roman, and others can seemingly send and receive messages beyond this life. To this end, digital afterlife technology can be used to benefit end-of-life care by not only providing a potential therapeutic outlet for grievers, but also by reminding them that even though their loved ones are dead, they are not forgotten.

REFERENCES

1. Beach SR, Schulz R, Friedman EE, Rodakowski J, Martsolf RG, James AE. Adverse consequences of unmet needs for care in high-need/high-cost older adults. *J Gerontol B-Psychol*. 2020;75(2):459–470.

2. Shunmugasundaram C, Rutherford C, Butow PN, Sundaresan P, Dhillon HM. Content comparison of unmet needs self-report measures used in patients with head and neck cancer: A systematic review. *Psycho-Oncol*. 2019;28:2295–2306.

3. Bell D, Brungraber-Ruttenberg M, Chai E. Care of geriatric patients with advanced illnesses and end-of-life needs in the emergency department. *Clin Geriatr Med*. 2018;34(3):453–467.

4. Staudt C. Whole-person, whole-community care at the end-of-life. *Virtual Mentor*. 2013;13(12):1069–1080.

5. Wright, F. *Frank Lloyd Wright: An Autobiography*. Duell, Sloan and Pearce; 1943.

6. World Health Organization. Preamble to the Constitution of the World Health Organiation. 1948. Available at: https://apps.who.int/gb/bd/PDF/bd47/EN/constitution-en.pdf?ua=1. Accessed March 1, 2021.

7. Gomersall T, Astel A, Nygård L, Sixsmith A, Mihailidis A, Hwang A. Living with ambiguity: A metasynthesis of qualitative research on mild cognitive impairment. *Gerontologist.* 2015;55(5):892–912.

8. Patra S. Public health: Infectious vs chronic diseases. *J Biomedical Sci.* 2018;7(4):15.

9. Cohen J, Deliens L. Applying a public health persepetive to end-of-life-care. In *A Public Health Perspective on End-of-life Care.* New York, NY: Oxford University Press; 2012:3–20.

10. Cerel J, Brown MM, Myfanwy M, et al. How many people are exposed to suicide? Not six. *Suicide Life Threat Behav.* 2018;29(2):529–534.

11. Ornstein KA, Kelley AS, Bollens-Lund E, Wolff JL. A national profile of end-of-life caregiving in the United States. *Health Aff.* 2017;36(7):1184-1192.

12. Öhman, C, Watson D. Are the dead taking over Facebook? A big data approach to the future of death online. *Big Data Soc.* 2019;6(1):1-13.

13. Vespa J. The graying of America: More older adults than kids by 2035. US Census Bureau. 2018. Available at: https://www.census.gov/library/stories/2018/03/graying-america.html. Accessed March 1, 2021.

14. Administration on Aging. 2017 Profile of older Americans. US Department of Health and Human Services. 2018. Available at: https://acl.gov/sites/default/files/Aging%20and%20 Disability%20in%20America/2017OlderAmericansProfile.pdf. Accessed March 1, 2021.

15. Xu J, Murphy SL, Kochanek KD, Arias E. Mortality in the United States, 2018. 2020. Centers for Disease Control and Prevention. Available at: https://www.cdc.gov/nchs/data/databriefs/ db355-h.pdf. Accessed March 1, 2021.

16. Kuluski K, Ho J, Kaur Hans P, Nelson ML. Community care for people with complex care needs: Bridging the gap between health and social care. *Int J Integr Care.* 2017;17(4):1–11.

17. Lewis ET, Harrison R, Hanly L, et al. End-of-life priorities of older adults with terminal illness and caregivers: A qualitative consultation. *Health Expect.* 2019;22(3):405–414.

18. Flaherty E, Bartels SJ. Addressing the community-based geriatric healthcare workforce shortage by leveraging the potential of interprofessional teams. *J Am Geriatr Soc.* 2019;67(S2):S400–S408.

19. Abramson TA. Older adults: The "panini sandwich" generation. *Clin Gerontologist.* 2015;38(4):251–267.

20. Rosenthal NA. Infections, chronic disease, and the epidemiological transition: A new perspective. *Clin Infect Dis.* 2015;61(3):489–490.

21. Warraich H. *Modern Death: How Medicine Changed the End-of-life.* New York, NY: St. Martin's Press; 2017:1–337.

22. Leach J. 'Give-up-itis' revisited: Neuropathology of extremis. *Med Hypotheses.* 2018;120: 14–21.

23. Institute of Medicine. Dying in America: Improving quality and honoring individual preferences near the end-of-life. National Academies Press. 2015. Available at: http://www.ahaphysicianforum.org/resources/appropriate-use/ICU/resources/IOM-Dying-in-America.pdf. Accessed March 1, 2021.

24. Coronado F, Koo D, Gebbie K. The public health workforce: Moving forward in the 21st Century. *Am J Prev Med.* 2014;47(5):S275–S277.

25. Centers for Disease Control and Prevention. 10 Essential Public Health Services. 2021. Available at: https://www.cdc.gov/publichealthgateway/publichealthservices/essentialhealthservices.html. Accessed March 1, 2021.

26. Cross S, Warraich H. Changes in the place of death in the United States. *N Engl J Med.* 2019;381(24):2369–2370.

27. Cardona-Morrell M, Kim J, Turner RM, Anstey M, Mitchell I.A, Hillman K. Non-beneficial treatments in hospital at the end-of-life: A systematic review on extent of the problem. *Int J Health Care Qual Assur.* 2016;28(4):456–469.

28. Maetens A, Beernaert K, De Schreye R, et al. Impact of palliative home care support on the quality and costs of care at the end-of-life: A population-level matched cohort study. *BMJ Open.* 2019;9(1):e025180.

29. National Institute on Aging. Providing care and comfort at the end-of-life. 2017. Available at: https://www.nia.nih.gov/health/providing-comfort-end-life. Accessed March 1, 2021.

30. Breen L, Aoun SA, O'Connor M, Johnson AR, Howting D. Effect of caregiving at end-of-life on grief, quality of life and general health: A prospective, longitudinal, comparative study. *Palliat Med.* 2020;34(1):145–154.

31. Jones, O, End-of-life care is vital. Why is it so neglected? The Guardian. January 2020. Available at: https://www.theguardian.com/commentisfree/2020/jan/31/end-of-life-care-britain-palliative-charity-public. Accessed March 1, 2021.

32. Goldstein J, Weiser B. 'I cried multiple times:' Now doctors are the ones saying goodbye. New York Times. April 2020. Available at: https://www.nytimes.com/2020/04/13/nyregion/coronavirus-nyc-doctors.html. Accessed March 1, 2021.

33. Sikstrom L, Saikaly R, Ferguson G, Mosher PJ, Bonato S, Soklaridis S. Being there: A scoping review of grief support training in medical education. *PLoS ONE.* 2019;14(11):e0224325.

34. Meller N, Parker D, Hatcher D, Sheehan A. Grief experiences of nurses after the death of an adult patient in an acute hospital setting: An integrative review of literature. *Collegian.* 2019;26(2):302-310.

35. PEW Charitable Trust. Patients seek better exchange of health data. PEW Issue Brief. March 2020. Available at: https://www.pewtrusts.org/en/research-and-analysis/issue-briefs/2020/03/patients-seek-better-exchange-of-health-data-among-their-care-providers. Accessed March 1, 2021.

36. Schulte F, Fortune EF. Death by a thousand clicks: Where electronic health records went wrong. Kaiser Health News. March 2019. Available at: https://www.healthleadersmedia.com/innovation/death-thousand-clicks-where-electronic-health-records-went-wrong. Accessed March 1, 2021.

37. US Bureau of Labor Statistics. The rising cost of dying, 1986–2017. The Economics Daily. October 2017. Available at: https://www.bls.gov/opub/ted/2017/the-rising-cost-of-dying-1986-2017.htm. Accessed March 1, 2021.

38. Morgan DG, Crossley M, Kirk A, et al. Evaluation of telehealth for preclinic assessment and follow-up in an interprofessional rural and remote memory clinic. *J Appl Gerontol.* 2011;30(3);304–331.

39. Calton B, Abedini N, Fratkin M. Telemedicine in the time of Coronavirus. *J Pain Symptom Manag.* 2020;S0885-3924(20):30170-6.

40. Klein BC, Busis NA. COVID-19 is catalyzing the adoption of teleneurology. *Neurology.* 2020;94(21):1–2.

41. Arora S, Smith T, Snead J, et al. Project ECHO: An Effective Means of Increasing Palliative Care Capacity. *Am J Manag Care.* 2017;23(7):1-9.

42. Sofka C, Noppe Cupit I, Gilbert K. *Dying, Death, and Grief in an Online Universe: For Counselors and Educators.* New York, NY: Springer Publishing Company; 2012:1–272.

43. Pombo N, Garcia N, Bousson K, Spinsante S, Chorbev I. Pain assessment–can it be done with a computerized system? A systematic review and meta-analysis. *Int J Environ Res Public Health.* 2016;13(415):1–27.

44. Domb M. Smart Home Systems Based on Internet of Things. In Y. Ismail, ed. *Internet of Things (IoT) for Automated and Smart Applications.* London, United Kingdom: IntechOpen; 2019:e1-e14.

45. Schwartz, M. Facebook promises to stop asking you to wish happy birthday to your friend who died. National Public Radio. April 2019. Available at: https://www.npr.org/2019/04/09/711399357/facebook-promises-to-stop-asking-you-to-wish-happy-birthday-to-your-friend-who-died. Accessed March 1, 2021.

46. Promobot. Robo-C: A humanoid robot with customized appearance for your office or home. Available at: https://promo-bot.ai/robots/robo-c. Accessed March 1, 2021.

47. Replika. The AI companion who cares. 2021. Available at: https://replika.ai. Accessed March 1, 2021.

48. WeCroak. Find happiness by contemplating your mortality. Available at: https://www.wecroak.com. Accessed March 1, 2021.

49. Weiner E. Bhutan's dark secret to happiness. British Broadcasting Corporation. April 2015. Available at: http://www.bbc.com/travel/story/20150408-bhutans-dark-secret-to-happiness. Accessed March 1, 2021.

50. Lang C. You can now get a tattoo that actually plays back your pre-recorded audio. TIME. May 2017. Available at: https://time.com/4781519/tattoo-plays-audio. Accessed March 1, 2021.

51. Tettlebaum HM, Billings JA. Getting comfortable with death: The culture change of life & death: Will health reform, demographics & the economy bring it about? *Mo Med.* 2014;11(2):120-125.

52. Green, P. The iPhone at the deathbed. The New York Times. February 2020. Available at: https://www.nytimes.com/2020/02/18/style/iphone-death-portraits.html. Accessed March 1, 2021.

53. Valentine C, Bauld L, Walter T. Bereavement following substance misuse: A disenfranchised grief. *OMEGA.* 2016;72(4):283–301.

54. Doka K. Disenfranchised grief. *Bereave Care.* 2009;18(3):37–39.

55. Fagundes C, Brown RL, Chen MA, et al. Grief, depressive symptoms, and inflammation in the spousally bereaved. *Psychoneuroendocrinology.* 2018;100:190–197.

56. Nielsen MK, Carlsen AH, Neergaard MA, Bidstrup PE, Guldin MB. Looking beyond the mean in grief trajectories: A prospective, population-based cohort study. *Soc Sci Med.* 2019;232:460–469.

57. Stroebe M, Schut H, Boerner K. Cautioning health-care professionals: Bereaved persons are misguided through the stages of grief. *OMEGA.* 2017;74(4):455–473.

58. Maddrell A. Mapping grief. A conceptual framework for understanding the spatial dimensions of bereavement, mourning and remembrance. *Soc Cult Geogr.* 2016;17(2):166–188.

59. Death Over Dinner. How death came to dinner. Available at: https://deathoverdinner.org/#about. Accessed March 1, 2021.

60. The Dinner Party. About us: The Dinner Party. Available at: https://www.thedinnerparty.org/about. Accessed March 1, 2021.

61. Bartone PT, Bartone JV, Violanti JM, Gileno ZM. Peer support services for bereaved survivors: A systematic review. *OMEGA.* 2018;8(1):137–166.

62. Nolan RD, Hallam JS. Construct validity of the Theory of Grief Recovery (TOGR): A new paradigm toward our understanding of grief and loss. *Am J Health Educ.* 2019;50(2):99–111.

63. Bartone T. Peer support for bereaved survivors; Systematic review of the evidence and identification of best practices. Tragedy Assistance Program for Survivors. 2017. Available at: https://www.taps.org/globalassets/pdf/about-taps/tapspeersupportreport2016.pdf. Accessed March 1, 2021.

64. Shakespeare W. *Much Ado About Nothing.* Miola R, ed. Sterling Publications; 2021. (Original work published 1600).

65. Art of Dying Institute. Who we are. Available at: https://www.artofdying.org/who-we-are. Accessed March 1, 2021.

66. US Department of Labor. Leave benefits. May 2020. Available at: https://www.dol.gov/general/topic/benefits-leave. Accessed March 1, 2021.

67. US Department of Labor. Fact sheet #28: The Family and Medical Leave Act. 2012. Available at: https://www.dol.gov/agencies/whd/fact-sheets/28-fmla. Accessed March 1, 2021

68. Employment Law Handbook. Bereavement leave. 2021. Available at: https://www.employmentlawhandbook.com/leave-laws/bereavement-leave-laws. Accessed March 1, 2021.

69. Kaiser Family Foundation. Paid family and sick leave in the US. 2020. Available at: https://www.kff.org/womens-health-policy/fact-sheet/paid-family-leave-and-sick-days-in-the-u-s. Accessed March 1, 2021.

70. Centers for Medicare and Medicaid Services. Medicare Learning Network Fact sheet: Advance care planning. October 2020. Available at: https://www.cms.gov/outreach-and-education/medicare-learning-network-mln/mlnproducts/downloads/advancecareplanning.pdf. Accessed March 1, 2021.

71. Death with Dignity. Death with Dignity Acts. Available at: https://www.deathwithdignity.org/learn/death-with-dignity-acts. Accessed March 1, 2021.

72. Shultz L. *A Chance to Say Goodbye: Reflections on Losing a Parent.* High Country Publications; 2017.

73. Armstrong N. The Astronaut Wings Ceremony: Research here is exploration and discovery. NASA Dryden Flight Research Center on Edwards Air Force Base, California, US. October 21, 2005. Available at: https://www.nasa.gov/centers/dryden/news/X-Press/stories/2005/102105_Wings.html. Accessed June 3, 2021.

74. Koffman J, Yorganci E, Murtagh F, et al. The AMBER care bundle for hospital inpatients with uncertain recovery nearing the end-of-life: The ImproveCare feasibility cluster RCT. *Health Technol Assess.* 2019;23(5):1–182.

75. Eues SK. End-of-life care: Improving quality of life at the end-of-life. *Prof Case Manag.* 2007;12(6):339–344.

76. Koffman J, Yorganci E, Yi D, et al. Managing uncertain recovery for patients nearing the end-of-life in hospital: A mixed-methods feasibility cluster randomized controlled trial of the AMBER care bundle. *Trials.* 2019;20(1):506.

77. Flåten AM, Stephens PA, Furnes B, Dysvik E. Group leaders' experiences in heterogenous grief. *Soc Work Groups.* 2019;42(2):101–116.

78. Worden JW. *Grief Counseling and Grief Therapy: A Handbook for the Mental Health.* 5th ed. New York, NY: Springer Publishing Company; 2018:1–317.

79. Nilsen P. Making sense of implementation theories, models and frameworks. *Implement Sci.* 2015;10(53):1–13.

80. Alder, S. Pandemic Pages. In: Newark A, ed. *Chicken Soup for the Soul: Listen to Your Dreams: 101 Tales of Inner Guidance, Divine Intervention and Miraculous Insight.* Chicken Soup for the Soul; 2020: 326.

81. Johnson KS, Kuchibhatla M, Payne R, Tulsky JA. Race and residence: Intercounty variation in Black-White Differences in Hospice Use. *J Pain Symptom Manag.* 2013;46(5):681–690.

82. Ornstein KA, Aldridge MD, Mair CA, Gorges R, Siu AL, Kelley AS. Spousal characteristics and older adults' hospice use: Understanding disparities in end-of-life care. *J Palliat Med.* 2016;19(5):1–8.

83. Carr D, Luth EA. Advance care planning: Contemporary issues and future directions. *Innov Aging.* 2017;1(1):1–10.

84. Corr CA, Corr DM. *Death & Dying, Life & Living.* 7th ed. Belmont, CA: Wadsworth Cengage Learning; 2013:1–816.

85. Doka KJ, Martin TL. *Grieving Beyond Gender: Understanding the Ways Men and Women Mourn.* 2nd ed. New York, NY: Routledge; 2010:1–264.

86. Coelho P. *The Devil and Miss Prym.* HarperCollins Publisher; 2006.

87. Frank M. Dignity in death: Why the fundamental right of the individual to choose their final moments outweighs the government's societal inter societal interests to preserve life. *U Balt L Rev.* 2020;49(2):1–17.

88. Neumann A. *The Good Death: An Exploration of Dying in America.* Boston, MA: Beacon Press; 2016:1–248.

89. Cherny N, Fallon M, Kaasa S, Portenoy RK, Currow DC. *Oxford Textbook of Palliative Medicine.* 5th ed. London, United Kingdom: Oxford University Press; 2015:1–1280.

90. Pearce C. *The Public and Private Management of Grief. Recovering Normal.* New York, NY: Palgrave MacMillan; 2019:1–233.

91. Engel, G. Is grief a disease? A challenge for medical research. *Psychosom Med.* 1961;23(1):18–22.

92. Friedman RA. Grief, depression, and the DSM-5. *N Engl J Med.* 2012;366(20):1855–1857.

93. Roulston A, Clarke MJ, Donnelly M, et al. Psychological therapies for major depressive disorder and prolonged grief in bereaved adults. *Cochrane Database Syst Rev.* 2018;12:CD013237.

94. Murphy, M. Replika: This app is trying to replicate you. Quartz. July 2017. Available at: https://qz.com/1698337/replika-this-app-is-trying-to-replicate-you. Accessed March 1, 2021.

IV. EDUCATION

Section IV addresses the components of the social determinant education, which are access to education and the impact of education on health outcomes and health literacy. This is accomplished through the lens of overall educational achievement, lifelong learning, retirement options, and workforce development.

This section is led with a chapter that discusses the role of education and educational attainment, and the connection with health outcomes and well-being. It makes the case for programs and interventions which can integrate educational strategies to promote health literacy and impact health outcomes.

Chapter 14 in this section will discuss the role of lifelong learning and continued education throughout the life span, as well as its relationships with healthy aging.

This text would be remiss if it did not address education within the context of workforce development and preparation. Preparing the workforce to be able to guide and direct initiatives will be important as a component of building healthy aging initiatives. Initiatives such as the Geriatric Education Centers, Geriatric Workforce Enhancement Programs, Age Friendly Health Systems, and Area Health Education Centers initiatives are addressed in Chapter 15.

The section concludes with a reflection on educational initiatives through technological considerations for healthy aging and health outcomes. Chapter 16 takes another approach to education, and educates the reader on the impact technology has upon various aspects of people growing older to include service delivery, infrastructure development, and resources available for the older adult, their caregivers, and the workforce.

Educational Factors for Healthy Aging

Brittany M. Chambers, MPH and Hengameh Hosseini, PhD

BACKGROUND AND CURRENT LITERATURE

As public health professionals, we work towards ensuring optimal care and wellness for all populations throughout their life span. Higher levels of educational attainment are linked with improved health and wellness. A clear understanding of how educational level predicts health outcomes for older adults is essential to being well-informed public health practitioners. Attention to educational attainment in older age is imperative. In this chapter, we describe how educational attainment is a key contributor to health outcomes and wellness for older adults.

Over the last few decades, the educational levels of older adults has improved significantly due to increased schooling at younger ages. Between 1970 and 2019, the number of older adults who completed high school increased from 28% to 88%.[1,2] The 2019 US Census Bureau shows 32% of the population aged 65 and older has a bachelor's degree or more education compared with 42% of adults ages 35–39 years and 40% of adults ages 25–29 years. Educational attainment differences are observed among racial and ethnic minority older adults. The 2019 Profile of Older Adults shows 92% of White adults have high school degrees compared with 79% of Black adults and 59% of Hispanic adults.[3]

According to the US Bureau of Labor Statistics, adults over the age of 55 in the workforce is predicted to rise to 25% by 2028; they are the fastest-growing segment of the labor force. Education levels are associated with older adult's likelihood to be employed. Ten percent of workers age 65 or older who had not completed high school were unemployed, compared with 5.8% of their counterparts with a college degree.[4] Higher levels of education are linked to higher incomes, better living conditions, and overall health and wellness. Households headed by older adults with a college degree had a median net worth almost four times more than older adults without a high school diploma.[5]

Educational attainment has also been found to be a predictor for older adults' plans to stay in the workforce. Those who continue to work post-retirement report that their employment provides financial assistance and daily routines, both important for cognitive stimulation.[2]

Continued education can have long-term positive effects throughout a person's life span. Additional education provides protective factors that help shape a person's health over the life course.[6] One study found that one additional year of education can improve basic literacy and numeracy skills, linked with better health outcomes.[7] Continued education can lead to job stability with access to financial resources that can be used to improve health and reduce mortality risks.[7] More educated older adults are more likely to live healthier lifestyles, live in a safer environment, and experience less stress and more social support than their less educated peers.[6] Older educated adults typically have a heightened sense of personal control such as seeking health-related information and adopting health behaviors that prolongs the length of their lives.[6] Older adults with higher levels of education tend to use preventative and specialty services more frequently.[8] Educated older adults are more likely to learn and retain crucial medical information during health care visits and hospitalizations.[6] Older adults with more education and with increased health literacy skills are better able to obtain health and medical information (e.g., through the use of the internet), and may assume greater roles in directing their own health care.[8] For instance, educated persons adhere better to treatments for diabetes and HIV than their less educated counterparts.[9]

Adults over the age of 60 with low socioeconomic status/household income are at greater risk of functional decline, including in their activities of daily living and mobility.[10] About one in three older adults with a chronic illness and low socioeconomic status cannot afford food, prescribed medications, or both.[11] Two contributing factors to older adult abuse in persons with dementia is poverty and low levels of education of both the victim and caregiver.[12,13]

At older ages, there are major differences between the labor force participation rates of more educated and less educated groups.[14] Those with limited education have low employment rates in old age. People with college and advanced degrees tend to remain in the workforce longer.[14] If less productive workers selectively exit the workforce at younger ages, the average productivity of the older workers who remain may compare favorably to the average productivity of the young.[14]

Workplaces are changing rapidly as technology advances, which can be particularly challenging for older adult workers, but can be mitigated through further educational and job training programs that will be described further on in this chapter.

There are a number of pressing issues that negatively impact the health of older adults with educational attainment being a contributor of those outcomes. The public health imperatives described in the upcoming sections are (1) mental health, (2) depression, (3) dementia, and (4) health literacy.

Mental Health

Depression is one of the most common mental health conditions among the older population and is discussed in more detail in Chapter 3. Low educational attainment, defined as less than high school education, is a risk factor for developing late onset depression, which occurs among people 65 years and older with no previous history of depression.[15-17] Consequently, older adults who are clinically depressed are more likely to be diagnosed with a physical illness.[17] These depressive symptoms can adversely impact a patient's disease trajectory leading to poorer outcomes. Studies show older adults suffering from depression are more likely to use more medications, visit the emergency department more often, and experience prolonged hospital stays compared with older adults who are not depressed.[17]

Less educated older adults with depression are at increased risk of experiencing older adult abuse, including physical, verbal, psychological, financial, and sexual abuse.[18] The Centers for Disease Control and Prevention estimates the proportion of older adults who are victims of older adult mistreatment range between 2%–10% of the population.[19] Those numbers are likely underreported, as establishing accurate estimates is challenging due to lack of a national database and standard definition of older adult abuse.[19] Public health professionals can address this challenge through monitoring and prioritization of depression rates though surveillance systems to support evidence-based programming for older adults at risk for depression.

It is critical to note that higher levels of education may be a protective factor to produce better health outcomes. Some studies indicate that older people with more education and a more positive perspective generally had better psychological adjustments concerning their health and aging.[20] These more educated older adults were also more likely to have social support, correlated with reduced risk of mental health problems, chronic conditions, and mortality.[20]

Dementia

According to the World Health Organization, dementia is attributed to low educational attainment.[21] Adults with more years of education are at lower risk for developing Alzheimer's and other dementias than those with fewer years of formal education.[22] Having more years of education is believed to build up a person's "cognitive reserve" (i.e, the brain's ability to cope with damage that would otherwise lead to dementia).[23]

It is believed that cognitive stimulation is a potential strategy for the prevention of dementia.[23] Cognitive stimulation also comes in the form of lifelong education, which is why many interventions that target older populations have an educational component.

Educational attainment is also associated with older adults' cognition quality over their life span. Research from the Health and Retirement Study found that life expectancy with good cognition is substantially higher among those with more education.[24] Adults over the age of 65 with a college degree or more can expect to spend more than 80% of their lifetime with good cognition compared with their counterparts with less than a high school education, who could expect to spend less than 50% with good cognition.[24] These findings were similar for those in the 85-year-old age groups. For 85-year-old adults with less than a high school education, they can expect about 20% of their life to be in good cognitive health, while those with some college education could expect 45%. These findings support the observation that older adults with lower levels of education have a considerably higher prevalence of dementia.[24]

Health Literacy

Health literacy is the degree to which people can obtain, process, and understand basic health information that can help inform health decision-making.[25] Lower health literacy is highly prevalent among older adults. According to the Centers for Disease Control and Prevention, 71% of adults older than age 60 find it challenging to use print materials.[26] Among this group, 68% had difficulty understanding numbers/calculations. Income and education level are believed to be the strongest predictors of health literacy when compared with other variables.

Older adults with lower health literacy have less income and education and often need assistance completing medical forms.[27] People with low health literacy are less likely to use preventative care measures, such as not receiving vaccinations or cancer screenings. They often find it challenging to navigate complex health systems, resulting in delaying routine appointments which can lead to more serious physical and cognitive issues in the long-term. For example, lower health literacy among the older population is associated with worse mental health, increased risk for heart failure, and mortality.[27] Medicare beneficiaries with low health literacy have higher medical costs and increased emergency room visits.[28]

Health literacy can be improved by working with older adults to enhance their self-management skills, improve their links to clinical care, and by providing ongoing social support. Patient educational materials written in simple, clear language can help older adults better discuss their concerns with their health care provider.[29] Health materials written at lower literacy levels have been shown to improve the use of preventive health measures.[30]

Public health professionals can help address health literacy among older adults through outreach efforts. Identifying and collaborating with agencies and organization that support older people is an effective approach. Improving health literacy leads to improved health care decision-making, better communication, increased compliance to treatment directions, and improved health status.[31]

EDUCATION LEVELS AND HEALTH OUTCOMES

Research suggests that generally, older adults are unlikely to proactively seek out preventive services that would reduce their risks of chronic conditions and debilitating illnesses. Educational attainment appeared to be associated with older adults' likeliness to utilize prevention opportunities. According to the Center for Health Studies, older adults with higher levels of education tended to use preventative services more frequently than their less educated counterparts. Vaccines are one of the most cost effective preventive services available to the public. There is optimistic data showing those over the age of 65 are doing well on obtaining vaccines compared with younger groups.[32] For the 2016–2017 influenza season, only 38.6% of adults aged 18–64 years were vaccinated compared with 71.3% of adults 65 years and over. It is important to take a closer look at disparities within the subgroup of older adults, as those without a high school degree are less likely to receive flu or pneumonia vaccines than those with more education.[33] In response to the COVID-19 pandemic, the Kaiser Family Foundation reports that adults 65 and older, including residents of long-term care facilities, make up more than 54% of all people who have received at least one COVID-19 vaccine as of February 2021.[34]

RELEVANT POLICIES AND LEGISLATION IMPACTING EDUCATION

Although there are a number of relevant policies and legislations that impact how educational achievement forecasts health outcomes for older adults, this section will briefly cover two areas: the Older Americans Act and Elder Abuse.

The Older Americans Act

In 1965, Congress passed the Older Americans Act (OAA) to address the gaps in community social services for older people. The OAA is one of the main dissemination routes for social and nutrition services to the older adult population. According to the Agency on Aging, about 70% of OAA funds (almost $1.4 billion) support essential programs, such as continued education, job training, senior centers and health promotion. The existence of those programs are essential to ensuring older adults have access to cognitive stimulation programs that leads to improved health outcomes.

Older Adult Abuse

Socioeconomic status (educational level and income) is linked with older adult abuse, which includes physical, emotional or sexual abuse, financial exploitation, and abandonment. The National Council on Aging reports one in 10 adults over the age of 60 have been victims of older adult abuse. Older adults who have been abused have a 300% higher risk of death.[35] To address this alarming public health problem, most states have enacted laws to penalize abusers. The Elder Justice Coalition (EJC) (available at: http://www.elderjusticecoalition.com) utilizes grassroots advocacy efforts to increase public awareness about older adult abuse and monitor legislation that impact the prevention of older adult neglect. The Ageless Alliance (available at: https://agelessalliance.org) is a national nonprofit organization that unites advocates to use personal stories and outreach strategies to combat older adult abuse through awareness, advocacy, and action. More information on older adult justice laws and state specific resources can be found on the National Center on Elder Abuse website (available at: https://ncea.acl.gov).

SPECIAL CONSIDERATIONS AND SPECIAL POPULATIONS

Racial and ethnically diverse older adults are particularly vulnerable with increased risk for poor health outcomes due to systemic racism and disadvantages. For instance, although dementia risk is a concern among all older adults, it is of particular concern to Black, Indigenous, and other people of color. Studies on racial and ethnic disparities in dementia prevalence show increased risk for Black and Hispanic/Latinx populations than among White populations, correlated to lower educational attainment levels among the former groups.[36] These health disparities are also observed among other relevant older adult health topics.

Older adults in general are less likely to use mental health services than younger adults; however, race and geography appear to be a factor in even lower use of those services. Research shows that older White adults in the southern United States are much more likely to use mental health services than older Black adults in the same region.[37] These findings are important because they have an impact on the mental health service utilization differences on a national level.[37] Culturally responsive interventions to engage older Black and Hispanic/Latinx adults in mental health care is a public health opportunity that would be impactful.[38]

CONCLUSION: CHALLENGES AND OPPORTUNITIES FOR PUBLIC HEALTH

As described in this chapter, there are a number of pressing public health issues and considerations related to educational level that manifests in the health outcomes of older adults. Public health professionals are well equipped to make a number of improvements through multilevel educational interventions to ensure an ideal health trajectory for the nation's older adults.

To improve outcomes and circumstances, there is dedicated funding through the OAA to support continued education and workforce training programs targeted to the needs of older adults, with promising outcomes and scalability. Public health practitioners are not alone in their effort to address the current problems that are plaguing older adults and reducing their likeliness of achieving wellness. There are many allies and thought partners to collaborate with to make the targeted goals a reality. One obvious partner is aging societies (e.g., American Society on Aging), who advocate on a number of educational related topics for older adults. Employers and industry associations can be impactful collaborators as they are sources of education and training for older workers already in the labor force. Finally, community based organizations are worthy partners as they can offer low cost or no cost educational opportunities and trainings to older adults in their communities. In addition, nontraditional partners such as social workers, occupational therapists, recreational therapists, and community health workers or public health educators can all play a role in health literacy.

Evidence-based recommended strategies for health professionals to implement and make improvements in the educational opportunities available to older adults are available. First, promoting the best practices and interventions that have been proven effective, such as the Wellness Initiative for Senior Education program (available at: https://acl.gov/sites/default/files/programs/2017-03/WISE_ACL_Summary.pdf) are an easy way to educate older adults and empower them to become their own health advocates. For public health professionals in the public policy sector, efforts should be made to improve access to higher education programs that have been proven to improve functional outcomes among older adults. Those working in higher education institutions should team up with their state officials and associations to better promote tuition waivers for older learners.[39]

For those that are particularly focused on addressing health inequities that exist for older adults, there are special approaches that could be implemented to make improvements for these traditionally oppressed communities. Those in the research sector should recruit racially and ethnically diverse older adults in studies to gain better understanding of mental health disparities, as well as develop culturally responsive interventions. Finally, certified health educators are well-equipped to improve health literacy among all older adults, but with emphasis on traditionally underserved communities with concentrated minority and immigrant populations.[40]

With increased collaboration and data sharing with those in other sectors who care about the health outcomes of older adults, there are many ways in which we can all ensure our older adult population thrives. With older adults making up close to 25% of the adult population in the coming decades, investments in their education to ensure optimal health is a key prevention strategy. Looking back at how far we have come, the high school completion rates have markedly improved over the last 50 years, with older adults who completed high school increasing 59%.[2] We should be proud of our successes, since educational levels are linked to health outcomes; however, as public health practitioners, we must continue the progress made and scale evidence-based educational interventions to take it to the next level.

CASE STUDY

Introduction to the Problem

Understanding and increasing adults' resilience to medical misinformation in online self-education behaviors is important from a public health perspective. A focus on older adults older than 60 years in particular is important in light of the spill down effect from older adults to other family members. For example, in a recent study, nearly 3 million school age children in the United States were being raised by, and thus receiving educational cues from, their grandparents.[41]

Since the democratization of the internet, one of the most critical components in education in the medical realm for the general public is online information, encompassing sources ranging from Wikipedia to discussion forums to social media platforms to formal online courses, newspapers, and medical journals. At least 65% percent of Americans reportedly self-educate about health-related and medicine-related topics on the internet.[42,43] One of the fastest growing cohorts of online health information seekers is those older than 60-years-old. This rise in use coincided with older Americans reporting that they have begun to trust online health information more than traditional media.[44]

One of the challenges in self-educating through online health information seeking is the amount of misinformation pervading the online space. Medical misinformation has been called one of the major global health threats of our time.[45] Here, we define misinformation as a health-related claim or fact that can be considered false due to lack of scientific evidence, and a closely related term, "disinformation," as a false claim put forth to intentionally mislead others.[46]

Adults older than 60-years-old exhibit several unique health information-seeking behaviors that deserve particular attention. First, people from this cohort are likely to be newer in their use of technology, and later adopters.[6] Second, they are more likely to have caretakers and relatives involved with their health care who do their own internet-based searches and pass that information, which might be discordant with physicians' advice or their own findings. Third, they tend to have significantly more intense, complex, and frequent clinical encounters and interaction with health institutions (e.g., long-term care facilities, rehabilitation) than younger people on average.[47] Fourth, the added intensity of interactions with health institutions introduces more opportunities to encounter bad or conflicting information. Fifth, they are more likely to suffer age-related cognitive issues and age-related health anxiety, which could interfere with critical assessment of information, learning, and retention of best practices, which can reinforce unhealthy information search practices and make people more susceptible to misinformation.[48]

What are the types of bad information that seniors are likely to encounter online? These include coordinated disinformation, which is a coordinated campaign of bad information meant to intentionally mislead; emotional contagion, which is the rapid, organic spread of fear and panic across users across online networks; hijacking of web-based informational tools with information known to be false or pseudoscientific; single-source misinformation, which encompasses the organic mistakes, omissions, mistranslations, misunderstandings, typographical errors, and other human error that pollute legitimate websites; and computational propaganda, which is the propagation of manipulated information by bots and other software programmed to spread (mis)information such as bot-based vaccine propaganda on Twitter.[47,49-51]

Description of the Intervention

Several freely available software solutions to the misinformation crisis have been published by academic and nonprofit civic groups over the last several years. Two of the best regarded include a toolkit of online misinformation training resources geared toward journalists published by First Draft news[52]; and open source dashboard Hoaxy, that allows users to type search terms into a web-based search box and see continuously updating sets of tweets on Twitter scored as being generated by bots posing as humans, potentially to push misinformation.[53] There exist few studies of the effectiveness of these tools in adults over 60 years of age.

This case was designed to evaluate the effectiveness of such tools in training technically unsophisticated "digital novice" adults over 60 years of age to identify misinformation in health care information. For the purposes of this case, we identified two over 60 volunteers enrolled as nondegree students in lifelong education courses at a US university. One, a male aged 67, has no health care experience; the second, a woman aged 65, is a retired nurse. Both consider themselves relative digital novices unfamiliar with social media or the previously listed tools, but are familiar with the basics of the internet (primarily browsing and using email). They have both used the internet to search for health-related news and information on a regular basis.

Both were initially given a short, untimed 20 item online quiz of their ability to identify general fake news text, videos, and images, from quizzes available on First Draft News website, and supplemented with a series of debunked Twitter and Facebook posts. Neither participant scored more than 40% accuracy.

Next, they were asked to read through seven total case studies, checklists, and training modules on how to identify online misinformation available on the First Draft website. Subsequently, both participants were shown how to use the well-studied Hoaxy search bar, asking them to focus on a feature presents a toolbar that allows users to search Twitter for keywords and phrases (e.g., Ebola vaccine, Sweden COVID deaths, cancer + vitamin D). The search bar produces a continuously updating series of tweets from influential sources that are rated as falling on a spectrum from "human" to "botlike" (i.e., a source programmed to put out automated content, possibly as part of a coordinated propaganda or misinformation farm). The two participants were instructed to spend at least five hours at home over the course of a week using that tool to search for at least 10 medical keywords and phrases from a preselected list of 40, and to focus on clicking through and reading posts all across the spectrum of credibility from "likely human" to "botlike."[54] Terms were selected to ensure participants would be exposed to accounts that published text as well as images and videos of health-related topics, and therefore exposed to misinformation in various forms. They were also encouraged to search the list of terms for articles and practice distinguishing real from fake using the previously referenced First Draft toolkit.

After one week, participants were again given an untimed 40 item quiz using a new set of posts, tweets, images, and videos drawn from the internet and focusing on health-related topics. They were asked to identify those that were false. In one attempt each, both participants completed this post quiz with over 80% accuracy, and reported an increased level of confidence in completing the quiz.

The "Why" of the Results

Post-training interviews with the two subjects revealed that their ability to identify non-credible sources and false online information related to health increased for several reasons. First, they reported that this training exercise made them aware of how much misinformation circulated online. Second, they reported this exercise showed them that bad information is circulated by sources that can look very credible, and that post other true information, but with efforts to conceal. Third, the exercise showed to them the importance of considering context clues within text and images for red flags. Outside the context of the quiz itself, they reported that this exercise and training taught them the ease with which they could double-check information presented to them: using online tools and strategies presented in the training modules and with minimal effort, and the importance of finding corroborating additional sources information from well-sourced resources when reading health-related online information.

How the Results Could Be Implemented for the Public Good

This case suggests that short courses of training with readily available online resources can be dramatically effective in training even technically less savvy older adults to recognize false or questionable medical information and sources online, and equipping them to self-educate about health care topics from online sources without pollution from incorrect information and propaganda.

REFERENCES

1. Centers for Disease Control and Prevention, National Center for Chronic Disease Prevention and Health Promotion. Promoting health for older adults. 2020. Available at: https://www.cdc.gov/chronicdisease/resources/publications/factsheets/promoting-health-for-older-adults.htm. Accessed March 2, 2021.

2. US Department of Health and Human Services, Administration for Community Living, Administration on Aging. 2017 Profile of older Americans. Available at: https://acl.gov/sites/default/files/Aging%20and%20Disability%20in%20America/2018OlderAmericansProfile.pdf. Accessed March 2, 2021.

3. US Department of Health and Human Services, Administration for Community Living, Administration on Aging. 2019 Profile of older Americans. 2020. Available at: https://acl.gov/sites/default/files/Aging%20and%20Disability%20in%20America/2019ProfileOlderAmericans508.pdf. Accessed on March 2, 2021.

4. The Sloan Center on Aging and Work at Boston College. Aging today: Educational attainment – fact sheet. 2012. Available at: https://www.bc.edu/research/agingandwork/archive_pubs/FS28.html Accessed March 2, 2021.

5. Federal Interagency Forum on Aging-Related Statistics. "Older Americans 2016: Key indicators of well-being." 2016. Available at: https://agingstats.gov/docs/LatestReport/Older-Americans-2016-Key-Indicators-of-WellBeing.pdf. Accessed March 2, 2021.

6. Hummer RA, Lariscy JT. Educational attainment and adult mortality. In Rogers RG, Crimmins EM, eds. *International Handbook of Adult Mortality.* Dordrecht, The Netherlands: Springer; 2011:241–261.

7. Zajacova A, Lawrence EM. The relationship between education and health: reducing disparities through a contextual approach. *Ann Rev Public Health.* 2018;39:273–289.

8. Center for Health Workforce Studies. The impact of the aging population on the health work force in the United States. 2006. Available at: https://www.albany.edu/news/pdf_files/impact_of_aging_full.pdf. Accessed March 2, 2021.

9. Goldman DP, Smith JP. Can patient self-management help explain the SES health gradient? *Proc Natl Acad Sci USA.* 2002;99(16):10929–10934.

10. Perissinotto CM, Cenzer IS, Covinsky KE. Loneliness in older persons: a predictor of functional decline and death. *Arch Intern Med.* 2012;172(14):1078–1084.

11. Gellad WF, Haas JS, Safran DG. Race/ethnicity and nonadherence to prescription medications among seniors: results of a national study. *J Gen Intern Med.* 2007;22(11):1572–1578.

12. Racic M, Kusmuk S, Kozomara L, Debelnogic B, Tepic R. The prevalence of mistreatment among the elderly with mental disorders in primary health care settings. *J Adult Prot.* 2006;8(4):20–24.

13. Laumann E, Leitsch S, Waite L. Elder mistreatment in the United States: prevalence estimates from a nationally representative study. *J Gerontol Series B Psychol Sci Soc Sci.* 2008;63(4):S248–S254.

14. Burtless G. The impact of population aging and delayed retirement on workforce productivity. Chestnut Hill, MA: Center for Retirement Research at Boston College; 2013.

15. Reeves WC, Pratt LA, Thompson W, et al. Mental illness surveillance among adults in the United States. *MMWR Morb Mortal Wkly Rep. Supp.* 2011;60(3):1–32

16. Conejero I, Olié E, Courtet P, Calati R. Suicide in older adults: current perspectives. *Clin Interv Aging.* 2018;13:691.

17. Centers for Disease Control and Prevention and National Association of Chronic Disease Directors. The state of mental health and aging in America Issue brief 1: What do the data tell us? 2008. Available at: https://www.cdc.gov/aging/pdf/mental_health.pdf. Accessed March 2, 2021.

18. Dong XQ, Simon MA, Beck TT, et al. Elder abuse and mortality: The role of psychological and social wellbeing. *Gerontology.* 2011;57(6):549–558.

19. National Prevention Council. Healthy aging in action. US Department of Health and Human Services, Office of the Surgeon General. 2016. Available at: https://www.cdc.gov/aging/pdf/healthy-aging-in-action508.pdf#:~:text=%20%20%20Title%20%20%20Healthy%20Aging,Created%20Date%20%20%2010/26/2016%203:42:38%20PM. Accessed March 2, 2021.

20. Belo P, Navarro-Pardo E, Pocinho R, Carrana P, Margarido C. Relationship Between Mental Health and the Education Level in Elderly People: Mediation of Leisure Attitude. *Front Psychol.* 2020;11:573.

21. World Health Organization. Dementia. 2020. Available at: https://www.who.int/news-room/fact-sheets/detail/dementia. Accessed March 2, 2021.

22. Alzheimer's Association. 2019 Alzheimer's disease facts and figures. Available at: https://www.alz.org/media/documents/alzheimers-facts-and-figures-2019-r.pdf. Accessed March 2, 2021.

23. Langa KM, Larson EB, Crimmins EM, et al. A comparison of the prevalence of dementia in the United States in 2000 and 2012. *JAMA Internal Medicine.* 2017;177(1):51–58.

24. Crimmins EM, Saito Y, Kim JK, Zhang YS, Sasson I, Hayward MD. Educational differences in the prevalence of dementia and life expectancy with dementia: changes from 2000 to 2010. *J Gerontol B Psycol Sci Soc Sci.* 2018;73(1):S20–S28.

25. Centers for Disease Control and Prevention. What is health literacy? 2021. Available at: https://www.cdc.gov/healthliteracy/learn/index.html. Accessed March 2, 2021.

26. Centers for Disease Control and Prevention. Older Adults. 2020. Available at: https://www.cdc.gov/healthliteracy/developmaterials/audiences/olderadults/index.html. Accessed March 2, 2021.

27. Cutilli CC, Simko LC, Colbert AM, Bennett IM. Health literacy, health disparities, and sources of health information in US older adults. *Orthop Nurs.* 2018;37(1):54–65.

28. US Department of Health and Human Services. Healthy People 2020: Health literacy. Office of Disease Prevention and Health Promotion. 2020. Available at: https://www.healthypeople.gov/2020/topics-objectives/topic/social-determinants-health/interventions-resources/health-literacy. Accessed March 2, 2021.

29. Centers of Disease Control and Prevention. CDC's health literacy action plan. 2020. Available at: https://www.cdc.gov/healthliteracy/planact/cdcplan.html. Accessed March 2, 2021.

30. World Health Organization. *World Report on Ageing and Health*. Geneva, Switzerland: World Health Organization; 2015. Available at: https://www.who.int/ageing/publications/world-report-2015/en/. Accessed June 1, 2021.

31. Chesser AK, Woods NK, Smothers K, Rogers N. Health literacy and older adults: A systematic review. *Gerontol Geriatric Med*. 2016;2:2333721416630492.

32. US Department of Health and Human Services. Healthy People 2020: immunization and infectious diseases. Office of Disease Prevention and Health Promotion. Available at: https://www.healthypeople.gov/2020/topics-objectives/topic/immunization-and-infectious-diseases/national-snapshot. Accessed March 2, 2021.

33. US Department of Health and Human Services. Healthy People 2020: Older adults with reduced physical or cognitive function who engage in leisure-time physical activities (percent, 65+ years) by educational attainment. Office of Disease Prevention and Health Promotion. Available at: https://www.healthypeople.gov/2020/data/Chart/4981?category=5.1&by=Educational%20attainment&fips=-1. Accessed March 2, 2021.

34. Hamel, L, Sparks, G, Brodie, M. KFF COVID-19 vaccine monitor: February 2021. Kaiser Family Foundation. February 2021. Available at: https://www.kff.org/coronavirus-covid-19/poll-finding/kff-covid-19-vaccine-monitor-february-2021/. Accessed June 1, 2021.

35. National Council on Aging. Elder abuse facts: What is elder abuse? 2020. Available at: https://www.ncoa.org/public-policy-action/elder-justice/elder-abuse-facts/. Accessed March 2, 2021.

36. Rodriguez FS, Aranda MP, Lloyd DA, Vega WA. Racial and ethnic disparities in dementia risk among individuals with low education. *Am J Geriatr Psychiatry*. 2018;26(9):966-976.

37. Kim G, Parton JM, DeCoster J, Bryant AN, Ford KL, Parmelee PA. Regional variation of racial disparities in mental health service use among older adults. *Gerontologist*. 2013;53(4):618–626.

38. Jimenez DE, Cook B, Bartels SJ, Alegría M. Disparities in mental health service use of racial and ethnic minority elderly adults. *J Am Geriatr Soc*. 2013;61(1):18–25.

39. Van Horn CE, Krepcio K, Heidkamp M. Improving education and training for older workers. AARP Public Policy Institute. 2015. Available at: https://www.aarp.org/content/dam/aarp/ppi/2015/improving-education-training-older-workers-AARP-ppi.pdf. Accessed March 2, 2021.

40. Du Y, Xu Q. Health disparities and delayed health care among older adults in California: A perspective from race, ethnicity, and immigration. *Public Health Nurs*. 2016;33(5):383–394.

41. Livingston, G. At grandmother's house we stay: One-in-ten children are living with a grandparent. Pew Research Center, 2013.

42. Gordon NP, Hornbrook MC. Older adults' readiness to engage with eHealth patient education and self-care resources: a cross-sectional survey. *BMC Health Serv Res*. 2018;18(1):220.

43. Medlock S, Eslami S, Askari M, et al. Health information–seeking behavior of seniors who use the internet: a survey. *J Med Internet Res*. 2015;17(1):e10.

44. Wu JT, McCormick JB. Why health professionals should speak out against false beliefs on the internet. *AMA J Ethics*. 2018;20(11):1052–1058.

45. Swire-Thompson B, Lazer D. Public health and online misinformation: challenges and recommendations. *Annu Rev Public Health*. 2020;41:433–451.

46. McDonough CC. Determinants of a Digital Divide Among Able-Bodied Older Adults: Does "Feeling Too Old" Play a Role? *Inter J Aging Res*. 2020;3(2):60.

47. Choi N. Relationship between health service use and health information technology use among older adults: analysis of the US National Health Interview Survey. *J Med Internet Res*. 2011;13(2):e33.

48. Huff MJ, Umanath S. Evaluating suggestibility to additive and contradictory misinformation following explicit error detection in younger and older adults. *J Exp Psychol Appl*. 2018;24(2):180–195.

49. Seo H, Blomberg M, Altschwager D, Vu HT. Vulnerable populations and misinformation: A mixed-methods approach to underserved older adults' online information assessment. *New Media & Society*. 2020. Available at: https://journals.sagepub.com/doi/metrics/10.1177/1461444820925041. Accessed June 1, 2021.

50. Hou R, Pérez-Rosas V, Loeb S, Mihalcea R. Towards automatic detection of misinformation in online medical videos. International Conference on Multimodal Interaction. 2019; 235–243.

51. Ruths D. The misinformation machine. *Science*. 2019;363(6425):348–348.

52. First Draft News. Training Resources. 2020. Available at: https://firstdraftnews.org/training/. Accessed March 2, 2021.

53. Hoaxy Beta. Bot search engine. 2021. Available at: https://hoaxy.iuni.iu.edu. Accessed March 2, 2021.

54. Shao C, Hui PM, Wang L, Jiang X, Flammini A, Menczer F., Ciampaglia GL. Anatomy of an Online Misinformation Network. *PloS one*. 2018;13:4, p.e0196087.

Lifelong Learning

Brittany M. Chambers, MPH and Elaine T. Jurkowski PhD, MSW

BACKGROUND

People today are living longer and have more time for leisure, both during their working years and the years beyond retirement. Gone are the days when people started working for a company and remained there at the same organization until retirement (more than 30 years), and potentially doing the same job. As Chapter 13 showcases, education is a key contributor to better health outcomes; thus the concept of learning and challenging one's mind across the life span can only help and promote healthy aging.

In today's world, the concept of automation and its impact across many employment sectors has had an impact on the workforce and has forced people to challenge their mental acuity to continuously advance their skills in specific areas, such as technology and practice-related advancements. These practices in the workforce have also forced the hand of community colleges and universities to address the needs of lifelong learning for people both across the life span and also for people advancing in age.

However, in portions of the lifelong learning continuum where the interaction between training and employment is poorly understood (or poorly functioning), there are opportunities for companies and government agencies to integrate and optimize existing interfaces, or to develop new ones altogether. For example, we have documented how some innovators are integrating to help those desiring to change careers into new industries, or retirees, find part-time employment, offering technical and soft skills training in an apprenticeship model, and then employing those who successfully complete the program.[1]

Postsecondary Education

All 50 states operate a postsecondary education system that consists of a network of community colleges and universities with programs available for older adults. Many of these high learning institutions offer reduced or free college tuition to adults over the age of 60. For example, the Senior Citizens Higher Education Act of 1974 allows Virginia residents aged 60 years and older to take college courses for free. In 1976, Ohio established a law that allows older adults (60 years of age or older) to enroll in noncredit graduate and undergraduate courses. Program 60 at the Ohio State University offers more than 100 courses with over 100,000 older adult students participating.[1]

Relevant Policies and Legislation Impacting Lifelong Learning

The Older Americans Act currently has a mandate to work with adults 60 years of age and older to help them retool their vocational skills through on-the-job training initiatives known as Job Corps, and through the Retired Senior Volunteer Programs (RSVP). The RSVP program is designed to recruit retired people over the age of 60, and place them in settings where they can utilize some of their skill set to contribute to some community need, while offering some opportunities to advance these skills. For example, a retired teacher may work with students in a mentoring after school training program. The mentoring may involve working with technology. The use of technology may be outside of the scope of the teacher's training, so in addition to the volunteer opportunity, the teacher also gains some technology skills through small group training sessions (Rindi Reeves, MSW, Egyptian Area Agency on Aging, oral communication, September 20, 2020).

GOVERNMENT-RELATED PROGRAMS

National and state programs that provide continued educational opportunities for older adults to enhance their personal enrichment or through career training are essential. Continued educational programs have many beneficial outcomes including improved cognitive and social engagement.

Senior Corps

One exemplar of mentally-stimulating and community engagement activities for older adults is Senior Corps. Senior Corps is a network of national service programs for adults over the age of 55, which provides local community service opportunities to over 200,000 older adults.[2] Older adults utilize their prior experience to make valuable contributions to society. There are three programs within the network: Foster Grandparents, RSVP, and Senior Companions. Foster Grandparents allow participants to serve as role models and mentors to children in need. The RSVP program allows seniors to use their prior occupational skills to serve in a variety of volunteer activities. The volunteers' demographic composition is usually unmarried women with an average age of 65, and who have completed some college. Most of the volunteers are White (47%) and 45% are Black.[3] The Senior Companions program provides an extra layer of support to older adults who need help with daily living tasks, such as cooking, cleaning, paying bills, and avoiding scams.

The network has demonstrated a number of positive participant outcomes. More than 80% of Senior Corps volunteers reported improved health and well-being, and a decrease in feelings of social isolation and improved social connections. Importantly, approximately 70% of the volunteers report experiencing fewer symptoms of depression.[2]

Age-Friendly University Network

The Age-Friendly University network includes global higher education institutions who commit to ensuring their university settings are welcoming for older students. With more than 60 member institutions, they promise to promote an inclusive approach to healthy aging through enhanced learning opportunities that address specific issues affecting older adults. Participating organizations endorsed the 10 Age-Friendly University Principles:[4]

1. To encourage the participation of older adults in all the core activities of the university, including educational and research programs.
2. To promote personal and career development in the second half of life and to support those who wish to pursue second careers.
3. To recognize the range of educational needs of older adults (from those who were early school-leavers through to those who wish to pursue Master's degree or PhD qualifications).
4. To promote intergenerational learning to facilitate the reciprocal sharing of expertise between learners of all ages.
5. To widen access to online educational opportunities for older adults to ensure a diversity of routes to participation.
6. To ensure that the university's research agenda is informed by the needs of an aging society and to promote public discourse on how higher education can better respond to the varied interests and needs of older adults.
7. To increase the understanding of students of the longevity dividend and the increasing complexity and richness that aging brings to our society.
8. To enhance access for older adults to the university's range of health and wellness programs, and its arts and cultural activities.
9. To engage actively with the university's own retired community.
10. To ensure regular dialogue with organizations representing the interests of the aging population.

ReGeneration

For older adults who need assistance with developing or enhancing technical and/or behavioral skills to obtain new or retain current employment, ReGeneration is a program designed for them. Through the support of the US Department of Labor and AARP Foundation, ReGeneration offers free career training in Information Technology and the health care sectors. Older adults can take advantage of these programs to obtain industry-recognized certifications. Upon program completion, participants are connected to local employers for job interviews and provided with ongoing support once hired.[5]

EVIDENCE-BASED INTERVENTIONS

The Wellness Initiative for Senior Education (WISE)[6] intervention provides older adults with the information and resources they need to live healthier lives and become their own health advocates. The program teaches older adults to use tools and manage health care, particularly regarding the use of medications. The participants are also trained to identify the early signs and symptoms of depression. The six-week WISE curriculum is delivered by substance use prevention specialists at small group sessions. The lessons are performed for a hybrid of learning: lectures, discussions, and individual exercises. To date, the intervention has reached over 40,000 older adults. It has shown to improve participant's psychological well-being, increase their knowledge of medication and alcohol interactions, and identify early symptoms of depression.

As technology advances, developing skills to remain competitive in the labor force is vital for older adults who want to continue to stimulate the economy. The Older Adults Technology Services (OATS)[7] is a social impact organization that helps older adults use technology to improve their health, finances, social engagement, and educational levels. They offer a variety of different types of programs based on the needs of their constituents. For example, Startup! is a 10-week course on entrepreneurship for older adults that helps them to post their products or services online and create social media accounts to promote their businesses. Through the ACTivate program, seniors learn key leadership skills and can improve their analytical abilities. Participation in the OATS programming has resulted in a number of positive outcomes. Seventy-three percent of the respondents reported gaining a new skill, 70% became aware of online banking features, and 62% reported making new friends and being socially engaged.

SPECIAL CONSIDERATIONS AND SPECIAL POPULATIONS

The concept of lifelong learning can be applied across various socioeconomic and ethnic groups who are growing older. However, the strategies that should be integrated may differ across socioeconomic groups or ethnic groups. Culture will play a role in terms of what types of activities one may want to engage in. In addition, access to resources may also play a role in the lives of people and the types of activities that will pique their interest as they grow older. Professionals who are now retired may be interested in using their skills, and may have the resources to utilize technology and travel as a part of their lifelong learning agenda. In contrast, this may be perceived as out of reach for someone on a fixed income with limited resources, but who is interested in accessing short educational programs offered in their neighborhood or local community at little or no cost.

Many assisted living programs, or housing campuses, offer a variety of educational and activity programs for their residents that span from sports to bridge to lectures. The programs are largely tailored to the needs and interests of their residents and community. Public health professionals developing educational materials for a specific target group will need to consider the literacy level and interests of their constituents when building health education offerings to their local constituents.

CONCLUSION: CHALLENGES AND OPPORTUNITIES FOR PUBLIC HEALTH

The opportunities for lifelong learning offer many opportunities for older adults in a variety of ways which can enhance the overall health of the population group. Programs focused upon the health literacy and promoting strategies for one's overall health can be dispatched through local public health departments or in conjunction with local senior centers and nutrition sites. These types of offerings, either face-to-face or via technology such as a computer or iPad, can also be the opportunity for computer training for older adults that can be delivered in collaboration with senior nutrition sites or senior centers.

A challenge within the lifelong education arena may be how public health practitioners can effectively work alongside allied health professionals to help deliver such educational programs or promote these programs. The medical model of service delivery often perceives older adults as having limitations, as opposed to growing human beings who can benefit from continual learning across their life span and into their upper years of life. As we have seen in the first section of the book, the strategy of ongoing education can be a protective factor against early onset of Alzheimer's disease or dementias.

In summary, lifelong learning provides the opportunity for older adults to remain engaged with others and within the world around them. It also helps foster a sense of well-being and confidence, as well as serve as a protective factor as we strive towards healthy aging.

CASE STUDY

Elizabeth is an 87-year-old widow currently living in the Midwest within the family home where she raised her four children. A stay at home housewife, Elizabeth busied herself with raising her children, chauffer duties, and being active in the local Parent Teacher Association, leaving little time for her to work outside the home. When Elizabeth turned 60, her husband retired and her youngest child became a freshman in college. Elizabeth did not have the opportunity to attend college following her high school graduation and had always fantasized about the opportunity. She lived vicariously through her first three children's college experiences and their after dinner debates about "worldly topics," but was herself interested in pursuing college attendance.

As a gift to herself, upon turning 60, Elizabeth decided that she wanted to take a class in her local neighborhood for credit at a local university. She enrolled into an introductory sociology course and was amazed at the opportunities for discussion and intellectual enrichment that the course opened up for her. She also learned that she was eligible for a program which entitled her to free tuition since she was 60 years of age. With this idea in mind, she continued to take classes, and discovered that she had nearly enough course credits to earn a bachelor's degree. At 65-years-old, she graduated with a bachelor's degree in developmental studies. Despite the fact that she could now retire, Elizabeth felt that the opportunity to earn a degree was more valuable in terms of how it expanded her thinking process, as opposed to preparing her for skills for the workforce.

Following the completion of Elizabeth's bachelor's degree, she decided to volunteer with her local health department that was in the process of setting up a nutrition program for people with cognitive disabilities. Through this process, she met a young dietitian, Gail, and became friends with the co-facilitator. Elizabeth was able to blend her skills in meal preparation with her newly acquired skills in working with people who had cognitive and learning issues to build a skill set.

When Elizabeth's husband suffered meningitis a few years later, she attributed her ability to be assertive with the health care team to her studies, and felt that the opportunity to make class presentations equipped her with the skills to become assertive with other professionals as a caregiver.

Fast forward this situation another 15 years, and we see a much older Elizabeth, who has been able to keep up with technological changes with her home computer and iPad. She credits her rehabilitation process poststroke to her ability to use her iPad to communicate with her children and health care professionals. She also credits her ability to use the devices as tools to enable her to learn about the poststroke rehabilitation process and to know what to expect, and what her potential can be. She also credits her ability to use these tools to the local senior center and public health department that offered short courses on utilizing the computer, social media, and offering health-oriented training programs as part of the process to learn how to use her technology tools.

REFERENCES

1. Price R. Today's economy demands lifelong learning skills. How can institutions keep pace? Christensen Institute. 2020 Available at: https://www.christenseninstitute.org/blog/todays-economy-demands-lifelong-learning-skills-how-can-institutions-keep-pace. Accessed March 2, 2021.

2. AmeriCorps. AmeriCorps Seniors. Available at: https://www.nationalservice.gov/programs/senior-corps. Accessed March 2, 2021.

3.   AmeriCorps and Corporation for National and Community Serivce. SeniorCorps:, Improving the Quality of Life for All Seniors. Available at: https://americorps.gov/sites/default/files/document/2019_02_05_LongitudinalStudyFactSheet_SeniorCorps.pdf. Accessed April 30, 2021.

4.   Gerontological Society of America. Age-friendly university (AFU) global network. Available at: https://www.geron.org/programs-services/education-center/age-friendly-university-afu-global-network. Accessed March 2, 2021.

5.   USA Generations. ReGeneration. Available at: https://usa.generation.org/regeneration. Accessed March 2, 2021.

6.   Wellness Initiative for Senior Education Program description. Available at: https://acl.gov/sites/default/files/programs/2017-03/WISE_ACL_Summary.pdf. Accessed March 2, 2021.

7.   Older Adults Technology Service (OATS). Available at: https://oats.org. Accessed March 2, 2021.

Workforce Development

Michelle Newman, MPH, Robyn L. Golden, LCSW, Erin Emery-Tiburcio, PhD, ABPP, Tara Sklar, JD, MPH, and Elaine T. Jurkowski, PhD, MSW

Preparing the workforce to be able to guide and direct initiatives at both a case and program level is an important component of building aging-focused initiatives and promoting aging well through the lens of social determinants of health. This chapter will address initiatives that promote a geriatric prepared workforce.

BACKGROUND AND DESCRIPTION OF THE TOPIC
Population Growth

In the United States, the population of older adults is growing. By 2030, all baby boomers (those born between 1946 and 1964) will be older than age 65, with 20% of people at retirement age.[1] As of 2017, with advances in technology, lifestyle changes, and public health interventions, the life expectancy in the United States was 81.1 years old for women and 76.1 years old for men.[2,3] This growth can be attributed to the aging of the baby boomers and increased longevity.[1]

Multiple Chronic Conditions

The increase in longevity is paired with older adults living with multiple chronic conditions (MCC). Living with two or more chronic conditions "that last a year or more and require ongoing medical attention and/or limit activities of daily living,"[4] impacts more than two-thirds of older adults, with 68.4% older adults living with two or more chronic conditions, and 36.4% with four or more.[5] As the number of chronic conditions increases, their clinical outcomes, such as mortality, hospitalizations, readmissions, adverse drug events, quality of life, and functional status worsen.[6]

Caregiving

Many older adults living with MCC or disability receive care, usually from an unpaid caregiver, to assist with activities of daily living. In 2015, about 34.2 million Americans provided unpaid care to an adult age 50 or older.[7] The care tasks can take a toll with unpaid caregivers reporting that positive activities in their daily lives were reduced by 27.2% as a result of their caregiving responsibilities.[7]

Workforce Needs

As the older adult population grows with MCC and social determinants of health needs (i.e., conditions in which people are born, live, learn, work, play, worship, and age),[8] so does our need for a geriatric prepared workforce. Meeting these needs is challenging due to the lack of geriatric training available and the small number of professionals pursuing geriatrics as a career. By 2030, it is estimated there will be a need for 3.5 million formal health care providers to maintain the current ratio of providers to the total population.[9] For geriatricians specifically, it is projected that by 2025, there will be roughly 6,200 practicing geriatrics when there is a need for over 33,000.[10]

Lack of Geriatric Training

Based on a national survey, the median time devoted to geriatric education in medicine in 2005 was only 9.5 hours.[11] Another survey of medical schools in the United States identified 41% of responding schools have a structured geriatrics curriculum and 23% require a geriatric clerkship.[12] In nursing, a survey of United States nursing programs suggested that more than 85% did not require any coursework in geriatrics.[13] In pharmacy, although all programs have practice experience options in geriatrics or long-term care, only 43% reported the option of an elective geriatrics course.[14]

Careers in Geriatrics

With lack of geriatric coursework and clinic exposure in training, it is not a surprise that only 4% of social workers and less than 1% of physician assistants identify themselves as specializing in geriatrics.[15,16] Additionally, there are less than 1% of pharmacists[17] and practicing professional nurses who are certified in geriatrics.[18] According to the National Resident Matching Program in 2008, 44% of the geriatric medicine first-year fellowship training slots were not filled.[19]

Compensation

For geriatricians, the median annual salary in 2018 was $189,879, which is less than half of what an average orthopedic surgeon or cardiologist earns.[20] Compared with a general internist, a geriatrician's median salary was less than their medicine colleagues. Similarly, differences exist where nurses in hospital settings earn higher wages than nurses working in long-term care facilities. The same differences exist for physician assistants who specialize in geriatrics compared to other types of physician assistants.[9]

Nature of the Work

Meiboom et al. conducted a study looking at factors affecting the disinterest among medical students to pursue a career in geriatrics. Common themes included students being discouraged because they are not able to see the direct effects of their treatment, older adults being too complex, and the fear of dealing with ethical dilemmas and unrealistic expectations.[21] There were positive factors identified which included students finding working with older adult patients a positive challenge, end-of-life care being rewarding, and being able to focus on the whole patient as opposed to organ systems.[22]

Preparing the Workforce

In response to the issues identified in this chapter, it is critical to prepare the health care workforce to meet the needs of older adults and their caregivers. By interfacing with other disciplines in an effort to address social determinants of health, health outcomes and quality of life can be improved. Public health practitioners need to align with primary care and allied health professionals on how to best address the needs of older adults and caregivers at micro, mezzo, and macro system levels.

Why Should Public Health as a Field Care About the Topic?

Public health interventions have contributed to longer longevity.[23] However, there are disparities in who benefits with living a longer life. According to a 2015 National Academies of Science, Engineering, and Medicine (NASEM) report, "The Growing Gap in Life Expectancy by Income,"[24] between 1980 and 2010, researchers found a 12.7–year difference in life expectancy between men in our society: the wealthiest men at 89 years and the poorest at 76 years. Disparities between women were even greater: the wealthiest women lived to 92 years, while the poorest lived to 78 years.[24] These and other disparities make it imperative that public health continues to focus on addressing social determinants of health as we age.

Although public health focuses on levels of prevention, many disease prevention and health promotion efforts have not been designed to reach disadvantaged and vulnerable older adults.[25] As described earlier, MCC and disability have a major impact on older adults and those providing care. There are opportunities for aging and public health to work together to advance quality of life as we age. Following are examples of system- and community-level programs:

- Federally Qualified Health Centers: Community-based health centers that provide primary care services in underserved areas,[26] which are beginning to respond to the fact that their patients are living longer with increased disability and MCC. Additionally, older adults tend to stay in these centers even when they receive Medicare, with the number of Medicare beneficiaries doubling between 2001 to 2011.[27]
- Age-Friendly Health Systems: These systems are an initiative of The John A. Hartford Foundation and the Institute for Healthcare Improvement, in partnership with the American Hospital Association and the Catholic Health Association of the United States. Age-Friendly Health Systems are designed to meet the challenge to reliably provide evidence-based practice to every older adult at every care interaction. The goal of the initiative is to rapidly spread the 4Ms Framework to 20% of US hospitals and medical practices by 2020.[28] The 4Ms include What Matters, Mentation, Medication, and Mobility. The 4Ms have been associated with key improvements; addressing What Matters is associated with decreased hospitalization, increased hospice use, and increased patient satisfaction[29]; addressing Mobility decreases falls and associated hospital costs[30]; addressing Medications decreases adverse drug events and related health care costs[31]; and addressing mentation (depression, delirium, and dementia) can increase function, quality of life, mortality, and decrease hospital cost.[32-34]

What Do We Know From the Best Evidence About the Topic?

The influential NASEM report, "Retooling for an Aging America: Building the Health Care Workforce,"[9] provides expert review and recommendations to train all health care providers in the basics of geriatric care and to prepare family members and other informal caregivers. The report recommended the following approach to improve the ability of the health care workforce to care for older adults:

1. Enhance the competence of all individuals in the delivery of geriatric care: The report recommends there be significant enhancements in the educational curricula and training programs provided. In addition to the educational challenges described earlier in this section, there is not sufficient faculty to teach, curricula varies, and there are overall a lack of training opportunities.
2. Increase the recruitment and retention of geriatric specialists and caregivers: The report recommends that health systems, payers, and states provide financial incentives to increase recruitment and retention. In addition to opportunities described in this chapter, the report recommends enhancing clinical reimbursement; authorizing more federal funding for programs like the Geriatric Care Achievement Award; and providing loan forgiveness, scholarships, and direct financial incentives for professionals who become geriatric specialists.

3. Redesign models of care and broaden provider and patient roles to achieve greater flexibility: Although not a focus of this chapter, the report acknowledges the challenges the health care system faces in providing quality care to older adults. The report recommends three key principles: (1) the health needs of the older population need to be addressed comprehensively, (2) services need to be provided efficiently, and (3) older persons need to be active partners in their own care. The Age-Friendly Health System framework may be an opportunity to achieve these principles.

Relevant Policies and Legislation

Title VII and VIII of the Public Health Service Act supports health professions education and training and are the "only federal programs designed to train providers in interdisciplinary settings to meet the needs of special and underserved populations, as well as increase minority representation in the health care workforce."[35]

In 2015, under Title VII and VIII, the Health Resources and Services Administration's (HRSA) Geriatrics Workforce Enhancement Program (GWEP) provided $35.7 million to 44 academic medical centers in the United States. The goal of this funding is to transform geriatric education and training for development of a health care workforce that maximizes patient and family engagement while improving health outcomes for older adults.[36] In 2019, HRSA funded its second cohort of 48 GWEP programs across 35 states and 2 territories (i.e., Guam and Puerto Rico), and provided extension grants to 15 former GWEP awardees.[37]

Another program under Title VII and VIII is the Geriatric Academic Career Award (GACA) which was established in 1998 to support junior level clinician educators in geriatrics. In 2019, 26 GACAs were awarded in 16 states. The goals of the program are to develop the necessary skills to lead health care transformation in a variety of settings, including rural and/or medically underserved settings, to be age-friendly, and to provide training in clinical geriatrics, including the training of interprofessional teams of health care professionals to provide health care for older adults.[38]

Other Related Programs

The following programs train and support the current and future workforce to work with older adults.

Tideswell, AGS and ADGAP Emerging Leaders in Aging Program

The Emerging Leaders in Aging program is an interdisciplinary experience that augments and leverages existing leadership skills for clinical, research, policy, and educational initiatives in aging. The program provides leadership training focused on the unique needs of leaders in aging-specific environments.[39]

Geriatric Interdisciplinary Team Training (GITT)

GITT is offered at Rush University Medical Center through CATCH-ON and provides advance practice students from a variety of disciplines the opportunity to learn the importance of interdisciplinary team care for older adults. The course is case-based and infuses principles of Age-Friendly Health Systems.[40,41]

GITT 2.0 Offered Through the Hartford Institute for Geriatric Nursing at NYU

GITT 2.0 aims to improve patient/caregiver-centered outcomes, health care costs, and overall population health by promoting interprofessional teams in practice academic collaboratives.[41]

Government-Funded

Under Medicaid, 21 states have implemented wage pass-through programs to help address the shortage of long-term care workers by increasing their compensation.

BEST PRACTICE INTERVENTIONS

As described in "Retooling for an Aging America: Building the Health Care Workforce,"[9] one of the key recommendations is ensuring professionals have competence in geriatric principles. Examples of best practices and interventions to achieve this recommendation are highlighted in activities of GWEP.

The mission of Rush University Medical Center's GWEP, or CATCH-ON, is to unify academic, health, and community organizations and resources to prepare a geriatric collaborative practice-ready health workforce optimizing health, while serving and improving person-centered health and wellness outcomes inside the walls of the clinic and into the community. CATCH-ON developed educational training initiatives for health professionals, students, direct care workers, and older adults and caregivers.[37,39] Select training initiatives include the following:

- CATCH-ON Evolving Cases: CATCH-ON's interprofessional education team developed four evolving cases to be used in graduate level health profession courses. The cases represent a compilation of the authors' experiences inspired by their work with older adults and their families. They are designed to help learners see older adults as individuals rather than compilations of symptoms. The cases highlight multiple social determinants of health needs (e.g., culture, language, socioeconomic status) that are critical to understanding and effectively treating older adults. Each section of the evolving case is accompanied by discussion questions designed to target a wide variety of health professionals. A CATCH-ON Instructor Guide accompanies the cases.

- Interprofessional Education Training Events: These events were developed to bring students from different disciplines (e.g., social work, medicine, nursing, physician assistant, psychology, law, and public health) together, working in interprofessional teams to move through a CATCH-ON evolving case, learning key points about older adult health and health care, including team skills.

- Geriatric Interprofessional Team Training (GITT): As noted earlier, GITT is a collaborative training for advanced practice students from multiple disciplines that teaches skills and techniques essential to interdisciplinary team practice. GITT incorporates CATCH-ON evolving cases throughout each session, adding specific behavioral skills for trainees to apply immediately to their practicum experiences.[41]

- CATCH-ON Learning Communities (LCs): These communities are telehealth educational interventions that are responsive to primary care requests for both less time away from patient care and highly practical clinical guidance for all clinic staff. CATCH-ON LCs are monthly one-hour video conferences where a participant clinician presents a case relevant to that month's geriatric primary care topic, then a geriatric expert provides a 20-minute lecture with specific behavioral recommendations for participants to apply immediately, followed by the full group discussing application of the content to the case. Similarly, the University of Chicago GWEP hosts the ECHO-Chicago Geriatrics curriculum that is an online educational initiative designed to "improve health outcomes for older adults by creating a robust, engaged network of interdisciplinary care providers who share resources and education to improve health for older adults on Chicago's South Side."[42]

- CATCH-ON Online Modules: As noted earlier, CATCH-ON developed free, online education for professionals, students, and consumers on important topics related to older adult health. Topics focus on normal aging, managing multiple chronic conditions, dementia, interprofessional geriatric health care teams, and communication. Five modules for older adults and families are available in English and Spanish CATCH-ON also developed online modules for health professionals on the 4Ms of an Age-Friendly Health System. The modules are available in two formats (i.e., for all health professionals and for those providing direct clinical care) on caregiving, delirium, dementia, depression, mobility, and medication. Many other GWEP programs have developed online education focused on different aging-related topics including the University of Illinois at Chicago's online education in interprofessional geriatrics[43] and the University of Iowa's GeriaLearning curriculum.[44] Specifically to address Alzheimer's disease and related dementias, HRSA created online training for the primary care workforce about dementia.[45]

Special Considerations and Special Populations

When preparing the workforce to work with older adults, we highlight two populations that are important for professionals to be aware of and professionally trained: lesbian, gay, bisexual, transgendered, and queer (LGBTQ) older adults and rural older adults.

LGBTQ Older Adults

By 2025, as many as 6 million people age 65 and older will identify as LGBTQ.[46] Older LGBTQ adults are at greater risk for more severe health issues, poorer health outcomes, and higher mortality rates than their heterosexual counterparts. Fear of facing insensitivity and discrimination can become a barrier to care, further reinforcing social isolation and leading to avoidance of needed health care.[47] As described earlier, health care professionals receive inadequate training in geriatrics and little to no training in health disparities and cultural competence as it pertains to aging LGBTQ populations.[48]

Supported through Rush's GWEP, an example of available training is the Nurses' Health Education About LGBTQ Elders (HEALE) curriculum. HEALE is a six-hour cultural competency continuing education training for nurses and health care professionals who serve older LGBTQ adults, and is provided for nurses and social workers free of charge.[49]

Rural and Urban Older Adults

As we have seen earlier in this chapter, training about older adults in medical and allied health programs is often limited. Even more limited is information and workforce development about rural communities. However, understanding the public health needs of older adults along with associated primary care and community service needs will become more crucial as demographics shift with the working age population migrating to metropolitan areas for better opportunities and averting a slower paced lifestyle found in rural areas.

Rural versus urban contexts for our workforce to practice leaves a host of differences and challenges to the public health and primary care workforce. In rural communities, the number one challenge is often transportation. Public transportation systems are limited, and are often ill-equipped to deal with a frail, chronic care individual. They are also limited in their routes and hours of operation. Unlike urban areas, ride share options are also limited for transportation in rural communities.

Limited caregiver support resources availability, especially within small communities, limit the caregiving options for older adults. Younger people tend to migrate to urban areas for jobs or schooling, leaving behind their older adult family members who are in need of home health workers and home care assistance. When one of the major oil companies pulled out of a rural Illinois town, over 60% of the community remaining after the working age population left were people over the age of 60.[50] This is not a unique situation and can be found across the United States.

Trained specialists and professionals with expertise in geriatrics and disabilities is a strong need in rural communities in order to build a workforce to provide care for older adults in these areas. Graduating specialists and geriatricians would prefer to work in an urban area to build a practice rather than settle in a rural community. Telehealth is beginning to address the disparity of available workforce with expertise to meet the needs of an older person and their family members.

The GWEP initiative has funded centers to address the rural as well as urban needs of our workforce. Through CATCH-ON, case studies with urban and rural dimensions have been built to meet the needs of the public health, primary care, and allied health workforces.

CONCLUSION: CHALLENGES AND OPPORTUNITIES FOR PUBLIC HEALTH

A number of opportunities and challenges exist for public health as we consider workforce development. As an opportunity, public health can provide education, incorporate aging into existing competencies/schools of public health, primary care, and allied health curriculum.

Challenges that are faced with respect to workforce development include ageism and trying to incorporate materials into already dense curriculum. Ideally, one needs to find a champion in program areas to push aging topics into workforce development, continuing education, and academic training. Another challenge (and potential opportunity) is to build alliances and partnerships with allies by working with the aging network, older adults, and consumers.

CASE STUDY: PALLIATIVE CARE IN RURAL ALABAMA

My husband succeeded in dying in his own damn bed, in his own damn house, but we did not have needed medical management ... It was terrible.
–Margaret Peterson[51]

An increasingly common dilemma that Americans are finding themselves in is, if they choose to die at home, they may face limited support with palliative care and pain medication. As more Americans opt to stay at home in their final days, which the majority of Americans are now choosing to do,[52] they face unknown and frightening thoughts for themselves and their family members as to how their death will be managed. There are also striking differences in place of death, with individuals who live in rural areas and who are non-White less likely to die at home.[53]

The University of Alabama at Birmingham (UAB) Health System is attempting to address this difficult predicament. This is being done by breaking down the traditional health care delivery approach by using in person care, so that it is not a choice between dying comfortably with pain appropriately managed in an intensive care unit away from loved ones, or with loved ones but in pain. End-of-life care is part of the care continuum where Rodney Tucker, a palliative medicine physician who directs the UAB Center for Palliative and Supportive Care says, "all patients should have access to all levels of care, not just curative and preventative, but also humane care for serious illness."[54] The reality is that resources are limited with "fewer than 40% of hospitals in Alabama offer[ing] palliative care services and 16% of households in rural Alabama (54 counties) lack a vehicle."[54]

The UAB approach represents a new model of care that will better prepare the health care force to support aging in place with telehealth combined with home health aides. Essentially, UAB has reallocated its resources from a hospital-based approach to working with older adults and their families to provide palliative care directly in their home. UAB has created a number of programs and established a governance approach to support this effort, including expanding house calls to include palliative care visits for patients; starting an advisory group of Black pastors to gain their insights on how to improve conversations with Black patients around end-of-life care; and conducting virtual palliative consults with clinicians and patients.[54]

This combination of including the end user in the design of the delivery model, utilizing telehealth technology with palliative care providers and personal touch with home health aides, and acting early can help reduce the hardship that individuals face as pain becomes more difficult to manage. Concerns regarding social isolation and loneliness are minimized with individuals being able to remain with their loved ones and have home health aides at their bedside, along with a virtual connection to the clinician. Many patients would have no way of receiving palliative care treatment in the home without this approach.

This approach is also assisting UAB to meet Medicare reimbursement requirements. Medicare has increased efforts to reduce excess admissions through their Hospital Readmissions Reduction Program, where they reduce payments to hospitals for care received within a 30–day window after discharge.[55] Hospitals are facing the difficult decision on whether to admit patients who fall into this window, but if they are facing a serious illness that is at the final stages, then these patients will likely need some form of palliative care.

The UAB program presents a way to provide quality end-of-life care in different settings, while reducing hospital readmissions and improving overall patient satisfaction. The program reflects the need for more education and training for clinicians and home health aides to provide palliative care with technological advancements in the areas of telehealth and remote patient monitoring. New and revised policies and procedures are needed to support the health system, provider, patient, and community health efforts. All these stakeholders have an interest in more programs, similar to the one at UAB, coming to fruition across the country, as they help improve quality end-of-life care availability across settings and delivered at lower costs.

REFERENCES

1. US Census Bureau. Older people projected to outnumber children. 2018. Available at: https://www.census.gov/newsroom/press-releases/2018/cb18-41-population-projections.html. Accessed March 3, 2021.

2. Arias E, Xu J. National vital statistics report: United States life tables 2017. US Department of Health and Human Services. 2019. Available at: https://www.cdc.gov/nchs/data/nvsr/nvsr68/nvsr68_07-508.pdf. Accessed March 3, 2021.

3. World Health Organization. Global health estimates: Life expectancy and leading causes of death and disability. 2019. Available at: http://www.who.int/gho/mortality_burden_disease/life_tables/situation_trends_text/en/. Accessed March 3, 2021.

4. Parekh AK, Goodman RA, Gordon C, Koh HK. Managing multiple chronic conditions: A strategic framework for improving health outcomes and quality of life. *Public Health Rep.* 2011;126(4):460–471.

5. Sambamoorthi U, Tan X, Deb A. Multiple chronic conditions and healthcare costs among adults. *Expert Rev Pharmacoecon Outcomes Res.* 2015;15(5):823–832.

6. Koh HK, Parekh AK. Supporting people with multiple chronic conditions: A health priority. Huff Post Life. Available at: https://www.huffpost.com/entry/supporting-people-with-mu_b_4394216. Accessed March 3, 2021.

7. Family Caregiver Alliance. Caregiver statistics: Demographics. 2016. Available at: https://www.caregiver.org/caregiver-statistics-demographics. Accessed March 3, 2021.

8. US Department of Health and Human Services. Social determinants of health. Healthy People 2020. Office of Disease Prevention and Health Promotion. 2020. Available at: https://www.healthypeople.gov/2020/topics-objectives/topic/social-determinants-of-health. Accessed March 3, 2021.

9. Institute of Medicine. Retooling for an aging America: Building the health care workforce. 2008. Available at: https://www.nap.edu/catalog/12089/retooling-for-an-aging-america-building-the-health-care-workforce. Accessed March 3, 2021.

10. American Geriatrics Society. State of the geriatrician workforce fast facts. Available at: https://www.americangeriatrics.org/sites/default/files/inline-files/State%20of%20the%20Geriatrician%20Workforce_10%2001%2018.pdf. Accessed March 4, 2021.

11. Eleazer GP, Doshi R, Wieland D, Boland R, Hirth VA. Geriatric content in medical school curricula: Results of a national survey. *J Am Geriatri Soc.* 2005;53(1):136–140.

12. Warshaw GA, Bragg EJ, Shaull RW, Lindsell CJ. Academic geriatric programs in US allopathic and osteopathic medical schools. *JAMA.* 2002;288(18):2313–2319.

13. Grocki JH, Fox GEB. Gerontology coursework in undergraduate nursing programs in the United States: a regional study. *J Gerontologl Nurs.* 2004;30(3):46–51.

14. Odegard PS, Breslow RM, Koronkowski MJ, Williams BR, Hudgins GA. Geriatric pharmacy education: A strategic plan for the future. *Am J Pharm Edu.* 2007;71(3):47.

15. American Academy of Pas. AAPA physician assistant census report. 2007. Available at: https://www.aapa.org/wp-content/uploads/2016/12/2007_AAPA_Census_Report.pdf. Accessed March 4, 2021.

16. McGinnis S, Moore J. The impact of the aging population on the health workforce in the United States—summary of key findings. *Cah Sociol Demogr Med.* 2006;46(2):193–220.

17. LaMascus AM, Bernard MA, Barry P, Salerno J, Weiss J. Bridging the workforce gap for our aging society: How to increase and improve knowledge and training. Report of an expert panel. *J Am Geriatr Soc.* 2005;53(2):343–347.

18. Alliance for Aging Research. Medical never-never land: 10 reasons why America is not ready for the coming age boom. Available at: https://www.agingresearch.org/document/medical-never-never- land-10-reasons-why-america-is-not-ready-for-the-coming-age-boom. Accessed March 4, 2021.

19. Meiboom AA, de Vries H, Hertogh CMPM, Scheele F. Why medical students do not choose a career in geriatrics: a systematic review. *BMC Medical Educ.* 2015;15(1):101.

20. Modern Healthcare. Geriatrics still failing to attract new doctors. Available at: https://www. modernhealthcare.com/article/20180227/NEWS/180229926/geriatrics-still-failing-to-attract-new-doctors. Accessed March 4, 2021.

21. Bagri AS, Tiberius R. Medical student perspectives on geriatrics and geriatric education. *J Am Geriatr Soc.* 2010;58(10):1994–1999.

22. Green SK, Keith KJ, Pawlson LG. Medical students' attitudes toward the elderly. *J Am Geriatr Soc.* 1983;31(5):305–309.

23. San Juan Basin Public Health. 200 years of public health has doubled our life expectancy. Available at: https://sjbpublichealth.org/200-years-public-health-doubled-life-expectancy. Accessed March 4, 2021.

24. National Academies of Sciences Engineering and Medicine. *The Growing Gap in Life Expectancy by Income: Implications for Federal Programs and Policy Responses.* Washington, DC: National Academies Press; 2015.

25. Anderson LA, Goodman RA, Holtzman D, Posner SF, Northridge ME. Aging in the United States: opportunities and challenges for public health. *Am J Public Health.* 2012;102(3):393–395.

26. US Health Resources and Services Administration. Federally qualified health centers. 2018. Available at: https://www.hrsa.gov/opa/eligibility-and-registration/health-centers/fqhc/index. html. Accessed March 4, 2021.

27. Center for Health and Research Transformation. Federally qualified health centers: An overview. 2013. Available at: https://chrt.org/publication/federally-qualified-health-centers-overview. Accessed March 4, 2021.

28. Institute for Healthcare Improvement. What is an age-friendly health system? 2021. Available at: http://www.ihi.org/Engage/Initiatives/Age-Friendly-Health-Systems/Pages/default.aspx. Accessed March 4, 2021.

29. AHRQ Health Care Innovations Exchange. System-integrated program coordinates care for people with advanced illness, leading to greater use of hospice services, lower utilization and costs, and high satisfaction. Available at: https://innovations.ahrq.gov/profiles/system-integrated-program-coordinates-care-people-advanced-illness-leading-greater-use. Accessed March 4, 2021.

30. Wong CA, Recktenwald AJ, Jones ML, Waterman BM, Bollini ML, Dunagan WC. The cost of serious fall-related injuries at three Midwestern hospitals. *Jt Comm J Qual Patient Saf.* 2011;37(2):81–87.

31. Field TS, Gilman BH, Subramanian S, Fuller JC, Bates DW, Gurwitz JH. The costs associated with adverse drug events among older adults in the ambulatory setting. *Medl Care.* 2005; 43(12):1171–1176.

32. Xu W, Collet J-P, Shapiro S, et al. Independent effect of depression and anxiety on chronic obstructive pulmonary disease exacerbations and hospitalizations. *Am J Respir Crit Care Med.* 2008;178(9):913–920.

33. Myers V, Gerber Y, Benyamini Y, Goldbourt U, Drory Y. Post-myocardial infarction depression: Increased hospital admissions and reduced adoption of secondary prevention measures—A longitudinal study. *J Psychosom Res.* 2012;72(1):5–10.

34 Nemeroff CB, Goldschmidt-Clermont PJ. Heartache and heartbreak—the link between depression and cardiovascular disease. *Nat Reviews Cardiol.* 2012;9(9):526–539.

35. Health Professions Nursing Professions Coalition. Health professions programs: Training providers, improving access. 2009. Available at: https://thehill.com/sites/default/files/AAMC_healthprofessionsprograms_0.pdf. Accessed March 4, 2021.

36. Health Resources and Services Administration Health Workforce Apply for a geriatrics grant. Available at: https://bhw.hrsa.gov/grants/geriatrics. Accessed March 4, 2021.

37. American Geriatrics Society. GWEP coordinating center. Available at: https://www.american-geriatrics.org/programs/gwep-coordinating-center. Accessed March 4, 2021.

38. Health Resources and Services Administration. Geriatrics academic career award. 2019. Available at: https://www.hrsa.gov/grants/find-funding/hrsa-19-007. Accessed March 4, 2021.

39. Tideswell at University of California San Franciso. Emerging leaders in aging program. 2021. Available at: http://www.tideswellucsf.org/tideswell-ags-adgap-national-leadership-development-program/. Accessed March 4, 2021.

40. CATCH-ON. Collaborative Action Team training for Community Health—Older Adult Network. Available at: http://catch-on.org. Accessed March 4, 2021.

41. New York University Hartford Institute of Geriatric Nursing. GITT 2.0 Toolkit. 2020. Available at: https://hign.org/consultgeri-resources/guides-and-competencies/gitt-20-toolkit. Accessed May 25, 2021.

42. The University of Chicago. ECHO-Chicago: Geriatrics. 2017. https://cme.uchicago.edu/ECHOGeriatrics17#group-tabs-node-course-default1. Accessed March 4, 2021.

43. Engage-IL. Online accredited learning in interprofessional geriatrics. Available at: https://engageil.com/health-professional-ce/. Accessed March 4, 2021.

44. Iowa Geriatric Education Center. GeriaLearning. 2021. Available at: https://igec.uiowa.edu/gerialearning. Accessed March 4, 2021.

45. Health Resources and Services Administration Health Workforce. Train health care workers about dementia. Available at: https://bhw.hrsa.gov/grants/geriatrics/alzheimers-curriculum. Accessed March 4, 2021.

46. Meyer IH. Prejudice, social stress, and mental health in lesbian, gay, and bisexual populations: Conceptual issues and research evidence. *Psychol Bull.* 2003;129(5):674–697.

47. Bonvicini KA, Perlin MJ. The same but different: clinician-patient communication with gay and lesbian patients. *Patient Educ Couns.* 2003;51(2):115–122.

48. Cahill S, Kim-Butler B. Policy priorities for the LGBT community: Pride survey 2006. New York: Policy Institute of the National Lesbian and Gay Task Force; 2006.

49. CATCH-ON. Education for Health Care Clinicians. 2020. Available at: http://catch-on.org/hp-home/hp-education/. Accessed July 21, 2021.

50. US Census Bureau. 2010. US Department of Commerce.

51. Cross SH, Warraich HJ. More Americans are dying at home. Is that a good thing? STAT. 2019. Available at: https://www.statnews.com/2019/12/11/more-americans-die-at-home/comment-page-1. Accessed March 4, 2021.

52. Kolata, G. More Americans are dying at home than in hospitals. The New York Times. 2019. Available at: https://www.nytimes.com/2019/12/11/health/death-hospitals-home.html. Accessed March 4, 2021.

53. Cross SH, Warraich HJ. Changes in the place of death in the United States. *N Engl J Med.* 2019;381(24):2369–2370.

54. Huff C. Bringing palliative care to underserved rural communities. *Health Aff (Millwood).* 2019;38(12):1971-1975

55. Centers for Medicare and Medicaid Services. Hospital readmissions reduction program (HRRP). 2020. Available at: https://www.cms.gov/Medicare/Medicare-Fee-for-Service-Payment/AcuteInpatientPPS/Readmissions-Reduction-Program. Accessed March 4, 2021.

Health Information Systems for Healthy Aging

Shenita Freeman, MSHIA, MPH and Danielle Ward, PhD, MPH

BACKGROUND

Aging in public health is not only about direct medical care and social determinants. It is also about technology! The world is developing, consuming, and relying on technology for everyday activities including the provisioning of health care and the implementation of public health interventions. Technology is even entrenched in the social determinants of health. The infrastructure of our communities is technology- and information systems-dependent; we rely on technology to support the surveillance of environmental hazards, the provision of safe and timely transportation, and the sharing of emergent communications and wireless emergency alerts. Both micro and macro economic and financial systems are technology-dependent. Education is stifled without access to computers and internet. The nation's safe food supply chain is technology-dependent. Postal communications and mail delivery of important supplies, medications, census forms, and voting materials are technology-dependent too. All of the nation's public health and public health-related systems rely on technology in one way or another, and these systems must be enhanced, maintained, and protected.

The US federal government continues to incentivize the use of health information technology. Health care professionals must strike a balance between the associated benefits and risks of implementation. The benefit of secure, well implemented, high functioning, and interoperable health information technology includes increasingly enhanced personal and public health communications, advanced clinical processes, and improved patient health outcomes. The risks of unsecured, low functioning, and unconnected health information technology include diminished or completely breached confidentiality and integrity of protected health information, disruption of health care operations, decreased patient safety, and even loss of life.[1-5]

In the health sector, technology-related domains include, but are not limited to, electronic medical records; patient portals; transaction processing, administrative, and decision support information systems; and internet connected medical devices. Health information technology encompasses all of the electronic systems that health care professionals, patients, patient families, and caregivers use to store, share, and analyze health information.[6] In fact, digital and mobile health tools and the health-related internet of things (IoT) are frequently being used to help aging populations with independent living and management of chronic diseases.[7] IoT devices include but are not limited to smartphones, smartwatches, digital scales, digital glucose meters, electronic stethoscopes, and mobile electrocardiograms. The data collected from these IoT devices and connected systems have become public health critical, helping to identify and contact high risk patients and populations.

The public health workforce should be both knowledgeable and prepared to educate the public about the cybersecurity risks associated with the internet-connected technologies that they are already using. Each public health stakeholder should be working toward protecting the public health and related infrastructure from crippling cyber threats while insuring that the public has informed and equitable access to important technologies.

How does the use of connected devices impact older adults and their health outcomes? Cisco predicts that the number of connected devices will be more than three times the global population by 2023.[8] These connected devices are being used by aging populations. In fact, in 2017, approximately 40% of seniors owned smartphones and a Pew Research Center survey found that seniors were moving towards having more digitally connected lives.[9] Participation in digital health care among patients of all ages increased dramatically during the COVID-19 pandemic when activities that were primarily done in person went virtual. This is likely to continue as a safety net for patients who are homebound or who are at increased risk of falls and/or infection. In terms of information security, this brings up a host of privacy and accessibility concerns that the public health workforce should be prepared for. The following sections define and provide examples of several public health-related security concepts.

Digital Health Literacy

Digital health literacy is the ability to look for, locate, understand, evaluate, and apply health information from electronic sources to address a health question or issue.[10] The Pew Research Center found that 35% of adults in the United States have gone online before or after seeking advice from a medical professional to better understand a medical condition.[9] Formally educated public health professionals are trained to scrutinize information sources for currency, relevance, authority, accuracy, and objectivity. However, on the internet, peer-to-peer health information sharing is a primary factor in shaping health-related attitudes, beliefs, and behaviors.[9]

Social media allows for quick and widespread dissemination of information, regardless of its accuracy or authenticity. The unrestricted and rapid spread of inaccurate health information, also known as a digital pandemic, can have a negative impact on public health efforts to protect and improve the health of people and their communities.

Disinformation and Misinformation

Disinformation and misinformation is intentionally false information designed to mislead. The distinction is that disinformation is usually related to governmental propaganda used to combat opposing geopolitical and/or media messages in the public; however, the terms are often used interchangeably. Deliberate deception, misinformation, and partial truths rely heavily on a population's low digital health literacy and motivation or inability to access accurate, timely, unbiased, and factual information.

Deep Fakes

Deep fakes are fraudulent audio and/or video recordings that look and sound like the real thing. Deep fakes are seemingly realistic but are falsified audio and video made with artificial intelligence and deep learning techniques. This type of disinformation and misinformation can be very difficult for the general public to detect and it is often used in the context of public health to sway political and medical public opinions.[11] Researchers have demonstrated that deep fakes can also be used to penetrate health care organizations and alter trusted medical images in a way that they are unable to be detected by expert radiologists.[12] In a study by Mirsky et al, the researchers demonstrated their ability to intercept and manipulate medical images by injecting and removing lung cancer from computed tomography scans.[13]

Protected Health Information

Protected health information (PHI) is "individually identifiable health information," which includes "health data created, received, stored, or transmitted by Health Insurance Portability and Accountability Act (HIPAA)-covered entities and their business associates in relation to the provision of healthcare, healthcare operations, and payment for healthcare services."[14] In electronic form, protected health information is called ePHI. Both forms of PHI, electronic and otherwise, include demographics, medical history, test results, insurance information, and other health information that can be linked back to a specific person. Protecting PHI is a critical public health function enforced by HIPAA's privacy and security rules. When PHI is not collected, stored, maintained, or destroyed in a secure manner that upholds confidentiality, a patient's identity, socioeconomic status, and health outcomes may be negatively affected. In addition to the negative patient impact, a health entity may suffer financial, operational, and reputation losses after a breach compromises the confidentiality, integrity, and/or availability of their data. This includes losses that are incurred as a result of cyber espionage or theft of intellectual property.[15]

Confidentiality

Confidentiality is the concept that data and information is only accessible by authorized custodians. Confidentiality upholds privacy principles and can be time and purpose limited (a need-to-know basis). Patients in the United States have the right to expect that all health communications and records that are transmitted electronically to or from a covered entity in the United States be treated as confidential and protected within the bounds of United States law.

In Europe, the General Data Protection Regulation (GDPR) requires all organizations, regardless of their geographical location, to protect data related to people in the European Union (EU). The GDPR requires global compliance to protect the personal data of EU citizens or residents. Under the GDPR, personal data is defined as, "any information that relates to an individual who can be directly or indirectly identified".[16] This can include names, email addresses, location, demographics, religious beliefs, web server data (cookies), and political opinions. The EU GDPR has a much broader scope than the legal protections afforded to citizens in the United States.

Permissions

Permissions, with respect to data, is the authorization to access or obtain information. In some cases, patients in the United States have the right to deny access to their information, but they do not necessarily have the right to rectification, objection, restriction of processing, and erasure as they do according to the rights afforded under the GDPR.

Integrity

Integrity, with respect to data, is the accuracy and validity of data throughout the data lifecycle. This means that each time the data is in transit or replicated, it remains intact and unaltered. Data integrity ensures appropriate health billing and care. Clinicians often site the 5Rs before providing treatment as an example of upholding medical integrity.[17] The 5Rs are right patient, right drug, right time, right dose, and right route. If any of the 5Rs are compromised, an error is likely to occur; the same is true for health information. The public health sector is responsible for ensuring that the digital information used in evidence-based decision-making is unaltered and presented to decision-makers intact.

Availability

Availability, with respect to data, is the ability to access data when it is needed. With electronic data, this means implementing and enforcing policies and procedures that keep computing hardware and software updated and in good working condition. It also means that data and information systems have regularly maintained backups, redundancies, and failover components. Having a functional disaster recovery plan for data centers and information systems supports the tenants of availability and business continuity. However, these measures alone will not prevent a ransomware attack that makes data unavailable.

Ransomware

Ransomware is malicious code (i.e., malware) that infects an organization's networks and information systems, encrypts (i.e., makes inaccessible) data and systems, and holds them hostage for a monetary ransom. Ransomware is generally spread via a malicious email that tricks the recipient into clicking a link, also known as a phishing attack. After the link has been clicked, the malware is downloaded without the recipient's knowledge, and it begins to search for and encrypt data on local and network drives.[18] The only way the data can be retrieved is by using an electronic key held by the author of the ransomware.

Defense in Depth

Defense in depth is a cybersecurity technique that employs layers of defense mechanisms to protect data and systems. With defense in depth, one defense mechanism may fail but it is not a single point of failure; there are additional mechanisms in place to prevent an attack or breach.

Data Breaches

Data breaches are an exposure of confidential, sensitive, or protected information to an unauthorized entity. The 2016 US Department of Health and Human Services' Healthcare and Public Health Sector (HPHS) Specific Plan states that nearly half of pharmaceutical and life science organizations experienced a breach of security within a 12-month timeframe.[19] These breaches specifically target PHI and electronic PHI that can be used for leverage in extortion schemes or sold on the dark web (anonymized areas of the internet not accessible by search engines) for nefarious use.

Emerging Example 1

In January 2015, the Anthem Blue Cross Insurance System suffered an attack in which 78.8 million health records were stolen. The stolen patient records included member names, identification numbers, dates of birth, social security numbers, addresses, telephone numbers, email addresses, employment information, and income data.[20,21] This data and systems breach violated confidentiality and availability; without functional data backups, the attack may also have violated the tenants of integrity.

In May 2017, the ransomware attack WannaCry infected more than 200,000 computers in 150 countries across multiple business sectors.[22] More than 600 organizations in the United Kingdom's National Health Service were directly or indirectly affected by WannaCry, including 34 hospital trusts providing acute and specialty care, mental health services, and emergency transportation services.[23] These hospitals were locked out of electronic systems and medical device technology. Over the next five to seven days, WannaCry created disruptions that included reverting back to paper records and manual processes, the cancellation of outpatient appointments, and diversion of emergency transportation services to several facilities.[23,24]

Another emerging threat is the breach into connected personal medical devices like insulin pumps and pacemakers with nefarious and potentially fatal intent. These connected technologies are vulnerable to cyberattack and subsequent malfunction. Attacks can include tampering with the operation of life altering medical devices in inpatient and outpatient care settings, which includes a patient's home where the technology is often connected to an unsecured home network.[4,5,7,25] Medical device safety and security also encompasses the manufacturing process. Not only do manufacturers need to be concerned with proper device operations, but they must ensure that the supply chain sourcing is free of fraudulent materials, malicious software, malicious hardware, and known security vulnerabilities.

In 2019, the US Department of Homeland Security reported security vulnerabilities in Medtronic implantable defibrillators that could allow attackers an opportunity to harm patients by altering the devices' programming.[26,27] These medical device vulnerabilities prompted the US Food and Drug Administration to issue guidelines describing how medical device manufacturers should manage security risks, both before and after products are put on the market.[28,29]

President Barack Obama defined critical infrastructure in an Executive Order as, "...systems and assets, whether physical or virtual, so vital to the United States that the incapacity or destruction of such systems and assets would have a debilitating impact on security, national economic security, national public health or safety, or any combination of those matters."[30]

The US Department of Health and Human Services is the designated Sector-Specific Agency for the HPHS. This sector protects all of the other sectors from terrorism, infectious disease outbreaks, and natural disasters by building and maintaining community health resilience, expanding medical capacity, improving health-related situational awareness capabilities, integrating with emergency management systems, and strengthening global health security.[19] The HPHS is highly dependent on communications, emergency services, food and agriculture, information technology, transportation, and water and wastewater systems. The HPHS is an attractive target for malicious actors because of its economic value, size, diversity, and openness. The threats to this sector are many. They include cybersecurity risks, since the health care and public health systems are increasingly reliant on health information technology.[19] The IBM Security and Ponemon Institute's 2019 Cost of a Data Breach Report points out that the health care industry has the highest average costs associated with a breach at $6.45 million, over 60% more than the global average of all industries.[31] The impact of critical infrastructure breaches have the potential to disproportionately affect older adults and other vulnerable populations.

Emerging Example 2

Power outages can negatively affect older adults and vulnerable populations by disrupting health care operations, refrigeration, heating and cooling, water pumping equipment in buildings with more than six floors, and elevators. New York City had major power outages in 2003 and 2019; the 2003 outage was associated with increased risk of all-cause mortality, according to an article published in the *Journal of Urban Health*.[32] Power outages can occur because of natural disasters, failed hardware and systems, and malicious threat actors. Power outages disrupt daily life and health care continuity, which includes functioning medical device operations (e.g., oxygen regulators, continuous positive airway pressure [CPAP] machines, dialysis machines).

The Administration for Community Living details an incident in 2019 when Pacific Gas and Electric Company cut power to hundreds of thousands of California residents in an effort to reduce wildfire risks.[33] This disruption, while not cybersecurity-related, caused older adults with major complications or comorbidities (MCCs) to suffer. One resident cited struggling to stay awake to watch her mother, who has severe sleep apnea, sleep without her CPAP machine. Another resident deciding between charging her electric wheelchair or heart monitor stated, "You don't know until it happens how it's really going to affect you."[33]

In Queensland Australia, a disgruntled job applicant sought revenge by hacking into the city's wastewater supervisory control and data acquisition (SCADA) systems. Over the course of a couple months, this threat actor directed the SCADA computer systems to discharge hundreds of thousands of gallons of raw sewage into local waterways.[34]

Cybersecurity is still an emerging field, especially within the public health sector. It has tremendous implications for personal and environmental health. The workforce must be prepared and ready to respond.

CONCLUSION: CHALLENGES AND OPPORTUNITIES FOR PUBLIC HEALTH

A robust and secure health information infrastructure is a critical component of the public health infrastructure. Our lives are increasingly tied to computers and other technological devices that assist in the management and treatment of complex health conditions. The ability to readily access and share health care data among interdisciplinary teams is necessary to ensure holistic treatment of individuals and communities. Yet, to date these systems have often operated in silos. Information is rarely shareable across systems, creating confusion and delays in delivering care. A lack of investment in the health technology infrastructure has made data accessible to subservient actors who aim to access data for malicious purposes, which can delay care and negatively affect health outcomes. At the same time, the overreliance on technological options may leave some behind. For example, older adults may not be able to access and use these systems at the same rate as other generations. Marginalized populations may lack the necessary computers, smartphones, and other devices needed to access these services. Individuals living in rural environments may not have the necessary infrastructure, including internet, to easily make use of these tools. In addition, smaller health entities and providers may go out of business as technology requirements and standards become more complex.

There is no doubt that we will increasingly rely on novel health information tools and technologies. Public health practitioners must work to ensure that all stakeholders, including patients and providers, are able to access and appropriately leverage the electronic information systems and technologies.

CASE STUDY

Local Programming and Technology Serve to Connect Older Adults

As discussed earlier in this book (see "Life Events and Resulting Disruption in Support Systems" in Chapter 9), there are major events that have the ability to impact an older person's social support system. Further, as adults age, opportunities to meet and form new relationships dwindle. This may be especially true as older adults retire from the workforce, relocate to be near family or to smaller or updated housing, and may experience decreased mobility or energy for social outings.

To combat this lack of opportunity, a national charity in England, Age UK, has started a program to provide adults above 60 years of age with opportunities to connect with other older adults with similar interests either via telephone or in-person meetings. The program, Call in Time, seeks to address loneliness in older adults by exploring low-cost and effective ways to increase opportunities for meeting other older adults and fostering companionship. Call in Time is a free befriending service that matches individuals with "a likeminded person who has similar interests and hobbies."[35] It is based upon the premise that having someone to talk to on a regular basis can ease feelings of loneliness. According to Charlesworth et al, befriending is "a form of social support where a supportive other is introduced to, or matched with, an individual who would otherwise be socially isolated."[36] Befriending services, which are usually one-to-one, typically provide support to a specific group of people such as at-risk children or older people. Befriending can take the form of in-person visits, letter writing, or by telephone.

Call in Time: A Program to Screen and Connect Older Adults

Call in Time has several locations across the United Kingdom, which are administered by voluntary and charitable organizations. Older adults and their family members can sign up for the program via the Age UK website. All members must be at least 60 years of age and have a landline or mobile phone. The member's contact information is provided to the program, but not to the other members, and software is used to help connect members based on a prearranged day and time. Call in Time has a sign up process which includes reference checks, online training, and an interview with the program administrators to ensure the safety of its members. Once an individual passes the requisite checks, they are then matched with an older person with similar interests. Once matched, they begin weekly 30-minute calls with their matched person. Additionally, members are encouraged to meet at the same time each week and to check in with the program ahead of time if they are unable to make their scheduled meeting. As such, the program is able to monitor regular use and can alert family members if something were amiss.

Users of this and other similar services indicated that what they want most from their conversations was normal, everyday dialogue, not problem- or health-focused. Users also wanted conversations to be reciprocal so that each person shares information about certain aspects of their life.

Is This Program Successful?

An evaluation of Call in Time demonstrated that the program had a positive impact on users' well-being. The majority of program users are self-described as socially isolated, and say they felt more connected to society with their weekly phone calls. Call in Time users also described feeling like they were still relevant and had something to offer through meaningful conversation. Users have indicated that the program has helped relieve loneliness and improved their mental and emotional well-being. Members also describe the weekly phone calls as positively impacting their overall happiness, and that they now have something to look forward to. Another positive outcome that users reported was that of wanting to get up, go outside and socialize with other people; these users noted a difference in their confidence levels and motivation to do things.

How Can Others Implement?

A befriending service, such as Call in Time, can be relatively easy to implement in that it does not require much effort on the part of its older members. The main requirements for implementation would be

1. A team of program administrators, including managers and counselors;
2. The ability to set up online recruitment, training, and registration processes;

3. Community engagement and advertising campaigns to attract a diverse pool of members; and

4. A software program to anonymize and connect phone calls between members.

Information about the Call in Time Programme in the United Kingdom can be found at the Age UK website (available at: https://www.ageuk.org.uk/services/befriending-services/sign-up-for-telephone-befriending).

REFERENCES

1. Burde H. Health law: The hitech act—an overview. *Virtual Mentor.* 2011;13(3):172–175.

2. Kwon J, Johnson ME. Meaningful healthcare security: Does meaningful-use attestation improve information security performance? *MIS Q.* 2018;42(4):1043–1067.

3. McKnight R, Franko O. HIPAA Compliance with mobile devices among ACGME programs. *J Med Syst.* 2016;40(5):129.

4. Slabodkin G. Mobile devices, cloud computing: What healthcare CIOs fear most. Fierce Healthcare. 2013. Available at: https://www.fiercehealthcare.com/mobile/mobile-devices-cloud-computing-what-healthcare-cios-fear-most. Accessed March 4, 2021.

5. Wetsman N. Health care's huge cybersecurity problem. The Verge. 2019. Available at: https://www.theverge.com/2019/4/4/18293817/cybersecurity-hospitals-health-care-scan-simulation. Accessed March 4, 2021.

6. Office of the National Coordinator for Health Information Technology. Health IT: Advancing America's health care. 2020. Available at: https://www.healthit.gov/sites/default/files/pdf/health-information-technology-fact-sheet.pdf. Accessed on March 4, 2020.

7. Wildenbos GA, Jaspers MWM, Schijven MP, Dusseljee-Peute LW. Mobile health for older adult patients: Using an aging barriers framework to classify usability problems. *Int J Med Inform.* 2019;124:68–77.

8. Cisco. Cisco annual internet report (2018–2023) white paper. 2020. Available at: https://www.cisco.com/c/en/us/solutions/collateral/executive-perspectives/annual-internet-report/white-paper-c11-741490.html. Accessed on March 4, 2021.

9. Fox S, Duggan M. Health online 2013. Pew Research Center. 2013. Available at: https://www.pewresearch.org/internet/2013/01/15/health-online-2013/. Accessed July 21, 2021.

10. Norman CD, Skinner HA. eHealth literacy: Essential skills for consumer health in a networked world. *J Med Internet Res.* 2006;8(2):e9.

11. Seymour B, Getman R, Saraf A, Zhang LH, Kalenderian E. When advocacy obscures accuracy online: Digital pandemics of public health misinformation through an antifluoride case study. *Am J Public Health.* 2015;105(3):517–523.

12. Rasser, M. Why are deepfakes so effective? Scientific American. 2019. https://blogs.
    scientificamerican.com/observations/why-are-deepfakes-so-effective. Accessed March 4,
    2021.

13. Mirsky Y, Mahler T, Shelef I, Elovici Y. CT-GAN: Malicious tampering of 3D medical imagery
    using deep learning. 2019. USENIX Security 2019. Available at: https://arxiv.org/
    pdf/1901.03597.pdf. Accessed on March 4, 2021.

14. US Department of Health and Human Services. Summary of the HIPAA privacy rule. 2013.
    Available at: https://www.hhs.gov/hipaa/for-professionals/privacy/laws-regulations/index.
    html. Accessed March 4, 2021.

15. Alder S. What is protected health information? HIPAA Journal. 2018. Available at: https://
    www.hipaajournal.com/what-is-protected-health-information. Accessed March 4, 2021.

16. European Union. Complete guide to GDPR compliance. 2021. Available at: https://gdpr.eu.
    Accessed March 21, 2021.

17. Grissinger M. The five rights: A destination without a map. PT. 2010;35(10):542.

18. Cyber Edu. What is defense in depth? Forcepoint. 2018. Available at: https://www.forcepoint.
    com/cyber-edu/defense-depth. Accessed March 4, 2021.

19. Department of Homeland Security. Healthcare and public health sector-specific plan, 2015.
    Cybersecurity and Infrastructure Security Agency. 2016. Available at: https://www.cisa.gov/
    publication/nipp-ssp-healthcare-public-health-2015. Accessed March 4, 2021.

20. Spence N, Bhardwaj N, Paul DP, Coustasse A. Ransomware in healthcare facilities: A harbin-
    ger of the future? Perspectives in health information management. 2018. Available at: https://
    perspectives.ahima.org/ransomwareinhealthcaretacilities. Accessed March 4, 2021.

21. California Department of Insurance. Anthem data breach. Available at: https://www.insurance.
    ca.gov/0400-news/0100-press-releases/anthemcyberattack.cfm. Accessed March 4, 2021.

22. Ghafur S, Kristensen S, Honeyford K, Martin G, Darzi A, Aylin P. A retrospective impact
    analysis of the WannaCry cyberattack on the NHS. NPJ Digit Med. 2019;2:98.

23. Slayton TB. Ransomware: The virus attacking the healthcare industry. J Leg Med.
    2018;38(2):287–311.

24. BBC News. Where has ransomware hit hardest? 2017. Available at: https://www.bbc.com/
    news/world-39919249. Accessed March 4, 2021.

25. Davis J. When medical devices get hacked, hospitals often don't know it. Healthcare IT News.
    2018. Available at: https://www.healthcareitnews.com/news/when-medical-devices-get-hacked-
    hospitals-often-dont-know-it. Accessed March 4, 2021.

26. Keane S. DHS reveals some Medtronic heart defibrillators are vulnerable to hacking. CNET. 2019.
    Available at: https://www.cnet.com/news/dhs-reveals-some-medtronic-heart-defibrillators-are-
    vulnerable-to-hacking. Accessed March 4, 2021.

27. US Department of Homeland Security. ICS medical advisory: Medtronic Valleylab FT10 and FX8. 2019. Cybersecurity and Infrastructure Security Agency. 2019. Available at: https://www.us-cert.gov/ics/advisories/icsma-19-311-02. Accessed March 4, 2021.

28. Schwartz S, Ross A, Carmody S, et al. The evolving state of medical device cybersecurity. *Biomed Instru Technol.* 2018;52(2):103–111.

29. US Food and Drug Administration. CFR-Code of Federal Regulations Title 21 Chapter 1 Subchapter H Medical Devices Section 820. US Department of Health and Human Services. 2020. Available at: https://www.accessdata.fda.gov/scripts/cdrh/cfdocs/cfcfr/CFRSearch.cfm?FR=820.30. Accessed March 4, 2021.

30. Obama B. Executive Order—Improving Critical Infrastructure Cybersecurity. The White House, President Barack Obama. 2013. Available at: https://obamawhitehouse.archives.gov/the-press-office/2013/02/12/executive-order-improving-critical-infrastructure-ybersecurity. Accessed March 4, 2021.

31. IBM Security. Cost of a data breach report 2019. Ponemon Intitute. 2019. Available at: https://clairelogic.net/wp-content/uploads/2019/09/SM-IBM-2019-cost-of-a-data-breach-report.pdf. Accessed March 21, 2021.

32. Dominianni C, Ahmed M, Johnson S, Blum M, Ito K, Lane K. Power outage preparedness and concern among vulnerable New York City residents. *J Urban Health.* 2018;95(5):716–726.

33. Chabria A, Luna T. PG&E power outages bring darkness, stress and debt to California's poor and elderly. Los Angeles Times. 2019. Available at: https://www.latimes.com/california/story/2019-10-11/pge-power-outage-darkness-stress-debt-vulnerable. Accessed March 4, 2021.

34. Janke R, Tryby ME, Clark RM. Protecting water supply critical infrastructure: An overview. In Clark RM, Hakim S, eds. *Securing Water and Wastewater Systems: Global Experiences.* 2014. Cham, Switzerland: Springer International Publishing; 2014:29-85.

35. Age UK Wigan Borough and Age UK. Call in Time. 2021. Available at: https://www.ageuk.org.uk/wiganborough/our-services/call-in-time/#:. Accessed June 2, 2021.

36. Charlesworth G, Shepstone L, Wilson E, Thalanany M, Mugford M, Poland F. Does befriending by trained lay workers improve psychological well-being and quality of life for careers of people with dementia, and at what cost? A randomised controlled trial. *Health Technol Assess.* 2008;12(4):iii, v–ix, 1–78.

V. ECONOMIC AND POLICY ISSUES

Section V examines the concept of economics and its impact on healthy aging. Factors such as pensions, economic resources, and policies that shape and play a role in these areas are discussed in this section. In relation to the social determinants of health, economic stability addresses key issues such as poverty, food security, and housing stability.

The lead chapter addresses economic issues that impact people as they grow older, and either influence or negate healthy aging. Socioeconomic factors that impact health and health outcomes are explored, as well as economic strategies that play a role in impacting one's overall health.

Chapter 18 examines policies that influence one's economic stability within the aging arena. Individual chapters briefly touch upon various governmental policies that have influenced the individual topics within this text. This chapter brings these policies together and discusses them in terms of the policy and the programs that flow from them for older adults. While public health practitioners may be familiar with the legislation related to public health and how various components impact people growing older, readers may not be as familiar with other major policies that impact people growing older, such as Social Security, Medicare, The Older Americans Act, The Americans with Disabilities Act, and the Elder Justice Act, to name a few.

This section concludes with an overall conclusion chapter for the entire book. Issues and opportunities discussed in individual chapters are revisited in Chapter 19, with future recommendations for the public health. These recommendations are made within the context of seeking to address social determinants of health in efforts to promote healthy aging.

Economic Issues in Healthy Aging

Lisa M. Lines, PhD, MPH, Jennifer A. Pooler, MPP, and Jason Burnett, PhD

BACKGROUND

An old saying suggests that "health is wealth." The reverse is often true: wealth is health. Poverty, at the individual, household, and neighborhood levels, is a significant risk factor for poorer health outcomes. The government's definition of poverty used to determine safety net program eligibility is called the poverty guideline.[1] The amount, which is equal to three times the income needed to provide for basic food needs in 1963, changes year to year and varies based on the number of people in the household. As of 2020, the guideline for a two-person household is $17,240.[1] The guideline is a simplified version of the US Census Bureau's official poverty measure (OPM), which has different measures depending on age and the number of children in the household.

The poverty guideline has been criticized as outdated.[3] This is why many researchers use a higher threshold, such as 200% or 250% of the OPM, or rely on the Supplemental Poverty Measure (SPM), to define poverty status.[4] The SPM poverty threshold is based on anticipated expenditures, such as shelter and utilities, health care costs, and taxes. Additionally, household resource calculations include income and additional benefits, such as food assistance and housing subsidies. According to the most recent data available, as many as 42% of older adults, over 21 million Americans, had incomes below 200% of the SPM (see Figure 17–1).[5]

It is likely that many more older Americans live in poverty than the official statistics imply. Both the Elder Economic Security Standard Index and the Institute on Assets and Social Policy's Senior Financial Stability Index suggest that three-quarters of older adults, even before the 2020 recession, struggled to meet their monthly expenses.[6] Most of them have incomes above the OPM. Among Medicare enrollees, dual enrollment in both Medicare and Medicaid, a marker of low income, is often associated with worse health outcomes.[7-9] Lack of adequate income has a cascading sequence of effects on many of the other social risk factors, such as housing and transportation. Individuals with lower incomes are also often less educated and have lower health literacy. The complex knot of relationships among social risk factors is one of the more under-researched topics in this area.

In the United States, far more is spent on health care than other wealthy countries, but far less on social services like housing and food assistance. This leads to gaps in the

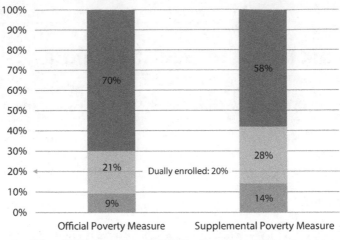

Source: Based on data presented in a Kaiser Family Foundation analysis of Current Population Survey, 2018 Annual Social and Economic Supplement data.[5]

Note: According to the same analysis, 20% of Medicare beneficiaries were dually enrolled in Medicaid.[5]

Figure 17-1. Percent of Medicare Beneficiaries Ages 65 and Older With Poverty-Level Incomes in 2017

social safety net that disproportionately affect older adults.[10] Additionally, the United States faces ongoing large policy concerns that affect older adults, such as how to finance health care, long-term care, and social services while ensuring universal coverage and quality care for all.

THE COSTS OF CARE AND HEALTH REFORM

The Social Security Amendments of 1965 created two publicly financed health insurance programs: Medicare, for older adults and permanently disabled adults; and Medicaid, initially only for poor parents and children, now expanded in some states to poor adults without children. Since nearly all legal US residents and citizens aged 65 and older are covered by Medicare, it might seem that the older population would have fewer concerns about paying for care than do younger Americans. In reality, between fixed incomes, higher prevalence of expensive conditions like cancer, and Medicare's cost-sharing requirements, older adults have much the same issues as the rest of society in terms of access to affordable care. Research shows that 17% of Medicare enrollees report having problems obtaining care due to the cost or paying medical bills, leaving them with hard choices between paying for health care, food, or housing.[11] In comparison, 23% of adults aged 19–64 who were insured all year reported at least one cost-related access problem in 2018.[12]

Older adults are more likely than younger people to need long-term services and supports, such as may be provided in assisted living or nursing homes. Such care is very expensive; in 2019, the median monthly cost for assisted living was over $4,000, and a semi-private room in a nursing facility cost over $7,500.[13] Although an estimated seven in ten Medicare beneficiaries will need long-term care in their lifetimes, traditional Medicare does not cover most long-term care. Long-term care insurance may be unobtainable or unaffordable by the time a person needs such care. Fewer than 10% of older adults have long-term care insurance.[14] Many older adults are forced to spend or transfer all their assets in order to qualify for Medicaid, the public health insurance program for the poor.[15]

In 2013, the average out-of-pocket burden among Medicare beneficiaries—the amount they are required to cover as part of the cost sharing structure of the program—was 41% of average per capita Social Security income. The burden increased with age and was higher for women than men, especially among people ages 85 and up. The average burden is expected to increase from 41% in 2013 to 50% in 2030.[16]

At the same time, the value of the amount spent on care is variable. Per federal policy, Medicare is not allowed to consider cost-effectiveness analyses in its reimbursement and formulary considerations.[17] By some estimates, a third of Medicare spending is either ineffective or wasteful.[18] These reports have led to widespread calls for health reform, including proposals to expand Medicare to cover all Americans, increasing access to care, and reducing total costs while redesigning the program to reward better quality care.[19]

Numerous government and academic reports have been issued in the past five years that delve deeply into the literature on economic issues for older adults. The National Academy of Medicine's report, "Accounting for Social Risk Factors in Medicare Payment," was published in 2017.[20] Experts examined the role of dual enrollment, living in a lower income area, Black race, Hispanic ethnicity, and rural residence as risk factors, along with disability, from the perspective of the current efforts in health reform, particularly value-based payment. The National Academies report issued in 2017 specifically stated that

> The trend toward [value-based payment] could result in certain adverse consequences for socially at-risk populations, such as leading providers and health plans to avoid patients with social risk factors, underpayment of providers disproportionately serving socially at-risk populations (e.g., safety-net providers), and thus exacerbating health disparities.[20]

Since 2017, the Centers for Medicare and Medicaid Services (CMS) has adjusted some publicly reported quality measures for dual enrollment, as a marker of poverty, and disability. In some states Medicaid Managed Care Organizations are reimbursed based on a formula that accounts for neighborhood stress and several other social risk factors.[21] These developments show that there is movement toward better understanding and consideration of poverty and other social risk factors as part of paying for care and/or assessing the quality of care.

HEALTH AND WEALTH DISPARITIES AMONG OLDER PEOPLE

Socioeconomic disparities are evident across a wide range of health outcomes, from heart disease to hypertension to frailty[22]; access to health services and medication adherence[23]; and mortality.[24] Research has identified both current and life-long economic factors as critical contributors to disease.[25] Socioeconomic health disparities may occur through multiple mechanisms, including food security, food access, and nutrition; affordable, safe, and stable housing; access to medical and dental care; discrimination; financial stress; and transportation access and mobility.

Recent studies estimate that 7% of older adults are food insecure,[26] 7% of older adults skip or cut medications to save money,[27] and 12% are sometimes or often unable to get to appointments due to transportation challenges.[28] Many of these barriers are co-occurring; among adults age 20 and older with chronic conditions, 11% reported both food insecurity and cost-related medication nonadherence.[29] Another study of adults aged 50 and older found that 64% of those reporting transportation challenges were also food insecure, compared with about 10% of adults reporting no transportation challenges.[28] Social risk factors are much more common among low-income populations.

When older adults are unable to meet their basic needs, whether due to a sudden financial shock (e.g., financial exploitation or unexpected medical bills) or insufficient income or savings, they often must choose which basic necessities to prioritize. Reducing expenditures on basic needs can have adverse short- and long-term consequences, including inadequate nutrition, poor chronic disease self-management, and eviction or homelessness.

RELEVANT POLICIES AND LEGISLATION

The Social Security Act of 1935 brought the United States in line with other industrial countries in providing financial assistance to people unable to work. The conditions of the Great Depression resulted in broad support for President Roosevelt's New Deal, which established, for the first time in US history, the beginnings of a social safety net. Funded by payroll taxes, the program has contributed greatly to reducing poverty rates among older adults.[30] Supplemental Security Income, a program for low-income older adults and people with disabilities, was created in 1972.

Research has shown that Social Security is the most important antipoverty program in the United States. In 1968, about 13% of all Americans and 25% of people over 65 years of age were living below the official poverty threshold; in 2016, the percentage of all Americans living in poverty was nearly the same, but the official poverty rate among older Americans had declined to 9%.[3] Relative to non-older adult incomes (rather than the official poverty guidelines), older adult poverty rates declined until the early 1980s and have remained steady since.[30] Each $1,000 increase in annual Social Security benefits has been associated with 2% to 3% lower poverty rates among older adult households.[30]

The Older Americans Act was passed in 1965. This legislation created the national network of the Administration on Aging at the federal level, Units on Aging at the state level, and local Agencies on Aging. These entities help provide funding for nutrition services, home and community based services, disease prevention and health promotion services, and older adult rights programs.

Separate legislation has established various food stamp programs since 1939. The current Supplemental Nutrition Assistance Program (SNAP), which provides resources for purchasing foods to low-income households, has been the subject of much research. Increasing household resources to purchase food may improve food security and nutrition and also free up financial resources to purchase other basic necessities. Participation among older adults in SNAP has been associated with a five percentage point decrease in cost-related medication nonadherence compared with nonparticipants, and this finding was nearly double for older adults at-risk of food insecurity.[31] Other studies have found associations between SNAP participation and better physical (but not mental) health outcomes for older adults[32] and lower health care expenditures for adults.[33] Participation in SNAP has been shown to be associated with 14% lower likelihood of hospital admission and 23% lower likelihood of nursing home care.[34] Home-delivered meals programs (e.g., Meals on Wheels) have also demonstrated positive results in improving nutrition among home-bound older adults,[35] while having other positive results, such as reducing isolation.[36]

GOVERNMENT PROGRAMS

A number of federal, state, and local programs are in place to help individuals and families who are struggling. Very few of these programs are intended to address the specific needs of older adults, and many are block-grant funded, and so are administered on a first-come-first-served basis.

A few government programs do target older people, particularly the large Medicare demonstration projects now organized by the Center for Medicare & Medicaid Innovation (CMMI). These programs often start out rather unevenly scattered across the country, but some eventually become standard practice for Medicare reimbursed patients. For example, under the CMMI funded State Innovation Models program, all providers in Maryland[37] currently get information about their patients' neighborhood-level relative deprivation, which allows them to better identify which patients may need what are referred to as "wraparound services"—generally services related to housing, food, or transportation.

A complete directory of government programs is beyond the scope of this chapter. However, the National Council on Aging's Benefits Check-Up (available at: www.benefits-checkup.org) can be used to identify potential programs for which older adults are eligible.

A growing body of evidence supports social safety net programs as a strategy to combat social risk factors for poor health among low-income older adults. A few of the most important government programs available to help older people with these services include the following:

- Food assistance: The Administration for Community Living operates the Elderly Nutrition Programs, which comprise home delivered meals and congregate meals site; and low-income older adults are entitled to participate in SNAP.
- Assistance with medical bills: Very low-income older adults may enroll in Medicaid and other programs that will reduce or cover the cost of their medical bills. States administer Medicare Savings Programs that can help low-income older adults pay for their Medicare premiums, copays/coinsurance, and deductibles. The Medicare Part D program is a subsidized prescription drug program that is available to all over age 65.
- Heating/energy assistance: The Low-Income Heating and Energy Assistance Program assists households with very low incomes that pay a high proportion of household income for home energy.
- Housing assistance: Low-income older adults can be eligible for housing subsidies from the US Department of Housing and Urban Development. These programs include Public Housing Assistance, the Housing Choices Voucher, and Supportive Housing for the Elderly programs.
- Financial assistance: While Social Security provides income for most older adults in the United States, Supplemental Security Income is intended to provide a basic minimum amount of support for living expenses, including for individuals who did not work enough to receive Social Security benefits. Many states offer services that provide free financial counseling, such as counseling to prevent foreclosure and loan refinancing.

Few of these are entitlement programs, meaning there can be long waiting lists for programs depending on the area in which older adults live. Many of these programs are also administered by different federal and state agencies, and processes for applying for these programs can be burdensome to older adults, especially when physical and/or cognitive limitations are present. Further, many older adults may find themselves struggling financially for the first time in their lives and may have no experience or knowledge of available programs or their eligibility to participate.

Highlighting the numerous barriers to accessing public assistance, only about half of older Americans eligible for SNAP were enrolled in the program in 2017.[34] Participation in the Medicare Savings Plans (MSP) are equally low. A recent analysis indicates that participation in the four MSP programs ranged from 15% to 58%, depending on the program.[37] The study authors attributed these low participation rates to lack of awareness, enrollment and eligibility requirements that conflict with other means-tested programs, and program administration that differs across states. While participation in other programs is not typically reported, programs such as subsidized housing and home delivered meals frequently have waiting lists due to limited resources. As the population of older adults continues to grow, it is likely the wait lists will grow without sufficient funding to serve all low-income older adults.

Health professionals, such as community health workers, health navigators, social workers, and nurses, have a large part to play in helping to bridge the gap between the large group of eligible people and the subset of enrolled beneficiaries. Programs that aim to increase enrollment and engagement in social service programs are most successful when case managers are empowered to reach out personally to eligible individuals, approaching people where they are and encouraging them to access available resources.

FINANCIAL EXPLOITATION

Definition and Prevalence

Financial exploitation (FE) of vulnerable adults, especially older adults, is a burgeoning public health problem.[38] The National Center on Elder Abuse defines FE as

> the illegal or improper use of an elder's funds, property, or assets. Examples include, but are not limited to, cashing an elderly person's checks without authorization or permission; forging an older person's signature; misusing or stealing an older person's money or possessions; coercing or deceiving an older person into signing any document (e.g., contracts or will); and the improper use of conservatorship, guardianship, or power of attorney.[38]

The most recent national prevalence study found that the prevalence of FE was 5% greater than all other forms of self-reported abuse.[39] While the true scope of the problem remains unknown, FE has become the most common form of older adult abuse in American society and has detrimental effects on older adults' health and wealth.[10]

FE occurs when someone other than the older adult asset owner illegally or dishonestly obtains and uses the older adult's assets or property for their own benefit.[41] These heinous acts are committed by "trusted others" such as family, neighbors, or caregivers and by fraudsters and scammers. The loss incurred by victims extends into the billions, and societal costs to investigate and respond are estimated to be well into the hundreds of millions.[42]

Health and Wealth Consequences

Financial loss is not the only negative impact that FE has on older adults. Victims may suffer psychological trauma after victimization,[43] financial ruin,[44] loss of independence,[45] decline in quality of life,[46] decreased resources for health care,[47] increased emergency department visits,[48] increased hospitalization,[49] and increased mortality.[50] These consequences may be difficult to overcome as older adults may experience physical and cognitive changes limiting their ability to effectively deal with victimization, and replenishing lost assets is difficult for most retirees.

Health and Wealth Risk Factors

Older adults are targeted for FE, fraud, and scams due to intersecting socioecological factors. Age-related changes in cognition, such as mild cognitive impairment, Alzheimer's disease and related dementias, and diminished levels of numeracy significantly affect the older adult's ability to manage their own finances.[51-53] Brain changes also result in a socioemotional response in older adults that causes them to overlook social "red flags" and ill-intent of others in favors of a positive world view.[54] In turn, they may engage in more risky financial transactions.[55,56] These risks also increase when an older adult is in close association with a family member or trusted other that misuses substances such as alcohol, illicit drugs, or opioids. Other health-related factors may also increase an older adult's dependency on others and thus, increase the risk for FE.

Financially, adults over the age of 50 years hold over 75% of society's assets.[57,58] Most of these assets are contained within defined benefit pension plans, defined contribution plans, and savings accounts. Wealth management responsibilities are being transferred from employers to individual retirees because of the shift from "defined benefit" retirement pension plans to riskier 401(k) accounts. This places individuals in control of their investments and savings, which can be very risky in the presence of the growing number of older adults, especially those over 85 years of age, suffering from cognitive decline.[51]

BEST PRACTICE INTERVENTIONS

Preventing Financial Exploitation

Unfortunately, the evidence identifying the best prevention and intervention practices to address older adult FE is lacking. However, steps have been taken at the federal, state, and local levels to help protect older adults from financial crimes and restore their dignity and resilience.[59] Creating awareness within communities regarding FE signs, how to report suspicion, and ways to intervene is a critical step towards effective intervention and prevention. The most updated list of state Adult Protective Services programs and how to make a report to them can be found on the American Bar Association Commission on Law and Aging website.[60] Triads consisting of law enforcement agencies, senior community members, and senior resources within communities are forming to help address FE.[61]

Older adult abuse forensic centers are showing great promise in providing increased protection and support for victims and potential victims of FE. Adding forensic accounting skills to older adult abuse multidisciplinary teams is also proving to be an effective intervention approach, especially for complex FE cases.[61-63] Daily money management programs could be helpful; these programs assist older Americans with tasks like paying bills, budgeting, and balancing checkbooks. Numerous states have passed laws giving financial firms freedom from liability for reporting older adult FE and placing limited account holds.[64,65] Finally, the best way to prevent FE is to take preemptive action through the use of revocable living trusts, financial power of attorney, and guardianship programs when necessary.[66]

Connecting People to Services

While many states have 2-1-1 hotlines to assist individuals in accessing information about public assistance programs, individual, tailored assistance is most effective for enrolling older adults in those programs. The National Council on Aging's Center for Benefits Access supports 84 Benefits Enrollment Centers around the country to help low-income people with Medicare access programs that pay for health care, food, and more.[67] Another organization, Benefits Data Trust, works with state governments to conduct outreach to Medicaid enrolled older adults and will help them complete and submit their public assistance program applications over the phone.

Some health systems have also implemented systematic screening and referral for patients who are struggling financially, finding that "warm handoffs" to social service agencies or community-based organizations are effective in obtaining assistance for older adults. For the most disadvantaged beneficiaries, three programs deserve special mention: the Program of All-Inclusive Care for the Elderly (PACE), Dual Special Needs Plans (D-SNPs), and the Medicare-Medicaid Financial Alignment Initiative.

Models of Wraparound Care: PACE

The roots of the PACE program go back to California in the 1970s to a program known as On Lok, designed as an alternative to nursing home care in the Chinese community.[68] From that single program, this model of comprehensive care for nursing home-eligible older adults has now spread to more than 60 sites nationwide.[69] The key difference between PACE and regular care is that PACE programs receive a set dollar amount per person enrolled, from which budget they provide all the health care their beneficiaries need. This form of health care reimbursement is known as capitation. In the case of PACE, it seems to provide the right incentives and level of reimbursement to ensure high quality across the full continuum of preventive, primary, acute, rehabilitative, and long-term care services for PACE program enrollees.[69]

Special Needs Plans

Special Needs Plans (SNPs), created by Congress in 2003, are a type of Medicare Advantage plan available to people with specific diseases or characteristics. Dual Eligible SNPs enroll only dual enrollees in Medicare and Medicaid. The level of integration varies widely, from those meeting minimum standards to Fully Integrated Dual Eligible (FIDE) SNPs, which achieve a high degree of integration between Medicare and Medicaid services. FIDE SNPs also offer additional benefits not typically covered by Medicare, such as vision, dental, hearing, durable medical equipment, transportation, and care coordination.[70]

Medicare-Medicaid Financial Alignment Initiative

One of the longstanding barriers to high-quality coordinated care for dual enrollees is the need to coordinate across two separate programs with different financing structures. Under this demonstration project, CMS is testing models to better align the financing of these two programs and integrate primary, acute, behavioral health, and long-term services and supports for their Medicare-Medicaid enrollees.

Special Considerations and Special Populations

The idea of intersectionality is useful for conceptualizing the many kinds of oppression and bias, and related stress and trauma that influence both health and wealth. For example, women are at higher risk of poverty than men. People of color are also at risk of both lower incomes and less wealth than White people. Gender nonconforming people and sexual minorities also face discrimination and bias. Adding the age-related processes affecting physical and mental functioning and health means that older vulnerable populations are among the most vulnerable people in our society. Age discrimination combined with other kinds of discrimination against vulnerable groups also affects the ability of older people to continue contributing to the economy and maintaining sufficient income to meet all their needs.

Typically, household income measurements in older populations fail to take into account other household assets. These are typically greater for White populations due to historic and contemporary disparities in education and salary attainment during one's working years, as well as the legacy of intergenerational wealth transfers (i.e., inheritances) that accrue less commonly to people of color. Black and Latinx older adults are more likely than White and Asian older adults to face economic insecurity.

Older adults of color are also more likely to have experienced negative stressful life events and trauma than their White counterparts. Many contemporary Black older adults are the grandchildren and great-grandchildren of enslaved people, and have been targeted by the most extended racist experiences of all age groups in the United States. For example, school segregation and the resulting disparities in educational quality, along with less well-resourced public schools, shorter school years, and fewer teachers available to youth of color, has been identified as one potential explanation for the much-greater incidence of dementia among Black and Hispanic older adults.[71] Educational quality affects a person's ability to get a good job with a high-paying salary, as well as health literacy and the ability to follow treatment plans.

Older women represent nearly two-thirds of all people 65 and older living in poverty. On average, women receive $4,000 less per year than men in Social Security payments; the disparity is even greater for women of color. Access to federal benefits is especially challenging for these individuals. Benefits associated with some safety net programs may be dependent on work and salary history. Given women's historically lower connections to the paid workforce and lower salaries, this can result in them having lower benefits.

Some lesbian, gay, bisexual, transgender, queer, and others (LGBTQ+) older adults face special economic barriers to healthy aging. LGBTQ+ older adults are twice as likely as heterosexual older adults to live alone, without close relatives or significant others to call for help. While some progress has been made in recent years in public attitudes towards LGBTQ+ people in general, discrimination may be more persistent in older generations.

Certain areas of the country, such as rural areas in the West, are also of special concern due to fewer providers (particularly geriatricians). Many rural hospitals have struggled and closed, and as of early 2020, one in four rural hospitals were at risk of closure.[72] People living in both rural and urban areas may be affected by lack of access to reliable transportation and long travel times to access care.

Many public health professionals focus their population health efforts on special populations, such as rural and frontier populations or LGBTQ+ individuals. The public health ethical principles of respect for autonomy and justice are particularly relevant when considering economic issues associated with aging. The public health concepts of solidarity and community responsibility underlie many of the local, state, and larger efforts to ensure universal coverage and quality care for all Americans.[73] These principles motivate many public health professionals and community members to advocate for better policies to protect vulnerable older adults.

CONCLUSION: CHALLENGES AND OPPORTUNITIES FOR PUBLIC HEALTH

We need to improve the public health awareness about the economic issues that older adults face and the impact of these issues. Public health needs to push more prevention as it relates to economic security. Younger generations need to understand the costs of aging so that proper planning can occur (e.g., costs of nursing homes, medications).

Programs for older adults need to be put into place, and rigorous program evaluations are needed to ensure that these programs are meeting the economic needs of the older adults. Challenges include growing disparity between the age of retirement and the life span. People are retiring early and living longer, therefore depleting savings accounts well before death. Older adults hold most of the money in the United States, making them the targets of financial exploitation, scams, and fraud. Preventive measures are important, so "soft" or sensitive public health campaigns are needed to address this very touchy and important topic.

The federal government has financial assistance programs, and most states and communities have AARP programs, local area Agencies on Aging, Meals on Wheels, and other programs for assisting with economic security and the loss of it. Yet, navigating these bureaucratic institutions can be especially hard for older people.

CASE STUDY

A 95-year-old woman who has been living alone for over 15 years receives a call from someone who claims to be the prize manager at Publisher's Clearinghouse. The man on the line uses the actual name of the prominent Publisher's Clearinghouse prize manager. He says he is calling because she has won the second prize, which is $2.5 million and a Mercedes sedan. He then mentions that because the winners have not been revealed, she is not allowed to tell anyone. He also lets her know that there are some fees that go along with gaining the prize, but assures her that if she keeps the receipts, she will be reimbursed.

The con man calls her frequently to check in on her and ask about her health. With each call there is a fee request. In some instances, it is a few hundred dollars, and in others, it is a few thousand. In the end, the thief steals $18,000 from the victim, leaving her with $8.75 in her savings account.

In contemporary news accounts, she describes feeling ashamed and in despair because she would not be able to replenish the money she lost. She also describes feeling stupid because she was unable to see the signs that she was being conned. Thankfully, the town rallied together with a dinner and not only raised $18,000 for her, but also used the dinner to bring awareness to the issue of financial scams against older adults.[74]

This case is highly relevant to the economic security of older adults because they are targeted daily by very convincing, seasoned scammers. They targeted an older woman living alone and used deceit to ensure that she kept the incident to herself. The outcomes of this case are very real in that she experiences psychological trauma in the forms of shame, despair, and self-doubt. She also became destitute, which affects all aspects of a person's well-being.

The best practice for a case like this is awareness of red flags related to scams. Unfortunately, intervening in scams is often futile since the scammers are hard to track down and may even be committing the act from another country. Reporting scams to the Better Business Bureau and federal agencies such as the Federal Bureau of Investigation can help prevent others from being scammed. Developing or using local Triads (consisting of law enforcement agencies, senior community members, and senior resources within communities), to raise community awareness about financial crimes against older adults, is helpful.[61]

This case study demonstrates how an individual's awareness and response can lead to community action against a problem that many older Americans face each day. There are federal and state programs along with safeguards in place to prevent and intervene in financial abuse of older adults. However, communities coming together to promote education and awareness of financial abuse of older adults is likely the best method for prevention. This case resulted in community agencies getting together to discuss, with community members, what their agency knows about financial abuse, how they work to protect the older adult, and what the community can do for prevention of financial abuse. It is this type of awareness that results in growing community networks against financial abuse, such as Triads, as well as community actions that result in legislative requests and changes such as criminal enhancements for crimes against vulnerable populations.

REFERENCES

1. Institute for Research on Poverty. What are poverty thresholds and poverty guidelines? 2019. Available at: https://www.irp.wisc.edu/resources/what-are-poverty-thresholds-and-poverty-guidelines. Accessed March 4, 2021.

2. Assistant Secretary for Planning and Evaluation. US Federal poverty guidelines used to determine financial eligibility for certain federal programs. 2021. Available at: https://aspe.hhs.gov/poverty-guidelines. Accessed March 4, 2021.

3. Institute for Research on Poverty. How is poverty measured? 2019. Available at: https://www.irp.wisc.edu/resources/how-is-poverty-measured. Accessed March 4, 2021.

4. Garner TI, Fox LE. A brief history of the supplemental poverty measure. In Haughwout A, Mandel B, eds. Handbook of US Consumer Economics. Cambridge, MA:Academic Press; 2019:389–426.

5. Cubanski J, Koma W, Damico A, Neuman T. How Many Seniors Live in Poverty? Kaiser Family Foundation. 2018. Available at: https://www.kff.org/report-section/how-many-seniors-live-in-poverty-appendix/. Accessed July 20, 2021.

6. Meschede T, Sullivan L, Shapiro T. From bad to worse: Senior economic insecurity on the rise. Institute on Assets and Social Policy. 2011. Available at: https://www.demos.org/research/bad-worse-senior-economic-insecurity-rise. Accessed March 4, 2021.

7. Halpern MT, Holden DJ. Disparities in timeliness of care for US Medicare patients diagnosed with cancer. Current oncology (Toronto, Ont). 2012;19(6):e404–413.

8. Lines LM, Cohen J, Halpern MT, Smith AW, Kent EE. Care experiences among dually enrolled older adults with cancer: SEER-CAHPS, 2005–2013. *Cancer Causes Control.* 2019;30(10): 1137–1144.

9. Walsh EG, Wiener JM, Haber S, Bragg A, Freiman M, Ouslander JG. Potentially avoidable hospitalizations of dually eligible Medicare and Medicaid beneficiaries from nursing facility and home-and community-based services waiver programs. *J Am Geriatr Soc.* 2012;60(5):821–829.

10. Bradley EH, Canavan M, Rogan E, et al. Variation in health outcomes: The role of spending on social services, public health, and health care, 2000–09. *Health Aff (Millwood).* 2016;35(5):760–768.

11. Cubanski J, Neuman T, Damico A. Problems getting care due to cost or paying medical bills among medicare beneficiaries. Kaiser Family Foundation. 2020. Available at: https://www.kff.org/coronavirus-covid-19/issue-brief/problems-getting-care-due-to-cost-or-paying-medical-bills-among-medicare-beneficiaries/. Accessed March 4, 2021.

12. Collins SR, Bhupal HK, Doty MM. Health insurance coverage eight years after the ACA. The Commonwealth Fund. 2019. Available at: https://www.commonwealthfund.org/publications/issue-briefs/2019/feb/health-insurance-coverage-eight-years-after-aca?omnicid=EALERT 1558577&mid=ggalvin@usnews.com. Accessed March 21, 2021.

13. Genworth. Cost of care survey. Genworth Financial. 2020. https://www.genworth.com/aging-and-you/finances/cost-of-care.html. Accessed March 4, 2021.

14. Favreault M, Dey J. Long-term services and supports for older Americans: Risks and financing research brief. Office of the Assistant Secretary For Planning and Evaluation. 2016. Available at: https://aspe.hhs.gov/basic-report/long-term-services-and-supports-older-americans-risks-and-financing-research-brief. Accessed March 4, 2021.

15. Salopek JJ. Medicaid coverage for nursing homes: Don't 'spend down' without a plan. AARP. 2019. Available at: https://www.aarp.org/caregiving/financial-legal/info-2019/medicaid-nursing-home-coverage.html. Accessed March 4, 2021.

16. Cubanski J, Neuman T, Damico A, Smith K. Medicare beneficiaries' out-of-pocket health care spending as a share of income now and projections for the future. Kaiser Family Foundation. 2018. Available at: https://www.kff.org/medicare/report/medicare-beneficiaries-out-of-pocket-health-care-spending-as-a-share-of-income-now-and-projections-for-the-future. Accessed March 4, 2021.

17. Gold MR, Sofaer S, Siegelberg T. Medicare and cost-effectiveness analysis: time to ask the taxpayers. *Health Aff.* 2007;26(5):1399–1406.

18. O'Neill DP, Scheinker D. Wasted health spending: Who's picking up the tab? Health Affairs Blog. 2018. Available at: https://www.healthaffairs.org/do/10.1377/hblog20180530.245587/full. Accessed March 4, 2021.

19. Galvani AP, Parpia AS, Foster EM, Singer BH, Fitzpatrick MC. Improving the prognosis of health care in the USA. *Lancet.* 2020;395(10223):524–533.

20. National Academies of Sciences, Engineering, Medicine. "Accounting for social risk factors in Medicare payment." Washington, D.C.:National Academies Press; 2017.

21. Ash AS, Mick EO, Ellis RP, Kiefe CI, Allison JJ, Clark MA. Social determinants of health in managed care payment formulas. *JAMA Intern Med.* 2017;177(10):1424–1430.

22. Szanton SL, Seplaki CL, Thorpe Jr RJ, Allen JK, Fried LP. Socioeconomic status is associated with frailty: The Women's Health and Aging Studies. *J Epidemiol Community Health.* 2010;64(1):63–67.

23. Almeida APSC, Nunes BP, Duro SMS, Facchini LA. Socioeconomic determinants of access to health services among older adults: A systematic review. *Rev Saude Publica.* 2017;51:50.

24. Braveman PA, Cubbin C, Egerter S, Williams DR, Pamuk E. Socioeconomic disparities in health in the United States: What the patterns tell us. *Am J Public Health.* 2010;100(suppl 1):S186–S196.

25. Tucker-Seeley RD, Li Y, Sorensen G, Subramanian SV. Lifecourse socioeconomic circumstances and multimorbidity among older adults. *BMC Public Health.* 2011;11:313.

26. Ziliak JP, Gundersen C. *The State of Senior Hunger in America in 2018, An Annual Report.* Feeding America. 2018:2–19.

27. Chung GC, Marottoli RA, Cooney LM, Rhee TG. Cost-related medication nonadherence among older adults: Findings from a nationally representative sample. *J Am Geriatr Soc.* 2019;67(12):2463–2473.

28. Pooler JA, Liu S, Roberts A. Older Adults and Unmet Social Needs: Prevalence and Health Implications. AARP Foundation and IMPAQ International. 2017. Available at: https://impaqint.com/sites/default/files/files/SDOH%20among%20older%20adults%202017_IssueBrief_COR2.pdf. Accessed May 19, 2021.

29. Berkowitz SA, Seligman HK, Choudhry NK. Treat or eat: Food insecurity, cost-related medication underuse, and unmet needs. *Am J Med.* 2014;127(4):303 310.e303.

30. Engelhardt GV, Gruber J. Social security and the evolution of elderly poverty. National Bureau of Economic Research Working Paper 10466. 2004. Available at: https://www.nber.org/papers/w10466. Accessed May 19, 2021.

31. Srinivasan M, Pooler JA. Cost-related medication nonadherence for older adults participating in SNAP, 2013–2015. *Am J Public Health.* 2017;108(2):224–230.

32. Pak TY, Kim GS. Food stamps, food insecurity, and health outcomes among elderly Americans. *Prev Med.* 2020;130:105871.

33. Berkowitz SA, Seligman HK, Rigdon J, Meigs JB, Basu S. Supplemental Nutrition Assistance Program (SNAP) participation and health care expenditures among low-income adults. *JAMA Intern Med.* 2017;177(11):1642–1649.

34. Benefits Data Trust. Seniors and SNAP. Available at: https://bdtrust.org/seniors-and-snap. 2020. Accessed March 5, 2021.

35. Walton K, do Rosario VA, Pettingill H, Cassimatis E, Charlton K. The impact of home-delivered meal services on the nutritional intake of community living older adults: a systematic literature review. *J Hum Nutr Diet.* 2020;33(1):38–47.

36. Thomas KS, Akobundu U, Dosa D. More than a meal? A randomized control trial comparing the effects of home-delivered meals programs on participants' feelings of loneliness. *J Gerontol B Psychol Sci Soc Sci.* 2017;71(6):1049–1058.

37. Kirchgraber K, Blom K. Improving participation in the Medicare Savings Programs. Medicaid and CHIP Payment and Access Commission. 2020. Available at: https://www.macpac.gov/wp-content/uploads/2020/01/Improving-Participation-in-the-Medicare-Savings-Programs.pdf. Accessed March 4, 2021.

38. Peterson JC, Burnes DP, Caccamise PL, et al. Financial exploitation of older adults: a population-based prevalence study. *J Gen Intern Med.* 2014;29(12):1615–1623.

39. Acierno R, Hernandez MA, Amstadter AB, et al. Prevalence and correlates of emotional, physical, sexual, and financial abuse and potential neglect in the United States: The National Elder Mistreatment Study. *Am J Public Health.* 2010;100(2):292–297.

40. Lachs MS, Pillemer KA. Elder abuse. *N Engl J Med.* 2015;373(20):1947–1956.

41. Hall JE, Karch DL, Crosby A. Elder abuse surveillance: uniform definitions and recommended core data elements for use in elder abuse surveillance. Centers for Disease Control and Prvention. 2016. Available at: https://www.cdc.gov/violenceprevention/pdf/EA_Book_Revised_2016.pdf. Accessed March 5, 2021.

42. Roberto K, Teaster P. The MetLife Study of Elder Financial Abuse: Crimes of occasion, desperation, and predation against America's elders. The MetLife Mature Market Institute. 2011. Available at: https://ltcombudsman.org/uploads/files/issues/mmi-elder-financial-abuse.pdf. Accessed March 5, 2021.

43. Acierno R, Watkins J, Hernandez-Tejada MA, et al. Mental health correlates of financial mistreatment in the National Elder Mistreatment Study wave II. *J Aging Health.* 2019;31(7):1196–1211.

44. Dessin CL. Financial abuse of the elderly. *Idaho L Rev.* 1999;36:203.

45. Choi NG, Kulick DB, Mayer J. Financial exploitation of elders: Analysis of risk factors based on county adult protective services data. *J Elder Abuse Negl.* 1999;10(3–4):39–62.

46. Coker J, Little B. Investing in the future: Protecting the elderly from financial abuse. *FBI L Enforcement Bull.* 1997;66:1.

47. Kemp BJ, Mosqueda LA. Elder financial abuse: An evaluation framework and supporting evidence. *J Am Geriatr Soc.* 2005;53(7):1123–1127.

48. Dong X, Simon MA. Association between elder abuse and use of ED: findings from the Chicago Health and Aging Project. *Am J Emerg Med.* 2013;31(4):693–698.

49. Dong X, Simon MA. Elder abuse as a risk factor for hospitalization in older persons. *JAMA Intern Med.* 2013;173(10):911–917.

50. Burnett J, Jackson SL, Sinha AK, et al. Five-year all-cause mortality rates across five categories of substantiated elder abuse occurring in the community. *J Elder Abuse Neg.* 2016;28(2):59–75.

51. Lichtenberg PA. Financial exploitation, financial capacity, and Alzheimer's disease. *Am Psychol.* 2016;71(4):312.

52. Plassman BL, Langa KM, Fisher GG, et al. Prevalence of cognitive impairment without dementia in the United States. *Ann Intern Med.* 2008;148(6):427–434.

53. Wood SA, Liu P-J, Hanoch Y, Estevez-Cores S. Importance of numeracy as a risk factor for elder financial exploitation in a community sample. *J Gerontol B Psychol Sci Soc Sci.* 2016;71(6):978–986.

54. Liu P-J, Wood S, Xi P, Berger DE, Wilber K. The role of social support in elder financial exploitation using a community sample. *Innov Aging.* 2017;1(1):igx016.

55. Asp EW, Manzel K, Koestner B, Denburg N, Tranel D. Benefit of the doubt: a new view of the role of the prefrontal cortex in executive functioning and decision making. *Front Neurosci.* 2013;7:86.

56. Gamble KJ, Boyle P, Yu L, Bennett D. The causes and consequences of financial fraud among older Americans. Center for Retirement Research at Boston College. 2014;13. Available at: https://crr.bc.edu/wp-content/uploads/2014/11/wp_2014-13.pdf. Accessed May 19, 2021.

57. Securities Industry and Financial Markets Association. Senior investor protection toolkit. 2021. Available at: https://www.sifma.org/resources/general/senior-investor-protection-toolkit. Accessed March 5, 2021.

58. US Census Bureau. Survey of income and program participation: Wealth, asset ownership, and debt of households. 2015. https://www.census.gov/data/tables/2015/demo/wealth/wealth-asset-ownership.html. Accessed March 5, 2021.

59. US Government Accountability Office. Elder justice: National strategy needed to effectively combat elder financial exploitation. Report to Congressional Requesters. 2012. Available at: https://www.gao.gov/assets/gao-13-110.pdf. Accessed June 2, 2021.

60. American Bar Association Commission on Law and Aging. Adult protective services reporting Laws. 2020. https://www.americanbar.org/content/dam/aba/administrative/law_aging/2020-elder-abuse-reporting-chart.pdf. Accessed March 5, 2021.

61. National Sherriffs Association. National association of triads. 2019. Available at: https://www.sheriffs.org/programs/national-triad. Accessed March 5, 2021.

62. Gassoumis ZD, Navarro AE, Wilber KH. Protecting victims of elder financial exploitation: The role of an elder abuse forensic center in referring victims for conservatorship. *Aging Ment Health.* 2015;19(9):790–798.

63. Navarro AE, Gassoumis ZD, Wilber KH. Holding abusers accountable: An elder abuse forensic center increases criminal prosecution of financial exploitation. *Gerontologist.* 2013;53(2): 303–312.

64. Deane S. Elder Financial Exploitation: Why it is a concern, what regulators are doing about it and looking ahead. Office of the Investor Advocate, US Securities and Exchange Commission. 2018. Available at: https://www.sec.gov/files/elder-financial-exploitation.pdf. Accessed March 5, 2021.

65. Senior Safe Act of 2017, HR 3758. 115th Congress (2017).

66. American Bar Association. Resources and research. Commission on Law and Aging. https://www.americanbar.org/groups/law_aging/resources. Accessed March 5, 2021.

67. Center for Benefits. Meet the BECs. National Council on Aging, Benefits Enrollment Centers. January 2021. Available at: https://www.ncoa.org/article/meet-our-benefits-enrollment-centers. Accessed March 5, 2021.

68. Kwiatkowski J, Gyurmey T. Program of All-Inclusive Care for the Elderly (PACE): Integrating Health and Social Care Since 1973. *R I Med J.* 2019;102(5)30–32.

69. Hirth V, Baskins J, Dever-Bumba M. Program of all-inclusive care (PACE): past, present, and future. *J Am Med Dir Assoc.* 2009;10(3):155–160.

70. Archibald N, Soper M, Smith L, Kruse A, Wiener JM. Integrating Care through Dual Eligible Special Needs Plans (D-SNPs): Opportunities and Challenges. US Department of Health and Human Services, Office of the Assistant Secretary for Planning and Evaluation. 2019. Available at: https://aspe.hhs.gov/basic-report/integrating-care-through-dual-eligible-special-needs-plans-d-snps-opportunities-and-challenges. Accessed March 5, 2021.

71. Glymour MM, Manly JJ. Lifecourse social conditions and racial and ethnic patterns of cognitive aging. *Neuropsychol Rev.* 2008;18(3):223–254.

72. Topchik M, Gross K, Pinette M, Brown T, Balfour B, Kein H. The Rural Health Safety Net Under Pressure: Rural Hospital Vulnerability. Chartis Center for Rural Health, The Chartis Group. 2020. Available at: https://www.chartis.com/forum/insight/the-rural-health-safety-net-under-pressure-rural-hospital-vulnerability. Accessed March 5, 2021.

73. Coughlin SS. How Many Principles for Public Health Ethics? *Open Public Health J.* 2008;1:8–16.

74. Free C. A 95-year-old woman was swindled out of nearly $18,000. Local towns rallied and got her money back. *The Washington Post.* January 29, 2020. Available at: https://www.washingtonpost.com/lifestyle/2020/01/29/95-year-old-woman-was-swindled-out-18000-town-rallied-got-her-money-back/. Accessed June 21, 2021.

Policies and Impacts for Healthy Aging

Patricia M. Alt, PhD, Elaine T. Jurkowski, PhD, MSW, and
Gwyneth M. Eliasson, JD, MPH

BACKGROUND AND DESCRIPTION

We have discussed a variety of programs and services throughout this book in efforts to understand how to address social determinants of health to support healthy aging. The backbone of the programs and services are social policies. This chapter will focus on several of the main policies that have been addressed throughout this text.

Public health as a field needs to be aware of the key factors which can help or hinder healthy aging. At a minimum, public health professionals should be aware of basic population changes, and of the public policies that have been put in place over time to help older adults maintain and sustain their health. This chapter will examine the major policies and programs affecting people as they grow older. It is particularly relevant as the population is living longer, which is projected to have a large impact on the health care system.

Key factors include significant projected growth in the older population, both in numbers and in percentage of the overall population. The 2018 Profile of Older Americans was developed by the Administration on Aging (AOA), using secondary data from the Center for Health Statistics and census data. It points out that the population aged 65 and older represented 15.6% of the population in 2017, and is projected to increase to 21.6% of the population by 2040, including a 123% increase in those older than 85 in that time period.[1]

As the Healthy People 2030 Framework[2] and the 10 Essential Public Health Services[3] point out, there are many areas where public health supports are key to advance healthy aging (see Appendix 19A and Appendix 19B). This chapter's focus is on the legal and administrative process which seeks to maintain those supports.

RELEVANT POLICIES AND LEGISLATION

There are multiple policies which have been passed over the years which have a direct impact on healthy aging. This section of the chapter provides an overview of some of their key features, the ways in which they continue to evolve, and the ongoing pressures faced in implementing them.

Social Security Act (1935), Public Law 74–271

Social Security was created as part of the New Deal response to the Great Depression in the 1930s. President Franklin Delano Roosevelt was a strong advocate, and it was seen as a way to ensure that workers have an income after their retirement. From the beginning, full eligibility has been linked to age, initially 65 years, but very gradual increases in the eligibility age for full benefits have been included to keep the system in financial balance as the population is living longer. Workers are required to pay into Social Security through a specific tax deduction from paychecks which is matched by their employers, and retirees receive a monthly amount related to their contributions, including cost-of-living increases determined by the Social Security Administration. The system was designed to be financed entirely by payroll taxes and initially covered only industrial workers. When it was created, the average life expectancy was less than 65, so the assumption was that it would be possible for individuals' benefits to be covered by their contributions. Over time, that has shifted, with people living longer and the number of beneficiaries drastically increasing, while the number of contributing workers has dwindled by comparison.[4]

The Social Security Act has expanded its focus over time, as it now covers both Old Age, Survivor, and Disability Insurance, and the Supplemental Security Income (SSI) program, which provides a means tested, income support program for low-income older adults, the blind, and the totally disabled. Initially, Social Security funded people with blindness, maternal and child health, as well as public health infrastructure and services. These areas are still currently funded under Social Security, however the list of titles has also expanded so that Social Security does not fund solely retirement. In 2020, Social Security was still based exclusively on payroll taxes and had funds to pay 100% of benefits for about 15 more years. If there are no changes before then, the revenues will be enough to support an estimated 80% of promised benefits. The last time there was a projected shortfall (i.e., in the 1980s), Congress increased Social Security taxes and changed benefits (e.g., delaying full retirement by 2 years). Something similar could still be done. Given the growth in numbers covered by these programs and the slower growth in the funds available, in addition to the tendency to tap into "prudent reserves" for other expenses, there is considerable worry that the programs will be unable to support future generations of retirees.[5]

Advocacy organizations such as the AARP and the National Committee to Preserve Social Security and Medicare have been actively lobbying to make sure that these benefits continue to exist as public insurance programs, in spite of various presidential efforts to privatize them. The three key projected trends being watched by policy advocates are the growth in federal spending on older adults (i.e., mostly Social Security and Medicare); the shrinking availability of caregivers, both family and paid; and the growing concentration of older adults in certain geographic areas.[6]

Medicare and Medicaid/Medical Assistance (1965), Public Law 89–97

In 1965, the federal government passed a key amendment to the Social Security Act, creating two programs affecting the health of older and disabled adults. These programs were created to fill coverage gaps left by private insurance, and were the result of negotiations among the supporters of a variety of proposals. Medicare was established as a federally funded program with two parts: Part A for hospital insurance, and optional Part B for care by physicians and preventative care. Part B is chosen by almost all beneficiaries because it is heavily subsidized by federal general revenues. Over time, Medicare has been expanded with Part C, allowing optional managed care plans encompassing Parts A and B, as well as additional services and optional Medicare Part D, providing a prescription drug coverage plan for enrollees.[7]

Medicaid was created as a state-federal program for the poor, but it also covers individuals who were both old enough for Medicare and poor enough to qualify for Medicaid. As Medicaid is administered by states, it has had considerable variation in coverage. It is also the key insurer for long-term care nursing homes and home and community services nationwide. The federal and state governments jointly set rules concerning who is covered and which services are provided. The federal government outlines which populations must be covered and which benefits must be offered, but the states have significant flexibility in determining how it operates in their state. It exists primarily to cover low-income adults, children, those with disabilities, and older adults for health care benefits.[8]

Both Medicare and Medicaid have been altered repeatedly, sometimes to improve care for recipients, sometimes in efforts to save funds and/or privatize benefits. Some of the key changes are described later in this chapter.

Older Americans Act (1965), Public Law 89–73

In 1965, the Older Americans Act (OAA) was passed, creating the AOA within the US Department of Health and Human Services. Working with state and local entities through the national aging services network, the OAA has provided a range of community-based services for older adults including congregate and home delivered meals, case management, specialized transportation services, adult day care, employment and volunteer programs, senior centers and activities, personal care, homemaker and chore services, legal support, health promotion, and disease prevention. As of 2012, the AOA was reorganized into the new Administration for Community Living (ACL), which includes both aging and disability services. It continues to focus strongly on the social determinants of health for older adults, and for their caregivers.[9]

The Fair Housing Amendments Act of 1988, Public Law 90–480

This legislation made it possible for older adults and people with disabilities to qualify for low cost public housing. The Fair Housing Amendments Act of 1988 required that a certain number of accessible housing units be created in all new multifamily housing to accommodate older adults, people with mobility impairments, and people with disabilities. The act covers both public and private homes, not only those in receipt of federal funding. It also addresses the needs of people with disabilities, while the Civil Rights Act of 1988 addressed minorities but did not give attention to people with disabilities, who are also often older adults.[10]

Americans With Disabilities Act (1990), Public Law 101–336

The Americans with Disabilities Act (ADA) was created in 1990. As a comprehensive piece of civil rights legislation, it prohibits discrimination and guarantees that people with disabilities have the same opportunities for employment, shopping, and receiving state and local government programs and services as all citizens. It was modeled after the Civil Rights Act of 1964, and the Rehabilitation Act of 1973, aiming to provide equal opportunity for people with disabilities. It was further strengthened by the case of *Olmstead v. LC* in 1999, in which the Supreme Court required states to eliminate unnecessary segregation of persons with disabilities and to ensure that they receive services in the most integrated setting appropriate to their needs.[10] The five titles within the ADA assure that not only people with disabilities, but also older adults, can participate as fully as possible in community life. It also mandates public services (Title II) as well as private services (Title III) to provide accommodations for retail and public services. Title IV mandates alternative communication, such as closed caption options on the television and movie theaters which benefits older adults with hearing loss.[10] In the ten-year anniversary of *Olmstead*, in 2009, the Civil Rights Division of the Justice Department launched an aggressive effort to better enforce *Olmstead v. LC*. Additionally, President Obama declared The Year of Community Living to address isolation and discrimination against people with disabilities across the age span.

Key Medicare and Medicaid Changes (1990–2010)

Multiple laws affecting healthy aging were passed during the decades since the creation of Medicare and Medicaid. They included the Balanced Budget Act of 1997, which built on a previous history of seeking to move Medicare beneficiaries into privately run managed care plans as a way to reduce costs. It sought severe cuts in overall spending, and encouraged seniors to join Medicare + Choice plans. In 2003, the Medicare Prescription Drug, Improvement, and Modernization Act changed the Medicare + Choice plan to Medicare Advantage, with the creation of an optional outpatient drug benefit (Medicare Part D), addition of Health Savings Accounts, and a variation in premium by participants' income level. It also created the doughnut hole in payments, where patients would pay an annual deductible, and about 25% of drug costs up to a certain annual limit ($2,250 at first), after which they paid 100% of costs until total costs for the year exceeded $5,100, when the program would cover 95% of the remaining costs for that year. The amounts went up every year, but the doughnut hole remained until the Affordable Care Act (ACA)was created, including provisions to gradually eliminate it.[11]

The Elder Justice Act (2010), Public Law 109–137

The Elder Justice Act was created to address the abuse, neglect, and exploitation of older adults at the federal level. It established the Elder Justice Coordinating Committee to coordinate activities related to older adult abuse, neglect, and exploitation across the federal government. It also provided authority for ACL programs including: Elder Abuse Prevention Demonstrations; Elder Justice Innovation Grants; state grants to enhance Adult Protective Services (APS); voluntary consensus guidelines for state APS systems; and the creation of a National Adult Maltreatment Reporting System.[12]

Patient Protection and Affordable Care Act (2010), Public Law 111–148

Also known as the ACA or Obamacare, this major federal health reform law passed in 2010, after decades of attempts to modernize and improve funding for the American health system. Its passage involved considerable negotiation and compromise, but it included some major changes in the health insurance system. These were

1. The individual mandate, requiring that individuals maintain minimum essential insurance coverage or face financial penalties. This was repealed in 2017 and effective in 2019. Some states have since instituted their own requirements. Subsidies were included for those who are not able to acquire minimum coverage, but do not qualify for Medicaid;
2. The second change was that insurers were prohibited from considering preexisting conditions when determining whether to accept an applicant, required to cover certain preventive and immunization services, and guarantee coverage for dependent children 26 years of age or younger;
3. The creation of health insurance exchanges or marketplaces nationwide, or in each state, to facilitate individuals' shopping for coverage; and

4. Finally, the ACA required expansion of Medicaid, although many states have resisted it and multiple court cases have ensued.

While the struggle over this law has waxed and waned over time, the Supreme Court did rule in 2012 that the individual mandate was a valid exercise of taxing power, although disagreements about its allowability under the Commerce Clause continue.[13]

Its implications for healthy aging are critical, as it not only requires insurance coverage but also prohibits discrimination against those with preexisting conditions, especially among older adults aged 60–64. Especially if individuals choose to use managed care models for their Medicare coverage and/or are low-income enough to be eligible for both Medicare and Medicaid, this law aims to ensure their access to preventive and sustainable care.

IMPACT and PAMA Acts (2014), Public Law 113–85

In 2014, following up on the ACA's requirement that the Centers for Medicare and Medicaid Services (CMS) explore ways to improve care coordination between and across providers, two key pieces of legislation were passed. The Protecting Access to Medicare Act (PAMA) required that CMS specify an all cause, all condition hospital readmission measure for nursing homes and an all condition, risk adjusted rate for potentially preventable hospital readmission.[14] The Improving Medicare Post-Acute Care Transformation (IMPACT) Act required that post-acute care (PAC) providers report standardized patient and resident assessment data, data on quality measures, and data on resource use and other measures. It also requires that the data be interoperable, allowing for its exchange among PAC and other providers.[15] Both of these acts work toward improving measurement of hospital readmissions and standardizing measures for resident assessment, resource use, and quality data. The timeline for implementation of these acts called for required standardized quality and resource use measures, and standardized assessment data to be in place by 2019.[15]

CHRONIC Care Act of 2018, Public Law 115–128

After multiple resubmissions and revisions, the Creating High-Quality Results and Outcomes Necessary to Improve Chronic Care Act was passed and signed in February 2018. It made significant policy changes to advance the goals of integrated person centered care for Medicare beneficiaries and those dually eligible for Medicare and Medicaid. It addresses three aspects of care; (1) it encourages the use of flexible new tools and strategies to better manage care for individuals with complex needs by giving Medicare Advantage and accountable care organization (ACO) plans greater flexibility to cover nonmedical benefits for high need members, telehealth benefits, and allowing ACOs to provide incentives for beneficiaries to choose high-value care; (2) it protects and builds on key programs serving individuals with complex care needs, including authorizing Special Needs Plans (SNPs) where managed care organizations can service high need Medicare beneficiaries, and extends and expands a demonstration of physicians serving very high need beneficiaries in their homes, rather than institutional care; and (3) it signals that care coordination and integration are explicit and essential purposes of SNPs, requiring that they create unified plans for dual eligible individuals and a single pathway for grievances and appeals.[16] The impact of this policy is still under evaluation through the Government Accountability Office.

RAISE Family Caregivers Act of 2018, Public Law 115–119

The Recognize, Assist, Include, Support, and Engage Family Caregivers Act (RAISE Family Caregivers Act) became law with strong bipartisan support in January 2018. It directs the Secretary of Health and Human Services to develop a national family caregiving strategy, led by the ACL. It required the establishment of a Family Caregiving Advisory Council to provide advice and recommendations and identify best practices for recognizing and supporting family caregivers. It defines "family caregiver" as "an adult family member or other individual who has a significant relationship with, and who provides a broad range of assistance to, an individual with a chronic or other health condition, disability, or functional limitation."[17]

In May 2019, the John A. Hartford Foundation awarded a three-year grant to the National Academy for State Health Policy to support the efforts of the council. It established the RAISE Act Family Caregiver Resource and Dissemination Center as a focal point for resources, technical assistance, and policy analysis for states and the stakeholder caregiver community. It also created a faculty of experts in the field to inform the work of the center and the council. The Council established three subcommittees for further discussion: (1) Assist Caregivers in Optimizing Care and Support for their Loved Ones; (2) Enable Caregivers to Provide Care While Maintaining their Health and Well-Being; and (3) Enhance Public Awareness and Education and Engage Nongovernmental Entities to Support Caregivers. As the Council moved forward, it maintained a strong emphasis on supporting the physical, emotional, and financial well-being of family caregivers and care recipients. There was a robust effort to gain public input, as well as an inventory of Federal efforts to support family caregivers. Their ongoing work continues, with meeting links available on the ACL website.[18]

SIGNIFICANT POLICIES PASSED IN 2020

In response to the COVID-19 health crisis in 2020, multiple laws were passed, several of which had significant meaning for healthy aging. While their funding streams and targeted programs sometimes overlapped, the basic public health goal was maintaining and improving programs during crisis situations. The following sections will highlight their likely impact on healthy aging.

The Coronavirus Preparedness and Response Supplemental Act, Public Law 116–123

Passed on March 6, 2020, this initial response gave emergency funding for federal agencies to begin to deal with the pandemic, including appropriations for research on potential treatments; money through the Centers for Disease Control and Prevention for state and local responses; and funding for grants under the Health Resources and Services Administration to improve care for people who were geographically isolated and economically or medically vulnerable.[19]

Families First Coronavirus Response Act, Public Law 116–127

Passed on March 18, 2020, the Families First Coronavirus Response Act aimed to address the outbreak's domestic outbreak, including strengthened support for nutrition services through the ACL, expanded emergency family and medical leave support, emergency paid sick leave due to quarantine or caregiving for someone in quarantine, and coverage for diagnostic procedures for the coronavirus. It eliminated Medicare cost sharing for outpatient visits and diagnostic procedures, and required Medicaid coverage of diagnostic testing, with greater federal financial support. The requirements of the Supplemental Nutrition Assistance Program (SNAP) were eased, allowing states to request expanded access to nutrition services for households in areas affected by the coronavirus. In addition, Personal Respiratory Protective Devices were covered when used during an "emergency period."[20]

Supporting Older Americans Act of 2020, Public Law 116–131

After multiple revisions, and after being renamed from the Dignity in Aging Act of 2019 to the Supporting Older Americans Act of 2020, the reauthorization of the 1965 OAA through 2024 was passed and signed into law in March 2020. It included "modernizing definitions" for the Administration on Aging's activities, expanding the focus on supporting the health of older adults across a spectrum of programs, and providing needed support in the midst of unanticipated crises. It also included a seven percent increase in funding for 2020, and a six percent per year increase for the next four fiscal years for each part of the OAA.[21]

Section 124 of the new Title I "modernizes the existing Interagency Coordinating Committee on Healthy Aging and Age-Friendly Communities"[21] as recommended by the committee. Under Title II – Improving Grants for State and Community Programs on Aging, the first section (Section 201) is entitled "Social Determinants of Health."[10] It aims to ensure that state and community programs on aging measure impacts related to social determinants of health of older individuals. In keeping with the Older Americans Act's history, the renewed law continues to support congregate and home-delivered meals, case management, specialized transportation services, employment and volunteer programs, adult day care, senior centers and activities, personal care, homemaker and chore services, legal support, health promotion, and disease prevention. It also emphasizes the importance of family caregivers.

Among the many programs reauthorized was the RAISE Family Caregivers Act for an additional year. The act makes improvements to the National Family Caregiver Support program by more clearly defining "caregiver assessment" and requiring the Assistant Secretary for Aging to identify best practices for caregiver assessment, award funds for activities of national significance to improve support provided to caregivers, and provide technical assistance on how to promote and implement caregiver assessments. It requires the Assistant Secretary on Aging to report to Congress on the use and impact of these assessments, including recommendations to state and area agencies on aging for implementing caregiver assessments.[22]

Coronavirus Aid, Relief, and Economic Security Act (CARES), Public Law 116–136

On March 27, 2020, the CARES Act was signed into law, as the third and largest legislative effort to address the COVID-19 outbreak. It is quite complicated, but it builds on the previous efforts in its health-related provisions affecting older adults. Its two main parts are Division A, addressing multiple programs and mandatory spending provisions, and Division B, containing emergency discretionary funding. The provisions listed below focus on the most relevant areas for the health of older adults.

Division A includes
- Provisions to address issues related to drug, device, and equipment supplies;
- An amendment to the Families First Coronavirus Response Act to clarify that tests for coronavirus are to be covered without cost-sharing by private insurance and Medicare, and by Medicaid, even if the test has not been approved by the US Food and Drug Administration;
- Provisions allowing broader use of telehealth services through Medicare, private health insurance, and other federally-funded providers (such as community health centers); and
- Reauthorization of multiple programs to strengthen rural community health.

Division B includes appropriations for multiple programs, including
- Overall, at least $242.4 billion provided for health or health-related activities, with more than half of it directed to the Department of Health and Human Services (HHS);

- More than $25 billion for domestic food assistance, including school programs, SNAP, and the emergency food assistance program; and
- $1 billion for the purchase of personal protective equipment and medical equipment such as ventilators.[23]

Telehealth may have a tremendous impact for older adults and the longest lasting impact since it provides access to services which otherwise may not be utilized.

Administration for Community Living Grants from CARES

In April 2020, HHS announced that the ACL would issue $955 million in grants to help meet the needs of older adults and those with disabilities as they face the spread of COVID-19. The CARES Act provides supplemental funding for programs in the network of community-based organizations established to help older adults and those with disabilities stay healthy and live independently in their communities. This network includes Area Agencies on Aging, Centers for Independent Living, native American Programs, Aging and Disability Resources Centers, senior centers, faith-based organizations, and other nonprofits serving older and disabled adults in the community.

The CARES Act funding included $200 million for Home and Community Based Services to help older adults minimize their exposure to COVID-19. These include personal care assistance; help with household chores and grocery shopping; transportation to essential services when necessary; and case management. It also included $480 million for home-delivered meals for older adults, including drive-through or "grab-and-go" meals in place of congregate meals, due to social distancing measures.

Other areas of expanded funding which particularly support healthy aging included $100 million for the National Family Caregiving Support Program, expanding a range of services to help family and informal caregivers provide support for their loved ones at home. These included counseling, respite care, training, and connecting people to needed information. Another $20 million was provided to support State Long-term Care Ombudsman programs in providing consumer advocacy services for residents of long-term care facilities, as their families were restricted in their ability to visit, and the disease took a heavy toll on both residents and staff.

Continuing the ongoing mission of the ACL, an additional $50 million was provided for Aging and Disability Resource Centers to fund programs to connect people most at risk of COVID-19 to services needed to practice social distancing, and to mitigate issues such as social isolation and the need for support in applying for services, care coordination, returning home after hospitalization, and other concerns. The funds were awarded to states, territories, and tribes in April 2020 for allocation to local service providers, using formulas defined under the programs' authorizing statutes.[24]

CONCLUSION: CHALLENGES AND OPPORTUNITIES FOR PUBLIC HEALTH

The realm of policy can be both a challenge and opportunity for public health, especially within the context of addressing social determinants of public health. A major challenge includes funding and the lack of available/appropriated funds for policies which have been signed into public law. Opportunities include the collaboration with a variety of partners, private, public and professional, to lobby for policies which will impact the public health arena which addresses older adults and their caregivers. It also includes the collaboration with other interest groups interested in the well-being of older adults and their health outcomes.

Shifting Situations

Given the rapidly changing situation of the nation's health, strengthening the social determinants of healthy aging has become more crucial. These include social support in the face of considerable isolation; preventive measures to avoid further spread of epidemic conditions; and expanded funding for development and access to care (i.e., potential treatments and vaccines). Older adults and their caregivers, whether in long-term care facilities, hospitals, or at home, have been some of the most vulnerable populations to public health initiatives and crises. Public health as a field has been active in identifying the problems, and in promoting advocacy to support valuable programs at all levels of government to meet the critical needs of our older adult population.

CASE STUDY

Practice Example: Medical-Legal Partnerships

Under the official poverty measure in 2017, 4.7 million adults ages 65 and older lived in poverty, with an annual individual income of $11,756 or less; under the Supplemental Poverty Measure, however, the total increased to 7.2 million older adults.[25] A 2017 study found that 56% of low-income older adult households had experienced a civil legal problem in the past year, but they faced a wide justice gap: 87% of their problems received inadequate or no professional legal help.[26] Often, these civil legal issues, such as economic insecurity (e.g., Social Security benefits); health care gaps (e.g., Medicare coverage); and food insecurity (e.g., Food Stamps (SNAP) applications) have the potential to adversely affect health.

Medical-legal partnerships (MLPs) embed legal services within health care settings, thus offering a holistic approach to determinants of health as well as systemic advances in both health promotion and disease prevention. Basically, MLPs place lawyers at hospitals and clinics to help patients with legal problems affecting their health, like housing conditions triggering asthma attacks that might require emergency room visits or even hospital stays.

As of 2020, 450 health organizations have successfully developed MLPs in 49 states and Washington, DC.[27] These partnerships are usually between health care institutions (i.e., hospitals, clinics, or medical schools) and legal assistance organizations (i.e., Legal Aid/Legal Services offices, bar associations, or law schools). Founded in 2006, the National Center for Medical-Legal Partnership (NCMLP) supports MLPs through education, research, and technical assistance; for MLPs working with older adults, NCMLP's resources include an issue brief [28] and a fact sheet.[29]

In 2020, NCMLP estimated that 40 MLPs, less than 10% of all MLPs, specified that they worked with older adults (Ellen Lawton, JD, email communication, July 16, 2020). One notable example is the Medical-Legal Partnership for Seniors (MLPS), a partnership among the University of California Hastings College of the Law, the University of California San Francisco Medical Center, and the San Francisco Veterans Administration Medical Center. The MLPS Clinic provides "advance health care, estate planning, public benefits, and wrap-around legal services to older adult patients."[30] The legal team meets clients in their home, at their hospital bed or clinic appointment, or in their long-term care facility.[31] Innovative MLPs for older adults offer lessons on implementation for new initiatives to advocate for this overlooked, and underserved, population.

REFERENCES

1. Administration for Community Living. 2018 Profile of older Americans. 2018. Available at: https://acl.gov/sites/default/files/Aging%20and%20Disability%20in%20America/2018Older-AmericansProfile.pdf. Accessed March 5, 2021

2. US Department of Health and Human Services. Healthy People 2030 framework. Office of Disease Prevention and Health Promotion. 2020. Available at: https://health.gov/healthypeople/about/healthy-people-2030-framework. Accessed March 5, 2021.

3. Centers for Disease Control and Prevention. 10 Essential public health services. Available at: https://www.cdc.gov/publichealthgateway/publichealthservices/essentialhealthservices.html. Accessed March 5, 2021.

4. Isaacs KP, Choudhury S. The growing gap in life expectancy by income: Recent evidence and implications for the social security retirement age. Congressional Research Service. 2017. Available at: https://crsreports.congress.gov/product/pdf/R/R44846. Accessed March 5, 2021.

5. Social Security Administration. Understanding the benefits. 2021. Available at: https://www.ssa.gov/pubs/EN-05-10024.pdf. Accessed March 5, 2021.

6. Super N. Three trends shaping the politics of aging in America. *Public Policy Aging Rep.* 2020;30(2):39–45.

7. Centers for Medicare and Medicaid Services Medicare program-general information. 2021. Available at: https://www.cms.gov/Medicare/Medicare-General-Information/MedicareGenInfo/index. Accessed March 5, 2021.

8. Centers for Medicare and Medicaid Services. Medicaid. Available at: https://www.medicaid.gov/medicaid/index.html. Accessed March 5, 2021.

9. Administration for Community Living. Older Americans Act. 2020. Available at: https://acl.gov/about-acl/authorizing-statutes/older-americans-act. Accessed March 5, 2021.

10. Jurkowski ET. *Policy and Program Planning for Older Adults and People With Disabilities: Practice Realities and Visions.* 2nd ed. New York, NY: Springer Publishing; 2019.

11. Bunis D. Understanding Medicare's options: Parts A, B, C, and D. AARP. 2021. Available at: https://www.aarp.org/health/medicare-insurance/info-01-2011/understanding_medicare_the_plans.html. Accessed March 5, 2021.

12. Administration for Community Living. The Elder Justice Act. 2017. Available at: https://acl.gov/about-acl/elder-justice-act. Accessed March 5, 2021.

13. Levitt L. The Affordable Care Act's enduring resilience. *J Health Polit Policy Law.* 2020; 45(4):609–616.

14. Centers for Medicare and Medicaid Services. PAMA Regulations. 2021. Available at: https://www.cms.gov/Medicare/Medicare-Fee-for-Service-Payment/ClinicalLabFeeSched/PAMA-Regulations.html. Accessed March 5, 2021.

15. Centers for Medicare and Medicaid Services. IMPACT Act of 2014 Data standardization and cross setting measures. 2018. Available at: https://www.cms.gov/Medicare/Quality-Initiatives-Patient-Assessment-Instruments/Post-Acute-Care-Quality-Initiatives/IMPACT-Act-of-2014/IMPACT-Act-of-2014-Data Standardization-and-Cross-Setting-Measures. Accessed March 5, 2021.

16. Tumlinson A, Burke M, Alkema, G. The CHRONIC Care Act of 2018: Advancing care for adults with complex needs. The SCAN Foundation. 2018. Available at: https://www.thescanfoundation.org/publications/the-chronic-care-act-of-2018-advancing-care-for-adults-with-complex-needs. Accessed March 5, 2021.

17. AARP. RAISE Family Caregivers Act promises federal help. 2019. Available at: https://www.aarp.org/politics-society/advocacy/caregiving-advocacy/info-2015/raise-family-caregivers-act.html. Accessed March 5, 2021.

18. Administration for Community Living. RAISE Family Caregiving Advisory Council. 2021. Available at: https://acl.gov/programs/support-caregivers/raise-family-caregiving-advisory-council. Accessed March 5, 2021.

19. Oum S, Wexler A, Kates J. The US response to Coronavirus: Summary of the Coronavirus Preparedness and Response Supplemental Appropriations Act, 2020. Kaiser Family Foundation. 2020. Available at: https://www.kff.org/global-health-policy/issue-brief/the-u-s-response-to-coronavirus-summary-of-the-Coronavirus-Preparedness-and-Response-Supplemental-Appropriations-Act. Accessed March 5, 2021.

20. Moss K, Dawson L, Long M, et al. The Families First Coronavirus Response Act: Summary of key provisions. Kaiser Family Foundation. 2020. Available at: https://www.kff.org/global-health-policy/issue-brief/the-families-first-coronavirus-response-act-summary-of-key-provisions. Accessed March 5, 2021.

21. Robertson L. A Renewed commitment to our nations older adults. Administration for Community Living. 2020. Available at: https://acl.gov/news-and-events/acl-blog/renewed-commitment-our-nations-older-adults. Accessed March 5, 2021.

22. Supporting Older Americans Act of 2020. Public Law 116-131-116th Congress. 2020. Available at: https://www.congress.gov/116/plaws/publ131/PLAW-116publ131.pdf. Accessed March 5, 2021.

23. Moss K, Wexler A, Dawson L, et al. The Coronavirus Aid, Relief, and Economic Security Act: Summary of key health provisions. Kaiser Family Foundation 2020. Available at: https://www.kff.org/global-health-policy/issue-brief/the-coronavirus-aid-relief-and-economic-security-act-summary-of-key-health-provisions. Accessed March 5, 2021.

24. Administration for Community Living. ACL announces nearly $1 Billion in CARES Act grants to support older adults and people with disabilities in the community during the COVID-19 emergency. 2020. Available at: https://acl.gov/news-and-events/announcements/acl-announces-nearly-1-billion-cares-act-grants-support-older-adults. Accessed March 5, 2021.

25. Cubanski J, Koma W, Damico A, Neuman T. How many seniors live in poverty? Kaiser Family Foundation. 2018. Available at: https://www.kff.org/medicare/issue-brief/how-many-seniors-live-in-poverty. Accessed March 5, 2021.

26. Legal Services Corporation. The justice gap: Measuring the unmet civil legal needs of low-income Americans. 2017. Available at: https://www.lsc.gov/sites/default/files/images/TheJusticeGap-FullReport.pdf. Accessed March 5, 2021.

27. National Center For Medical Legal Partnership. Home page. 2021. Available at: https://medical-legalpartnership.org. Accessed March 5, 2021.

28. Tobin Tyler E. Socially vulnerable older adults and medical-legal partnership. National Center for Medical Legal Partnership. 2019. Available at: https://medical-legalpartnership.org/wp-content/uploads/2019/03/Socially-Vulnerable-Older-Adults-and-MLP.pdf. Accessed March 5, 2021.

29. National Center for Medical-Legal Partnership and National Center for Equitable Care for Elders. The role of medical-legal partnerships for socially vulnerable older adults. National

Center for Medical-Legal Partnership. 2020. Available at: https://medical-legalpartnership. org/wp-content/uploads/2020/07/Elder-Fact-Sheet-July-2020.pdf. Accessed March 5, 2021.

30. UC Hastings Law San Francisco. Medical-legal partnership for seniors (MLPS). 2020. Available at: https://www.uchastings.edu/academics/centers/consortium/initiatives/mlps. Accessed March 5, 2021.

31. Hooper S, Teitelbaum J, Parekh A, Fabiny A. Legal advocacy to improve care for older adults with complex needs. Health Affairs Blog. May 17, 2019. Available at: https://www.healthaffairs. org/do/10.1377/hblog20190514.199890/full. Accessed March 5, 2021.

Conclusions and Visions for the Future

Elaine T. Jurkowski, PhD, MSW and M. Aaron Guest, PhD, MPH, MSW

Throughout this book, we have attempted to weave through the social determinants of health to examine the issues associated with healthy aging. We also examine potential interventions and resources that the public health and allied health professional can utilize when understanding the issues, building interventions, conducting assessments, and evolving policies. In this chapter, we re-examine the central issues developed throughout the chapters and propose some visions for the future. We hope that our visions will be embraced by practitioners throughout the public health system as we strive towards healthier communities for people growing older.

HEALTH AND HEALTH CARE

Within this section, we examine dementia and brain changes in aging, polypharmacy, hearing, oral health care, vision, and mental health and aging. Access to care and quality care is also a theme within many of the chapters; thus, we did not develop a specific chapter for this social determinant. In summary, each of the specific areas are reviewed and recommendations for the future are proposed.

Dementia and Brain Changes in Aging

As our understanding of dementia continues to evolve, it is necessary to adopt culturally sensitive and relevant programming to meet the needs of an increasingly diverse population of older adults. Moreover, considering recent evidence suggesting that changes in the brain associated with Alzheimer's Disease may begin years or even decades before symptoms emerge, these efforts should not be restricted to older age but instead should be viewed within the context of the life course. While researchers are working to identify underlying pathways and mechanisms that may shape trajectories of poor cognitive health, state and federal public health agencies are shifting more resources in response to the expected increases in the number of adults affected by dementia. However, in many circumstances, state and federal funding are insufficient to target and fund programs related to healthy aging.

Specifically, public health can do the following:

1. Recognize the role of aging across the life span and how healthy behaviors that protect physical health can also protect cognitive health,
2. Utilize existing infrastructure for chronic conditions to also address dementia, and
3. Employ broad-based changes to policies, systems, and environments to ensure access to services, a competent and dementia capable workforce, and a public educated in cognitive aging, risk reduction, and early detection.

Polypharmacy and Medication Safety in Older Adults

Polypharmacy is a real issue and factor that plays a role in the functioning or lack of functioning among people growing older. The number of medications that individuals often have prescribed is staggering, and a grasp of what these medications are and how they interact with each other is also paramount to optimal functioning within older adults. Challenges addressed include the increased cost of medications and the management of multiple chronic conditions with medications to optimize functioning. In terms of future visions, public health can

1. Monitor and assess the extent of medications which potentially can be over prescribed and work with providers to ensure that such medications do not become overly depended upon leading to other health programs,
2. Advocate for, promote, and evaluate the Prescription Drug Monitoring Program across all states, and
3. Advocate for policies to provide access to affordable medications for older people.

Hearing Within Healthy Aging

Hearing can impact one's functioning and quality of life. Degenerative diseases which impact one's auditory sense can play a central role in the ability to function in the least restrictive environment day to day. Auditory issues can also impact balance and falls. Occupational exposures across one's life span can definitely have an impact on one's hearing later in life. In terms of future visions, public health can do the following:

1. Facilitate public awareness through accurate and relevant health information, and
2. Utilize evidence to promote policy recommendations and promote interventions.

Oral Health and Vision Care

This chapter affirms the relationship between oral health and overall health. Oral health impacts not only one's overall health, but has many other manifestations including nutrition, self-esteem, and quality of life. Access to oral health care can also be limited by health literacy and the assumption that being edentulous means that one does not need to seek oral health examinations.

Many cancers associated with oral health can be detected through regular screenings, which also leads to the importance of public education and access to oral health services. In terms of oral health and vision care, and future visions, public health can

1. Promote public awareness and create health literacy for older adults within the area of oral health,
2. Expand access to clinical care and routine screenings through local venues to include senior nutrition sites, community events, and parish nursing programs,
3. Enhance public health capacity through assessment, assurance, and policy development, and
4. Develop partnerships with other allied health partners working to advance these issues.

Mental Health and Healthy Aging

Adequate mental health care across the life span and for older adults has long been a struggle within the United States, and has been often perceived as the stepchild to other specialties. However, mental health concerns should not be a normal part of aging. Public health visions for the future of mental health and aging include the following:

1. Promoting advocacy through organizations such as the National Coalition for Mental Health and Aging for improved funding via the Older Americans Act for mental health services to older adults.
2. Promoting the lens of social determinants of health when addressing the development and evaluation of federal programs to address mental health needs for older adults.
3. Promoting assessment and advocacy of evidence to support the connection between mental health and one's overall health, especially among older adults.

NEIGHBORHOOD AND BUILT ENVIRONMENT

Factors such as one's residential setting and the structure of one's community will also play a critical role in terms of access to services, functionality, and quality of life. This section examines some environmental factors that impact healthy aging. It explores the use of the International Classification of Functioning, Disability, and Health (ICF) as an assessment tool and explores different housing options available for older adults. This social determinant and its relationship to overall health outcomes is also explored.

Built Environment for Healthy Aging

The built environment influences all levels of the social determinants of health. The fact is, there are built environments that are conducive to aging and those that are not.

As discussed in this chapter, the built environments not only influence older adults' perceptions of safety and walkability, but also their access to healthy food and appropriate programming. Public health practitioners who focus on aging should look to engage colleagues in diverse fields such as architecture, land developers, community planners, and local policymakers to encourage an approach to development grounded in healthy aging principles. They should also work to inform their nonaging-focused colleagues on how to ensure their programming is accessible to all. Visions for the future include the following:

1. Public health's use of principles of universal design when considering the built environment and older adults,
2. The use of public education and awareness to help public health professionals and the general public become more attuned with principles of universal design, and
3. The utilization of the core functions of public health (i.e., assessment, assurance, and policy development) to promote and advocate for environmental factors for healthy aging.

Housing

This chapter examines living arrangements for older adults, and addresses housing options for people growing older. It also explores the continuum of options available for residential settings ranging from the least restrictive to skilled care and nursing home care facilities. The chapter discusses various housing strategies which have been designed to promote healthy aging, and examines the benefits and needs to optimize housing options for older adults. Public health professionals need to examine challenges and embrace opportunities to include the following interventions:

1. Affordable housing options for low-income and fixed-income living older adults,
2. Programs and services which will promote aging in place and enable the older adult to remain in their own home for as long as possible, and
3. Policy development which ensures that predatory lending or occupancy practices are safeguarded against.

The World Health Organization's International Classification of Functioning, Disability, and Health (ICF)

The World Health Organization's ICF is presented in this text as a framework for the classification of specific conditions or diagnoses, and a case is made that this classification system can help with creating assessment data that is comparable across systems, countries, and cultures. In the future, public health can do the following:

1. Adopt the use of ICF within health care systems to promote comparable assessment data for public health and resource planning,
2. Utilize the ICF data to assure that community and neighborhood needs are met, and
3. Promote the use of ICF as a framework through policy development.

SOCIAL AND COMMUNITY CONTEXT

Social support and the community context is a social determinant that is sometimes underrated in relation to health outcomes; however, it is well documented that there is a strong correlation between social support and health outcomes. This section of the book examines social and community context through the lens of social support, caregiving, mobility, and end-of-life care.

Social Support for Healthy Aging

This chapter examines a host of social support factors that play a role in the healthy aging process. Factors such as social relationships and cognition, life events that disrupt the social support system, and neglect are all explored as components of social support. Visions for the future which public health can support in this area include

1. Stronger infrastructure and support for older adult abuse and neglect assessment and intervention,
2. Public education to help foster and support enhanced supports to people growing older, and
3. Strategies to address life events which disrupt the social support system and build in interventions to mitigate these impacts.

Mobility and Falls Among Older Adults

Ideally, public health practitioners, geriatricians, and other medical and allied health professionals such as nurses and social workers, as well as aging service organizations, would work together in integrated teams to engage in detection and early intervention of older adults to address known multifactorial risks for mobility and falls. Public health efforts in the future should include the following strategies:

1. The development of effective and accessible services to improve in-home and community mobility,
2. Coordinated efforts related to fall prevention and mobility which drive research, practice, and policy initiatives to advance older adult health, and reduce health disparities among this population, and
3. Public awareness initiatives which help educate the workforce and public on falls prevention strategies.

Caregiving

Caregiving is an important factor in the lives of people advancing in age and healthy aging. Paid and unpaid caregivers contribute widely to the health and well-being of older adults. The dynamics of caregiving are addressed in this chapter, along with the role caregivers play and the impact formal and informal caregiving plays in healthy aging. One of the biggest challenges in public health research is the accurate identification of caregivers. Many individuals do not self-identify as caregivers because they do not realize their actions are a part of caregiving; caregiving is what they do naturally. Future directions for public health to embark upon within the realm of caregiving include the following strategies:

1. Public education and recognition of the important role caregivers play in the lives of those they support,
2. Public policies that support the role of formal and informal caregivers to include benefits to those who are caregivers, and
3. Public education and health education on strategies to enable caregivers to self-care and prevent burnout within their role as caregivers.

The Intersection of End-of-Life and Grief

While public health long has focused on well-being, and not merely an absence of disease, "well-being" may often be interpreted as resulting from efforts to control communicable or chronic disease with the goal of establishing healthy environments and populations. Issues related to death, dying, and grief do not fit neatly into this conceptualization. These issues include the inherent right of all individuals to die with their dignity intact or the ability for dying persons to have autonomy over their own dying processes, as well as the ability to make decisions as to where and how they prefer to die. In fact, achieving the preferred manner and place of death is many times a hallmark of a "good death," a death that is in concordance with the wishes of both the dying and the grieving. In the future, public health can address challenges such as

1. Ensuring agreement about what constitutes normal or abnormal outcomes following loss,
2. The creation of reliable criteria to assess normal and abnormal grief reactions, and
3. The development of valid instrumentation for assessment grief and loss outcomes.

EDUCATION

Education as a social determinant of health plays a critical role in health outcomes. Research has provided evidence to the field, demonstrating that as one increases their education level, their quality of life, economic potential, and health outcomes all improve. This section views health outcomes from the vantage point of education across different sectors, from consumers to the workforce.

Educational Factors for Healthy Aging and Lifelong Learning

These two chapters highlight the relationship between education attainment and health outcomes, and summarize how one's education level also plays a role in life span, health conditions, and quality of life. Visions for the future include the following:

1. Consideration of literacy levels when preparing materials related to health education or training for older adults.
2. Promotion of age friendly campuses to support the idea of lifelong education for older adults.
3. Promotion of public policies and funding to support education across the life span and not specifically for children and young adults.

Workforce Development

A number of opportunities and challenges exist for public health as we consider workforce development. As an opportunity, public health can provide education and incorporate aging into existing competencies and schools of public health, primary care, and allied health curriculum. Challenges that are faced with respect to workforce development include ageism and trying to incorporate materials into already dense curriculum. Ideally, one needs to find a champion in program areas to push aging topics into workforce development, continuing education, and academic training. Another challenge, and potential opportunity, is to build alliances and partnerships, such as working with the aging network, older adults, and consumers. Retired professionals and students within academic settings are also strong allies who can help foster and advocate for training in professional and academic settings to help build an age-friendly workforce. In the future, public health can advocate for the following:

1. Strategies for interprofessional development which aim to promote competencies and team collaboration on older adult health issues,
2. Workforce development strategies that utilize low-cost venues such as webinars and online teaching options, and
3. A consistent review of continuing education training needs for the workforce since the field of working with older adults is evolving at a quick pace and older adults are more consumer-oriented now than at any time in history.

Health Information Systems for Healthy Aging

The increasing reliance on the changing technology for the delivery of health care can be difficult for both consumers and providers to fully grasp. It is critical that we do not overstate the benefits while underweighting the potential consequences or threats that technology may pose for healthy aging. We also cannot overlook the real disparities that exist among populations, and particularly among the aging population. As public health continues to adopt and develop new technologies to promote health across the life span, we must advocate for and consider the following:

1. Methods for ensuring the equitable distribution of technological resources across the life span and to all populations,
2. The development of secure, shareable health systems that can communicate and follow individuals across the continuum of care, and
3. A constant quality improvement process to ensure data is protected and not vulnerable to outside actors who wish to use the information for harm.

ECONOMIC STABILITY AND POLICIES

Economics and economic stability also form a critical component of healthy aging. Unfortunately, one's economic status as an older adult is often an outcome of one's economic well-being across the life span. This section examines economic factors in healthy aging as well as policies designed to promote economic stability and healthy aging outcomes.

Economic Issues in Healthy Aging

This chapter addresses economic issues that impact people as they grow older, and either influence or negate healthy aging. Socioeconomic factors that impact health and health outcomes are explored in this chapter, as well as economic strategies that play a role in impacting one's overall health. Specifically, within this social determinant of health, public health can do the following:

1. Improve the public health awareness about the economic issue's faced by older adults and the impact of these issues,
2. Push more prevention as it relates to economic security. The younger generation needs to understand the costs of aging so that proper planning for aging can occur (e.g., costs of nursing homes, medications), and
3. Evaluate the impact of current economic policies (e.g., Social Security versus private pensions) as a strategy to advocate for changes or revisions to current economic policies.

Policies and Impact for Healthy Aging

This chapter examines policies that influence the aging arena. Individual chapters briefly touch upon various governmental policies that have influenced the individual topics within this text. This chapter brings all of these policies together and discusses them in terms of the policy and programs that flow from the policies for older adults. Public health practitioners may be familiar with the legislation related to public health and how various components impact people growing older. However, readers may not be as familiar with other major policies that impact people growing older such as Social Security, Medicare, The Older Americans Act, The Americans with Disabilities Act, and the Elder Justice Act, which are addressed within this chapter. Specifically, within the area of policy development, public health can do the following:

1. Inform and educate the public on issues related to policies and how their voice can strengthen support on the part of elected officials,
2. Mobilize community partnerships for the purpose of strengthening existing and new public policies, and
3. Address gaps in services through advocacy and policy development.

CONCLUSION

This book attempts to enable the public health practitioner to be versed in various areas that will improve the lives of older adults who live in our communities, regardless of the setting. We hope that the tools and information presented in this book will empower readers and public health professionals, and help you gain the knowledge, values, and skills to be effective advocates and change agents.

Appendix 19A: Healthy People 2030 Alignment With Chapters in This Book

Healthy People 2030 Objective	Chapter 1	Chapter 2	Chapter 3	Chapter 4	Chapter 5	Chapter 6	Chapter 7	Chapter 8	Chapter 9	Chapter 10	Chapter 11	Chapter 12	Chapter 13	Chapter 14	Chapter 15	Chapter 16	Chapter 17	Chapter 18
Increase the proportion of older adults with physical or cognitive health problems who get physical activity — OA-01	X					X		X		X								
Reduce the rate of pressure ulcer-related hospital admissions among older adults — OA-04		X													X	X		
Reduce the rate of hospital admissions for diabetes among older adults — OA-05		X				X		X										
Increase the proportion of older adults with dementia, or their caregivers, who know they have It — DIA-01	X				X			X			X				X			
Reduce the proportion of preventable hospitalizations in older adults with dementia — DIA-02	X	X			X			X			X							X
Increase the proportion of adults with subjective cognitive decline who have discussed their symptoms with a provider — DIA-03	X				X						X				X			
Reduce infections caused by *Listeria* — FS-03															X	X		
Reduce the rate of hospital admissions for urinary tract infections among older adults — OA-07		X											X		X			

(Continued)

Healthy People 2030 Objective	Chapter 1	Chapter 2	Chapter 3	Chapter 4	Chapter 5	Chapter 6	Chapter 7	Chapter 8	Chapter 9	Chapter 10	Chapter 11	Chapter 12	Chapter 13	Chapter 14	Chapter 15	Chapter 16	Chapter 17	Chapter 18
Reduce fall-related deaths among older adults – IVP-08	X	X	X		X	X		X		X	X							
Reduce the proportion of older adults who use inappropriate medications – OA-02		X			X			X							X			
Reduce the rate of emergency department visits due to falls among older adults – OA-03	X					X		X		X								
Reduce the proportion of older adults with untreated root surface decay – OH-04		X	X						X						X			
Reduce the proportion of adults aged 45 years and over who have lost all their teeth – OH-05		X	X						X						X			
Reduce the proportion of adults aged 45 years and over with moderate and severe periodontitis – OH-06		X	X						X						X			
Reduce hip fractures among older adults – O-02						X	X	X		X								
Increase the proportion of older adults who get screened for osteoporosis – O-D01											X				X		X	X
Increase the proportion of older adults who get treated for osteoporosis after a fracture – O-D02								X			X				X			
Reduce the rate of hospital admissions for pneumonia among older adults – OA-06									X			X			X	X		X
Reduce hospitalizations for asthma in adults aged 65 years and over – RD-D03						X		X										X
Reduce vision loss from age-related macular degeneration – V-07			X					X				X			X			

Source: Based on US Department of Health and Human Services. Healthy People 2030. Older Adults. Office of Disease Prevention and Health Promotion. 2020. Available at: https://health.gov/healthypeople/objectives-and-data/browse-objectives/older-adults. Accessed June 21, 2021.

Appendix 19B: Core Functions of Public Health Alignment With Chapters in This Book

	Core Functions of Public Health	Chapter 1	Chapter 2	Chapter 3	Chapter 4	Chapter 5	Chapter 6	Chapter 7	Chapter 8	Chapter 9	Chapter 10	Chapter 11	Chapter 12	Chapter 13	Chapter 14	Chapter 15	Chapter 16	Chapter 17	Chapter 18
Assessment	Assess and monitor population health status, factors that influence health, and community needs and assets.	X	X			X	X	X	X		X	X		X				X	X
Assessment	Investigate, diagnose, and address health problems and hazards affecting the population.						X	X	X									X	X
Policy Development	Communicate effectively to inform and educate people about health, factors that influence it, and how to improve it.	X	X	.		X	X			X	X	X	X	X	X	X	X	X	X
Policy Development	Strengthen, support, and mobilize communities and partnerships to improve health.	X				X	X	X			X	X	X		X		X	X	X
Policy Development	Create, champion, and implement policies, plans, and laws that impact health						X	X								X		X	X
Policy Development	Utilize legal and regulatory actions designed to improve and protect the public's health.						X	X	X							X		X	X
Assurance	Assure an effective system that enables equitable access to the individual services and care needed to be healthy.	X	X		X	X	X	X	X	X	X	X	X	X	X	X	X	X	X
Assurance	Build and support a diverse and skilled public health workforce.		X		X							X				X		X	X
Assurance	Improve and innovate public health functions through ongoing evaluation, research, and continuous quality improvement.						X									X		X	X
Assurance	Build and maintain a strong organizational infrastructure for public health.				X			X								X	X	X	X

Source: Based on Centers for Disease Control and Prevention. 10 Essential Public Health Services. 2020. Available at: https://www.cdc.gov/publichealthgateway/publichealthservices/essentialhealthservices.html. Accessed June 21 2021.

Resources

CHAPTER 1: AGING AND DEMENTIA

Website Resources

1. National Institute on Aging. Available at: www.alzheimers.gov. Accessed March 6, 2021. This is a federal government portal on information about Alzheimer's and all dementia care, research, and support.
2. Alzheimer's Disease and Healthy Aging Program (ADHAP), Centers for Disease Control and Prevention. Available at: www.cdc.gov/aging. Accessed March 6, 2021. The ADHAP houses the Healthy Brain Initiative, a public-private initiative aimed to fully integrate cognitive health into public health practice.
3. Alzheimer's Association. Available at: www.alz.org. Accessed March 6, 2021. This is a website for voluntary health organization dedicated to advancing Alzheimer's research, care and support, and education. A microsite, www.alz.org/publichealth, offers unique information for state, local, and tribal public health agencies on cognitive health, dementia, and caregiving.

Additional Reading

1. National Academies of Sciences, Engineering, and Medicine. Preventing cognitive decline and dementia: A way forward. Washington, DC: The National Academies Press; 2017.
2. Alzheimer's Association and Centers for Disease Control and Prevention. Healthy brain initiative, state and local public health partnerships to address dementia: The 2018–2023 Road Map. 2018. Available at: https://www.alz.org/media/Documents/healthy-brain-initiative-road-map-2018-2023.pdf. Accessed March 6, 2021.

YouTube Video

Centers for Disease Control and Prevention. Healthy aging: promoting well-being in older adults. 2017. Available at: https://youtu.be/G5Z4JAcCflM. Accessed March 6, 2021.

CHAPTER 2: POLYPHARMACY AND MEDICATION SAFETY IN OLDER ADULTS

Website Resources

Adverse Event Monitoring and Report Systems

1. US Food and Drug Administration MedWatch. Available at: https://www.fda.gov/safety/medwatch-fda-safety-information-and-adverse-event-reporting-program. Accessed March 6, 2021.
2. World Health Organization VigiBase. Available at: https://www.who-umc.org/vigibase/vigibase. Accessed March 6, 2021.

Adverse Drug Events in Adults

1. Centers for Disease control and Prevention. Adverse drug events. Available at: https://www.cdc.gov/medicationsafety/adult_adversedrugevents.html. Accessed March 6, 2021. CDC website that provides information for adverse drug events with an emphasis on older adults.
2. HealthyAging.org. Available at: https://www.healthinaging.org. Accessed March 6, 2021. A product of the American Geriatrics Society, HealthyAging.org provides interactive tools based on the Beers Criteria.

Additional Reading

2019 American Geriatrics Society Beers Criteria Update Expert Panel. American Geriatrics Society 2019 updated AGS Beers criteria for potentially inappropriate medication use in older adults. *J Am Geriatr Soc.* 2019;67(4):674–694.

CHAPTER 3: HEARING WITHIN HEALTHY AGING

Website Resources

1. National Institute on Deafness and Other Communication Disorders. Age-related hearing loss. Available at: https://www.nidcd.nih.gov/health/age-related-hearing-loss. Accessed March 6, 2021. This website provides information on the signs of hearing loss and how to seek hearing care.
2. Centers for Disease Control and Prevention. Loud noise can cause hearing loss. Available at: https://www.cdc.gov/nceh/hearing_loss. Accessed March 6, 2021. The Centers for Disease Control and Prevention National Center for Environmental Health provides information on preventing adult hearing loss from noise and other exposures.
3. Centers for Disease Control and Prevention. Progress Review Webinar: Hearing and other sensory or communication disorders and vision: slides 52–70. Healthy People

2020: Office of Disease Prevention and Health Promotion. 2018. Available at: www.cdc.gov/nchs/data/hpdata2020/hp2020_ENT_VSL_and_V_Progress_Review-Presentation_R.pdf. Accessed March 23, 2021. The link takes one to a terrific and informative presentation on the senses and hearing health.

Additional Reading

1. National Academies of Sciences, Engineering, and Medicine. Making eye health a population health imperative: Vision for tomorrow. Washington, DC: The National Academies Press; 2016. Free download available at: https://www.nap.edu/catalog/23471/making-eye-health-a-population-health-imperative-vision-for-tomorrow. Accessed March 6, 2021.
2. National Academies of Sciences, Engineering, and Medicine. Hearing health care for adults: Priorities for improving access and affordability. Washington, DC: The National Academies Press; 2016. Free download available at: https://www.nap.edu/atalog/23446/hearing-health-care-for-adults-priorities for-improving-access-and. Accessed March 6, 2021.

YouTube Videos

1. Better Together as ONE. Vision loss and depression in older adults. 2017. Available at: https://www.youtube.com/watch?v=OZzjikmLEBk. Accessed March 6, 2021.
2. Twin Cities PBS. Hearing loss matters: older adults. 2018. Available at: https://www.youtube.com/watch?v=KksFfn4bhCs. Accessed March 6, 2021.

CHAPTER 4: ORAL AND VISION CARE FOR HEALTHY AGING

ORAL HEALTH

Website Resources

1. National Institute of Dental and Craniofacial Research. Tooth loss in seniors. Available at: www.nidcr.nih.gov/research/data-statistics/tooth-loss/seniors. Accessed March 6, 2021. This website specifically explains tooth loss in seniors.
2. Centers for Disease Control and Prevention. Older adult oral health. Available at: www.cdc.gov/oralhealth/basics/adult-oral-health/adult_older.htm. Accessed March 6, 2021. This website gives an overview of oral health in seniors.

Additional Reading

Shuman S, Chen X, Friedman PK, Ghezzi EM, Saunders MJ, Wu B. Oral health: An essential element of healthy aging. In What's Hot, A Newsletter of the Gerontological Society of America. The Gerontological Society of America. 2017.

YouTube Videos

GEC MedEdVids. SA STGEC Opus: An oz of prevention. 1990. Available at: https://youtu.be/el1LRmIZUiI. Accessed March 6, 2021. Oral Health Videos: All 7 English versions are posted on YouTube at one link and play sequentially. All 7 Spanish versions are also posted at another YouTube link and also play sequentially. Available at: https://youtu.be/QN5YI-zHpH4. Accessed March 6, 2021.

VISION LOSS

Website Resources

1. Prevent Blindness. Living well with low vision. Available at: https://lowvision.preventblindness.org/vision-related-web-sites. Accessed March 6, 2021. This website provides a host of resources for low vision, and provides the viewer with strong recommendations on strategies to improve one's lifestyle.
2. American Foundation for the Blind Accessibility Resources. Available at: https://www.afb.org/about-afb/what-we-do/afb-consulting/afb-accessibility-resources. Accessed March 6, 2021. This website provides the viewer with ideas on how to make websites accessibility to one with vision loss. It also provides a host of resources for consumers, families and caregivers.

CHAPTER 5: MENTAL HEALTH AND HEALTHY AGING

Website Resources

1. Health Promotion Research Center. Healthy Aging Research Network Archives. Centers for Disease Control and Prevention Healthy Aging Research Network. 2021. Available at: https://depts.washington.edu/hprc/research/thematic-networks/healthy-aging-research-network-archives. Accessed March 6, 2021. The CDC Healthy Aging Research Network brought together diverse communities and multidisciplinary expertise from across the country to identify and address health promotion needs for healthy aging.
2. Substance Abuse and Mental Health Services Administration. Available at: https://www.samhsa.gov. Accessed March 6, 2021. The Substance Abuse and Mental Health Services Administration is the agency within the US Department of Health and Human Services that leads public health efforts to advance the behavioral health of the nation.

YouTube Videos

1. Suicide Prevention Resource Center. Reaching older adults, community mental health. Available at: https://youtu.be/xNkKN_otejc. Accessed March 6, 2021.

2. The John A. Hartford Foundation. Mental health and the older adult. Available at: https://youtu.be/tRJUniDRnAU. Accessed March 6, 2021.
3. Centers for Disease Control and Prevention. Healthy aging: Promoting well-being in older adults. https://www.youtube.com/watch?v=G5Z4JAcCflM. Accessed March 6, 2021.

CHAPTER 6: BUILT ENVIRONMENTS FOR HEALTHY AGING: A SOCIAL DETERMINANTS APPROACH

Website Resources

1. AARP. AARP livable communities. Available at: https://www.aarp.org/livable-communities/: Provides a guide for the development of age-friendly and liveable communities. Accessed March 6, 2021.
2. World Health Organization. WHO global network for age-friendly cities and communities. 2021. Available at: https://www.who.int/ageing/projects/age_friendly_cities_network/en. Accessed March 6, 2021. Resource page for the World Health Organization Age-Friendly Initiatives.
3. Kaye N, Long K. Toolkit: State strategies to support older adults aging in place in rural areas. National Academy for State Health Policy. 2019. Available at: https://nashp.org/toolkit-state-strategies-to-support-older-adults-aging-in-place-in rural-areas. Accessed March 6, 2021.

Additional Reading

Scharlach AE, Lehning AJ. *Creating Aging-friendly Communities.* New York, NY: Oxford University Press; 2016. A detailed introductory text to the development of aging-friendly communities.

YouTube Video

Palacios, K. The 7 principles of universal design–A non-lecture. 2015. Available at: https://www.youtube.com/watch?v=d-GzKyK0iw4. Accessed March 6, 2021. Overview of the seven principles of universal design with examples.

CHAPTER 7: HOUSING

Websites Resources

1. US Center for Medicare and Medicaid Services. What are my other long-term care choices? Available at: https://www.medicare.gov/what-medicare-covers/part-a/other-long-term-care-choices.html. Accessed March 6, 2021. This website, published by

Medicare.gov provides a range of housing options that can be covered by Medicare. The options range from independent living to those with care needs.

2. National Institute on Aging. Caregiving: Long-term care. Available at: https://www.nia.nih.gov/health/caregiving/long-term-care. Accessed March 6, 2021. This website provides an opportunity for the reader to become familiar with a variety of evidence based opportunities for long-term care. Published by the National Institute of Aging, the information is forthright and timely.

3. National Association of Home Builders. Certified Aging-In-Place Specialist (CAPS). Available at: https://www.nahb.org/education-and-events/education/Designations/Certified-Aging-in-Place-Specialist-CAPS. Accessed March 6, 2021. The Certified Aging-In-Place Specialist (CAPS) is a program of the National Home Builders Association.

Additional Reading

Rowles GD. Housing for Older Adults. In Devlin AS, ed. *Environmental Psychology and Human Well-Being*. Cambridge, MA: Academic Press; 2018:77–106.

CHAPTER 8: INTERNATIONAL CLASSIFICATION OF FUNCTIONING, DISABILITY, AND HEALTH

Website Resource

Swiss Paraplegic Research. ICF case studies. 2018. Available at: https://www.icf-casestudies.org. Accessed March 6, 2021. The World Health Organization offers various case studies on the International Classification of Functioning, Disability, and Health (ICF) across several different populations (e.g., walking recovery environmental accessibility).

Additional Reading

1. Byrne K, Orange JB. Conceptualizing communication enhancement in dementia for family caregivers using the WHO-ICF framework. *Adv Speech Lang Pathol.* 2005;7(4):187–202.

2. Martins AI, Queirós A, Nelson MC, Teixeira RA. The International Classification of Functioning, Disability and Health as a conceptual model for the evaluation of environmental factors. *Procedia Comput Sci.* 2012;14:293–300.

3. Spoorenberg SLW, Reijneveld SA, Middel B, Uittenbroek RJ, Kremer HPH, Wynia K. The Geriatric ICF Core Set reflecting health-related problems in community-living older adults aged 75 years and older without dementia: development and validation.

Disabl Rehabil. 2015;37(25):2337–2343. A customized set of ICF codes for persons 75 and over.

4. World Health Organization. 2013. How to use the ICF: A practical manual for using the International Classification of Functioning, Disability and Health (ICF). Geneva: World Health Organization.

CHAPTER 9: SOCIAL SUPPORT AND AGING

Website Resources

1. AmeriCorps. AmeriCorps Seniors. Available at: https://www.nationalservice.gov/programs/senior-corps. Accessed March 6, 2021.
2. Administration for Community Living. Available at: https://acl.gov. Accessed March 6, 2021.
3. Geller, H. The importance of socialization in aging. Elder Care Alliance. 2017. Available at: https://eldercarealliance.org/blog/importance-of-socialization-in-aging. Accessed March 6, 2021.

Additional Reading

1. Campaign to End Loneliness. Guidance for local authorities developed by the Campaign to End Loneliness. Available at: http://www.campaigntoendloneliness.org.uk/toolkit. Accessed March 6, 2021.
2. The National Academies of Sciences, Engineering, Medicine. Social isolation and loneliness in older adults: Opportunities for the health care system. 2020. Available at: https://www.nap.edu/download/25663. Accessed March 6, 2021.

YouTube Videos

1. Tufts Health Plan Foundation. Social Isolation in Older Adults. 2014. Available at: https://youtu.be/6j8L7ghNmiF. Accessed March 6, 2021.
2. American Sociological Association. Connected Seniors. 2018. Available at: https://youtu.be/bKvmUkbFCl0. Accessed March 6, 2021.

CHAPTER 10: MOBILITY AND FALLS AMONG OLDER ADULTS

Website Resources

1. Centers for Disease Control and Prevention. Keep on your feet-preventing older adult falls. 2020. Available at: https://www.cdc.gov/injury/features/older-adult-falls/index.html.

Accessed March 6, 2021. This Center for Disease Control and Prevention's (CDC) website provides an overview of falls among older people.

2. Centers for Disease Control and Prevention. Plan to stay safe, mobile, and independent. 2021. Available at: https://www.cdc.gov/injury/features/older-adults-mobility/index.html. Accessed March 6, 2021. The CDC's MyMobility Plan can help older people plan how to stay mobile and independent as they age.

3. Rural Health Information Hub. Aging in place in rural communities. 2021. Available at: https://www.ruralhealthinfo.org/toolkits/aging/1/rural-issues. Accessed March 6, 2021. The Rural Health Information Hub also has an interesting guide with some helpful links, etc. This is specific to rural aging and mobility.

Additional Reading

1. Rantanen T. Promoting mobility in older people. *J Prev Med Public Health.* 2013;46(suppl 1):S50–S54.
2. Satariano WA, Guralnik JM, Jackson RJ, Marottoli FA,. Mobility and aging: New directions for public health action. *Am J Public Health.* 2012;102(8):1508–1515.

YouTube Videos

1. Kram Gallery. Health and independence for older adults–Mobility matters. 2015. Available at: https://www.youtube.com/watch?v=fuOyuO5Jzkg. Accessed March 6, 2021. Using a whiteboard animation scheme, this video illustrates some of the statistics for falls and consequences of falls in the United States.

2. YaleCampus. The effect of physical activity on mobility in older adults. 2016. Available at: https://www.youtube.com/watch?v=5UNHeR_IG_w. Accessed March 6, 2021. This video provides an overview of a study conducted at Yale University examining the impacts of a physical activity program on the mobility of older adults.

3. UFHealth. Study proves physical activity helps maintain mobility in older adults. Available at: https://www.youtube.com/watch?v=b6Q_KvvM_o4. Accessed March 6, 2021. This short video explains the importance of mobility and highlights the Life Study, conducted at the University of Florida, that compares older adults enrolled in a physical activity program compared with those receiving an educational program only.

CHAPTER 11: CAREGIVING

Website Resources

1. National Alliance on Caregiving. 2021. Available at: https://www.caregiving.org. Accessed March 6, 2021. Established in 1996, the National Alliance for Caregiving is

a 501(c)(3) nonprofit coalition dedicated to improving quality of life for friend and family caregivers and those in their care, by advancing research, advocacy, and innovation.

2. National Council on Aging. Available at: https://www.ncoa.org. Accessed March 6, 2021. The National Council on Aging is a respected national leader and trusted partner to help people aged 60+ meet the challenges of aging.

Additional Reading

1. AssistGuide Information Services. Available at: http://www.agis.com. Accessed March 6, 2021. AssistGuide provides caregivers with free access to the broadest possible range of worthwhile older adult care information.
2. Aging In Place. Available at: https://www.aginginplace.org/caregiving. Accessed March 6, 2021. AginginPlace.org strives to make desire a reality for more people by helping seniors, their family members, and their caregivers prepare their homes and their lives for successful aging in place.

YouTube Videos

1. Caregiver Action Network-Caregiver Resource Video Center. Available at: https://caregiveraction.org/resources/videos. Accessed March 6, 2021.
2. mmLearn.org. Caregiver Training Videos. Available at: https://training.mmlearn.org/caregiver-training-videos. Accessed March 6, 2021.

CHAPTER 12: THE INTERSECTION OF END-OF-LIFE AND GRIEF

There are many additional resources you might wish to access to learn more. Here we recommend several programmatic, digital, and print selections.

Community Grief Programs

1. Actively Moving Forward: A national support network for grieving young adults aged 18–30.
2. Outward Bound: A national support network for grieving teenagers aged 14–18.
3. Grief Resource Network: A national resource and service network for those suffering from loss.
4. The Grief Recovery Method: An international, evidence-based program for grief and loss.

5. Tragedy Assistance Program for Survivors: A national network for grieving military families.
6. Traditions Program: A family-based program for children grieving the loss of a parent.
7. National Alliance for Grieving Children: A national network of child bereavement supports.
8. GriefShare: A national network of interpersonal support groups for bereavement and loss.
9. Good Grief Network: A national network of resources and supports to reduce collective grief.
10. A Safe Place to Grieve: A therapeutic self-guided program for grief and loss.

Website Resources

1. Death over Dinner. Available at: https://deathoverdinner.org. Accessed March 6, 2021.
2. The Dinner Party. Available at: https://www.thedinnerparty.org. Accessed March 6, 2021. Death over Dinner and The Dinner Party provide uplifting and interactive dialogue to transform the difficult conversation of death into one of deep engagement, insight, and empowerment.
3. Endwell. Design + tech. Available at: https://www.endwellproject.org/watch/design-tech-end-of-life-technology. Accessed March 6, 2021. The End Well Project develops cutting-edge solutions and new models of end-of-life care to better support the experience of death and dying in America.
4. National Institute on Aging. End-of-life. Available at: https://www.nia.nih.gov/health/end-of-life. Accessed March 6, 2021.
5. National Institute on Aging. Providing care and comfort at the end-of-life. Available at: https://www.nia.nih.gov/health/providing-comfort-end-life. Accessed March 6, 2021.
6. Administration on Aging. Eldercare locator. Available at: https://eldercare.acl.gov/public/resources/advanced_care/index.aspx. Accessed March 6, 2021. The National Institute on Aging and the Administration on Aging aggregate useful information by topic, such as the difference between hospice and palliative care. They also provide resources related to end-of-life and comfort care, essential aspects of public health.

Additional Reading

1. Cohen J, DeLiens L. *A Public Health Perspective on End of Life Care*. New York, NY: Oxford University Press; 2012.

2. Öhman C, Floridi L. An ethical framework for the digital afterlife industry. *Nat Hum Behav*. 2018;2(5):318–320.

YouTube Videos

1. TEDx Talks. Future death technology and the shock of the past: John Troyer at TEDx-BathUniversity. Available at: https://www.youtube.com/watch?v=Y3J13BQYv_c& app=desktop&ab_channel=TEDxTalks. Accessed March 6, 2021.
2. TED-ED. Let's talk about dying-Peter Saul. Available at: https://www.youtube.com/watch?v=lkvKGafoyIY&ab_channel=TED-Ed. Accessed March 6, 2021.

CHAPTER 13: EDUCATIONAL FACTORS FOR HEALTHY AGING

Website Resources

1. Centers for Disease Control and Prevention. Older adults: Are you communicating effectively with older adults? Available at: https://www.cdc.gov/healthliteracy/developmaterials/audiences/olderadults. Accessed March 6, 2021. This collection of tools can be used to assist public health practitioners improve their communication with older adults about health issues.
2. National Council for Aging Care. Available at: https://www.ncoa.org. Accessed March 6, 2021. This national organization partners with nonprofit organizations, government, and business entities to provide creative and effective community programs and services with a plethora of resources related to economic security, healthy living, public policy, along with blogs and action oriented resources.
3. National Prevention Strategy. Healthy aging in action. 2018. Available at: https://www.cdc.gov/aging/pdf/healthy-aging-in-action508.pdf. Accessed March 6, 2021. This report identifies specific actions for healthy aging and highlights federal and nonfederal programs that advance the four Strategic Directions of the National Prevention Strategy where the older adult population is concerned: Healthy and Safe Community Environments, Clinical and Community Preventive Services, Empowered People, and Elimination of Health Disparities.

YouTube Video

AmeriCorps. RSVP: Making an impact. 2011. https://youtu.be/voJIlDYAMqM. Accessed March 6, 2021. A seven-minute video describing the Senior Corps RSVP program, one of the largest volunteer networks in the nation for people older than 55.

CHAPTER 14: LIFELONG LEARNING

Website Resource

Road Scholar. Available at: https://www.roadscholar.org. Accessed March 6, 2021. The Road Scholar programs offers educational options for people 50 years of age or greater. Elderhostel is now part of the Road Scholar program.

YouTube Videos

1. Simpleshow Foundation. Lifelong learning. Available at: https://www.youtube.com/watch?v=NljvcJUoNt4. Accessed March 6, 2021. This YouTube video provides an overview of the value and importance of lifelong learning.
2. GoConqr Videos. 10 ways to engage in lifelong learning. Available at: https://www.youtube.com/watch?v=YMAGgPoZSvs. Accessed March 6, 2021. This YouTube video provides the viewer with an overview of why lifelong learning is essential and provides 10 easy steps to pursue lifelong learning.

CHAPTER 15: WORKFORCE DEVELOPMENT

Website Resource

Institute for Healthcare Improvement. Age friendly health systems. Available at: http://www.ihi.org/Engage/Initiatives/Age-Friendly-Health-Systems/Pages/default.aspx. Accessed March 6, 2021. This site prepares the practitioner to understand how to deal with working within primary care or community care settings.

Additional Reading

Institute of Medicine. *Retooling for an Aging America: Building the Health Care Workforce*. Washington DC: The National Academies Press; 2008. Available at: https://www.nap.edu/catalog/12089/retooling-for-an-aging-america-building-the-health-care-workforce. Accessed March 6, 2021.

CHAPTER 16: HEALTH INFORMATION SYSTEMS FOR HEALTHY AGING

Website Resources

1. USA.gov. Online safety. 2020. Available at: https://www.usa.gov/online-safety. Accessed March 6, 2021. USA.gov Online Safety website is a consumer facing government website set-up to warn consumers of emerging technology threats.

2. American Public Health Association. Health informatics information technology. 2021. Available at: https://www.apha.org/apha-communities/member-sections/health-informatics-information-technology. Accessed March 6, 2021. This professional organization has a member section dedicated to improving the public's health and promoting prevention and early intervention by advancing the use of innovative and effective information technology and informatics applications.
3. HealthIt.Gov. Health IT standards. 2019. Available at: https://www.healthit.gov/topic/standards-technology/health-it-standards. Accessed March 6, 2021. HealthIT.Gov is the governments clearing-house for IT Standards and recommendations.

Additional Reading

Marcolino MS, Oliveira J, D'Agostino M, Ribeiro AL, Alkmim M, Novillo-Ortiz D. The impact of mHealth interventions: Systematic review of systematic reviews. *JMIR Mhealth Uhealth*. 2018;6(1):e23.

CHAPTER 17: ECONOMIC ISSUES IN HEALTHY AGING

Website Resources

1. Kaiser Family Foundation. Medicare. 2021. Available at: https://www.kff.org/medicare. Accessed March 6, 2021. This website is a hub for information about Medicare by the Kaiser Family Foundation.
2. National Center on Elder Abuse. Available at: https://ncea.acl.gov. Accessed March 6, 2021. This is the website of the National Center on Elder Abuse, one of the 27 Administration on Aging-funded Resource Centers.
3. National Council on Aging. Benefits for Older Adults. Available at: https://www.ncoa.org/older-adults/benefits. Accessed March 6, 2021. This Benefits Check-up website, presented by the National Council on Aging, helps people understand what benefits for which they are eligible.

YouTube Videos

1. Milliken Institute. Race, gender, and work: The economics of healthy aging. 2018. Available at: https://www.youtube.com/watch?v=6vWAg_Rbb8k. Accessed March 6, 2021. This session explores the intersectional issues facing women as they age and opportunities to address them.
2. CBS Sunday Morning. Aging in America: Crisis in long-term care. 2014. Available at: https://www.youtube.com/watch?v=oLKTThGrAxw. Accessed March 6, 2021. Rita Braver reports on a group of older adults who have banded together and found a way to make their golden years not just affordable, but truly "golden."

CHAPTER 18: POLICIES AND IMPACTS FOR HEALTHY AGING

Website Resources

1. AARP. Available at: www.aarp.org. Accessed March 6, 2021. This website of a leading advocacy group for older persons, has a fantastic section on policy issues and current legislation being considered by Congress.
2. Administration for Community Living. Available at: www.acl.gov. Accessed March 6, 2021. This website provides a link to the Administration for Community Living and the Administration on Aging, including an array of programs.
3. Centers for Disease Control and Prevention. Available at: www.cdc.gov. Accessed March 6, 2021. This website provides updates on public health concerns, including those of older adults.
4. Social Security Administration. Available at: www.ssa.gov. Accessed March 6, 2021. This website provides an excellent overview of the Social Security program, its history, current program materials, and calculation tables.

Additional Reading

1. Di Biasi A, Wolfe M, Carmody J, Fulmer T, Auerbach J. Creating an age friendly public health system. *Innov Aging.* 2020;4(1):igz044.
2. Lepore M. Building momentum for a new future in politics and aging. *Pub Pol Aging Rep.* 2020;30(2). This issue contains multiple excellent articles on the likely direction of aging politics in the American future.

YouTube Videos

1. AARP Answers. How does Social Security work? 2020. Available at: https://www.youtube.com/watch?v=3N5xeWyU128. Accessed March 6, 2021.
2. Boomer Benefits. Social Security basics with Devin Carroll. 2019. Available at: http://www.youtube.com/watch?v=kLE4eKBLk8o. Accessed March 6, 2021. Two pragmatic YouTube videos that provide the viewer with a quick overview of the Social Security and available resources.
3. SWKMontevallo. The Older Americans Act of 1965. Available at: http://www.youtube.com/watch?v=F8dFWM94arE. Accessed March 6, 2021. This video provides the viewer with an overview of the history of Older Americans Act and the services provided.
4. Medicare on Video. Medicare explained 2020 – Medicare basics. Available at: https://www.youtube.com/watch?v=JKNFO7xioDg. Accessed March 6, 2021. This video covers the evolution of Medicare since its creation in 1965.

Contributors

EDITORS

In addition to her academic appointment as a Professor in the School of Social Work at Southern Illinois University Carbondale, **Elaine T. Jurkowski, PhD, MSW**, has been an active member of the American Public Health Association (APHA). She has served as Chair and section counselor for the Social Work Section, and more recently, has served as the Program Planner and Governing Councilor for the Aging and Public Health Section. Significantly, Dr. Jurkowski is the author or editor of eight books, all published by Springer Publishing, including the book: *Policy and Program Planning for Older Adults: Realities and Visions*. She is an experienced podcaster and has created podcast interviews of leading experts for chapters of two of her Springer Publishing books. Dr. Jurkowski has influenced aging services in several countries outside of the United States, including Canada, Russia, Egypt, and Niger, West Africa. She is active in a number of aging-oriented organizations which help her fuel her passion for aging-related education and public health scholarship.

As an Assistant Professor of Aging within the Center for Innovation in Healthy and Resilient Aging at Arizona State University, **M. Aaron Guest, PhD, MPH, MSW**, specializes in aging among rural marginalized populations, particularly around the topics of isolation, loneliness, and the influence of social networks on health. When he was a student, he was one of the elected students to serve on APHA's Executive Board. Dr. Guest has also served in leadership positions in three sections of APHA (Aging, Public Health Education and Health Promotion, and Environment), on the Student Assembly, and the LGBTQ Health Caucus. Dr. Guest was awarded the Distinguished Member Award in 2019 by the APHA Environment Section. He is also active in other national aging-related organizations, developing a strong network of like-minded aging and public health scholars.

AUTHORS

Jon Agley, PhD, MPH, Associate Professor, Indiana University

Talha Ali, PhD, MS, Postdoctoral Fellow, Yale School of Medicine

Patricia M. Alt, PhD, Professor Emerita, Towson University

Caroline D. Bergeron, DrPH, MSc, Senior Policy Analyst, Public Health Agency of Canada

Godfred O. Boateng, PhD, MPhil, Assistant Professor, The University of Texas at Arlington

Jason Burnett, PhD, Associate Professor of Geriatric and Palliative Medicine, The University of Texas Health Science Center, McGovern Medical School

William Cabin, PhD, MPH, MSW, Assistant Professor of Social Work, Temple University

Brittany M. Chambers, MPH, Associate Director of Education, Icahn School of Medicine at Mount Sinai

Stephanie T. Child, PhD, MPH, Assistant Professor, Harvard University

Steven A. Cohen, DrPH, MPH, Assistant Professor, University of Rhode Island

Darren Cosgrove, PhD, MSW, Assistant Professor, Miami University

Jude des Bordes, MBChB, DrPH, CPH, Research Scientist, The University of Texas Health Science Center at Houston, McGovern Medical School

Charles R. Doarn, MBA, Professor, University of Cincinnati

Gwyneth M. Eliasson, JD, MPH, Adjunct Professor, Montclair State University

Jeananne Elkins, PhD, DPT, MPH, Associate Professor, Brenau University

Erin Emery-Tiburcio, PhD, ABPP, Associate Professor, Rush Center for Excellence in Aging

Shenita Freeman, MSHIA, MPH, Senior Director Analytics and Informatics, Centurion Managed Care

Amy Funk, PhD, Assistant Professor, Illinois Wesleyan University

Robyn L. Golden, LCSW, Associate Vice President of Population Health and Aging, Assistant Professor of Medicine, Nursing, Psychiatry, and Health Systems Management, Rush University Medical Center

Howard J. Hoffman, MA, Director, Epidemiology and Statistics Program, National Institute on Deafness and Other Communication Disorders, National Institutes of Health

Hengameh Hosseini, PhD, Professor, University of Scranton

Elizabeth G. Hunter, PhD, OTR/L, Assistant Professor of Gerontology, University of Kentucky

Aliza R. Karpes Matusevich, PhD, Postdoctoral Research Fellow, The University of North Texas Health Sciences Center at Fort Worth

Lisa M. Lines, PhD, MPH, Senior Health Services Researcher, RTI International

Nicole S. MacFarland, PhD, MSW, Executive Director, Senior Hope Counseling, Clinical Associate Professor, University at Albany, State University of New York

Andrea P. Medeiros, MPH, Director of Programs, Policy, and Membership, National Osteoporosis Foundation

Isis S. Mikhail, MD, DrPH, MPH, Section Chief, National Institute on Aging

Kristine A. Mulhorn, PhD, MHSA, Professor and Chair of the Health Administration Department, Drexel University

Michelle Newman, MPH, Program Coordinator, Rush University Medical Center

Emily J. Nicklett, PhD, MSW, Associate Professor of Social Work, University of Texas at San Antonio

Rachael D. Nolan, PhD, MPH, CPH, Assistant Professor, University of Cincinnati

Jennifer A. Pooler, MPP, Senior Study Director, Insight Policy Research

Minakshi Raj, PhD, MPH, Assistant Professor, University of Illinois at Urbana Champaign

Rafia S. Rasu, MPharm, MBA, PhD, Professor, The University of North Texas Health Sciences Center at Fort Worth

Nahid Rianon, MD, DrPH, Associate Professor, The University of Texas Health Science Center at Houston

Michelle J. Saunders, DMD, MS, MPH, Adjunct Professor, University of Texas Health Science Center at San Antonio

John Shean, MPH, Associate Director of Public Health, Alzheimer's Association

Tara Sklar, JD, MPH, Professor of Health Law and Director of Health Law and Policy Program, University of Arizona

Matthew Lee Smith, PhD, MPH, Associate Professor, Texas A&M University

Donna Beth Stauber, PhD, System Program Manager, Innovations, Spiritual Care Delivery, Baylor Scott and White Health

Shana D. Stites, PsyD, MS, MA, Assistant Professor, University of Pennsylvania

Christa L. Themann, MA, CCC-A, Scientific Researcher, Centers for Disease Control and Prevention, The National Institute for Occupational Safety and Health

Danielle Ward, PhD, MPH, Independent Researcher

Jordan Weiss, PhD, Postdoctoral Scholar, University of California, Berkeley

Rana Zalmai, PharmD, Postdoctoral Research Fellow, The University of North Texas Health Sciences Center at Fort Worth

Index

technology for, 241
types of, 241–242
workforce knowledge about, 242
Health Insurance Portability and Accountability Act (HIPAA), 243
health literacy, 28–29, 208, 242
Health Resources and Services Administration (HRSA, Department of Health and Human Services), 61, 280
Healthy Brain Initiative (Centers for Disease Control and Prevention), 10
Healthy People 2030 Framework, 10, 273, *299–300*
hearing loss, 39–57
    best practice interventions, 48
    case study, 50–51
    challenges and opportunities, 45–47, 49–50
    hearing aids/assistive devices for, 40, 41, *42*, 43, 46–51
    hyperacusis, 40, 43
    issues of, 43–45
    policies and legislation, 47–48
    prevalence and public health importance, 39–43
    special populations and, 48–49
    tinnitus, 41, 43, 45
heating assistance, 260
Hendrich II Fall Risk Model™, 152
Hoaxy, 213
hospice care. *See* palliative and hospice care
housing, 109–117
    Age-Friendly City Framework, 98–100
    assistance for low-income older people, 260
    case study, 115
    challenges and opportunities, 114
    community dwelling vs. institutionalized care statistics, 109–110
    continuum of, *110*, 110–112
    Fair Housing Amendments Act (1988), 276
    homeless population, 113
    within least restrictive environment, 110, 112, 114
    for specialized populations, *112*, 112–114
hyperacusis, 40, 43
hyperpolypharmacy, 23–24

I

IBM, 247
ICF. *See* International Classification of Functioning, Disability, and Health
Improved Prescribing in the Elderly Tool (IPET, "Canadian Criteria"), 30
Improving Medicare Post-Acute Care Transformation (IMPACT Act, 2014), 278
informational support, 132
Institute of Medicine, 76, 185
Institute on Assets and Social Policy, 255
institutionalized living arrangements. *See* assisted living facilities; skilled nursing facilities
instrumental support, 132
insurance (private)
    data breaches in, 245–247
    Family and Medical Leave Act and, 173
    Health Insurance Portability and Accountability Act (HIPAA), 243

hearing loss and, 47, 48, 50
long-term care and, 257
mental health and, 76
oral health and, 61
integrity (data), 244
International Classification of Diseases, 74
International Classification of Functioning, Disability, and Health (ICF), 119–128
    best practice interventions, 120–121
    case studies, 121–122, *123–127*
    challenges and opportunities, 121
    ICF model, overview, 119–120, *120*
    policies and relevant government programs, 120
    special considerations and special populations, 121
internet of things (IoT), 242
isolation, 132–133, 173 (*See also* rural lifestyle)

J

Job Corps, 220
John A. Hartford Foundation, 230, 279
Joint Commission, 28

L

labor force participation, education and, 205, 206
least restrictive environment, 110, 112, 114
Lewy body disease, 4
LGBTQ (lesbian, gay, bisexual, transgendered, and queer) population
    built environment practices and, 101
    dementia and, 11
    economic issues of, 265
    housing and, 113
    workforce development and needs of, 234
life events, social support disruption and, 136–137
lifelong learning, 219–225
    case study, 223–224
    challenges and opportunities, 223
    evidence-based interventions, 222
    policy and legislation, 220–222
    postsecondary education, 219–220
    for special populations, 222–223
    See also education
Lifespan Respite Care Program, 175–176
loneliness, 132–133, 173 (*See also* isolation)
longevity
    dementia and, 3, 6
    fear of death vs. longevity expectations, 184–185 (*See also* end-of-life and grief)
    "The Growing Gap in Life Expectancy by Income" (NASEM), 229
long-term care insurance, 257
Lubben Social Network Scale (LSNS), 135

M

Maine
    AARP Network of Age-Friendly States and Communities, 99